THE ARCTIC
p 143

SOUTHERN OCEAN

STUDENT
WORLD
ATLAS

Penguin
Random
House

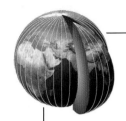

Penguin
Random
House

FOR THE EIGHTH EDITION

Senior Cartographic Editor Simon Mumford
Senior Producer Vivienne Yong   Producer, Pre-Production Luca Frassinetti
Jacket Design Development Manager Sophia MTT   Publisher Andrew Macintyre   Art Director Karen Self
Publishing Director Jonathan Metcalf   Associate Publishing Director Liz Wheeler

FOR PREVIOUS EDITIONS

MANAGING EDITOR   MANAGING ART EDITOR
Lisa Thomas   Philip Lord

PROJECT EDITORS   PROJECT DESIGNERS
Debra Clapson, Wim Jenkins, Jill Hamilton (US)   Rhonda Fisher, Karen Gregory

EDITORIAL CONTRIBUTORS   DESIGNERS
Thomas Heath, Kevin McRae, Constance Novis,   Carol Ann Davis, David Douglas,
Iris Rossoff (US), Siobhan Ryan   Nicola Liddiard

MANAGING CARTOGRAPHER   SENIOR CARTOGRAPHIC EDITOR
David Roberts   Roger Bullen

DATABASE MANAGER   DIGITAL MAPS CREATED IN DK CARTOPIA BY
Simon Lewis   Phil Rowles, Rob Stokes

PLACENAMES DATABASE TEAM   EDITORIAL DIRECTION
Natalie Clarkson, Julia Lynch,   Andrew Heritage

CARTOGRAPHERS
Pamela Alford, James Anderson, Chris Atkinson, Dale Buckton, Tony Chambers, Jan Clark,
Martin Darlison, Damien Demaj, Paul Eames, Sally Gable, Jeremy Hepworth, Michael Martin,
Ed Merritt, Simon Mumford, John Plumer, Gail Townsley, Julie Turner,
Sarah Vaughan, Jane Voss, Peter Winfield

PICTURE RESEARCH
Louise Thomas

EDUCATIONAL CONSULTANTS
Dr. David Lambert, Institute of Education, University of London, David R Wright, BA MA

TEACHER REVIEWERS
US: Ramani DeAlwis; UK: Kevin Ball, Pat Barber, Stewart Marson

First published in Great Britain in 1998 by
Dorling Kindersley Limited,
80 Strand, London WC2R ORL

Second Edition 2002, Reprinted 2003, Third Edition 2004, Fourth Edition 2006,
Fifth Edition 2008, Sixth Edition 2011, Reprinted with revisions 2012,
Seventh Edition 2013, Eighth Edition 2015

ACKNOWLEDGMENTS

The publishers are grateful for permission to reproduce the following photographs:

t=top, b=bottom, a=above, l=left, r=right, c=centre
Axiom: Jiri Rezac 64br; J Spaull 92br. **Bridgeman Art Library:** Hereford Cathedral, Trustees of the Hereford Mappa Mundi 8tr. **J Allan
Cash:** 120cr. **Bruce Coleman Ltd:** C Ott 28cr (below); Dr E Pott 4bc; H Reinhard 19cr; J Murray 130bl; Peter Terry 19cr. **Colourific:** Black
Star/R Rogers 113br; Frank Herrmann 119bc. **Comstock:** 17tc. **Corbis:** Bob Daemmrich 30bl. **James Davis Travel Photography:** 44tr,
119tr. **Robert Harding Picture Library:** 6tr (below), 21c, 21cr, 22br, 92cr (above), 28bl, 30cr, 30br, 31bl, 38tr, 118bl; A Tovy 120br; Adam
Woolfitt 62br; C Bowman 112tr; Charcrit Boonson 90cr (below); David Lomax 20tr; Franz Joseph Land 19tr; G Boutin 120cl (below); G
Renner 17c, 118cr(above); Gavin Hellier 31tr; Geoff Renner 39cr (above); H P Merten 23tl; Jane Sweeney 23bl; Louise Murray 93tr; Peter
Scholey 91tr; Robert Francis 23cr; Schuster/Keine 62cr (above); Simon Westcott 90br. **Hutchison Library:** A Zvoznikov 19cl; J Nowell 93bl;
R Ian Lloyd 10cl. **Image Bank:** Carlos Navajas 17bl; M Isy-Schwart 17bc; P Grumann 64cr (below); Steve Proehl 30cr (below); Terje Rakke
17br. **Images Colour Library:** 19c, 62cr (below), 118br. **Impact:** Jeremy Nicholl 121cr (below); Mark Henley 20bl; Paul O'Driscoll 63cr;
Robin Lubbock 118br. **Frank Lane Picture Agency:** D Smith 19bc; W Wisniewski 17cr. **Magnum:** Chris Steele Perking 120tr (below); Jean
Gaumy 65cl. **N.A.S.A:** 9tc. **N.H.P.A:** M Wendler 4cl, 110bl. **Oxford Scientific Films:** Konrad Wothe 19tc; L Gould 4tr; Nobert Rosing 28cl.
Panos Pictures: Alain le Garsheur 92cr; Alain le Garsmeur 31cl (below); Alberto Arzoz 63tr; Bruce Paton 121bl; Jeremy Hartley 120bl;
Maria Luiza M Cavalho 112cl (below); Paul Smith 11cr; Rhodri Jones 113bl; Ron Gilling 119cr; Trygve Bolstad 22bl. **Edward Parker:**
17cr (above). **Pictor International:** 4tc, 10bc, 18tr, 20br, 36bc, 38br. **Planet Earth Pictures:** J Waters 113bc. **South American Pictures:**
Robert Francis 29br; Tony Morrison 110cr, 111cl. **Spectrum Colour Library:** 29br. **Frank Spooner Pictures:** Gamma/E. Baitel 91cl.
Still Pictures: J Frebet 113cr; R Seitre 90cr (above). **Tony Stone Images:** 17tr, 112cl; A Sacks 28cr; Alan Levenson 92cr; Charles Thatcher
39tr; D Austen 131cr; D Hanson 17cl; Donald Johnson 62bc; Earth Imaging 6tr (above); G Johnson 90bl; H Strand 113tr; Hans Schlapfer
38bc; J Jangoux 19bcr; J Warden 110bc; John Garrett 121br; L Resnick 121tr; Larry Ulrich 37br; P Chesley 130tr; Paul Chesley 36br; Randy
Wells 19br; Robert Frerck 65tr; Tom Walker 36bl; Tony Craddock 65cr. **Telegraph Colour Library:** 29tr. **Travel Ink:** Colin Marshall 22bc.
Trip: A Kuznetsov 92bc; H Rogers 90cr; M Barlow 112bl; N Ray 10tr; Robert Belbin 92bl; V Kolpakov 93cr (below); V Sidoropolev 64cr; W
Jacobs 130c. **World Pictures:** 131tr. **ZEFA Picture Library:** 19bcl, 19cll, 63bc; Damm 119cl; Heilman 11cr (below); K Siewert 110cl; Kitchen
19bll; Sunak 91cr; Surpress 111tr. **JACKET IMAGES:** Front: **Corbis:** Richard Berenholtz br; Bob Krist tc, bl; JamesRandklev tr, bl; Keren Su
tl.; **Science Photo Library/NOAA.** Back: **Corbis:** Robert Y. Ono bc; James Randklevbl; Paul A. Souders br; Royalty Free Images: Cobis tc;
Corbis tr. Spine: **Corbis:** Robert Y. Ono

CONTENTS

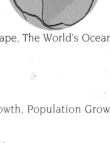

LEARNING MAP SKILLS

THE WORLD ABOUT US

THE WORLD ATLAS

NORTH AMERICA

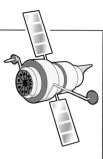

▓ KEY TO MAP SYMBOLS ON FRONT ENDPAPER

▓ FLAGS ON BACK ENDPAPER

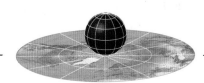

AMAZING EARTH

Earth is unique among the nine planets that circle the Sun. It is the only one that can support life, because it has enough oxygen in its atmosphere and plentiful water. In fact, seen from space, the Earth looks almost entirely blue. This is because about 70% of its surface is under water, submerged beneath four huge oceans: the Pacific, Atlantic, Indian and Arctic oceans. Land makes up about 30% of the Earth's surface. It is divided into seven landmasses of varying shapes and sizes called continents. These are, from largest to smallest: Asia, Africa, North America, South America, Antarctica, Europe and Australia.

THE SHAPE OF THE EARTH

Photographs taken from space by astronauts in the 1960s, and more recently from orbiting satellites, have proven beyond doubt what humans had already worked out long ago – that the Earth is shaped like a ball. But it is not perfectly round. The force of the Earth's rotation makes the world bulge very slightly at the Equator and go a little flat at the North and South poles. So the Earth is actually a flattened sphere, or a 'geoid'.

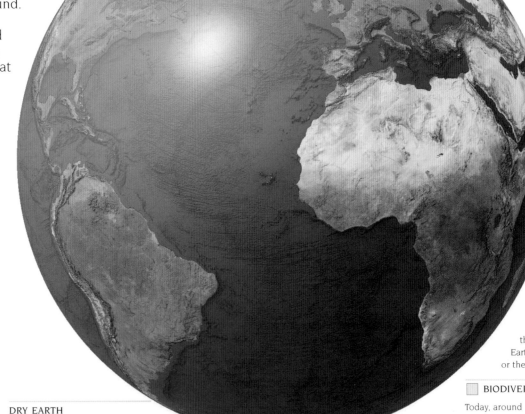

WATERY WORLD

The Earth's oceans and seas cover more than 367 million sq km – that is twice the surface of Mars and nine times the surface of the moon.

Beneath the ocean waves lies the biggest and most unexplored landscape on Earth. Here are coral reefs, enormous, open plains, deep canyons and the longest mountain range on Earth – the Mid-Atlantic Ridge – which stretches almost from pole to pole.

HEIGHTS AND DEPTHS

The Pacific Ocean contains the deepest places on the Earth's surface – the ocean trenches. The very deepest is Challenger Deep in the Mariana Trench which plunges 10,920 m into the Earth's crust. If Mount Everest, the highest point on land at 8,848 m, was dropped into the trench, its peak wouldn't even reach the surface of the Pacific.

WATER

Over 97% of the Earth's water is salt water. The total amount of salt in the world's oceans and seas would cover the whole of Europe to a depth of five km. Less than 3% of the Earth's water is fresh. Of this, 2.06% is frozen in ice sheets and about 0.9% is stored underground as groundwater. The remainder is in lakes and rivers.

COASTS

The total length of the Earth's coastlines is more than 350,000 km – that is the equivalent of 8.75 times around the globe. A high percentage of the world's people live in coastal zones: of the ten most populated cities on Earth, seven are situated on estuaries or the coast.

BIODIVERSITY

Today, around 7,200,000,000 humans, an estimated 7.7 million animal species and 300,000 known plant species depend on the air, water and land of planet Earth.

WET EARTH

Tropical rainforests grow in areas close to the Equator, where it is wet and warm all year round. Although they cover just 7% of the Earth's land, these thick, damp forests form the richest ecosystems on the planet. More plant and animal species are found here than anywhere else on Earth.

DRY EARTH

Deserts are among the most inhospitable places on the planet. Some deserts are scorching hot, others are freezing cold, but they have one thing in common – they are all dry. Very few plant and animal species can survive in these harsh conditions. The world's coldest and driest continent, Antarctica (*left*), is a cold desert.

VANISHING FORESTS

10,000 years ago, thick forests covered about half of the Earth's land surface. Today, 33% of those forests no longer exist, and more than half of what remains has been dramatically altered. During the 20th century, more than 50% of the Earth's rainforests were felled.

DIFFERENT WORLD VIEWS

Because the Earth is round, we can only see half of it at any one time. This half is called a hemisphere, which means 'half a sphere'. There are always two hemispheres – the half that you see and the other half that you don't see. Two hemispheres placed together will always make a complete sphere.

Equator 0°

NORTH AMERICA
EUROPE
AFRICA
SOUTH AMERICA

NORTH AND SOUTH

The Equator is an imaginary line drawn around the middle of the Earth, where its circumference is greatest. If we cut along the Equator, the Earth separates into two hemispheres: the northern and southern hemispheres. Most of the Earth's land is in the northern hemisphere. Europe and North America are the only continents which lie entirely in the northern hemisphere. Australia and Antarctica are the only continents that lie wholly in the southern hemisphere.

The southern hemisphere contains three of the Earth's four great oceans: the Pacific, Indian and Atlantic oceans.

Prime Meridian (0°)

North Pole

NORTH AMERICA
EUROPE
AFRICA
SOUTH AMERICA

180°

EAST AND WEST

The Earth can also be divided along two other imaginary lines – the Prime Meridian (0°) and 180° – which run opposite each other between the North and South poles. This creates eastern and western hemispheres. The continents in the eastern hemisphere are traditionally called the Old World while those in the western hemisphere – the Americas – were named the New World by the Europeans who explored them in the 15th century.

PLANET WATER, PLANET LAND

The Earth can also be divided into land and water hemispheres. The land hemisphere shows most of the land on the Earth's surface. The water hemisphere is dominated by the vast Pacific Ocean – from this view, the Earth appears to be almost entirely covered by water.

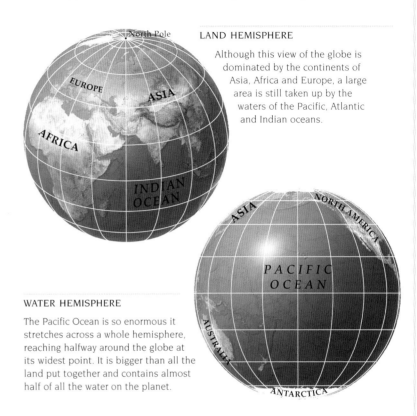

North Pole

EUROPE
ASIA
AFRICA
INDIAN OCEAN

LAND HEMISPHERE

Although this view of the globe is dominated by the continents of Asia, Africa and Europe, a large area is still taken up by the waters of the Pacific, Atlantic and Indian oceans.

ASIA
NORTH AMERICA
PACIFIC OCEAN
AUSTRALIA
ANTARCTICA

WATER HEMISPHERE

The Pacific Ocean is so enormous it stretches across a whole hemisphere, reaching halfway around the globe at its widest point. It is bigger than all the land put together and contains almost half of all the water on the planet.

THE SEASONS

As the Earth orbits the Sun, it is also spinning around an imaginary line called its axis, which joins the North and South poles. The Earth's axis is not quite at right angles to the Sun, but tilts over at an angle of 23.5°. As a result, each place gradually moves closer to the Sun and then further away from it again. Summer in the northern hemisphere is when the north is closest to the Sun. In winter, the northern hemisphere tilts away from the Sun, receiving far less heat and light. In the southern hemisphere the seasons are reversed, with summer in December and winter in June.

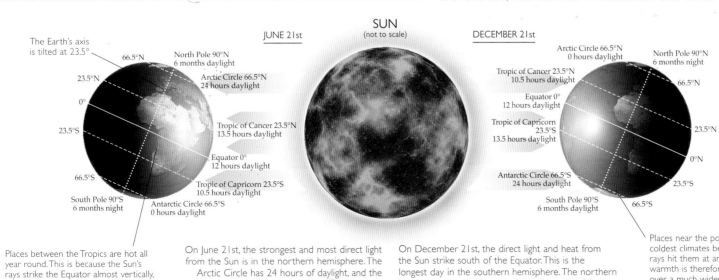

SUN
(not to scale)

JUNE 21st

The Earth's axis is tilted at 23.5°
66.5°N
North Pole 90°N
6 months daylight
23.5°N
Arctic Circle 66.5°N
24 hours daylight
0°
Tropic of Cancer 23.5°N
13.5 hours daylight
23.5°S
Equator 0°
12 hours daylight
66.5°S
Tropic of Capricorn 23.5°S
10.5 hours daylight
South Pole 90°S
6 months night
Antarctic Circle 66.5°S
0 hours daylight

DECEMBER 21st

Arctic Circle 66.5°N
0 hours daylight
North Pole 90°N
6 months night
Tropic of Cancer 23.5°N
10.5 hours daylight
66.5°N
Equator 0°
12 hours daylight
Tropic of Capricorn 23.5°S
13.5 hours daylight
23.5°N
0°N
Antarctic Circle 66.5°S
24 hours daylight
23.5°S
South Pole 90°S
6 months daylight
66.5°S

Places between the Tropics are hot all year round. This is because the Sun's rays strike the Equator almost vertically, heating the land more intensely.

On June 21st, the strongest and most direct light from the Sun is in the northern hemisphere. The Arctic Circle has 24 hours of daylight, and the northern hemisphere has its longest day.

On December 21st, the direct light and heat from the Sun strike south of the Equator. This is the longest day in the southern hemisphere. The northern hemisphere has its shortest day and longest night.

Places near the poles have the coldest climates because the Sun's rays hit them at an angle. The Sun's warmth is therefore spread out over a much wider area.

MAPPING THE WORLD

The main purpose of a map is to show, or locate, where things are. The only truly accurate map of the whole world is a globe – a round model of the Earth. But a globe is impractical to carry around, so map-makers (cartographers) produce flat paper maps instead. Changing the globe into a flat map is not simple. Imagine cutting a globe in half and trying to flatten the two hemispheres. They would be stretched in some places, and squashed in others. In fact, it is impossible to make a map of the round Earth on flat paper without some distortion of area, distance or direction.

MODELS OF THE WORLD

Satellite images can show the whole world as it appears from space. However, this image shows only one half of the world, and is distorted at the edges.

A globe (*right*) is the only way to illustrate the shape of the Earth accurately. A globe also shows the correct positions of the continents and oceans and how large they are in relation to one another.

LATITUDE

We can find out exactly how far north or south, east or west any place is on Earth by drawing two sets of imaginary lines around the world to make a grid. The horizontal lines on the globe below are called lines of latitude. They run from east to west. The most important is the Equator, which is given the value 0°. All other lines of latitude run parallel to the Equator. and are numbered in degrees either north or south of the Equator.

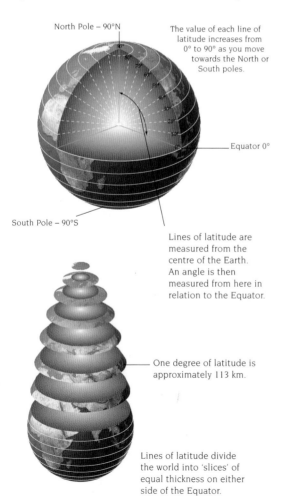

North Pole – 90°N

The value of each line of latitude increases from 0° to 90° as you move towards the North or South poles.

Equator 0°

South Pole – 90°S

Lines of latitude are measured from the centre of the Earth. An angle is then measured from here in relation to the Equator.

One degree of latitude is approximately 113 km.

Lines of latitude divide the world into 'slices' of equal thickness on either side of the Equator.

LONGITUDE

The vertical lines on the globe below run from north to south between the poles. They are called lines of longitude. The most important passes through Greenwich, London and is numbered 0°. It is called the Prime Meridian. All other lines of longitude are numbered in degrees either east or west of the Prime Meridian. The line directly opposite the Prime Meridian is numbered 180°.

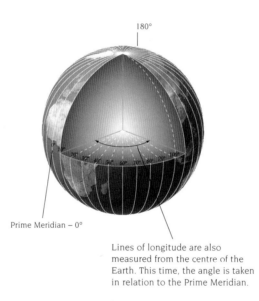

180°

Prime Meridian – 0°

Lines of longitude are also measured from the centre of the Earth. This time, the angle is taken in relation to the Prime Meridian.

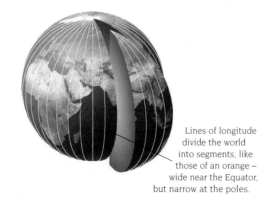

Lines of longitude divide the world into segments, like those of an orange – wide near the Equator, but narrow at the poles.

WHERE ON EARTH?

When lines of latitude and longitude are combined on a globe, or as here, on a flat map, they form a grid. Using this grid, we can locate any place on land, or at sea, by referring to the point where its line of latitude intersects with its line of longitude. Even when a place is not located exactly where the lines cross, you can still find its approximate position.

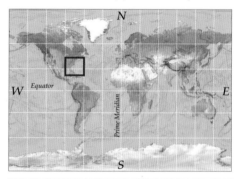

N

W   Equator   E

Prime Meridian

S

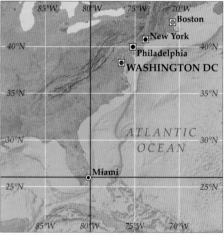

85°W   80°W   75°W   70°W

Boston

New York

40°N   Philadelphia   40°N

WASHINGTON DC

35°N   35°N

30°N   ATLANTIC OCEAN   30°N

Miami

25°N   25°N

85°W   80°W   75°W   70°W

The map above is of the eastern USA. It is too small to show all the lines of latitude and longitude, so they are given at intervals of 5°. Miami is located at about 26° north of the Equator and 80° west of the Prime Meridian. We write its location like this: 26°N 80°W.

MAKING A FLAT MAP FROM A GLOBE

Cartographers use a technique called projection to show the Earth's curved surface on a flat map. Many different map projections have been designed. The distortion of one feature – either area, distance, or direction – can be minimized, while other features become more distorted. Cartographers must choose which of these things it is most important to show correctly for each map that they make. Three major families of projections can be used to solve these questions.

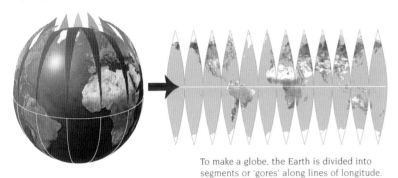

To make a globe, the Earth is divided into segments or 'gores' along lines of longitude.

1 CYLINDRICAL PROJECTIONS

These projections are 'cylindrical' because the surface of the globe is transferred onto a surrounding cylinder. This cylinder is then cut from top to bottom and 'rolled out' to give a flat map. These maps are very useful for showing the whole world.

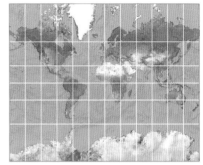

The cylinder touches the globe at the Equator. Here, the scale on the map will be exactly the same as it is on the globe. At the northern and southern edges of the cylinder, which are furthest away from the surface of the globe, the map is most distorted. The Mercator projection (*above*), created in the 16th century, is a good example of a cylindrical projection.

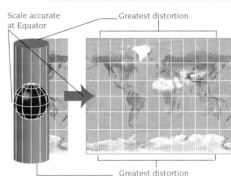

Scale accurate at Equator — Greatest distortion

Greatest distortion

2 AZIMUTHAL PROJECTIONS

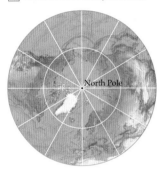

North Pole

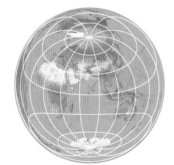

Azimuthal projections put the surface of the globe onto a flat circle. 'Azimuthal' means that the direction or 'azimuth' of any line coming from the centre point of that circle is correct. Azimuthal maps are useful for viewing hemispheres, continents and the polar regions. Mapping any area larger than a hemisphere gives great distortion at the outer edges of the map.

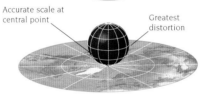

Accurate scale at central point — Greatest distortion

The circle only touches the globe's surface at one central point. The scale is only accurate at this point and becomes less and less accurate the further away the circle is from the globe. This kind of projection is good for maps centering on a major city or on one of the poles.

3 CONIC PROJECTIONS

Conic projections are best used for smaller areas of the world, such as country maps. The surface of the globe is projected onto a cone which rests on top of it. After cutting from the point to the bottom of the cone, a flat map in the shape of a fan is left behind.

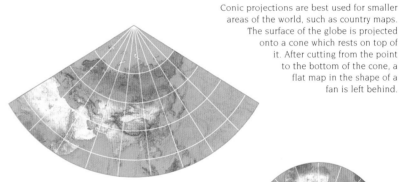

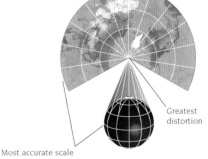

The conic projection touches the globe's surface at one latitude. This is where the scale of the map will be most accurate. The parts of the cone furthest from the globe will be the most distorted and are usually omitted from the map itself.

Greatest distortion

Most accurate scale

PROJECTIONS USED IN THIS ATLAS

The projections which are appropriate for showing maps at a world, continental or country scale are quite different. The projections for this atlas have been carefully chosen. They are ones that show areas as familiar shapes and ensure that they are distorted as little as possible.

1 World Maps

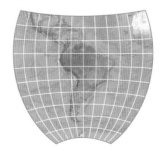

The Wagner VII projection is used for our world maps as it shows all the countries at their correct sizes relative to one another.

2 Continents

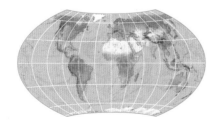

The Lambert Azimuthal Equal Area is used for continental maps. The shape distortion is relatively small and countries retain their correct sizes relative to one another.

3 Countries

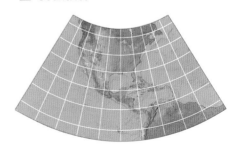

The Lambert Conformal Conic shows countries with as little distortion as possible. The angles from any point on the map are the same as they would be on the surface of the globe.

HOW MAPS ARE MADE

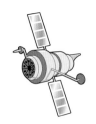

New technologies have revolutionized map making. Computers and information from satellites have replaced drawing boards and drafting pens, and the process of creating new maps is now far easier. But map making is still a skilled and often time-consuming process. Information about the World must be gathered, sorted and checked. The cartographer must make decisions about the function of the map and what information to select in order to make it as clear as possible.

Maps have been made for thousands of years. The 13th century Mappa Mundi, meaning 'known world' shows the Mediterranean Sea and the Don and Nile rivers. Asia is at the top, with Europe on the left, and Africa to the right. The oceans are shown as a ring surrounding the land. The map reflects a number of biblical stories.

HISTORICAL MAP MAKING

This detailed hand-drawn map of the southern coast of Spain was made in about 1750. The mountains are illustrated as small hills and the labels have been hand lettered.

For centuries, maps were drawn by hand. Very early maps were no more than a pictorial representation of what the surface of the ground looked like. Where there were hills, pictures were drawn to represent them. Later maps were drawn using information gathered by survey teams. They would carefully mark out and calculate the height of the land, the positions of towns and other geographical features. As knowledge and techniques improved, maps became more accurate.

NEW TECHNIQUES

Computers make it easier to change map information and styles quickly. This map of the southern coast of Spain, made in 1997 has been made using digital terrain modelling (see below) and traditional cartography.

Today, cartographers have access to far more data about the Earth than in the past. Satellites collect and process information about its surface. Further elements may then be added in the traditional way. Computers are now widely used to combine these different sorts of map information. More recently, the use of Global Positioning Systems (GPS) linked to satellites, and the increased availability of Internet based mapping, has revolutionised the way that maps are created and used.

MODERN MAP MAKING

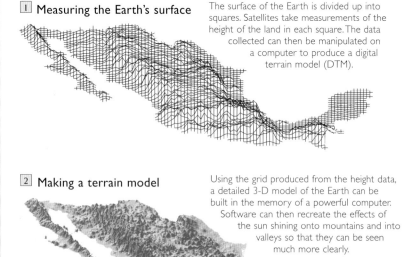

1 Measuring the Earth's surface
The surface of the Earth is divided up into squares. Satellites take measurements of the height of the land in each square. The data collected can then be manipulated on a computer to produce a digital terrain model (DTM).

3 Adding detail to the land surface
The height of the land can be shown using bands of colour, or by contour lines, which are applied to the digitally-created surface of the Earth. Colour can also be used to show different kinds of vegetation, such as deserts, forests and grasslands.

2 Making a terrain model
Using the grid produced from the height data, a detailed 3-D model of the Earth can be built in the memory of a powerful computer. Software can then recreate the effects of the sun shining onto mountains and into valleys so that they can be seen much more clearly.

4 Adding map detail
Features such as roads, rivers, towns and cities can now be added to the map. They are selected, and compiled and scanned digitally into the computer. The information can then be 'draped' on top of the terrain model to create a map.

SHOWING INFORMATION ON A MAP

A map is a selective diagram of a place. It is the cartographer's job to decide what kind of information to show on a map. They can choose to highlight certain kinds of features – such as roads, rivers and land height. They can also show other features such as sea depth, place names, and borders which would be impossible to see either on the ground or from a photograph. The information that can be shown in a map is influenced by a number of factors, most notably by its scale.

This is a satellite photograph of the harbour area of Rio de Janeiro in Brazil. Although you can see the bay and where most of the housing is, it is impossible to see roads or get any sense of the position of places relative to one another.

This is a map of the same area as you can see in the photograph. Much of the detail has been greatly simplified. Towns are named and marked; contours indicate the height of the land; and roads, railways and borders between districts have been added.

SCALE

To make a map of an area it needs to be greatly reduced in size. This is known as drawing to scale. The scale of the map shows us by how much the area has been reduced. The smaller the scale, the greater the area of land that can be shown on the map. There will be far less detail and the map will not be as accurate. The maps below show the different kinds of information that can be shown on maps of varying scales.

When using a map to work out what areas or distances are in reality, we need to refer to the scale of that particular map. Map scales can be shown in several ways.

WAYS TO SHOW SCALE

1 **Representative fraction**
One unit on the map would be equal to 1,000,000 units on the ground. **1:1,000,000**

2 **Linear scale**
The line is marked off in units which represent the real distances of the map, given in both miles and kilometres.

SCALE BAR

3 **Statement of scale**
It means that 1-mm on the map represents 1-km on the ground.
1 mm represents 1 km

LONDON 1:21,000,000

This small-scale map shows the position of London in relation to Europe. Very little detail can be seen at this scale – only the names of countries and the largest towns.

LONDON 1:5,500,000

At a scale of 1 to 5,500,000 you can see the major road network in the southeast of the UK. Many towns are named and you can see the difference in size and status.

LONDON 1:900,000

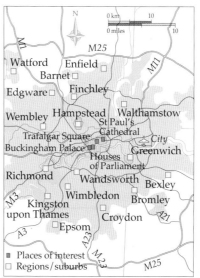

This map is at a much larger scale. You can see the major roads that lead out from London and the names of many suburbs, places of interest and airports.

LONDON 1:12,500

This is a street map of central London. The streets are named, as are places of interest, train and underground stations. The scale is large enough to show plenty of detail.

READING MAPS

Maps use a unique visual language to convey a great deal of detailed information in a relatively simple form. Different features are marked out using special symbols and styles of print. These symbols are explained in the key to the map and you should always read a map alongside its key or legend. This page explains how to look for different features on the map and how to unravel the different layers of information that you can find on it.

PHYSICAL FEATURES

All the regional and country maps in this atlas are based on a model of the Earth's surface. The computer-generated relief gives an accurate picture of the surface of the land. Colours are used to show the relative heights of the land; green is for low-lying land, and yellows, browns and greys are for higher land. Water features like streams, rivers and lakes are also shown.

1 WATER FEATURES

On this map extract, the blue lines show a number of rivers, including the Salween and the Irrawaddy. The Irrawaddy forms a huge delta, splitting into many streams as it reaches the sea.

2 RELIEF

These mountains are in the north of Southeast Asia. The underlying relief on the map and the coloured bands help you to see the height of the land.

HUMAN FEATURES

Maps also reveal a great deal about the human geography of an area. As well as showing where towns and roads are, different symbols can tell you more about the size of towns and the importance of a road. Borders between countries or regions can only be seen on a map.

3 BORDERS

Borders on the map are marked by a thick purple line. The boundary between Laos and Vietnam is in sparsely populated mountainous terrain, with the border generally running along a mountain range.

4 SETTLEMENTS

The symbol for a settlement can tell you its position, population and political status. Most towns are shown by a circle or a square. These represent the size of their population. Where a town is coloured red, this shows that it is a capital city such as Kuala Lumpur in Malaysia.

KEY TO MAP SYMBOLS

BOUNDARIES

‒‒‒‒‒	Full international border
‑ ‑ ‑ ‑	Disputed border

COMMUNICATION FEATURES

	Major road
	Minor road
	Railway
✈	International airport

DRAINAGE FEATURES

	Major river
	Minor river
	Lake
	Wetland

LANDSCAPE FEATURES

△	Mountain

POPULATED PLACES

●	Capital city
▣	Greater than 500,000
◉	100,000–500,000
○	50,000–100,000
○	Less than 50,000

NAMES

LAOS	Country
PARACEL ISLANDS (disputed by China, Taiwan & Vietnam)	Dependent territory
JAKARTA	Capital city
Sarawak	Cultural region
Chin Hills	Landscape feature
Puncak Jaya 5040m	Mountain/pass
Red River	River/lake
Java Sea	Sea feature

FINDING PLACES

Alphanumeric grid references

All the maps in this book are indexed using their alphanumeric grid reference – for example, G4. To find a place you must first look up its page number and then its grid reference. Read the letters and numbers off the bottom and side of the grid. Using rulers held at right angles to one another you will find the point where the lines meet. The place will be located within this square.

Latitude and longitude references

The lines of latitude and longitude are known as graticules. They are shown on the map as thin blue lines with the value of their latitude or longitude given as a blue number at the edge of the map.

LAND HEIGHT

	Above 4000 m
	2000–4000 m
	1000–2000 m
	500–1000 m
	250–500 m
	100–250 m
	0–100 m

SEA DEPTH

	0–250 m
	250–500 m
	500–1000 m
	1000–2000 m
	2000–3000 m
	3000–4000 m
	Below 4000 m

CITIES AND TOWNS

▣	Over 500,000 people
◉	100,000–500,000
○	50,000–100,000
○	Less than 50,000

MALAYSIA'S TWO CAPITALS
KUALA LUMPUR - capital
PUTRAJAYA - administrative capital

5 ROADS AND RAILWAYS

[a] The major road and railway links between Hue and Nha Trang hug the Vietnamese coast. A string of coastal towns is often connected by road and rail in this manner.

Chiang Mai, in northern [b] Thailand, is linked to the capital Bangkok to the south by railway and road. At Chiang Mai, the mountains are too high for the railway to continue, and only roads go north into Myanmar (Burma).

USING THE ATLAS

This Atlas has been designed to develop map-reading skills and to introduce readers to a wide range of different maps. It also provides a wealth of detailed geographic information about the world today. The Atlas is divided into four sections: **Learning Map Skills**; **The World About Us**, covering global geographic patterns; the **World Atlas**, dealing with the world's regions, and an **Index**.

LEARNING MAP SKILLS

Maps show the Earth – which is three-dimensional – in just two dimensions. This section shows how maps are made; how different kinds of information are shown on maps; how to choose what to put on a map and the best way to show it. It also explains how to read the maps in this Atlas.

THE WORLD ABOUT US

These pages contain a series of world maps which show important themes, such as physical features, climate, life zones, population and the world economy, at a global scale. They give a worldwide picture of concepts which are explored in more detail later in the book.

Text introduces themes and concepts in each spread.

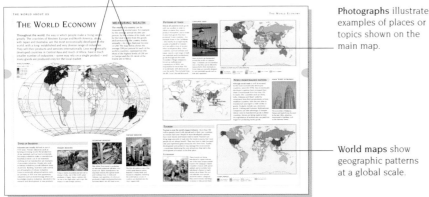

Photographs illustrate examples of places or topics shown on the main map.

World maps show geographic patterns at a global scale.

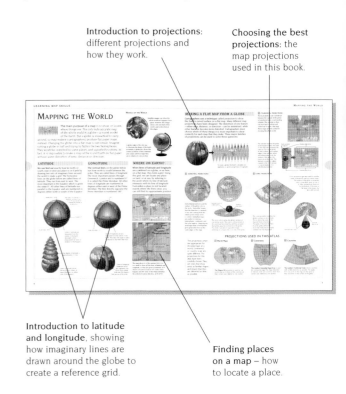

Introduction to projections: different projections and how they work.

Choosing the best projections: the map projections used in this book.

Introduction to latitude and longitude, showing how imaginary lines are drawn around the globe to create a reference grid.

Finding places on a map – how to locate a place.

CONTINENTAL MAPS

A cross-section through the continent shows the relative height of certain features.

A detailed physical map of the continent shows major natural geographic features, including mountains, lakes and rivers.

Photographs and locator maps illustrate the main geographic regions and show you where they are.

The industry map shows the main industrial towns and cities and the main industries in each continent. It also shows the wealth of each country relative to the rest of the world.

CONTINENTAL GEOGRAPHY PAGES

Humans have colonized and changed all the continents except Antarctica. These pages show the factors which have affected this process: climate, the availability of resources such as coal, oil and minerals, and varying patterns of land use. Mineral resources are directly linked to many industries, and most agriculture is governed both by the quality of the land and the climate.

The climate map shows the main types of climates across the continent and where the hottest and coldest, wettest and driest places are.

The mineral resources map shows where the most important reserves of minerals, including coal and precious metals, are found.

CONTINENTAL PAGES

These pages show the physical shape of each continent and the impact that humans have made on the natural landscape – building towns and roads and creating borders between countries. They show where natural features such as mountain ranges and rivers have created physical boundaries, and where humans have created their own political boundaries between states.

The political map of the continent shows country boundaries and country names.

The land use map shows different types of land and the main kinds of farming that take place in each area.

REGIONAL MAPS

The main part of the Atlas contains detailed maps of countries and regions. Each of these is accompanied by a series of small thematic maps, models and charts, which give information about the climate, where people live, how they use the land, the different kinds of industry, and important environmental issues.

TERRAIN MODEL

A computer-generated landscape model shows what the land really looks like. There are no roads or towns to mask the physical geography of the country or region. Mountain ranges, plains and river basins can be easily seen.

COLOURED THUMB TAGS

Each section has its own colour code.

- Learning Map Skills
- The World About Us
- North America
- South America
- Africa
- Europe
- Asia
- Australasia and Oceania
- Antarctica and the Arctic

CLIMATE MAPS

These maps show the temperature and rainfall patterns in January and July. Coloured bands indicate temperatures: blue for low temperatures, orange for high ones. Rainfall is represented by black lines with a number giving the average amount of rain. These are called isohyets.

Isohyets show the rainfall patterns in millimetres per year. The areas between the lines are either over or under the figures shown on the isohyets.

JULY

The hottest areas are coloured orange.

JANUARY

Here the rainfall is between 50 and 100 mm per year.

Less than 50

LOCATOR GLOBE

This shows the location of the country or region both within its continent, and in relation to the rest of the world.

EUROPE
Eastern Europe

NORTH AMERICA · ASIA · AFRICA · SOUTH AMERICA · AUSTRALASIA AND OCEANIA · ANTARCTICA

MAP GRID

Each main map has a grid. Using the grid will help you to find a place on the map. Grid references are expressed as letters (running from left to right across the frame), and numbers (running from the top to the bottom of the frame), for example, A-4, G-6. Everything on the map is referenced in the **Index** at the back of the book.

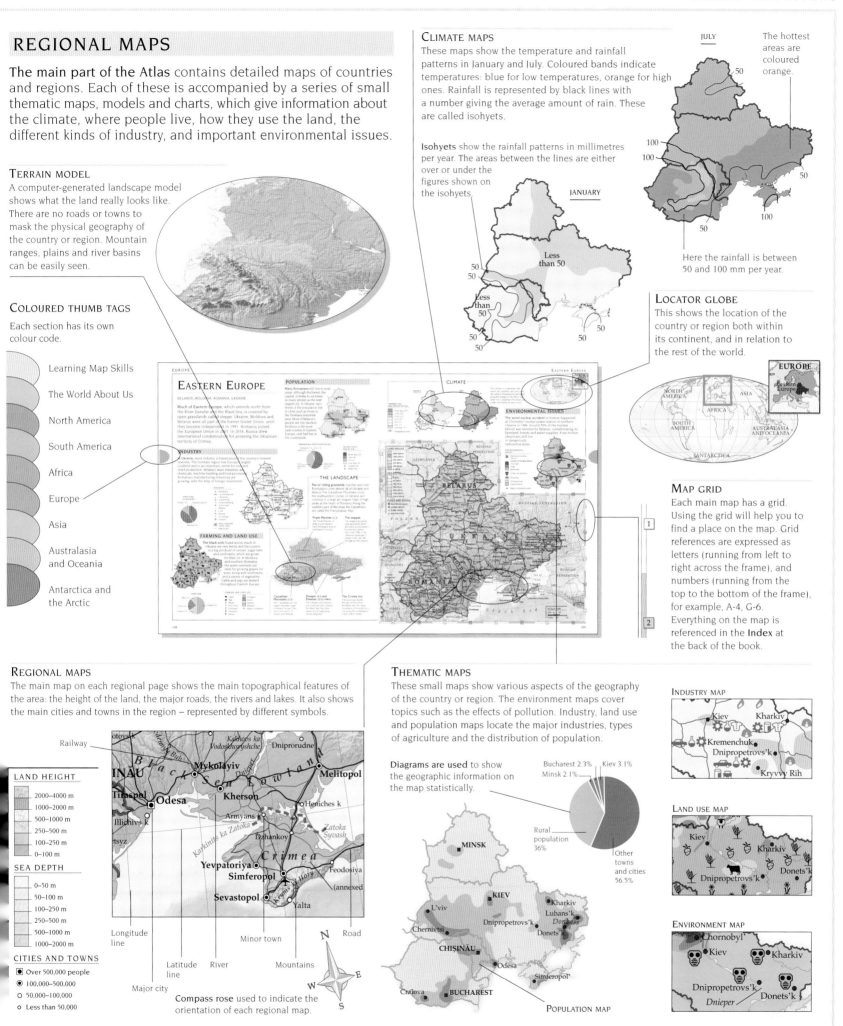

EASTERN EUROPE

REGIONAL MAPS

The main map on each regional page shows the main topographical features of the area: the height of the land, the major roads, the rivers and lakes. It also shows the main cities and towns in the region – represented by different symbols.

Railway

LAND HEIGHT

- 2000–4000 m
- 1000–2000 m
- 500–1000 m
- 250–500 m
- 100–250 m
- 0–100 m

SEA DEPTH

- 0–50 m
- 50–100 m
- 100–250 m
- 250–500 m
- 500–1000 m
- 1000–2000 m

CITIES AND TOWNS

- ◼ Over 500,000 people
- ◉ 100,000–500,000
- ◌ 50,000–100,000
- ○ Less than 50,000

Black Sea Lowland

MYKOLAYIV · Melitopol · Tiraspol · Odesa · Kherson · Heniches'k · Illichivs'k · Armyans · Dzhankoy · Zatoka Syvash · Crimea · Yevpatoriya · Simferopol · Feodosiya · Sevastopol · Yalta · (annexed)

Longitude line · Latitude line · River · Mountains · Major city · Minor town · Road

Compass rose used to indicate the orientation of each regional map.

THEMATIC MAPS

These small maps show various aspects of the geography of the country or region. The environment maps cover topics such as the effects of pollution. Industry, land use and population maps locate the major industries, types of agriculture and the distribution of population.

Diagrams are used to show the geographic information on the map statistically.

Bucharest 2.3% Kiev 3.1%
Minsk 2.1%
Rural population 36%
Other towns and cities 56.5%

MINSK · KIEV · L'viv · Chernivtsi · Kharkiv · Luhans'k · Dnipropetrovs'k · Donbass · Donets'k · CHIŞINĂU · Odesa · Simferopol' · Craiova · BUCHAREST

POPULATION MAP

INDUSTRY MAP

Kiev · Kharkiv · Kremenchuk · Dnipropetrovs'k · Kryvvy Rih

LAND USE MAP

Kiev · Kharkiv · Dnipropetrovs'k · Donets'k

ENVIRONMENT MAP

Chornobyl · Kiev · Kharkiv · Dnipropetrovs'k · Donets'k · Dnieper

THE PHYSICAL WORLD

This map shows the main physical features of the world: the mountain ranges, the great rivers and lakes, deserts, grassland plains, seas and oceans. No human settlements are named on this map – only the physical or landscape features.

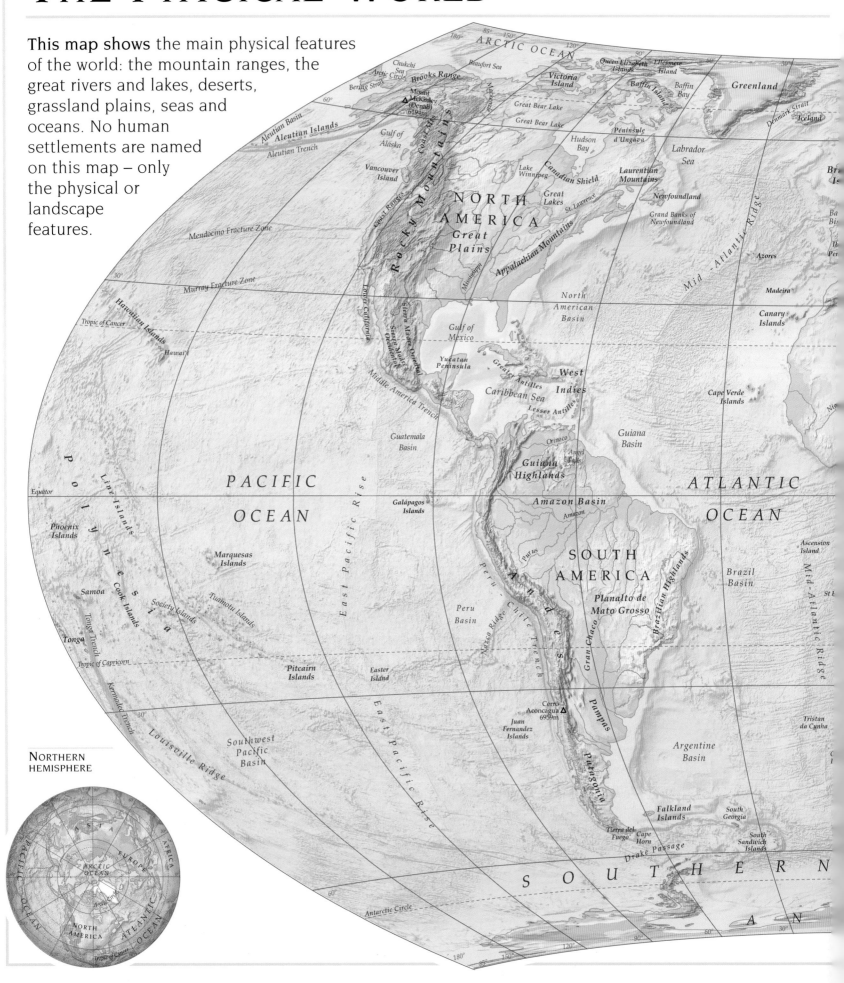

ARCTIC OCEAN

Chukchi Sea
Arctic Circle
Bering Strait
Brooks Range
Beaufort Sea
Mackenzie
Victoria Island
Queen Elizabeth Islands
Ellesmere Island
Baffin Island
Baffin Bay
Greenland
Denmark Strait
Iceland

Mount McKinley (Denali) 6194m
Gulf of Alaska
Coast Ranges
Great Bear Lake
Great Bear Lake
Hudson Bay
Péninsule d'Ungava
Labrador Sea

Aleutian Basin
Aleutian Islands
Aleutian Trench

Vancouver Island

Lake Winnipeg
Canadian Shield
Laurentian Mountains
Newfoundland
Grand Banks of Newfoundland

NORTH AMERICA
Great Plains
Great Lakes
St. Lawrence

Mendocino Fracture Zone

Rocky Mountains

Appalachian Mountains
North American Basin

Mid-Atlantic Ridge

Azores

30°
Murray Fracture Zone
Mississippi

Madeira

Hawaiian Islands
Tropic of Cancer

Sierra Nevada
Lower California

Gulf of Mexico
Yucatan Peninsula

Canary Islands

Hawai'i
Sierra Madre Occidental
Sierra Madre Oriental

Greater Antilles
West Indies
Caribbean Sea
Lesser Antilles

Cape Verde Islands

Middle America Trench

Guatemala Basin

Guiana Basin

Orinoco
Angel Falls
Guiana Highlands

PACIFIC

Equator
Linе Islands

OCEAN

Galápagos Islands

Amazon Basin
Amazon

ATLANTIC
OCEAN

Phoenix Islands

Polynesia

East Pacific Rise

Ascension Island

Marquesas Islands

Purus
SOUTH AMERICA
Brazilian Highlands
Brazil Basin

Samoa
Cook Islands
Society Islands
Tuamotu Islands

Peru Basin
Andes
Planalto de Mato Grosso

St

Tonga
Tonga Trench

Nazca Ridge
Peru-Chile Trench
Gran Chaco

Tropic of Capricorn

Pitcairn Islands

Easter Island

Juan Fernandez Islands
Cerro Aconcagua 6959m

Pampas

Tristan da Cunha

East Pacific Rise

Kermadec Trench
Louisville Ridge

Southwest Pacific Basin

Argentine Basin

Patagonia

Falkland Islands
South Georgia

Tierra del Fuego
Cape Horn
South Sandwich Islands

Drake Passage

SOUTHERN

60°

Antarctic Circle

120°
90°

180°

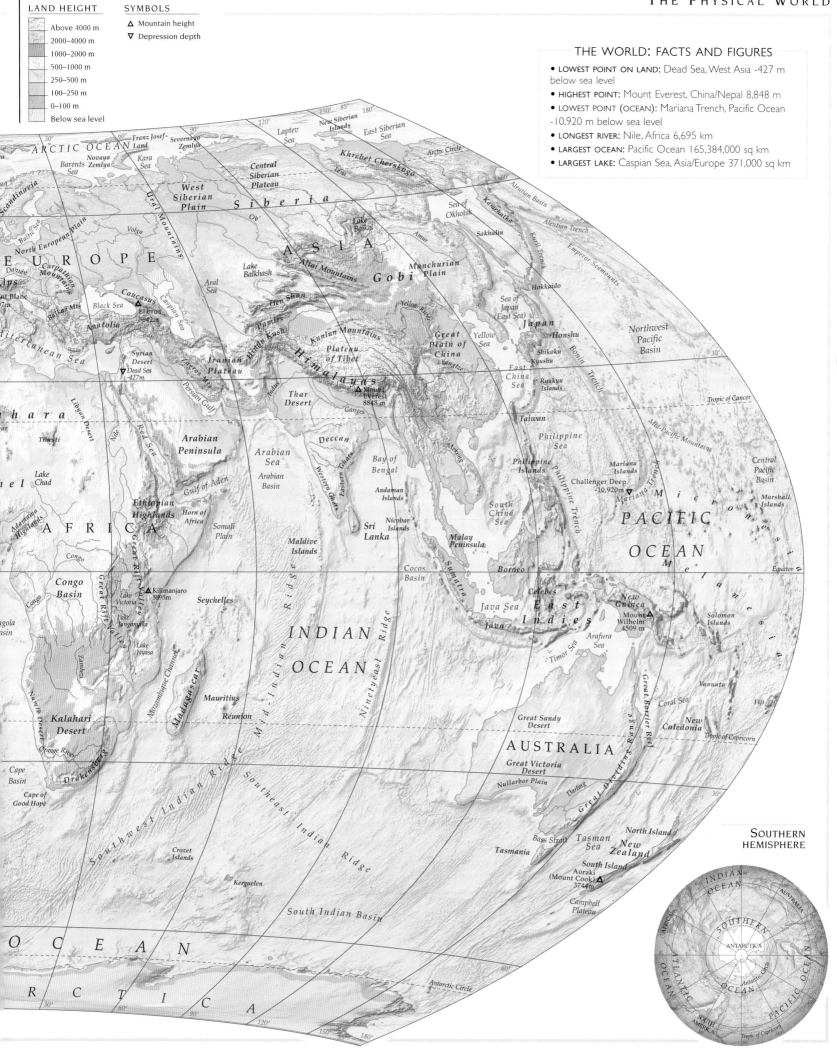

LAND HEIGHT

Above 4000 m
2000–4000 m
1000–2000 m
500–1000 m
250–500 m
100–250 m
0–100 m
Below sea level

SYMBOLS

△ Mountain height
▽ Depression depth

THE WORLD: FACTS AND FIGURES

- **LOWEST POINT ON LAND:** Dead Sea, West Asia -427 m below sea level
- **HIGHEST POINT:** Mount Everest, China/Nepal 8,848 m
- **LOWEST POINT (OCEAN):** Mariana Trench, Pacific Ocean -10,920 m below sea level
- **LONGEST RIVER:** Nile, Africa 6,695 km
- **LARGEST OCEAN:** Pacific Ocean 165,384,000 sq km
- **LARGEST LAKE:** Caspian Sea, Asia/Europe 371,000 sq km

SOUTHERN
HEMISPHERE

THE EARTH'S STRUCTURE

The shape and position of the Earth's oceans and continents make a familiar pattern. This is just the latest in a series of forms which the Earth has taken in the hundreds of millions of years since its creation. Massive forces inside the Earth cause the continents and oceans to move apart and together again, forming larger landmasses and then breaking them apart – a process known as plate tectonics. The movement is very slow – but over millions of years, the changes can be enormous.

DYNAMIC EARTH

The heart of the Earth is a solid core of iron surrounded by several layers of very hot – sometimes liquid – rock. The crust is relatively thin and is made up of a series of 'plates' which fit closely together. Movement of the molten rock deep within the mantle of the Earth causes the plates to move, creating changes in the surface features of the Earth.

THE EARTH'S PLATES

Continental plate

Oceanic plate

Plate boundary or margin

Continental and oceanic plates are tectonic plates – made from crustal rock

INSIDE THE EARTH

Rocky crust

Outer core – liquid iron and nickel

Inner core – made of iron

Mantle – ma from solid a molten ro

TECTONIC PLATES, VOLCANOES AND EARTHQUAKES

▲ Volcanic zone

▨ Earthquake zone on land

⇨ Direction of plate movement

〰 Rift valley

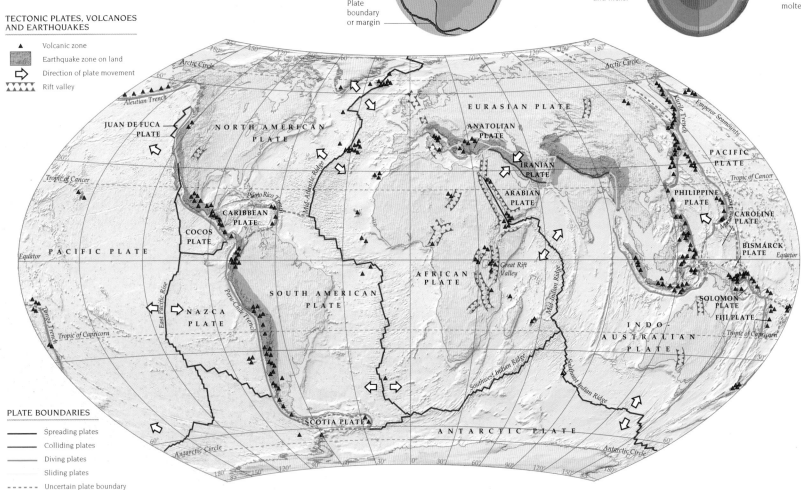

PLATE BOUNDARIES

—— Spreading plates

—— Colliding plates

—— Diving plates

—— Sliding plates

---- Uncertain plate boundary

PLATE BOUNDARIES

The point where two plates meet is known as a plate boundary. As the Earth's plates move together or apart or slide alongside one another, the great forces which result cause great changes in the landscape. Mountains can be created, earthquakes occur and there may be frequent volcanic eruptions.

SPREADING PLATES

Earthquake zone   Ocean floor

Magma pushed upwards   Solid mantle

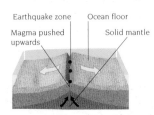

As plates move apart, magma rises through the outer mantle. When it cools, it forms new crust. The Mid-Atlantic Ridge is caused by spreading plates.

COLLIDING PLATES

Colliding plate   Mountains thrust upwards

Earthquake zone

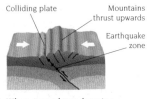

When two plates bearing landmasses collide with one another, the land is crumpled upwards into high mountain peaks such as the Alps, and the Himalayas.

DIVING PLATES

Earthquake zone   Mountains

Ocean plate   Continental plate

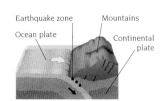

When an ocean-bearing plate collides with a continental plate it is forced downwards under the other plate and into the mantle. Volcanoes occur along these boundaries.

SLIDING PLATES

Earthquake zone   Fault line

Plate   Plate

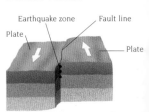

As two plates slide past each other, great friction is set up along the fault line which lies between them. This can lead to powerful earthquakes.

SHAPING THE LANDSCAPE

The Earth's surface is made from solid rock or water. The land is constantly re-shaped by external forces. Water flowing as rivers or in the oceans erodes and deposits material to create valleys and lakes and to shape coastlines. When water is built up and compressed into solid sheets of ice, it can erode more deeply, creating deeper, wider valleys. Wind also has a powerful effect; stripping away vegetation and transporting rock particles vast distances.

RIVERS

Most rivers have their sources in mountain areas. They flow fast through the mountains, eroding deep V-shaped valleys. As they reach flatter areas they begin to meander in great loops, both eroding and then depositing rock particles as they slow down.

GLACIERS

In cold areas, close to the poles or on mountain tops, snow is built up into rivers of ice called glaciers. They move slowly, eroding deep U-shaped valleys. When the glacier melts, ridges of eroded rock called moraines are left at the sides and end of the glacier.

SEA ACTION

The oceans change the landscape in two major ways. They batter cliffs, causing rock to break away and the land to retreat, and they carry eroded material along the coast, to make beaches and sand bars.

WIND

Wind can erode and break down rock into smaller boulders and stones and eventually into sand. Desert sand dunes are shaped by the force of the wind and vary from ripples to hills 200 m high.

LANDSLIDES

Heavy rain can loosen soil and rock beneath the surface of slopes. As this moves, the top layers slip forward, to form heaps of rubble at the base of the slope.

THE WORLD'S OCEANS

Just over two-thirds of the Earth's surface is covered by water and more than 97% of this water is contained in the oceans. Movements within the Earth shape the ocean floor in the same way as they do the land surface, creating mountain ranges, trenches and plateaus, and changing the shape and size of the oceans. The difference between an ocean and a sea is simply its size; oceans are much bigger.

POLAR OCEANS

The Southern and Arctic Oceans contain large icebergs, that have broken away from the ice shelf.

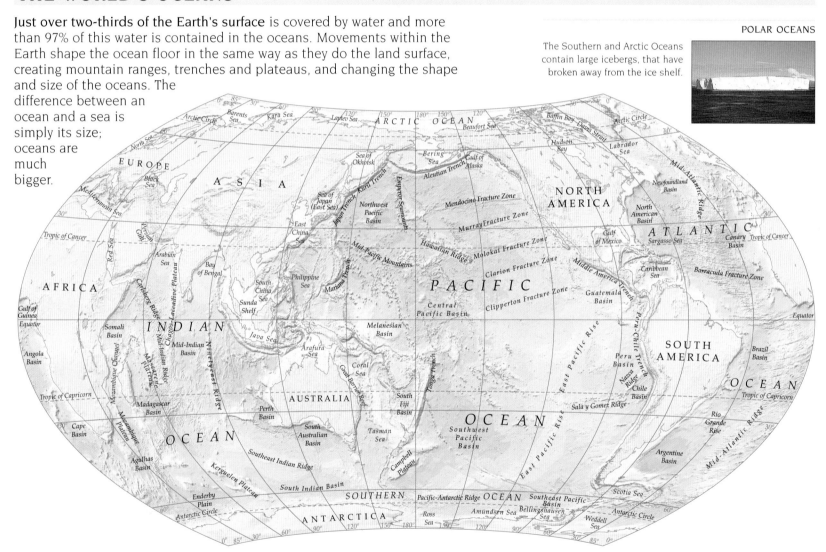

INDIAN OCEAN

The Indian Ocean covers about 20% of the world's surface. Ocean swells, starting deep in the Southern Ocean, often cause flooding in Sri Lanka and the Maldives.

PACIFIC OCEAN

The Pacific is the largest and deepest ocean in the world. It is surrounded an arc of volcanoes, including Japan, Indonesia and the Andes, known as the 'Ring of Fire'.

ATLANTIC OCEAN

The Atlantic Ocean was formed about 180 million years ago. The land which now forms Europe and Africa pulled apart from the Americas to create an ocean 3,000 km wide.

CLIMATE AND LIFE ZONES

This map shows the different climates found around the world. Climates are particular combinations of temperature and humidity. Climates are affected by latitude, the height of the land, winds and ocean currents. Climates can change, but not overnight. Weather is local and consists of short-term events such as thunderstorms, hurricanes and blizzards.

HURRICANES

Hurricanes are violent cyclonic windstorms, driven by heat energy gathered from tropical seas. The Caribbean islands and the east coast of the USA are particularly prone to hurricanes.

PREVAILING WINDS

→ Cool wind
→ Warm wind

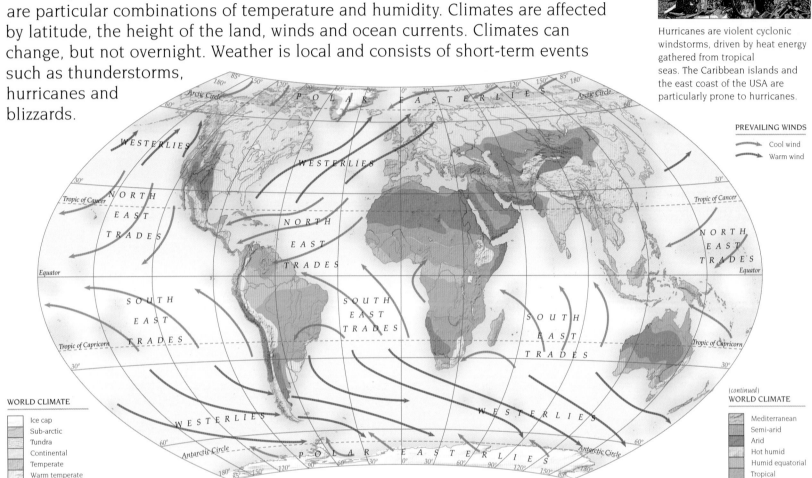

WORLD CLIMATE

- Ice cap
- Sub-arctic
- Tundra
- Continental
- Temperate
- Warm temperate

WORLD CLIMATE (continued)

- Mediterranean
- Semi-arid
- Arid
- Hot humid
- Humid equatorial
- Tropical

CLIMATE CHANGE

The Earth's climate is a constantly changing system resulting from a complex interaction of different geographical factors. Throughout history there have been several periods when the Earth's climate has been either hotter or colder than today. However, many scientists think that human activity is causing problems to this system by increasing levels of 'greenhouse gases' in the atmosphere. These gases, including carbon dioxide (CO_2), allow heat from the Sun to enter the atmosphere and then trap some of this heat like a greenhouse. Most scientists believe that unless action is taken to reduce greenhouse gases, temperatures will rise in a process known as global warming.

MAP KEY

Predicted change in average surface air temperature between 1960–1990 and 2070–2100

- 4 to 5°C
- 3 to 4°C
- 2 to 3°C
- 1 to 2°C
- 0 to 1°C

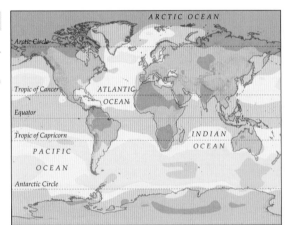

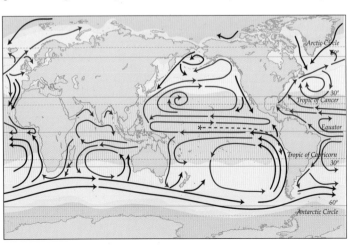

OCEAN CURRENTS

Ocean currents help to distribute heat around the Earth and have a great influence on climate. Convection currents circulate massive amounts of warm and cold water around the oceans. Warm water is moved away from the tropics to higher latitudes and cold water is moved toward the tropics.

OCEAN CURRENTS AND SURFACE TEMPERATURES

- ⤴ Cold currents
- ⤴ Warm currents
- *--→ El Niño

- 20 to 30°C
- 10 to 20°C
- 0 to 10°C
- Sea-water −2° to 0°C
- Sea-ice (average) below −2°C

LIFE ZONES

The map below shows the Earth divided into different biomes – also called biogeographical regions. The combination of climate, the type of landscape, and the plants and animals that live there, are used to classify a region. Similar biomes are found in very different places around the world.

POLAR REGIONS

The North and South poles are permanently covered by ice. Only a few plants and animals can live here.

TUNDRA

Tundra is flat, cold and dry with few trees. Plants such as mosses and lichens grow close to the ground.

DESERTS
Very little rain falls in desert areas, whether they are hot deserts such as the Sahara or cold deserts like the Gobi.

NEEDLELEAF FORESTS
Tall coniferous trees such as pine and spruce, with spines or needles instead of leaves, grow in the far north of Scandinavia, Canada and the Russian Federation.

BROADLEAF FORESTS
Broadleaf or deciduous forests once covered temperate regions over most of the northern hemisphere. They contain trees of many varieties – all of which shed their leaves every year.

TEMPERATE RAINFORESTS
Evergreen, broadleaved trees need a warmer, wetter climate than deciduous trees. They are known as temperate rainforests.

MEDITERRANEAN
Close to the shores of the Mediterranean Sea, the vegetation consists mainly of herbs, shrubs and drought-resistant trees.

BIOME TYPES
- Mountains
- Polar regions
- Tundra
- Tropical rainforests
- Dry woodlands
- Savannah
- Temperate grasslands

(continued)
BIOME TYPES
- Mediterranean
- Needleleaf forests
- Temperate rainforests
- Broadleafs forests
- Cold deserts
- Hot deserts
- Wetlands

TEMPERATE GRASSLANDS
Grasslands cover the central areas of the continents. They are known in the middle latitudes as prairies, steppe and pampas.

SAVANNAH
The savannah consists of woodland, interspersed with grassland. These regions lie between the tropical rainforest and hot desert regions.

DRY WOODLANDS
Dry woodlands are found at the edge of grasslands. They contain small trees and shrubs adapted to dry conditions.

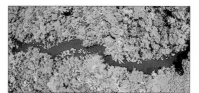

TROPICAL RAINFORESTS
Around the Equator, where temperatures are high and there is plenty of rain, tropical rainforests can flourish. Trees grow continuously and are tall with huge, broad leaves.

WETLANDS
Low-lying swamps and marshes are known as wetlands. They are often home to a rich variety of animal, plant and bird species.

WORLD POPULATION

Favelas – or shanty towns – have grown up around many South American cities because of overcrowding.

There are now an estimated **7.2 billion people** on Earth. The population has increased nearly four times since 1900. Before that date, the number of people increased slowly as people were born and died at similar rates. With improved living conditions, better medical care and more efficient food production, more people survived to adulthood and the population began to grow much faster. If growth continues at the present rate, the world's population is likely to reach 7.7 billion by the year 2020.

POPULATION STRUCTURES

Measuring the numbers of old and young people gives the age structure of a country or continent. If there are large numbers of young people and a high birth rate, the population is said to be youthful – as is the case in many African, Asian and South American countries. If the birth-rate is low but many people survive into old age, the population distribution is said to be ageing – this is true of much of Europe, Japan, Canada and the USA. Extreme events like wars can distort the population, leading to a loss of population in certain age groups.

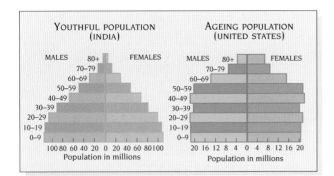

POPULATION DENSITY

The main map (*centre*) and the map below both show population density – the number of people who live in a given area. The map below shows the average population density per country. You can see that European countries and parts of Asia are very densely populated. The large map shows where people actually live. While the average population density in Brazil and Egypt is quite low, the coasts of Brazil and the areas close to the River Nile in Egypt are very densely populated.

DENSE POPULATION

Huge crowds near the Haora Bridge in Kolkata (Calcutta), India – one of the world's most densely populated cities.

POPULATION DENSITY (BY COUNTRY)

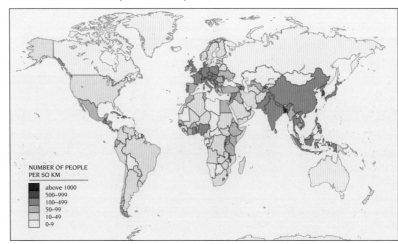

NUMBER OF PEOPLE PER SQ KM
- above 1000
- 500–999
- 100–499
- 50–99
- 10–49
- 0–9

SPARSE POPULATION

The cold north of Canada has one of the lowest population densities in the world. Some people live in extreme isolation, separated from others by lakes and forests.

URBAN GROWTH

The 20th century saw a huge increase in the number of people living in cities. This has led to more large cities and the development of some 'super cities' such as Mexico City and Tokyo, each with more than 20 million people. In 1900, only about 10% of the population lived in cities. Now it is closer to 50% and soon the figure may be nearer two in three people. Some continents are far more 'urbanized' than others: in South America nearly 80% of people live in cities, whereas in Africa the figure is only about 30%.

LEVELS OF URBANIZATION

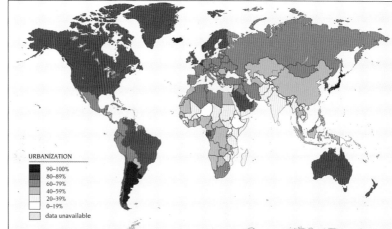

URBANIZATION
- 90–100%
- 80–89%
- 60–79%
- 40–59%
- 20–39%
- 0–19%
- data unavailable

POPULATION GROWTH

The rate of population growth varies dramatically between the continents. Europe has a large population but it is increasing slowly. Africa is still sparsely populated, but in some countries such as Kenya, the population is growing very rapidly, increasing pressure on the land. China and India have the world's largest populations. Both countries now have laws to try and curb the birth rate.

CONTROLLING GROWTH

In 1980, fewer than 25% of women in less developed countries used birth control. Education programmes and more widely available contraceptives are thought to have doubled this figure. But many families still have no access to contraception.

AN AGEING POPULATION

In some countries, a low birth-rate, and an increasingly long-lived elderly population has greatly increased the ratio of old people to younger people, putting a strain on health and social services. For example, in Japan, most people can now expect to live to at least 80 years of age.

MAIN MAP:
POPULATION DENSITY
(People per sq km)
- Below 1
- 1–5
- 6–10
- 11–20
- 21–50
- 51–100
- 101–200
- Above 200

Arctic Circle
Tropic of Cancer
Equator
Tropic of Capricorn
Antarctic Circle

BIRTH RATE

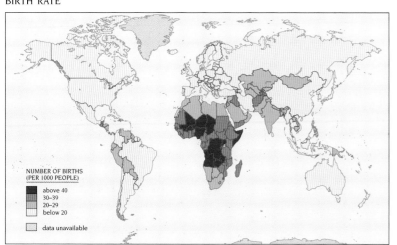

NUMBER OF BIRTHS
(PER 1000 PEOPLE)
- above 40
- 30–39
- 20–29
- below 20
- data unavailable

LIFE EXPECTANCY

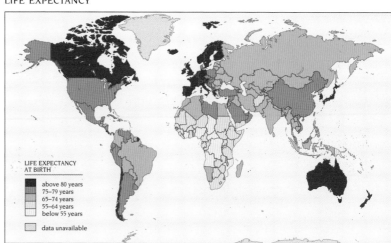

LIFE EXPECTANCY
AT BIRTH
- above 80 years
- 75–79 years
- 65–74 years
- 55–64 years
- below 55 years
- data unavailable

THE WORLD ECONOMY

Throughout the world, the way in which people make a living varies greatly. The countries of Western Europe and North America, along with Japan and Australia, are the most economically developed in the world, with a long- established and very diverse range of industries. They sell their products and services internationally. Less economically developed countries in Central Asia and much of Africa, have a much smaller number of industries – some may rely on a single product – and many goods are produced only for the local market.

MEASURING WEALTH

The wealth of a country can be measured in several ways: for example, by the average annual income per person; by the volume of its trade; and by the total income from the goods and services that the country trades annually – its Gross National Income or GNI. The map below shows the average GNI per person for each of the world's countries, expressed in US$. Most of the highest levels of GNI are in Europe and the US; most of the lowest are in Africa.

WORLD ECONOMIES

GNI per capita (in US$)

- above 45,000
- 30,000–45,000
- 15,000–30,000
- 6,500–15,000
- below 6,500
- data unavailable

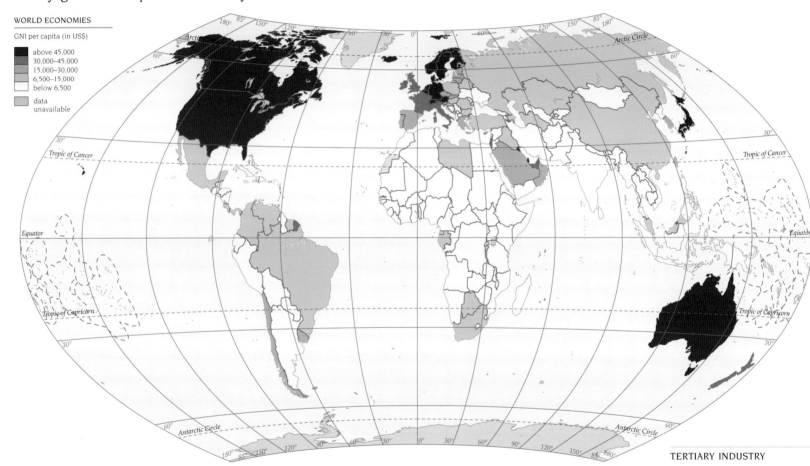

TYPES OF INDUSTRY

Industries are usually defined in one of three ways. Primary industries such as farming or mining involve the production of raw materials such as food or minerals. Secondary industries make or manufacture finished products out of raw materials: clothing and car manufacture are examples of secondary industries. People who work in tertiary industries provide different kinds of services. Banking, insurance and tourism are all examples of tertiary industries. Some economically advanced nations such as Germany or USA now have quaternary industries such as biotechnology which are knowledge-creation industries, devoted to the research and development of new products.

PRIMARY INDUSTRY

Tobacco leaves are picked and laid out for drying in Cuba, one of the world's great producers of cigars. Many countries rely on one or two high-value 'cash crops' like tobacco to earn foreign currency.

SECONDARY INDUSTRY

This skilled Thai weaver is producing an intricately patterned silk fabric on a hand loom. Fabric manufacture is an important industry throughout South and Southeast Asia. In India and Pakistan, vast quantities of cotton are produced in highly mechanized factories, but many fabrics are still hand woven.

TERTIARY INDUSTRY

The City of London is one of the world's great finance centres. Branches of many banks and insurance companies, including the world famous Lloyds of London, are clustered into the City's 'square mile'.

PATTERNS OF TRADE

Almost all countries trade goods
with one another in order to
obtain products they cannot
produce themselves, and to make
money from goods they have
produced. Some countries – for
example those in the Caribbean
– rely mainly on a single export,
usually a foodstuff or mineral,
and can suffer a loss of income
when world prices drop. Other
countries, such as Germany and
Japan, export a vast range of both
raw materials and manufactured
goods throughout the world.
A number of huge companies,
known as multinational
corporations or MNCs, are
responsible for more than 70%
of world trade, with divisions all
over the world. They include firms
like BP, Coca Cola and Microsoft.

CONTAINER SHIPS

Many products are transported
around the world on container
ships. Containers are of a standard
size so that they can be efficiently
transported to their destinations.
Some ships are specially designed
to carry perishable goods such as
fruit and vegetables.

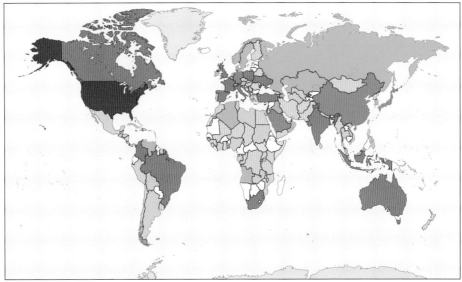

CURRENT ACCOUNT BALANCE (MILLIONS US$)

Deficit		Surplus		
Over 450,000	1,000–10,000	0–10,000	Over 100,000	Data unavailable
10,000–450,000	0–1,000	10,000–100,000		

NEWLY INDUSTRIALISED NATIONS

Although world trade is still dominated
by the more economically developed
countries, since the 1970s, less economically
developed countries have increased their
share of world trade from less than 10%
to nearly 30%. Countries such as China,
India, Malaysia and Brazil, aided by
investment from their governments or from
wealthier countries, have become able to
manufacture and export a wide variety of
goods. Products include cars, electronic
goods, clothing and footwear. Multinational
companies can take advantage of cheaper
labour costs to manufacture goods in these
countries. Moves are being made to limit
the exploitation of workers who are paid low
wages for producing luxury goods.

ASIAN 'TIGER' ECONOMIES

The economies of Malaysia,
Taiwan and South Korea, boomed
in the late 1980s, attracting
investment for buildings such
as the Petronas Towers.

TOURISM

Tourism is now the world's largest industry. More than 700
million people travel both abroad and in their own countries
as tourists each year. People in more developed countries
have more money and leisure time to travel. Tourism can
bring large amounts of cash into the local economy, but local
people do not always benefit. They may have to take low-paid
jobs and experience great intrusions into their lives. Tourist
development and pollution may damage the environment
– sometimes destroying the very attractions that led to the
development of tourism in the first place.

ECOTOURISM

These tourists are being
introduced to a giant tortoise,
one of the many unique animals
found in the Galapagos Islands.
A number of places with special
animals and ecosystems have
introduced schemes to teach
visitors about them. This not
only educates more people
about the need to safeguard
these environments, but brings
in money to help protect them.

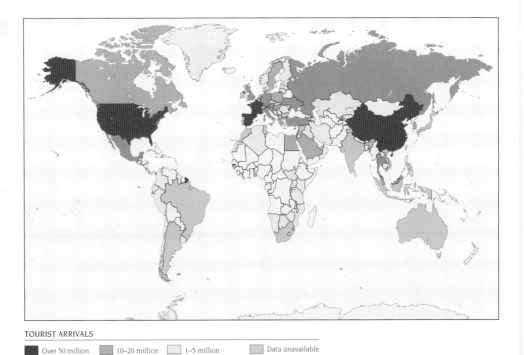

TOURIST ARRIVALS

Over 50 million	10–20 million	1–5 million	Data unavailable
20–50 million	5–10 million	below 1 million	

BORDERS AND BOUNDARIES

There are more countries in the world today than ever before – almost 200 – whereas in 1950, there were only 82. Since then, many former European colonies and Soviet states have become independent. The establishment of borders for each of these countries has often been the subject of disagreement.

Military borders

At the end of wars, new borders are often drawn up between the countries – frequently along ceasefire lines. They may remain there for many years. At the end of the Korean War in 1953, North and South Korea were divided close to the 38° line of latitude. This border has remained heavily fortified.

Long borders

The border between the USA and Canada is the second longest continuous border in the world. It cuts through the centre of the Great Lakes. To the west of the Great Lakes, the border runs along the 49° line of latitude.

Enclaves

If part of a country's territory has become separated from the rest of the country, and is surrounded by foreign territory, it is called an enclave. Kaliningrad is part of the Russian Federation, but is cut off from it by Lithuania and Belarus.

River borders

Over one-sixth of the world's national borders are formed by rivers. Long stretches of the Danube form natural borders in southeastern Europe.

NORTH AMERICA

SOUTH AMERICA

EUROPE

ASIA

AFRICA

AUSTRALASIA AND OCEANIA

ATLANTIC OCEAN

PACIFIC OCEAN

PACIFIC OCEAN

ATLANTIC OCEAN

INDIAN OCEAN

Mountain borders

Mountain ranges such as the Pyrenees, Alps and Himalayas form natural borders between many countries. In the Andes, border disputes between Chile and Argentina centred on finding the highest point in the mountain range which divided them.

Straight line borders

The borders of many countries in Africa and other former colonial territories are straight lines. This was the simplest solution for colonial administrators, who often knew little of the country's geography or population.

Lake boundaries

Countries which lie next to lakes usually fix their borders in the middle of the lake. Complicated agreements between colonial powers led to the awkward division of Lake Nyasa in Africa.

Territorial disputes

There are still many disputed territories and borders. One of the most serious territorial disputes is between India and Pakistan over Jammu and Kashmir, which has led to three wars since 1947.

The Atlas
OF THE
WORLD

THE NATIONS OF THE WORLD

The world is divided into 196 independent countries, and about 60 overseas territories or dependencies. The largest country is the Russian Federation covering 17,075,200 sq km; the smallest is Vatican City in Rome, with an area of 0.44 sq km.

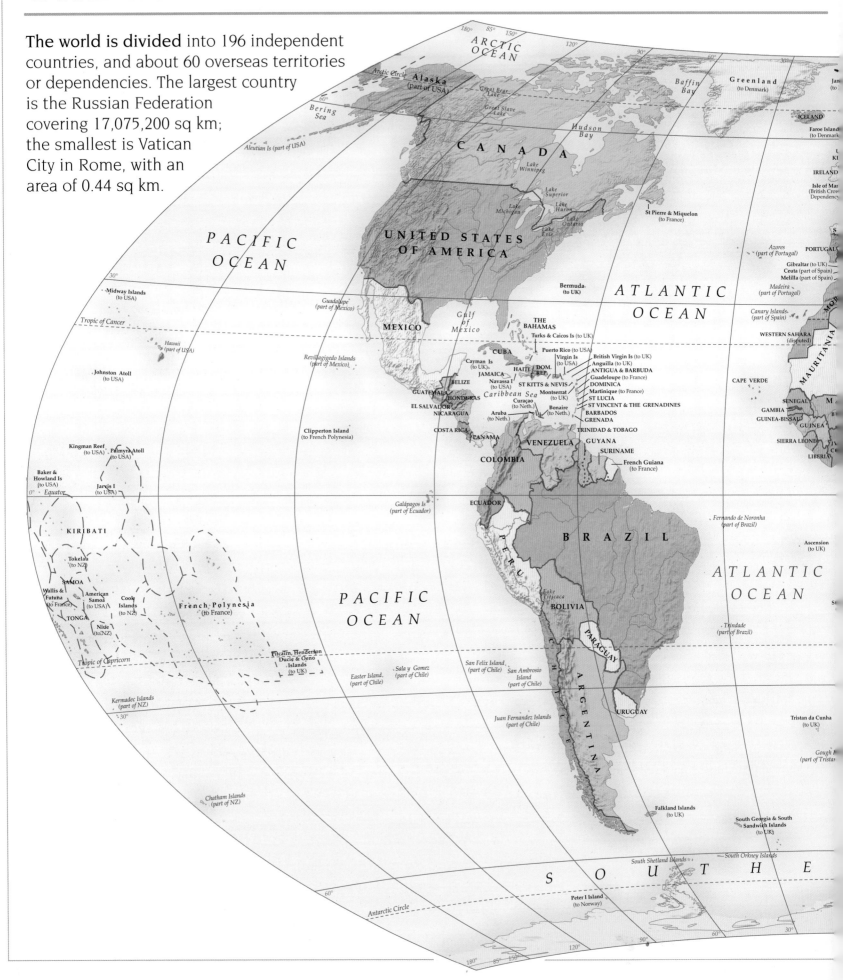

ARCTIC OCEAN

Arctic Circle Alaska (Part of USA)

Great Bear Lake

Great Slave Lake

Bering Sea

CANADA

Hudson Bay

Baffin Bay

Greenland (to Denmark)

ICELAND

Faroe Islands (to Denmark)

Aleutian Is (part of USA)

Lake Winnipeg

Lake Superior

Lake Michigan

Lake Huron

Lake Ontario

Lake Erie

St Pierre & Miquelon (to France)

IRELAND

Isle of Man (British Crown Dependency)

UNITED STATES OF AMERICA

PACIFIC OCEAN

Azores (part of Portugal) PORTUGAL

ATLANTIC OCEAN

Bermuda (to UK)

Gibraltar (to UK)
Ceuta (part of Spain)
Melilla (part of Spain)

Madeira (part of Portugal)

Midway Islands (to USA)

Guadalupe (part of Mexico)

Tropic of Cancer

MEXICO

Gulf of Mexico

THE BAHAMAS

Turks & Caicos Is (to UK)

Canary Islands (part of Spain)

WESTERN SAHARA (disputed)

Hawaii (part of USA)

Revillagigedo Islands (part of Mexico)

CUBA

Cayman Is (to UK)

JAMAICA

Puerto Rico (to USA)
Virgin Is (to USA)
British Virgin Is (to UK)
Anguilla (to UK)
ANTIGUA & BARBUDA
Guadeloupe (to France)
DOMINICA
Martinique (to France)
ST LUCIA
ST VINCENT & THE GRENADINES
BARBADOS
GRENADA

MAURITANIA

CAPE VERDE

Johnston Atoll (to USA)

HAITI DOM. REP.

BELIZE

Navassa I (to USA)

ST KITTS & NEVIS

Montserrat

Curaçao (to Neth.)

GUATEMALA

HONDURAS

Caribbean Sea

SENEGAL

GAMBIA

GUINEA-BISSAU

GUINEA

SIERRA LEONE

LIBERIA

EL SALVADOR

NICARAGUA

Aruba (to Neth.)

Bonaire (to Neth.)

TRINIDAD & TOBAGO

COSTA RICA

Clipperton Island (to French Polynesia)

PANAMA

Kingman Reef (to USA)

Palmyra Atoll (to USA)

VENEZUELA

COLOMBIA

GUYANA

SURINAME

French Guiana (to France)

Baker & Howland Is (to USA)

Jarvis I (to USA)

0° Equator

Galápagos Is (part of Ecuador)

ECUADOR

Fernando de Noronha (part of Brazil)

KIRIBATI

BRAZIL

Ascension (to UK)

Tokelau (to NZ)

PERU

ATLANTIC OCEAN

SAMOA

Wallis & Futuna (to France)

American Samoa (to USA)

Cook Islands (to NZ)

French Polynesia (to France)

Lake Titicaca

BOLIVIA

TONGA

Niue (to NZ)

PACIFIC OCEAN

Trindade (part of Brazil)

Pitcairn, Henderson Ducie & Oeno Islands (to UK)

San Felix Island (part of Chile)

San Ambrosio Island (part of Chile)

PARAGUAY

Tropic of Capricorn

Easter Island (part of Chile)

Sala y Gomez (part of Chile)

CHILE

ARGENTINA

URUGUAY

Tristan da Cunha (to UK)

Kermadec Islands (part of NZ)

30°

Juan Fernandez Islands (part of Chile)

Gough I (part of Tristan

Chatham Islands (part of NZ)

Falkland Islands (to UK)

South Georgia & South Sandwich Islands (to UK)

South Shetland Islands

South Orkney Islands

S O U T H E

Antarctic Circle

Peter I Island (to Norway)

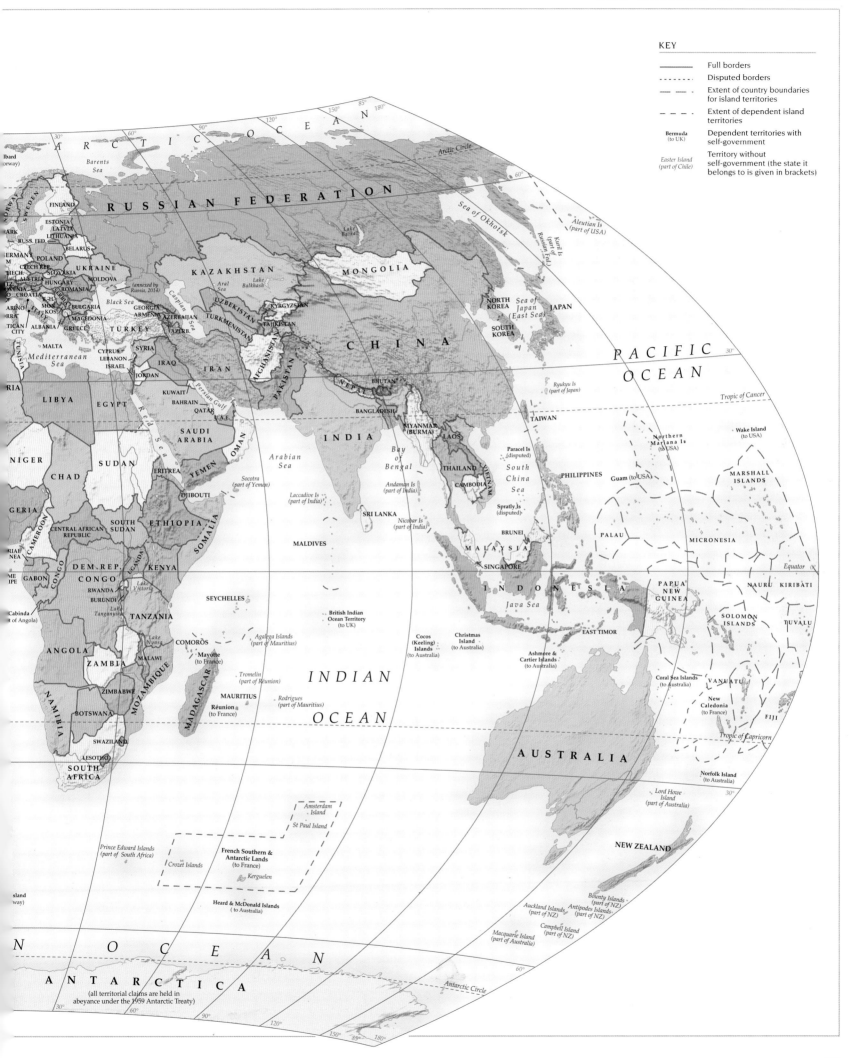

CONTINENTAL NORTH AMERICA

North America is the world's third largest continent, stretching from icy Greenland to the tropical Caribbean. The first people came from Asia more than 20,000 years ago. Their descendants spread across the continent, ate fish, meat, and wild and cultivated plants, and developed a wide variety of cultures and languages. About 500 years ago, immigrants from Europe, Africa, and Asia began to arrive in North America, bringing their own languages and cultures.

CROSS-SECTION THROUGH NORTH AMERICA

In the west, the land rises from the Pacific Ocean to the coastal ranges and the Rocky Mountains. Further east, the continent flattens into the Great Plains and the Great Lakes – gouged out by glaciers at the end of the last Ice Age. The Appalachian Mountains are older than the Rockies, and very worn down.

PHYSICAL NORTH AMERICA

The high peaks of the Rocky Mountains of Canada and the USA tower above the lower ranges of the western coasts. These ranges stretch from the icy north of Alaska, south to Mexico and Central America. The heart of the continent is flatter, and much of it is drained by the mighty Mississippi-Missouri river system.

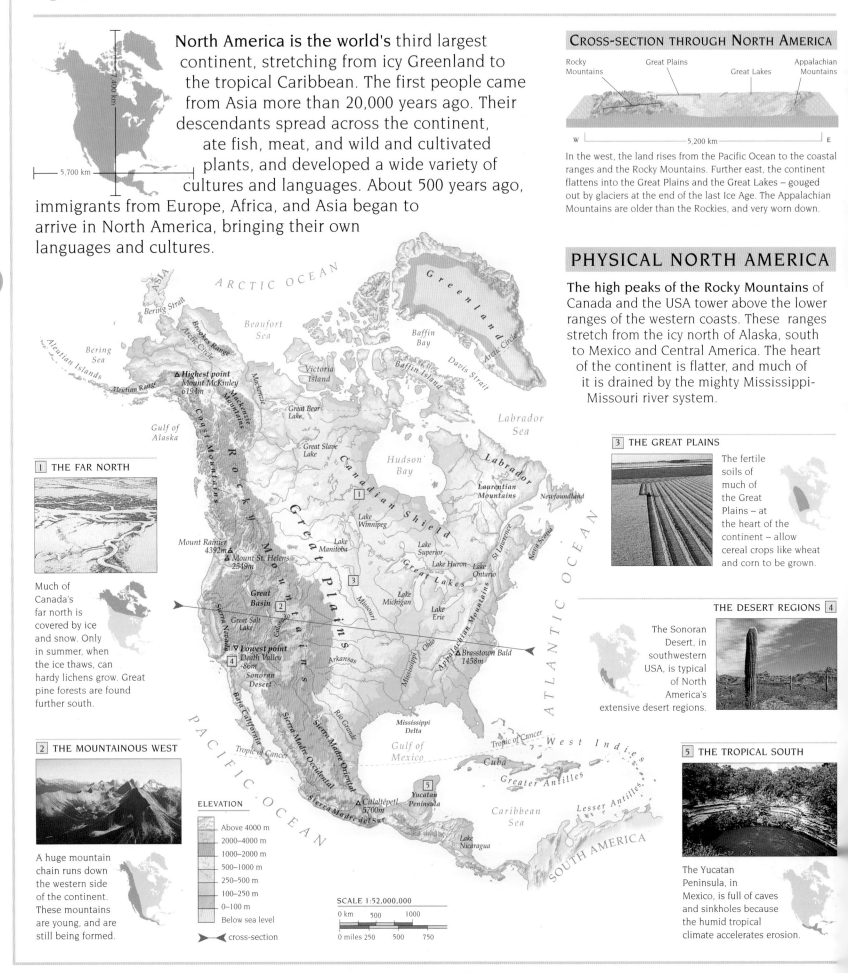

1 THE FAR NORTH

Much of Canada's far north is covered by ice and snow. Only in summer, when the ice thaws, can hardy lichens grow. Great pine forests are found further south.

2 THE MOUNTAINOUS WEST

A huge mountain chain runs down the western side of the continent. These mountains are young, and are still being formed.

3 THE GREAT PLAINS

The fertile soils of much of the Great Plains – at the heart of the continent – allow cereal crops like wheat and corn to be grown.

4 THE DESERT REGIONS

The Sonoran Desert, in southwestern USA, is typical of North America's extensive desert regions.

5 THE TROPICAL SOUTH

The Yucatan Peninsula, in Mexico, is full of caves and sinkholes because the humid tropical climate accelerates erosion.

ELEVATION

- Above 4000 m
- 2000–4000 m
- 1000–2000 m
- 500–1000 m
- 250–500 m
- 100–250 m
- 0–100 m
- Below sea level
- cross-section

SCALE 1:52,000,000

0 km 500 1000

0 miles 250 500 750

POLITICAL NORTH AMERICA

The USA, Canada and Mexico are all federal countries. This means that political power is shared between the national government and the state or provincial governments. Canada and the USA are democracies with a long history of freedom and equal rights. Governments in the countries south of the USA have been less stable, often ruled by dictators or harsh regimes. Many people have suffered for their political beliefs. During the 1960's and 1970's many of the Caribbean islands gained independence from their European colonial rulers.

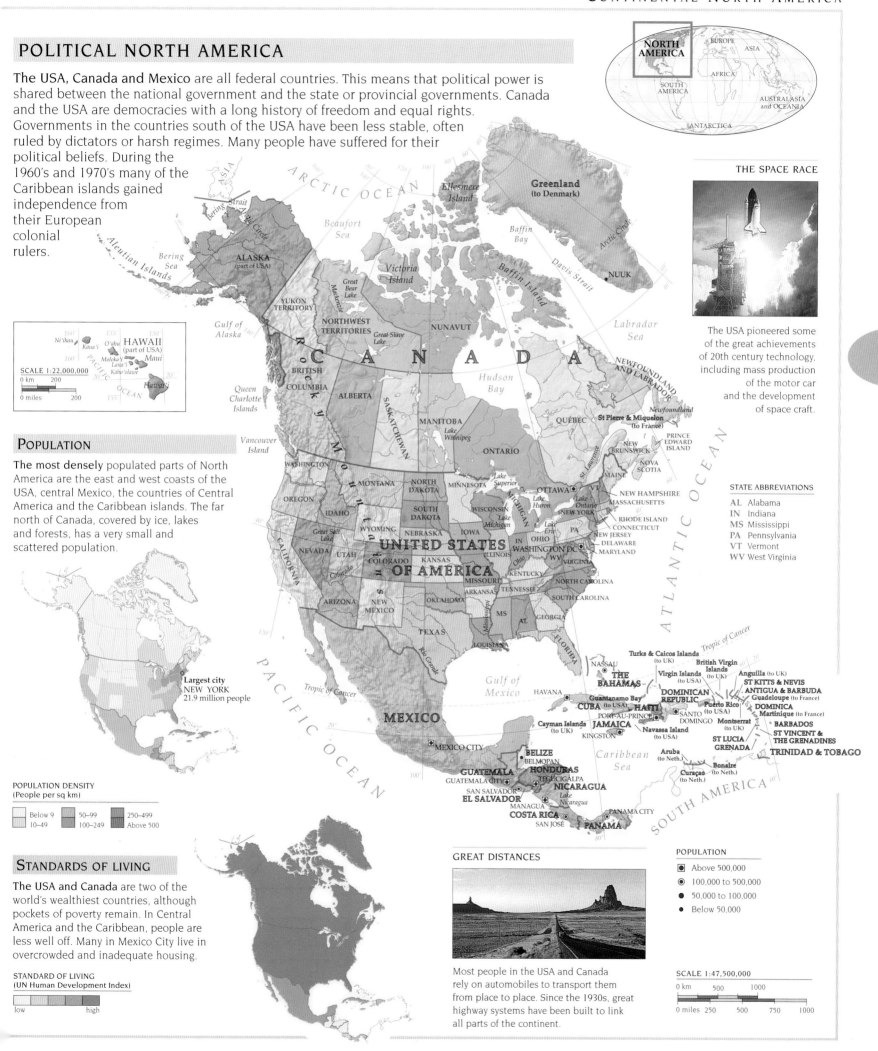

THE SPACE RACE

The USA pioneered some of the great achievements of 20th century technology, including mass production of the motor car and the development of space craft.

POPULATION

The most densely populated parts of North America are the east and west coasts of the USA, central Mexico, the countries of Central America and the Caribbean islands. The far north of Canada, covered by ice, lakes and forests, has a very small and scattered population.

Largest city
NEW YORK
21.9 million people

POPULATION DENSITY
(People per sq km)

Below 9	50–99	250–499
10–49	100–249	Above 500

STATE ABBREVIATIONS

AL Alabama
IN Indiana
MS Mississippi
PA Pennsylvania
VT Vermont
WV West Virginia

STANDARDS OF LIVING

The USA and Canada are two of the world's wealthiest countries, although pockets of poverty remain. In Central America and the Caribbean, people are less well off. Many in Mexico City live in overcrowded and inadequate housing.

STANDARD OF LIVING
(UN Human Development Index)

low   high

GREAT DISTANCES

Most people in the USA and Canada rely on automobiles to transport them from place to place. Since the 1930s, great highway systems have been built to link all parts of the continent.

POPULATION

- ◉ Above 500,000
- ◎ 100,000 to 500,000
- ● 50,000 to 100,000
- • Below 50,000

SCALE 1:47,500,000

0 km   500   1000

0 miles 250   500   750 1000

SCALE 1:22,000,000

0 km   200

0 miles 200

NORTH AMERICAN GEOGRAPHY

Canada and the USA are among the world's wealthiest countries. They have rich natural resources, good farmland and thriving, varied industries. The range of different industries in Mexico is growing, but other Central American countries and the Caribbean islands rely on one or two important cash crops and tourism for most of their incomes. They have a lower standard of living than Canada and the USA.

INDUSTRY

The USA and Canada have an extremely wide range of industries, from mining and the processing of farm produce, to heavy and light manufacturing and service industries like banking. A variety of goods are produced, including aeroplanes, cars and computers. Oil exports and machine assembly are Mexico's main industries. In Central America and the Caribbean nations, most industry is based on agricultural produce.

INDUSTRY

- ✈ Aerospace
- ♦ Brewing
- 🚗 Car/vehicle manufacture
- ♨ Chemicals
- ⛏ Coal
- ⚜ Defence
- ✿ Engineering
- ✵ Film industry
- Ｓ Finance
- 🗗 Food processing
- 💻 Hi-tech industry
- 🚂 Iron & steel
- ♦ Oil & gas
- ✎ Pharmaceuticals
- 📖 Printing & publishing
- ☢ Research & development
- ◑ Shipbuilding
- ⏚ Textiles
- ♣ Timber processing

GNI per capita (US$)

- Below 2,500
- 2,500-9,999
- 10,000-14,999
- 15,000-34,999
- 35,000-49,999
- Above 50,000
- • Industrial centre

MANUFACTURING

Mexico has many car part assembly plants. Labour costs in Mexico are low, making it cheap to assemble car parts here.

MINERAL RESOURCES

North America still has large amounts of mineral resources. Canada has important nickel reserves, Mexico is renowned for its silver, and bauxite – used to make aluminum – is found in Jamaica. Oil and gas are plentiful, particularly in the arctic northwest by the Beaufort Sea, and further south by the Gulf of Mexico.

MINERAL RESOURCES

- ♠ Bauxite
- ♦ Copper
- ♦ Iron
- ♦ Nickel
- ♦ Phosphates
- ♦ Silver
- ♠ Uranium
- ▨ Oil/gas field
- ▨ Coal field

TIMBER PROCESSING

Huge tracts of forest are found toward the north of the continent; nearly 30% of Canada is covered by forest. Timber is processed to make paper in cities such as Portland and Vancouver.

HI-TECH INDUSTRY

The Santa Clara Valley, just south of San Francisco is also known as Silicon Valley, because of the number of firms producing computer hardware and software and micro-electronics which have set up in the area.

FOOD PROCESSING

Jamaica has been famous for its rum since the 16th century. Syrup is extracted from sugar cane which is then fermented to make rum.

CLIMATE

Much of northern Canada lies within the Arctic Circle and is permanently covered by ice or the sparse vegetation known as tundra. Southern Canada and much of central USA have a continental climate, with hot summers and cold winters. The southern parts of the USA, Central America and the Caribbean have a hot, humid tropical climate. The Caribbean and the eastern and central states of the USA often experience hurricane-force winds, waterspouts and tornadoes.

EXTREME WEATHER EVENTS

Symbols indicate climatic extremes

Coldest place
NORTHICE (Greenland)
Temperature −66°C

Wettest place
HENDERSON LAKE (BC, Canada)
Annual rainfall 6650mm

Hottest place
DEATH VALLEY (CA, USA)
Temperature 57°C

Driest place
BATAQUES (Mexico)
Annual rainfall 30mm

CLIMATE

- Ice cap
- Tundra
- Sub-arctic
- Cool continental
- Warm temperate
- Mediterranean
- Semi-arid
- Arid
- Humid equatorial
- Tropical
- Hot Humid

NORTH AMERICA'S HOTTEST PLACE

Death Valley in California is the hottest and driest place in the USA. Strong, dry winds sweep through the valley, constantly reshaping the sand and salt deposits which cover its floor.

LAND USE AND AGRICULTURE

On the Great Plains and Prairies of the USA and Canada, vast quantities of cereal crops, including corn and wheat, grow in the fertile soils. Cattle are also raised on great ranches throughout these regions and on the foothills of the Rocky Mountains. In California, vegetables and fruits are grown with the aid of irrigation. Bananas, coffee and sugar cane are grown for export in Central America and the Caribbean, while sorghum and maize are grown as subsistence crops.

BANANA PLANTATION

Banana plantations are common in the Caribbean and Central America. The fruit is grown for local consumption and for export to the USA and Europe, where they are valued for their flavour and nutritional qualities.

FISHING

The Grand Banks off the eastern coast of Canada were once home to almost limitless fish stocks. Overfishing has reduced the number of fish to very low levels. Quotas limiting the numbers of fish caught are helping numbers to rise.

LAND USE AND AGRICULTURE

- Cattle
- Poultry
- Pigs
- Reindeer
- Sheep
- Bananas
- Cereals
- Citrus fruits
- Coffee
- Corn (maize)
- Cotton
- Fishing
- Fruit
- Peanuts
- Rice
- Shellfish
- Soya beans
- Sugarcane
- Timber
- Tobacco
- Vineyards

- Cropland
- Desert
- Forest
- Ice cap
- Mountain region
- Pasture
- Tundra
- Wetland
- Major conurbation

WESTERN CANADA

ALBERTA, BRITISH COLUMBIA, MANITOBA, NORTHWEST
TERRITORIES, NUNAVUT, SASKATCHEWAN, YUKON TERRITORY

The first inhabitants of Canada's western provinces
were Native Americans. By the late 1800s, the Canadian
Pacific Railroad was completed and European settlers
moved west, turning most of the prairie into huge grain
farms. North of the prairies lie the vast, empty territories
that have significant Native American populations.
In 1999, part of the Northwest Territories, known as
Nunavut, became a self-governing Inuit homeland.

INDUSTRY

The major industries in the prairie provinces
are related to agriculture, such as
meat-processing in Manitoba. Alberta
has huge reserves of fossil fuels,
and the other provinces are rich in
minerals, including zinc, nickel, silver
and uranium. British Columbia's
economy depends on manufacturing,
especially automobiles, chemicals
and machinery, along with paper
and timber
industries.

STRUCTURE OF
INDUSTRY

Primary 6%
Services 64%
Manufacturing 30%

INDUSTRY

🚗 Car manufacturing	△ Metal refining	⛴ Tourism
🛢 Chemicals	⬦ Oil and gas	▣ Major industrial centre / area
⚙ Engineering	⛏ Mining	
🥫 Food processing	🏭 Timber processing	— Major road

ENVIRONMENTAL ISSUES

For hundreds of years sailors have searched in vain for
a route from Europe to Asia via the Northwest Passage,
through the north of this region. In recent summers the sea
ice has retreated further north, and in 2007 the route was
completely navigable.
Many of the extensive forests in
British Columbia are used for
commercial lumbering. The
province produces more than
half of Canada's timber.

ENVIRONMENTAL
ISSUES

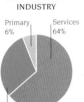 Lumbering activity

Permafrost zone

● Major industrial centre

---- Northwest Passage - direct route

FARMING AND LAND USE

More than 20% of the world's wheat is
grown in Canada's prairie provinces:
Manitoba, Alberta and
Saskatchewan. Beef cattle graze
on the ranches of Alberta and
British Columbia. Fruits,
especially apples, flourish
in the sheltered southern
valleys of British Columbia,
and Pacific salmon and
herring are caught off
the west coast.

LAND USE

Pasture 5%
Cropland 4%
Forest 38%
Other (including mountains) 53%

FARMING AND LAND USE

🐄 Cattle		Pasture
🐟 Fishing		Cropland
🌿 Cereals		Forest
🐖 Fruit		Mountain region
🌲 Timber		Barren
● Major conurbation		Tundra

THE LANDSCAPE

The prairie provinces are mostly flat. Occasionally,
the level plains are broken up by river valleys such
as that of the Qu'Appelle in Saskatchewan. In the
west, the jagged peaks and steep passes of the Rocky
Mountains and the Coast Mountains are covered
in snow for months on end. West of the Rockies,
the land descends sharply towards the coast of
British Columbia. The far north is covered by dense
forests and many glacial lakes.

The Arctic
Most of Canada's northern
islands are within the Arctic
Circle. They are covered by
ice year-round.

Mount Logan (B 5)
Mount Logan is Canada's
tallest peak. It rises 5,959 m.

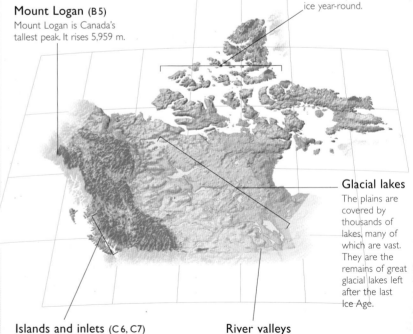

Glacial lakes
The plains are
covered by
thousands of
lakes, many of
which are vast.
They are the
remains of great
glacial lakes left
after the last
Ice Age.

Islands and inlets (C 6, C7)
The British Columbia coast is peppered
with islands and fjord-like inlets, created
by the force of the Pacific Ocean.

River valleys
Prairie river valleys such as the Qu'Appelle (F 7)
(French for 'who calls') were cut by glacial
meltwater thousands of years ago.

POPULATION

Most of the people in western Canada live near the Canada/USA border, taking advantage of the warmer climate and convenient transport routes. In the cold, forested north, the population is sparse, with only a few people per 100 sq km – many of them Native Americans such as the Inuit.

CLIMATE

Parts of northern Canada are frozen all year round. The prairie provinces have warm summers and cold winters. Coastal British Columbia is mild and wet.

January

July

TEMPERATURE AND PRECIPITATION

More than 20°C	0 to -5°C
15 to 20°C	-5 to -10°C
10 to 15°C	-10 to -15°C
5 to 10°C	Less than -15°C
0 to 5°C	100 ── Precipitation (mm)

NORTH AMERICA
Western Canada

URBAN/RURAL POPULATION DIVISION

Vancouver 22.7%
Other towns and cities 38%
Calgary 10.8%
Edmonton 10.5%
Rural population 18%

INHABITANTS PER SQ KM

More than 10
1–10
Less than 1
● Major city

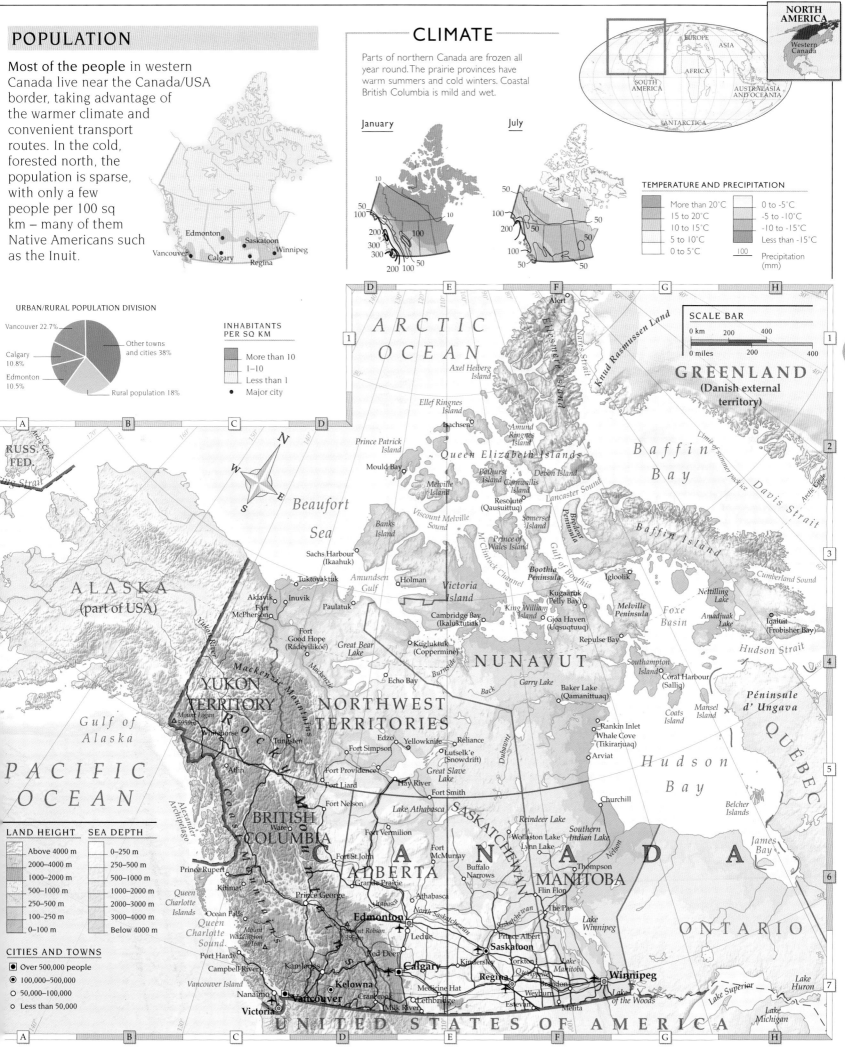

SCALE BAR
0 km   200   400
0 miles   200   400

ARCTIC OCEAN

GREENLAND (Danish external territory)

Alert
Axel Heiberg Island
Ellesmere Island
Knud Rasmussen Land
Nares Strait

Baffin Bay
Davis Strait

Prince Patrick Island
Ellef Ringnes Island
Isachsen
Amund Ringnes Island
Queen Elizabeth Islands

Mould Bay
Melville Island
Bathurst Island
Cornwallis Island
Devon Island
Lancaster Sound
Resolute (Qausuittuq)

Beaufort Sea
Banks Island
Viscount Melville Sound
Prince of Wales Island
Somerset Island
Boothia Peninsula
Gulf of Boothia
Brodeur Peninsula
Baffin Island
Cumberland Sound

Sachs Harbour (Ikaahuk)
Amundsen Gulf
Holman
Victoria Island
M'Clintock Channel
Igloolik
Nettilling Lake

Tuktoyaktuk
Paulatuk
Cambridge Bay (Ikaluktutiak)
King William Island
Kugaaruk (Pelly Bay)
Melville Peninsula
Amadjuak Lake
Iqaluit (Frobisher Bay)

ALASKA (part of USA)
Aklavik
Inuvik
Fort McPherson
Fort Good Hope (Rádeyilikóe)
Great Bear Lake
Kugluktuk (Coppermine)
Gjoa Haven (Uqsuqtuuq)
Repulse Bay
Foxe Basin

Echo Bay
Burnside
Back
Garry Lake
NUNAVUT
Southampton Island
Coral Harbour (Sallig)
Hudson Strait

YUKON TERRITORY
Mackenzie Mountains
Mackenzie
NORTHWEST TERRITORIES
Baker Lake (Qamanittuaq)
Coats Island
Mansel Island
Péninsule d' Ungava

Gulf of Alaska
Mount Logan 5959m
Whitehorse
Tungsten
Rocky Mountains
Edzo
Yellowknife
Reliance
Fort Simpson
Lutselk'e (Snowdrift)
Dubawnt
Rankin Inlet
Whale Cove (Tikirarjuaq)
Arviat
Hudson Bay
QUÉBEC

PACIFIC OCEAN
Atlin
Fort Providence
Fort Liard
Hay River
Great Slave Lake
Fort Smith
Churchill
Belcher Islands

Fort Nelson
Lake Athabasca
SASKATCHEWAN
Reindeer Lake
James Bay

BRITISH COLUMBIA
Fort Vermilion
Fort St John
Fort McMurray
Buffalo Narrows
Wollaston Lake
Lynn Lake
Southern Indian Lake
Nelson
Thompson

Prince Rupert
Kitimat
Grande Prairie
Athabasca
Flin Flon
MANITOBA
ONTARIO

Queen Charlotte Islands
Ocean Falls
Prince George
Athabasca
North Saskatchewan
ALBERTA
CANADA
The Pas
Lake Winnipeg

Port Hardy
Mount Waddington 4016m
Mount Robson 3954m
Edmonton
Leduc
Prince Albert
Saskatchewan
Lake Superior

Queen Charlotte Sound
Campbell River
Kamloops
Red Deer
Saskatoon
Kindersley
Yorkton
Lake Manitoba
Lake Winnipeg

Vancouver Island
Kelowna
Calgary
Qu'Appelle
Winnipeg
Lake Huron

Nanaimo
Cranbrook
Medicine Hat
Regina
Brandon
Weyburn
Lake of the Woods
Lake Michigan

Victoria
Milk River
Lethbridge
Estevan
Melita

UNITED STATES OF AMERICA

RUSS. FED.
Bering Strait
Arctic Circle
Beaufort Sea

LAND HEIGHT

Above 4000 m
2000–4000 m
1000–2000 m
500–1000 m
250–500 m
100–250 m
0–100 m

SEA DEPTH

0–250 m
250–500 m
500–1000 m
1000–2000 m
2000–3000 m
3000–4000 m
Below 4000 m

CITIES AND TOWNS

◼ Over 500,000 people
◉ 100,000–500,000
◎ 50,000–100,000
○ Less than 50,000

EASTERN CANADA

NEW BRUNSWICK, NEWFOUNDLAND AND LABRADOR,
NOVA SCOTIA, ONTARIO, PRINCE EDWARD ISLAND, QUÉBEC

The first European settlements grew up in the Atlantic provinces, and along the St. Lawrence River, where Québec City and Montréal were founded. People gradually migrated further west along the St. Lawrence River and the Great Lakes, establishing other cities including Toronto. Although the majority of Canadians speak English, people in Québec speak mainly French, and both English and French are official languages in Canada.

INDUSTRY

In the Atlantic provinces the traditional fishing industry has declined, causing unemployment. However, Newfoundland has a thriving food processing industry. Ontario and Québec have a wide range of industries, including the generation of hydro-electricity, mining, and chemicals, car manufacturing and fruit canning in the great cities. Large amounts of wood pulp and paper are also produced.

STRUCTURE OF INDUSTRY

Primary 7%
Services 64%
Manufacturing 29%

INDUSTRY

- 🚗 Car manufacture
- 🧪 Chemicals
- 🐟 Fish processing
- 🥫 Food processing
- ⊣⊢ Hydro-electric power
- △ Metal refining
- ⛏ Mining
- 🌲 Timber processing
- 💻 Hi-tech industry
- 🏛 Tourism
- ⊡ Major industrial centre / area
- — Major road

Labrador City, St. John's, Thunder Bay, Timmins, Chicoutimi, Sydney, Sudbury, Québec, Saint John, Sault Ste. Marie, Ottawa, Montréal, Halifax, Toronto, Yarmouth

FARMING AND LAND USE

The best farmland lies on the flat, fertile plains close to the St. Lawrence River and on the strip of land between Lake Erie and Lake Ontario. It is used to grow fruits such as grapes, cherries and peaches, and to raise cattle. Nova Scotia has fruit farms, and the rich red soils of Prince Edward Island produce a big potato crop. The vast forests that grow across the north are a major source of timber.

Thunder Bay, St. John's, Ottawa, Québec, Montréal, Toronto, Halifax

LAND USE

Pasture 2%   Cropland 2%
Other (including mountains) 32%
Forest 64%

FARMING AND LAND USE

- 🐄 Cattle
- 🎣 Fishing
- 🦞 Fruit
- 🥔 Potatoes
- 🌲 Timber
- Pasture
- Cropland
- Forest
- Tundra
- ● Major conurbation

ENVIRONMENTAL ISSUES

Acid rain caused by emissions from factories in the USA and along the St. Lawrence River destroys forests and kills marine life. Massive hydro-electric power projects in James Bay on Hudson Bay have flooded huge areas of land, affecting the environment and the local Cree people. Overfishing in the Atlantic has led to limits being set on the number of fish that can be caught.

ENVIRONMENTAL ISSUES

- 🐟 Depleted fish stocks
- 🏭 Major dam
- ☠ Urban air pollution
- Affected by acid rain
- Severe sea/lake pollution
- ● Major industrial centre

James Bay, Sudbury, Montréal, Hamilton, Toronto

THE LANDSCAPE

A huge, ancient mass of rock called the Canadian Shield lies beneath much of eastern Canada. It is covered by low hills, rocky outcrops, thousands of lakes, and huge areas of forest. Much of the Canadian Shield is permanently frozen. The St. Lawrence River flows out of Lake Ontario and into the Atlantic Ocean. It is surrounded by rolling hills and flat areas of very fertile farmland.

Scoured by ice

About 20,000 years ago, Labrador and northern Québec were completely covered by ice. The glaciers scraped hollows in the rock beneath. When the ice melted, lakes were left in the hollows that remained.

Lake Superior (B5)

Lake Superior is the largest freshwater lake in the world. It covers an area of 83,270 sq km and lies between Canada and the USA.

St. Lawrence River (E5)

The St. Lawrence River is 1,197 km long. Parts of it have become silted up, causing it to be braided into many different channels. Between December and mid-April the river freezes over.

Highlands

The highlands of New Brunswick, Nova Scotia and Newfoundland are the most northerly part of the Appalachian mountain chain.

The Bay of Fundy (F5)

This bay has the world's highest tides. It is shaped like a funnel, and as the Atlantic flows into it, the ever narrowing shores cause the water level to rise 6–15 m at every high tide.

NORTH AMERICA
Eastern Canada

POPULATION

Colonists from both France and Britain settled in Canada from the early 1600s onward. Ontario and the Atlantic provinces are mainly English speaking. Québec is the centre of French settlement; 80% of the people there have French as a first language. Most people in eastern Canada now live in large towns and cities close to the St. Lawrence River.

Thunder Bay
St. John's
Québec
OTTAWA
Montréal
Toronto
Halifax
Windsor
London

URBAN/RURAL POPULATION DIVISION

Toronto 19.7%
Montréal 14.5%
Ottawa 3.7%
Other towns and cities 46.1%
Rural population 16%

INHABITANTS PER SQ KM

More than 50
10–50
1–10
Less than 1

■ Capital city
● Major city

CLIMATE

Winters are very cold, but warm winds from the Gulf of Mexico can bring hot summers to southern Ontario and the areas bordering the St. Lawrence River.

January
July

TEMPERATURE AND PRECIPITATION

More than 20°C
15 to 20°C
10 to 15°C
5 to 10°C
0 to 5°C
0 to -5°C
-5 to -15°C
-15 to -25°C
Less than -25°C

100 Precipitation (mm)

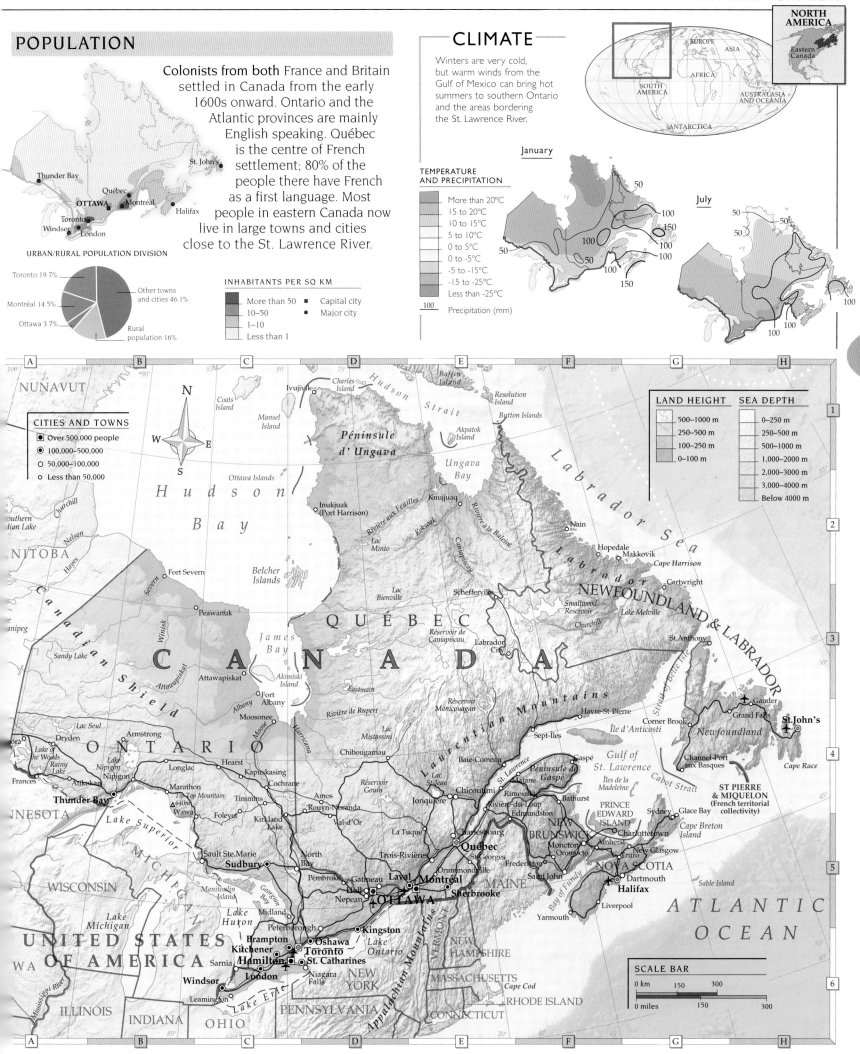

LAND HEIGHT
500–1000 m
250–500 m
100–250 m
0–100 m

SEA DEPTH
0–250 m
250–500 m
500–1000 m
1,000–2000 m
2,000–3000 m
3,000–4000 m
Below 4000 m

CITIES AND TOWNS
■ Over 500,000 people
◉ 100,000–500,000
○ 50,000–100,000
○ Less than 50,000

SCALE BAR
0 km 150 300
0 miles 150 300

USA: THE NORTHEASTERN STATES

CONNECTICUT, DELAWARE, MAINE, MASSACHUSETTS, NEW-HAMPSHIRE, NEW JERSEY, NEW YORK, PENNSYLVANIA, RHODE ISLAND, VERMONT

The dynamic 200-year boom of the northeastern states has been the result of a combination of factors. Between 1855 and 1924, over 20 million people poured into the region from all over the world, hoping to build a new life. Natural resources, including coal and iron, fuelled new industries and fertile farmland provided food for the region's growing population. The 'gateway' cities of the Atlantic seaboard, New York and Boston, enabled manufacturers to export their goods worldwide.

INDUSTRY

Boston, New York and Philadelphia are international centres of industry and commerce. Electronics and communications are growing throughout the Northeast alongside traditional industries such as fishing and wood products. Tourism is vital for the northeastern states, particularly along the Atlantic coast.

STRUCTURE OF INDUSTRY

Manufacturing 16.5%
Primary 0.5%
Services 83%

INDUSTRY

- 🜹 Chemicals
- ⚙ Engineering
- 🍴 Food processing
- ⛏ Iron and steel
- ⚗ Pharmaceuticals
- 👕 Textiles
- 🪵 Timber processing
- 🛡 Defence
- $ Finance
- 💻 High-tech
- 🔬 Research and development
- 🏛 Tourism

▪ Major industrial centre / area
— Major road

ENVIRONMENTAL ISSUES

The high level of industry and the large population puts great pressure on the environment. Air pollution from vehicles and industry led to poor air quality in many cities and caused acid rain. The problem is worse close to the Great Lakes, where severe lake pollution has occurred.

ENVIRONMENTAL ISSUES

- Urban air pollution
- Wind farm
- Affected by acid rain
- Severely affected by acid rain
- Polluted rivers
- Sea/lake pollution
- Severe sea/lake pollution
- • Major industrial centre

FARMING AND LAND USE

The varied landscape of the northeastern states supports a great range of farming. Livestock, including cattle, horses, poultry and pigs, are raised throughout the region. The main crops are fruits and vegetables. Fishing is important, especially off the Atlantic coast of Maine.

FARMING AND LAND USE

- 🐂 Cattle
- 🐖 Pigs
- 🦃 Poultry
- 🎣 Fishing
- 🌾 Cereals
- 🍒 Cranberries
- 🍓 Fruit
- 🍁 Maple syrup
- 🌲 Timber

- Cropland
- Forest
- Pasture
- • Major conurbation

LAND USE

Pasture 6%
Cropland 14%
Other 16%
Forest 64%

THE LANDSCAPE

The Appalachian and Adirondack Mountains form a barrier between the marshy lowlands of the Atlantic coast and the lowlands further west. The interior consists of rolling hills, fertile valleys and thousands of lakes created by the movement of glaciers.

Appalachians (E 3)
The Appalachian Mountains, which run through most of this region, are the eroded remnants of peaks that were once much higher.

Rocky coastline (G 3)
The coast of Maine is made up of rocky bays, islands, and inlets. If the shoreline were stretched out, it would be 4,000 km long.

Adirondacks (E 3)
The Adirondacks are a broad, wide mountain range, formed when older rocks were forced into a 'dome' shape by movements in the Earth's crust many millions of years ago.

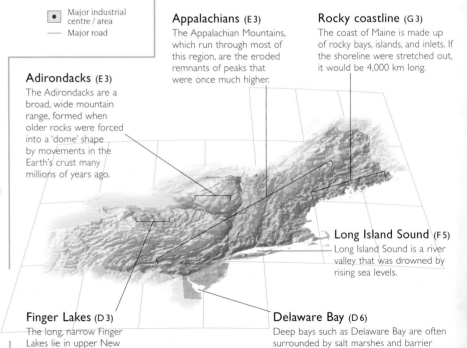

Long Island Sound (F 5)
Long Island Sound is a river valley that was drowned by rising sea levels.

Finger Lakes (D 3)
The long, narrow Finger Lakes lie in upper New York state. They were cut by glaciers.

Delaware Bay (D 6)
Deep bays such as Delaware Bay are often surrounded by salt marshes and barrier beaches that create ideal breeding conditions for a wide variety of birds and animals.

POPULATION

The areas along the eastern seaboard were settled by some of the earliest European colonists. The Northeast is now one of the most densely populated parts of the USA. A few of the largest cities in the USA, such as New York and Philadelphia, are in this region, but in the six states known as New England many towns and cities have populations of less than 30,000 inhabitants.

CLIMATE

Although the climate is mild during spring and autumn, summers can be hot and extremely humid, while winters are often very cold with heavy snowfall.

NORTH AMERICA

USA: The Northeastern States

January

July

INHABITANTS PER SQ KM

More than 200
100–200
50–100
25–50
Less than 25

• Major city

URBAN/RURAL POPULATION DIVISION

New York 14.6%
Philadelphia 2.7%
Boston 1.1%
Rural population 17%
Other towns and cities 64.6%

TEMPERATURE AND PRECIPITATION

More than 20°C
15 to 20°C
0 to 5°C
-5 to 0°C
-10 to -5°C
Less than -10°C
100 Precipitation (mm)

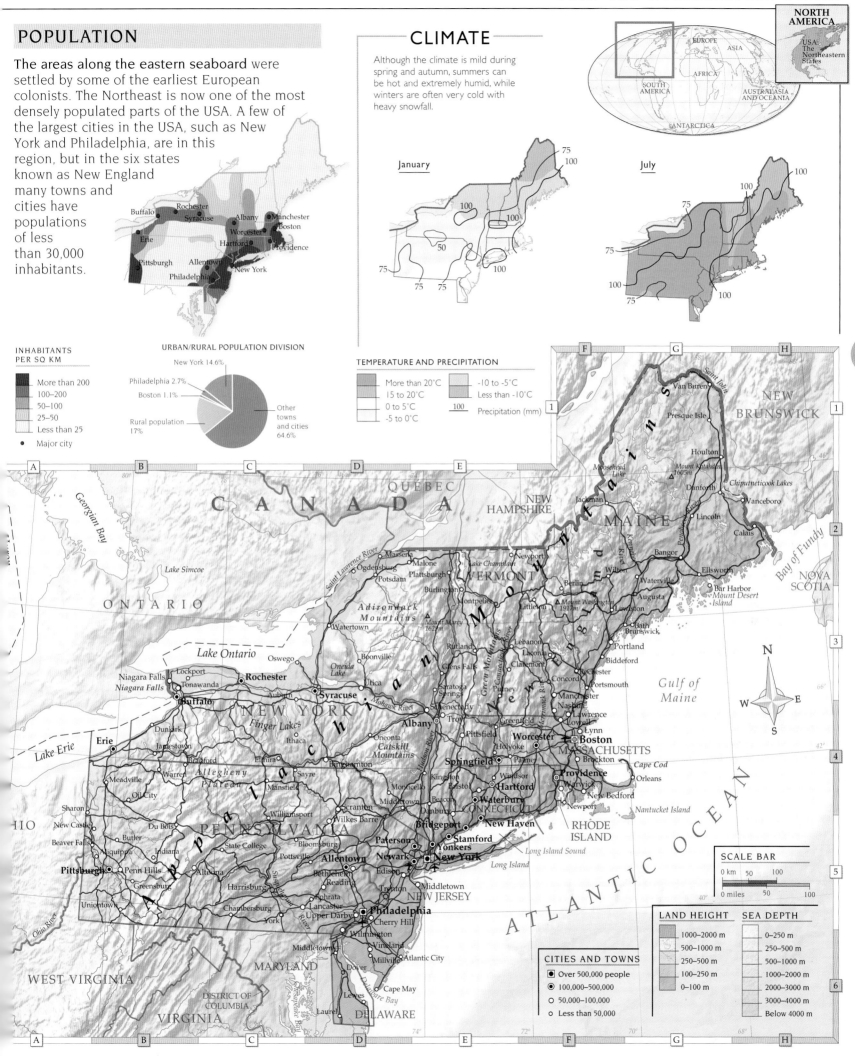

SCALE BAR

0 km   50   100

0 miles   50   100

LAND HEIGHT
1000–2000 m
500–1000 m
250–500 m
100–250 m
0–100 m

SEA DEPTH
0–250 m
250–500 m
500–1000 m
1000–2000 m
2000–3000 m
3000–4000 m
Below 4000 m

CITIES AND TOWNS
■ Over 500,000 people
◉ 100,000–500,000
○ 50,000–100,000
○ Less than 50,000

USA: The Southern States

ALABAMA, ARKANSAS, DISTRICT OF COLUMBIA, FLORIDA, GEORGIA, KENTUCKY, LOUISIANA, MARYLAND, MISSISSIPPI, NORTH CAROLINA, SOUTH CAROLINA, TENNESSEE, VIRGINIA, WEST VIRGINIA

The southern states suffered great devastation and poverty as a result of the Civil War (1861–65). Recovery has come with the discovery and exploitation of resources and the development of major commercial and industrial centres. Yet these states retain the vibrant mix of cultures that reflect their French, Spanish, English and African heritage.

INDUSTRY

Tourism is a major industry in the 'sunbelt' states, especially Florida, and many people move to the area when they retire to enjoy the climate. Oil and gas are extracted along the coast of the Gulf of Mexico, and there are many related chemical industries. Textiles are still produced in North and South Carolina, but aerospace and other high-tech industries have been established as well.

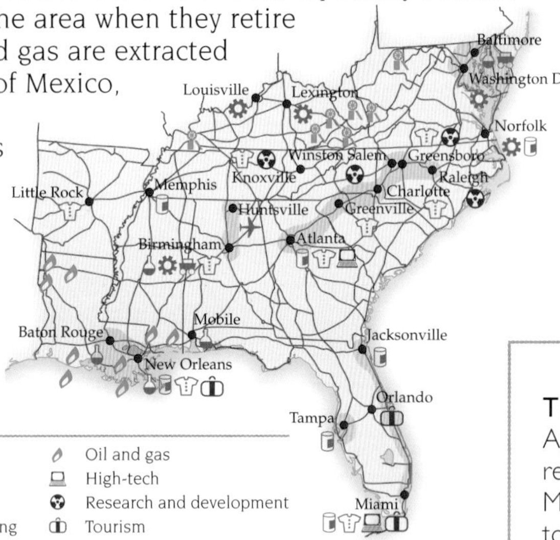

STRUCTURE OF INDUSTRY

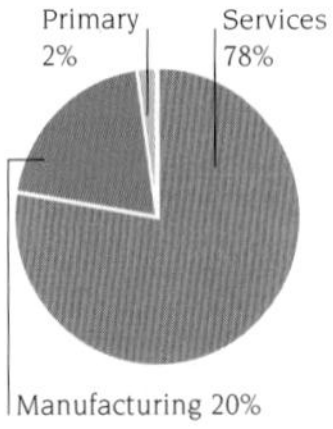

INDUSTRY

- Aerospace
- Chemicals
- Engineering
- Food processing
- Iron and steel
- Textiles
- Coal
- Oil and gas
- High-tech
- Research and development
- Tourism
- Major industrial centre / area
- Major road

POPULATION

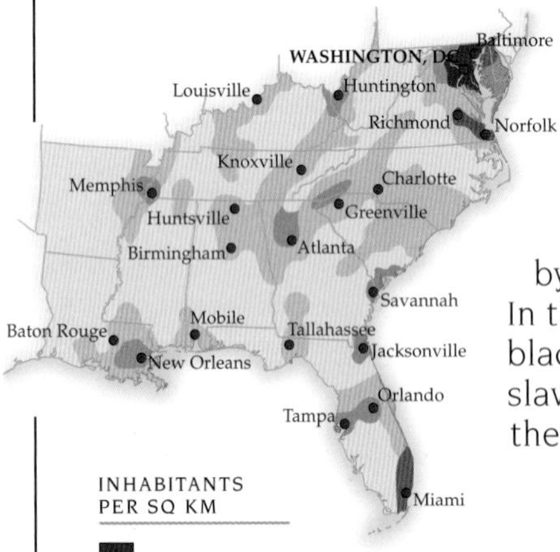

INHABITANTS PER SQ KM

- More than 200
- 100–200
- 50–100
- 25–50
- Less than 25
- Capital city
- Major city

Creoles, descended from Spanish and French colonizers, and Cajuns, of French-Canadian ancestry, live in the south of this region. Florida has a large Hispanic population, increased by migration from the Caribbean. In the early 20th century, five million black people, the descendants of slaves, left the South for cities in the North.

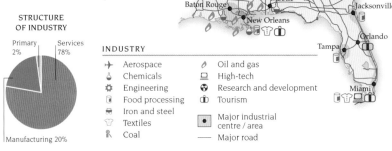

URBAN/RURAL POPULATION DIVISION

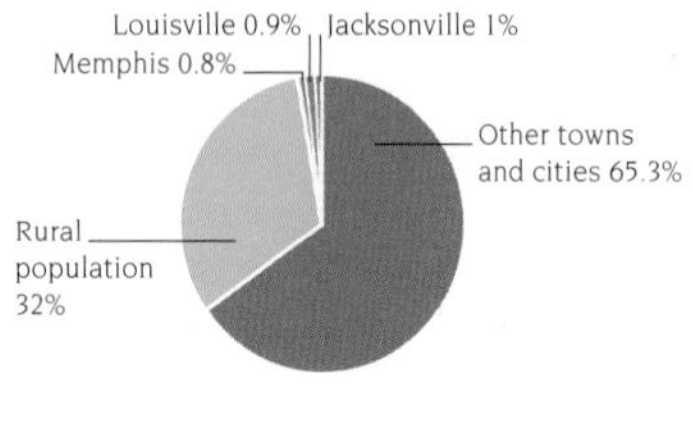

FARMING AND LAND USE

Cotton is still the South's main crop, but many old cotton fields are now pastures where all types of livestock are raised. Florida is famous for citrus fruits, while Georgia is renowned for peanuts. Sugarcane, soya beans, tobacco, corn, fruits and rice are grown in other areas.

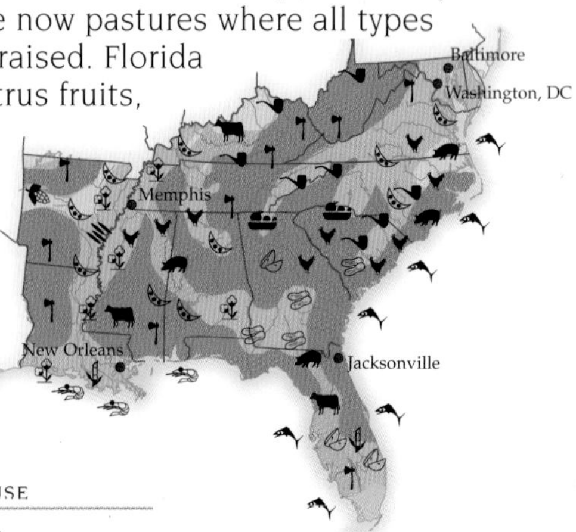

FARMING AND LAND USE

- Cattle
- Fishing
- Pigs
- Poultry
- Shellfish
- Citrus fruit
- Corn
- Cotton
- Fruit
- Peanuts
- Rice
- Soya beans
- Sugarcane
- Timber
- Tobacco
- Cropland
- Forest
- Pasture
- Wetland
- Major conurbation

LAND USE

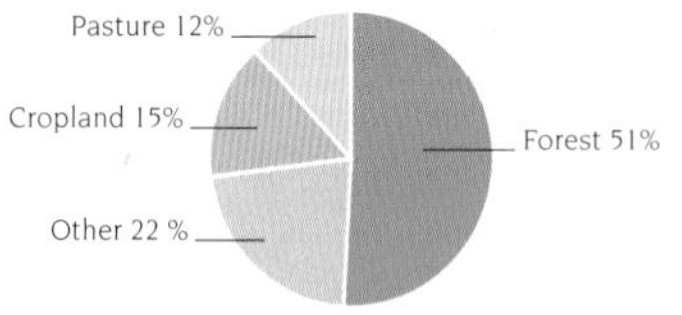

THE LANDSCAPE

The South is a land of contrasts – the uplands of the Appalachians, the foothills of the Piedmont, and low-lying coastal regions are all featured. The interior lowlands are drained by the Mississippi. Florida is dotted with thousands of lakes and is home to the Everglades, a giant sawgrass swamp.

Mississippi River (C 4)
A major transport artery, the Mississippi was an essential route in opening up the interior region. With its main tributary, the Missouri, it is nearly 6,115 km long, making it the world's fourth-longest river.

Kentucky Bluegrass (E 2)
The gently rolling bluegrass landscape of northern Kentucky is ideal country for raising horses and livestock.

Barrier beaches (I 3)
Sandy barrier beaches and islands line the eastern and southern coasts, along with sheltered lagoons and salt marshes.

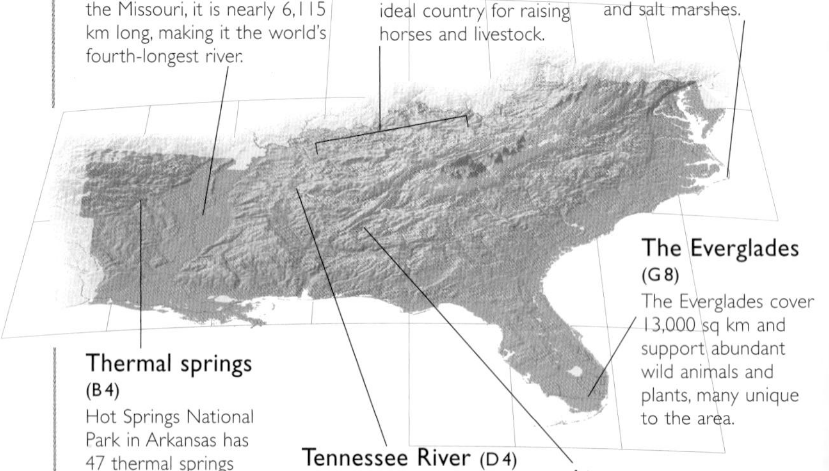

The Everglades (G 8)
The Everglades cover 13,000 sq km and support abundant wild animals and plants, many unique to the area.

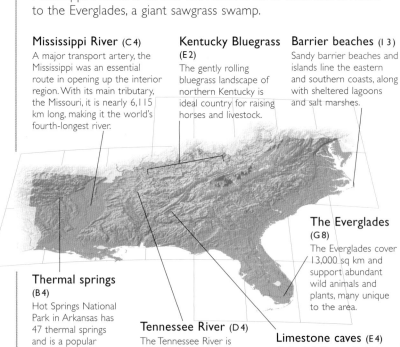

Thermal springs (B 4)
Hot Springs National Park in Arkansas has 47 thermal springs and is a popular tourist and health resort. Visitors relax here in the hot water that trickles from the hillsides.

Tennessee River (D 4)
The Tennessee River is 1,000 km long. Dams along the river generate hydro-electricity to provide most of the region's energy needs.

Limestone caves (E 4)
Cathedral Caverns in Alabama is a collection of enormous limestone caves. The main entrance is more than 300 m high and 45 m wide.

ENVIRONMENTAL ISSUES

Factories in the Great Lakes region have contributed to the large blanket of acid rain across the northern part. Towards the south, hurricanes sweep in from the Atlantic Ocean and Gulf of Mexico during the hurricane season, which lasts from May to October each year.

ENVIRONMENTAL ISSUES

- - - -🌀- - ▸ Path of recent, devastating hurricane
- Affected by acid rain
- Polluted river
- Sea pollution
- • Major city

NORTH AMERICA

USA: The Southern States

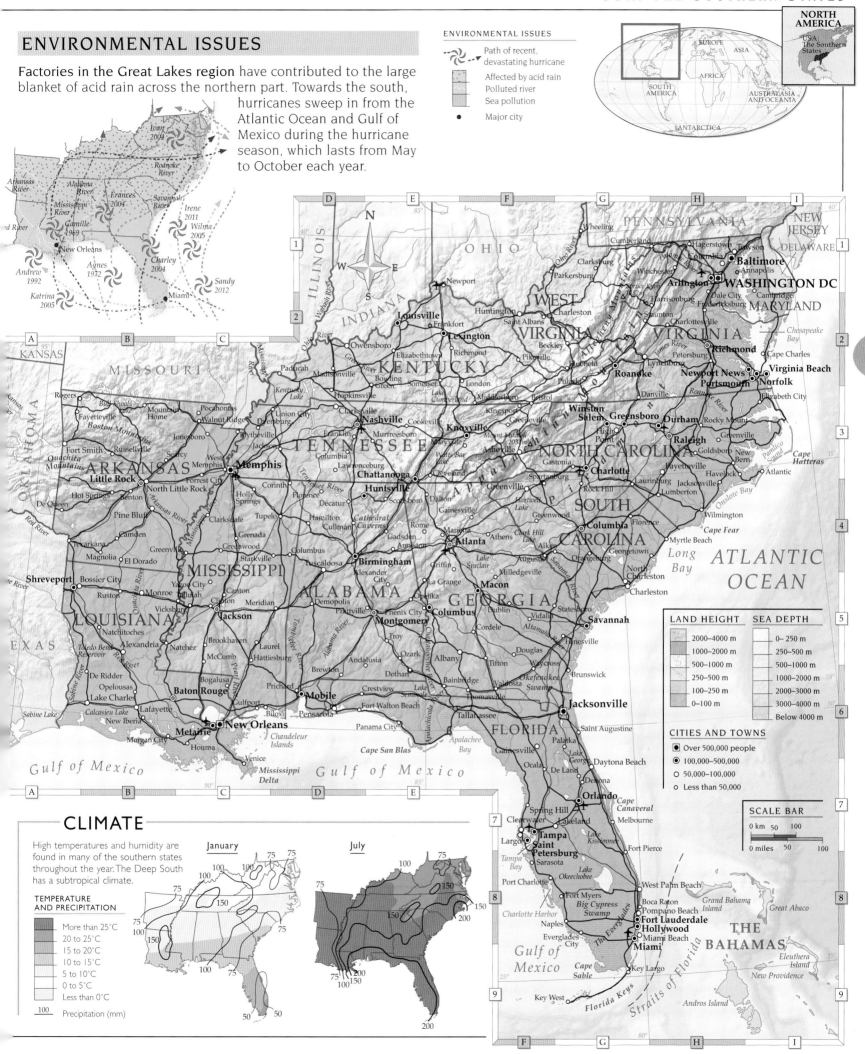

LAND HEIGHT
- 2000–4000 m
- 1000–2000 m
- 500–1000 m
- 250–500 m
- 100–250 m
- 0–100 m

SEA DEPTH
- 0– 250 m
- 250–500 m
- 500–1000 m
- 1000–2000 m
- 2000–3000 m
- 3000–4000 m
- Below 4000 m

CITIES AND TOWNS
- ▣ Over 500,000 people
- ⊙ 100,000–500,000
- ○ 50,000–100,000
- ∘ Less than 50,000

SCALE BAR

0 km 50 100

0 miles 50 100

CLIMATE

High temperatures and humidity are found in many of the southern states throughout the year. The Deep South has a subtropical climate.

TEMPERATURE AND PRECIPITATION
- More than 25°C
- 20 to 25°C
- 15 to 20°C
- 10 to 15°C
- 5 to 10°C
- 0 to 5°C
- Less than 0°C

100 ⎯ Precipitation (mm)

January

July

USA: THE GREAT LAKES STATES

ILLINOIS, INDIANA, MICHIGAN, OHIO, WISCONSIN

Good transport links, excellent farmland and a wealth of natural resources drew settlers from Europe and the south and east of the USA to the Great Lakes states during the late 19th century. By the 1930s, they had become one of the world's most prosperous industrial and agricultural regions. In recent years, the decline in traditional heavy industries has hit some cities hard, leading to unemployment and a rising crime rate.

POPULATION

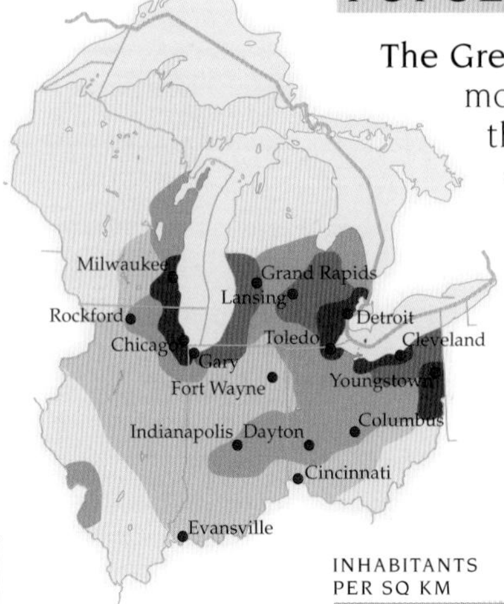

The Great Lakes states are one of the most densely populated parts of the USA. Many of the largest cities in this region – Chicago, Detroit and Milwaukee – grew up on the banks of the lakes and are connected to each other and the rest of the USA by an impressive road and rail network.

INHABITANTS PER SQ KM

- More than 200
- 100–200
- 50–100
- 25–50
- Less than 25
- Major city

URBAN/RURAL POPULATION DIVISION

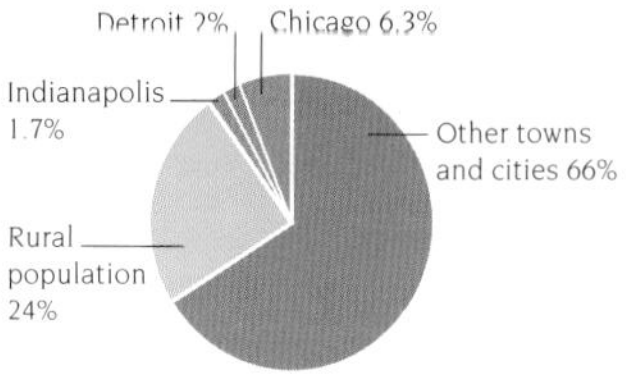

Detroit 2% Chicago 6.3%
Indianapolis 1.7%
Other towns and cities 66%
Rural population 24%

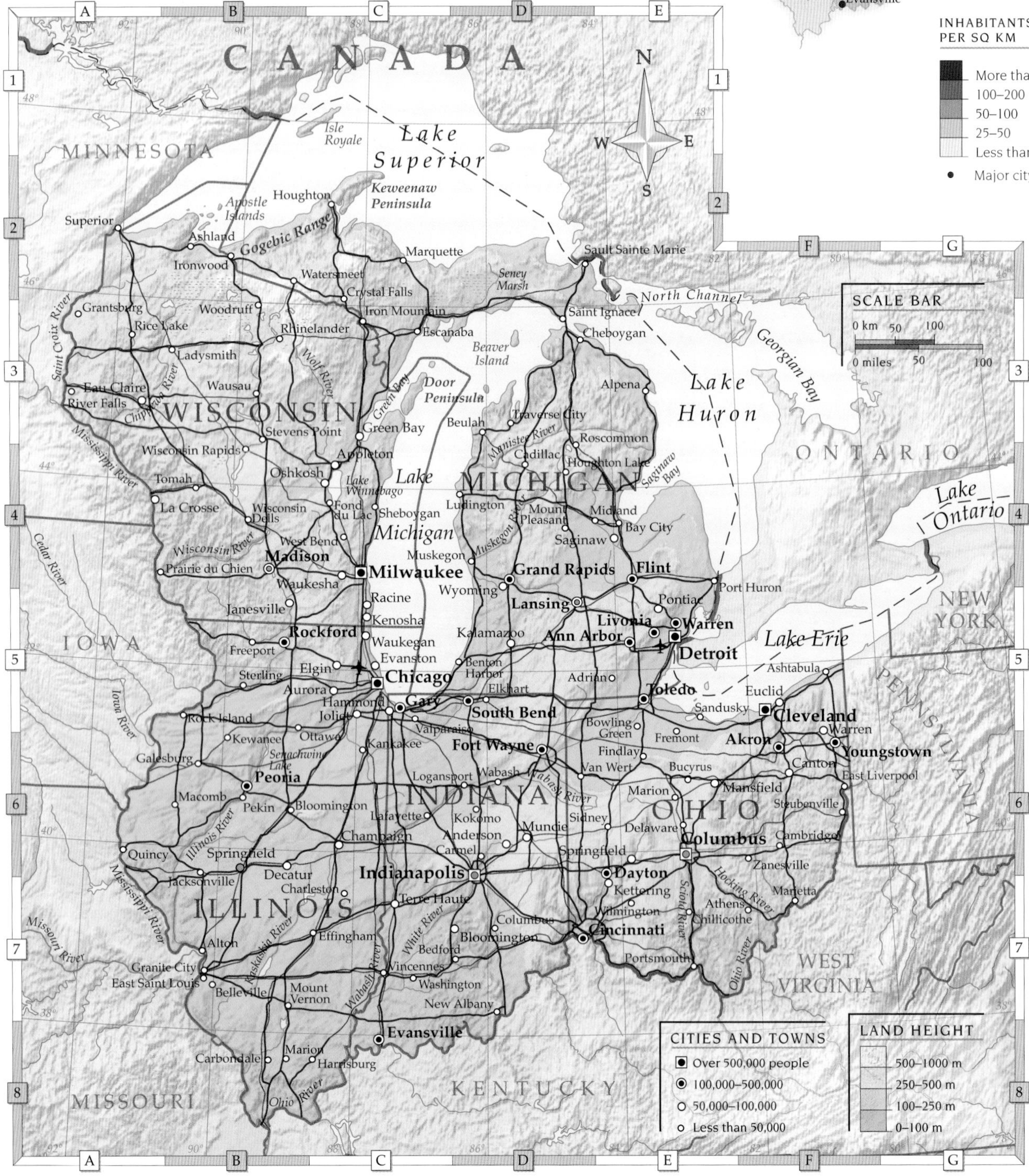

CLIMATE

Plentiful rainfall waters the agricultural lands. In winter, strong winds sweep across the lakes, and water close to the shore may freeze.

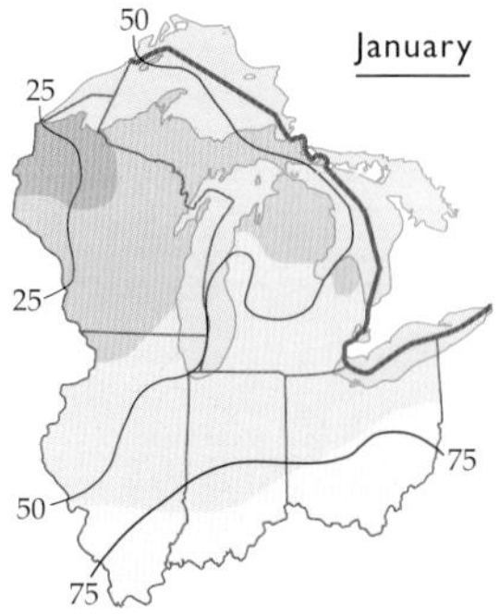

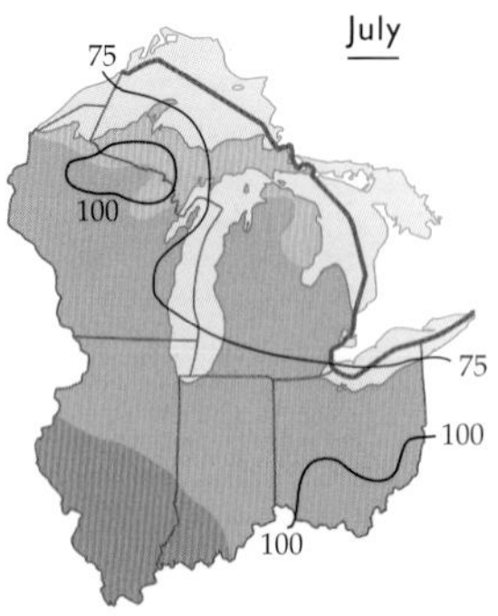

January

July

SCALE BAR

0 km 50 100

0 miles 50 100

TEMPERATURE AND PRECIPITATION

- More than 25°C
- 20 to 25°C
- 15 to 20°C
- 0 to 5°C
- -5 to 0°C
- -10 to -5°C
- Less than -10°C
- 100 Precipitation (mm)

CITIES AND TOWNS

- ● Over 500,000 people
- ● 100,000–500,000
- ○ 50,000–100,000
- ○ Less than 50,000

LAND HEIGHT

- 500–1000 m
- 250–500 m
- 100–250 m
- 0–100 m

Map labels: CANADA, MINNESOTA, Isle Royale, Lake Superior, Apostle Islands, Houghton, Keweenaw Peninsula, Superior, Ashland, Gogebic Range, Ironwood, Watersmeet, Marquette, Seney Marsh, Sault Sainte Marie, North Channel, Grantsburg, Rice Lake, Woodruff, Crystal Falls, Iron Mountain, Saint Ignace, Cheboygan, Georgian Bay, Saint Croix River, Ladysmith, Rhinelander, Escanaba, Beaver Island, Alpena, Lake Huron, ONTARIO, Eau Claire, River Falls, Wausau, Door Peninsula, Green Bay, Beulah, Traverse City, Roscommon, Lake Ontario, WISCONSIN, Stevens Point, Cadillac, Houghton Lake, Wisconsin Rapids, Appleton, Lake Winnebago, MICHIGAN, Tomah, Oshkosh, Fond du Lac, Sheboygan, Ludington, Mount Pleasant, Midland, Bay City, La Crosse, Wisconsin Dells, West Bend, Lake Michigan, Muskegon, Saginaw, Madison, Milwaukee, Wyoming, Grand Rapids, Flint, Waukesha, Racine, Pontiac, Port Huron, Janesville, Kenosha, Lansing, Livonia, Warren, NEW YORK, Rockford, Waukegan, Kalamazoo, Ann Arbor, Detroit, Lake Erie, Freeport, Elgin, Evanston, Benton Harbor, Adrian, Ashtabula, Sterling, Aurora, Chicago, Elkhart, Toledo, Euclid, PENNSYLVANIA, Rock Island, Joliet, Hammond, Gary, South Bend, Bowling Green, Sandusky, Cleveland, Kewanee, Ottawa, Valparaiso, Fremont, Akron, Warren, Galesburg, Kankakee, Fort Wayne, Findlay, Van Wert, Bucyrus, Canton, Youngstown, East Liverpool, Peoria, Logansport, Wabash, Marion, Mansfield, Steubenville, Macomb, Pekin, Bloomington, Lafayette, Kokomo, Sidney, Delaware, Cambridge, INDIANA, Anderson, Muncie, Springfield, Columbus, OHIO, Zanesville, Quincy, Springfield, Carmel, Marietta, Jacksonville, Decatur, Indianapolis, Terre Haute, Dayton, Kettering, Charleston, Columbus, Wilmington, Athens, Chillicothe, Alton, Effingham, White River, Bloomington, Cincinnati, Portsmouth, WEST VIRGINIA, Granite City, East Saint Louis, Vincennes, Bedford, Washington, Belleville, Mount Vernon, New Albany, Evansville, Marion, Carbondale, Harrisburg, MISSOURI, KENTUCKY, IOWA, Mississippi River, Wisconsin River, Illinois River, Missouri River, Ohio River

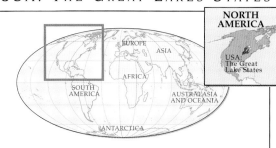

FARMING AND LAND USE

Michigan is renowned for its cherries and apples. Corn and soya beans are the main crops produced in the region's southern states. Livestock-rearing includes pig and poultry farms – many very large – in Illinois, Indiana and Ohio. Cattle rearing and dairy farming are common in Michigan and Wisconsin.

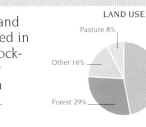

LAND USE

- Cropland 47%
- Forest 29%
- Other 16%
- Pasture 8%

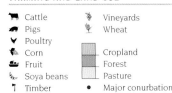

FARMING AND LAND USE

- 🐂 Cattle
- 🐗 Pigs
- 🦃 Poultry
- Corn
- 🐟 Fruit
- Soya beans
- Timber
- Tobacco
- 🍇 Vineyards
- 🌾 Wheat

- Cropland
- Forest
- Pasture
- Major conurbation

THE LANDSCAPE

Until about 10,000 years ago, much of this region was covered by great ice sheets that extended south to Illinois and Ohio. When the ice melted the Great Lakes were left in large hollows that the ice had scoured. The ice sheets changed the course of many rivers, so today most rivers flow south into the Mississippi/Missouri River system.

Lakes and marshes (B3)

Wisconsin is scattered with thousands of smaller lakes and many marshy areas. Like the Great Lakes, they were formed by erosion by the retreating ice at the end of the last Ice Age.

Underground water

In northern Illinois much of the water is pumped from underground reservoirs. In some places, the water table has dropped by 215 m over the last century, so many areas now face a water shortage.

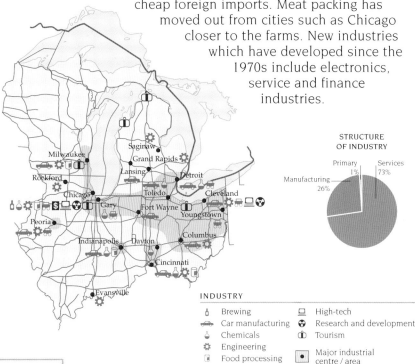

INDUSTRY

The US vehicle industry grew up on the banks of the Great Lakes, supported by the manufacture of iron and steel. Both industries have suffered in recent years from competition from cheap foreign imports. Meat packing has moved out from cities such as Chicago closer to the farms. New industries which have developed since the 1970s include electronics, service and finance industries.

STRUCTURE OF INDUSTRY

- Services 73%
- Manufacturing 26%
- Primary 1%

INDUSTRY

- 🍶 Brewing
- 🚗 Car manufacturing
- 🧪 Chemicals
- ⚙ Engineering
- Food processing
- Iron and steel
- Ⓢ Finance
- 🖥 High-tech
- ☢ Research and development
- 🎡 Tourism
- Major industrial centre / area
- — Major road

ENVIRONMENTAL ISSUES

The heavy industries on the banks of the Great Lakes have caused terrible pollution over the last century. Industrial effluent has polluted the lakes themselves, and factory emissions have led to severely acidic rain, which affects forests and lakes both here and further away in Canada.

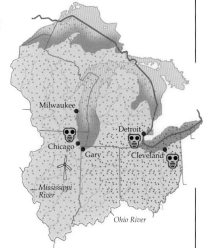

ENVIRONMENTAL ISSUES

- Urban air pollution
- Wind farm
- Affected by acid rain
- Severely affected by acid rain
- Polluted rivers
- Lake pollution
- Severe lake pollution
- • Major industrial centre

Moraines

When the last ice age ended, the retreating ice sheets left long ridges and piles of rock to the south of Lake Michigan. Some of these ridges, known as moraines, can be up to 90 m high.

Limestone region

Limestone in the hills of southern Indiana has been dissolved by acid rainwater. This has produced features such as sinkholes and underground caves.

Lake Erie (F5)

Lake Erie is the shallowest of the Great Lakes. Its average depth is about 19 m. Storms that sweep across from Canada have eroded its shores and caused the silting of its harbours.

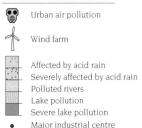

USA: THE CENTRAL STATES

IOWA, KANSAS, MINNESOTA, MISSOURI, NEBRASKA,
NORTH DAKOTA, OKLAHOMA, SOUTH DAKOTA

The prairie states of the central USA became one of America's richest agricultural regions in the mid-19th century. Despite the 'Dustbowl' crisis of the 1930s, which led many farmers to leave their ruined lands, agriculture is still crucial to the economy, and one third of the people still live in rural areas rather than large cities.

FARMING AND LAND USE

Wheat and corn grow on the fertile plains. Kansas is the leading grower of wheat in the entire USA, while Iowa is one of the leaders in corn and livestock. Irrigation projects to combat drought are crucial in large areas. Livestock – including cattle in vast herds; pigs, particularly in Iowa, the Dakotas and Nebraska; sheep; and turkeys – are raised throughout these states.

LAND USE

Other 37%

Cropland 43%

Forest 11%

Pasture 9%

FARMING AND LAND USE

- Cattle
- Pigs
- Poultry
- Sheep
- Corn
- Soya beans
- Wheat
- Cropland
- Forest
- Pasture
- Major conurbation

INDUSTRY

Industries related to agriculture, such as food processing and the production of farm machinery, are traditional in these states but high-tech industries – such as aeronautical engineering – are increasing and large aerospace plants are found in Wichita and Saint Louis. Oil and gas are extracted in great quantities toward the south of the region, especially in Oklahoma and Kansas.

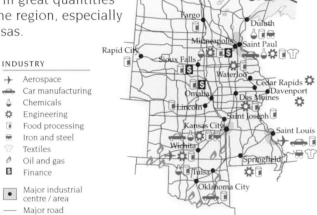

STRUCTURE OF INDUSTRY

Primary 4%

Services 76%

Manufacturing 20%

INDUSTRY

- ✈ Aerospace
- 🚗 Car manufacturing
- ⚗ Chemicals
- ⚙ Engineering
- 🍴 Food processing
- Iron and steel
- 👕 Textiles
- ⬧ Oil and gas
- S Finance
- ▣ Major industrial centre / area
- — Major road

THE LANDSCAPE

Most of the eastern edge of this region is marked by the Mississippi River, while the Missouri bisects it, running from northwest to southeast. The Great Plains cover most of this area, gradually rising towards the Rocky Mountains at the far western edge of the Central States.

The Badlands (A 4)

The Badlands cover an area of about 5,200 sq km in South Dakota. Heavily eroded by wind and water, almost nothing grows there.

Minnesota

Minnesota is filled with lakes, hills strewn with boulders, and mineral-rich deposits that have been left behind by the scouring movement of glaciers.

Chimney Rock (A-5)

Chimney Rock stands 150 m above the plains. It is a remnant of an ancient land surface that was eroded by the North Platte River.

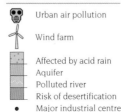

ENVIRONMENTAL ISSUES

Intensive agriculture requires large quantities of water to grow crops. Over-intensive use of the land has destroyed the balance of soil and water in the past, leading to fertile farmland being turned into useless areas of 'Dustbowl'. These states have a great underground store of water known as the Ogallala Aquifer, but over-extraction for irrigation is reducing the amount of available water.

ENVIRONMENTAL ISSUES

- Urban air pollution
- Wind farm
- Affected by acid rain
- Aquifer
- Polluted river
- Risk of desertification
- Major industrial centre

Great Plains (D 7)

Little more than a century ago the great flat plains that cover most of these states were home to wild grasses and massive herds of buffalo. In areas where lack of water has made farming impossible, large tracts of land are being allowed to return to grassland.

Great Salt Plains (D 7)

These arid salt plains cover about 120 sq km of northern Oklahoma. An ancient salt lake once occupied the area. When the salt evaporated, only the salt flats were left.

POPULATION

The inhabitants are largely the descendants of Europeans who came to the region in the late 1800s. The entire region is primarily rural, with enormous tracts of land devoted to growing crops. North Dakota has no city with a population greater than 100,000.

URBAN/RURAL POPULATION DIVISION

Kansas City 1.9% Oklahoma City 2.3%
Omaha 1.8%
Other towns and cities 60%
Rural population 34%

NORTH AMERICA

USA: The Central States

INHABITANTS PER SQ KM

More than 50
25–50
Less than 25
● Major city

CLIMATE

The Central States have a continental climate, with hot, dry summers and long, cold winters. Unreliable rainfall can be a problem for farmers on the Great Plains.

January

July

TEMPERATURE AND PRECIPITATION

More than 25°C
20 to 25°C
15 to 20°C
10 to 15°C
5 to 10°C
0 to 5°C
-5 to 0°C
-10 to -5°C
-15 to -10°C
Less than15°C
100 Precipitation (mm)

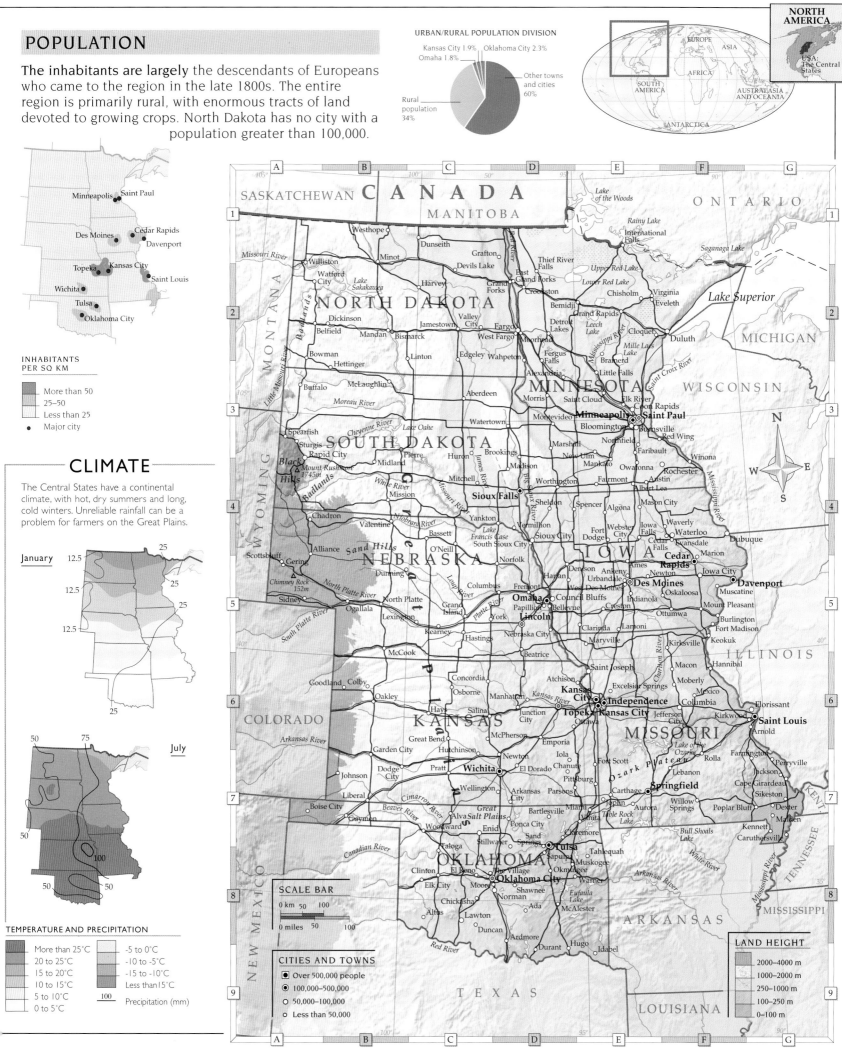

SCALE BAR

0 km 50 100

0 miles 50 100

CITIES AND TOWNS

◉ Over 500,000 people
◎ 100,000–500,000
○ 50,000–100,000
• Less than 50,000

LAND HEIGHT

2000–4000 m
1000–2000 m
250–1000 m
100–250 m
0–100 m

USA: THE SOUTHWESTERN STATES

ARIZONA, NEW MEXICO, TEXAS

Large parts of the southwestern states were purchased from Mexico in 1848. This land of expansive plateaus, spectacular canyons, prairies and deserts is home to several distinct peoples, whose customs and traditions are still practised. The Navaho and Hopi own one-third of the land in Arizona, and the ruins of thousand-year-old cliff dwellings built by the Anasazi people are still preserved there today.

ENVIRONMENTAL ISSUES

Desertification is a serious problem in the southwestern states. Lack of water combined with intensive farming has allowed soils to erode. Drought is held at bay by irrigation, but falling water table levels are a cause for concern. New Mexico was the site for many early nuclear weapons tests, and some places remain contaminated.

ENVIRONMENTAL ISSUES

- Urban air pollution
- Former nuclear test site
- Path of recent, devastating hurricane
- Wind farm

- Desert area
- Risk of desertification
- Polluted river
- Major industrial centre

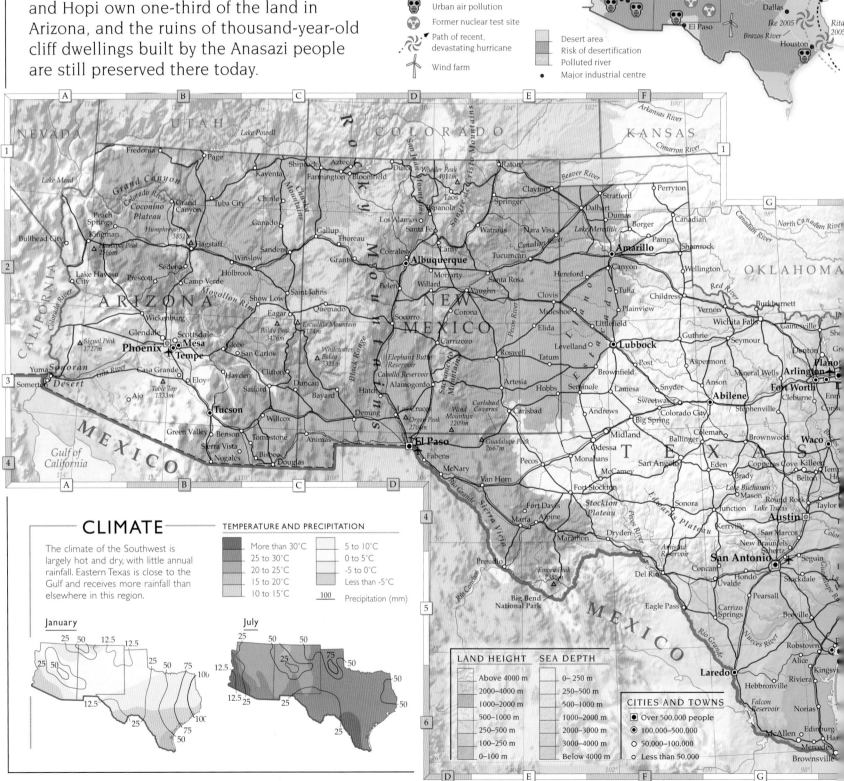

CLIMATE

The climate of the Southwest is largely hot and dry, with little annual rainfall. Eastern Texas is close to the Gulf and receives more rainfall than elsewhere in this region.

TEMPERATURE AND PRECIPITATION

More than 30°C	5 to 10°C
25 to 30°C	0 to 5°C
20 to 25°C	-5 to 0°C
15 to 20°C	Less than -5°C
10 to 15°C	Precipitation (mm)

January

July

LAND HEIGHT

- Above 4000 m
- 2000–4000 m
- 1000–2000 m
- 500–1000 m
- 250–500 m
- 100–250 m
- 0–100 m

SEA DEPTH

- 0 – 250 m
- 250–500 m
- 500–1000 m
- 1000–2000 m
- 2000–3000 m
- 3000–4000 m
- Below 4000 m

CITIES AND TOWNS

- Over 500,000 people
- 100,000–500,000
- 50,000–100,000
- Less than 50,000

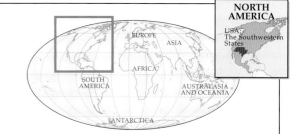

NORTH
AMERICA

USA:
The Southwestern
States

THE LANDSCAPE

The arid, mountainous Colorado Plateau covers nearly half of Arizona, dipping towards the south to form desert basins. Parts of northern New Mexico are forested, but the south consists primarily of semi-arid plains. Eastern Texas is bordered by the waters of the Gulf of Mexico, and the farmland of this area is well watered. Western Texas is covered by the Llano Estacado and, in the south, much of the land is arid.

Big Bend (E5)
Big Bend National Park gets its name from the 90° bend that the Rio Grande makes there.

Invading sea
The crust of southeastern Texas is warping, causing the land to subside and allowing the sea to invade. Hurricanes make the situation worse.

Grand Canyon (B1)
The Grand Canyon is a dramatic gorge cut in the rock by the Colorado River. It is about 350 km long, 675 km wide, and up to 1.6 km deep.

Carlsbad Caverns (B3)
Carlsbad Caverns are a series of underground caves, consisting of a three-level chain of limestone chambers studded with towering stalactites and stalagmites. They are millions of years old.

Rio Grande (G5)
The Rio Grande, or 'Great River' forms all of the border between Texas and Mexico. It flows from its source high up in the Rocky Mountains, to the Gulf of Mexico.

INDUSTRY

Mining and related industries are one of the most important sources of income in the Southwest. Great deposits of oil lie under about 65% of Texas; copper and coal are mined in Arizona and New Mexico. Defence-related industries, including NASA have encouraged the development of many high-tech companies in Texas – and high-tech is also growing in larger cities such as Santa Fe and Phoenix.

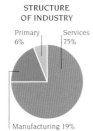

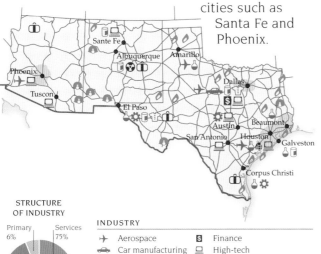

STRUCTURE
OF INDUSTRY

Primary
6%
Services
75%
Manufacturing 19%

INDUSTRY

- ✈ Aerospace
- 🚗 Car manufacturing
- ⚗ Chemicals
- ⚙ Engineering
- Food processing
- ⛏ Mining
- ⬤ Oil and gas
- Defence
- 🅂 Finance
- 🖳 High-tech
- ☢ Research and development
- Tourism
- ⦿ Major industrial centre / area
- — Major road

N
W — E
S

SCALE BAR
km   100
miles   100

FARMING AND LAND USE

Many cattle and sheep ranches have been set up on the open plateaus. Fruit and vegetables, grown in hothouses and cotton, hay and wheat are among the major crops. Beef cattle and broiler chickens are raised on huge farms while sheep graze the drier parts of Texas. Extensive irrigation has made farming possible in even the most arid areas.

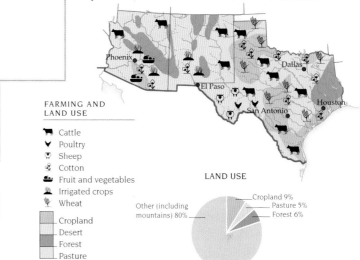

FARMING AND
LAND USE

- Cattle
- Poultry
- Sheep
- Cotton
- Fruit and vegetables
- Irrigated crops
- Wheat
- Cropland
- Desert
- Forest
- Pasture
- ● Major conurbation

LAND USE

Other (including mountains) 80%
Cropland 9%
Pasture 5%
Forest 6%

POPULATION

The descendants of Mexican and Spanish settlers and numerous groups of Native Americans live in the southwestern states. The great cities of Texas grew up on income from cattle-ranching and the oil industry. Much of Arizona and New Mexico is sparsely populated, but today people are moving to these states to escape the cold winters elsewhere.

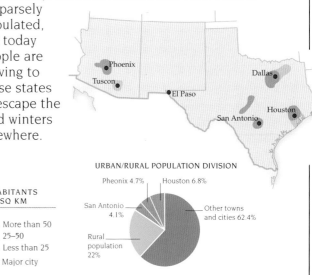

INHABITANTS
PER SQ KM

- More than 50
- 25–50
- Less than 25
- ● Major city

URBAN/RURAL POPULATION DIVISION

Pheonix 4.7%
Houston 6.8%
San Antonio 4.1%
Other towns and cities 62.4%
Rural population 22%

45

USA: THE MOUNTAIN STATES

COLORADO, IDAHO, MONTANA, NEVADA, UTAH, WYOMING

These states are home to some of the nation's most fantastic landscapes: endless treeless plains, craggy peaks, incredible desert landforms, and the salt flats of Utah. Although this was one of the last regions of the USA to be settled, great mineral reserves have been exploited here in recent years, and new industries have grown up in some of the larger cities. Utah is the headquarters of the Mormon religion.

INDUSTRY

Rich mineral reserves, including coal, oil and gas, are mined throughout the region and forests are a source of good-quality timber. In the larger cities of Colorado and Utah, growing industries include high-tech computer firms. Many tourists are drawn to this region to ski in the resorts of Colorado and to explore the wilderness.

STRUCTURE OF INDUSTRY

Manufacturing 16%
Primary 4%
Services 80%

INDUSTRY

- ⚗ Chemicals
- 🥫 Food processing
- 👕 Textiles
- ⛏ Coal
- ⚒ Mining
- 🛢 Oil and gas
- 🪵 Timber processing
- 🎰 Gambling
- 💻 High-tech
- ☢ Research and development
- 🎭 Tourism
- ● Major industrial centre / area
- — Major road

FARMING AND LAND USE

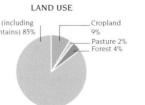

In the southern mountain states, cattle ranching is the main form of farming. Wheat and corn are grown in the eastern states, and the fertile soils of the Snake River valley in Idaho produce large crops of potatoes and many other vegetables. The northern states have many large commercial forests.

FARMING AND LAND USE

- 🐄 Cattle
- 🌽 Corn
- 💧 Irrigated crops
- 🥔 Potatoes
- 🌲 Timber
- 🌾 Wheat

- Cropland
- Desert
- Forest
- Pasture
- ● Major conurbation

LAND USE

Other (including mountains) 85%
Cropland 9%
Pasture 2%
Forest 4%

POPULATION

Colorado, with the growing city of Denver, is the most populous of the mountain states. In other states, people have settled close to sources of water such as Great Salt Lake in Utah. Many towns have less than 10,000 people and are far apart.

INHABITANTS PER SQ KM

- More than 50
- 25–50
- Less than 25
- ● Major city

URBAN/RURAL POPULATION DIVISION

Las Vegas 4.3%
Denver 4.7%
Colorado Springs 3%
Other towns and cities 64%
Rural population 24%

THE LANDSCAPE

The great Rocky Mountains and many smaller mountain ranges cover almost all of this region. Only eastern Montana is not mountainous. Here western parts of the Great Plains rise to meet the mountains. Parts of the southern mountain states are very arid with spectacular scenery, including block-like mesas, formed by erosion.

Continental Divide
From this watershed, crossing the Lewis Range, rivers flow in different directions across North America. Some flow east to Hudson Bay, some south to the Gulf of Mexico and others west to the Pacific Ocean.

Yellowstone National Park (D 3)
Yellowstone was set up in 1872 as the first national park in the USA. Water from hot springs has deposited minerals as it cools, forming white rock terraces close to the springs.

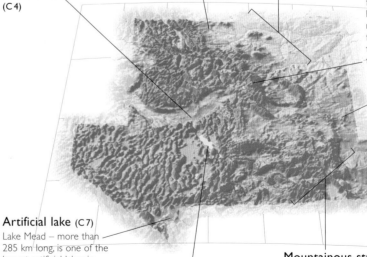

Snake River (C 4)

Great Plains (E 2)

North Platte River (F 4)

Artificial lake (C 7)
Lake Mead – more than 285 km long, is one of the largest artificial lakes in the world. It was formed in 1936, when the Hoover Dam was built across the Colorado River.

Great Salt Lake (C 5)

Mountainous state
Colorado has more than 1,500 peaks more than 3000 m high – this is six times the number of high mountains found in the Swiss Alps.

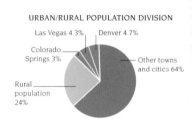

NORTH
AMERICA

USA:
The Mountain
States

ENVIRONMENTAL ISSUES

Parts of the Rocky Mountains, including the National Parks, have become major centres for outdoor pursuits. The sheer number of people puts pressure on the land leading to soil erosion, and increasing the possibility of landslides. Nevada remains the main testing ground for the US nuclear arsenal, and there are many older, disused sites here.

ENVIRONMENTAL ISSUES

- Former nuclear test site
- Nuclear test site
- Urban air pollution
- Wind farm
- National Park
- Winter tourist resort
- Major industrial centre

CLIMATE

In the lowland areas, particularly in the south, summers are often very hot and dry. Parts of the Rocky Mountains are permanently covered by snow, and some of the high passes are cut off by snow in the winter.

January

July

TEMPERATURE AND PRECIPITATION

More than 30°C	0 to 5°C
25 to 30°C	-5 to 0°C
20 to 25°C	-10 to -5°C
15 to 20°C	Less than -10°C
10 to 15°C	100 Precipitation (mm)
5 to 10°C	

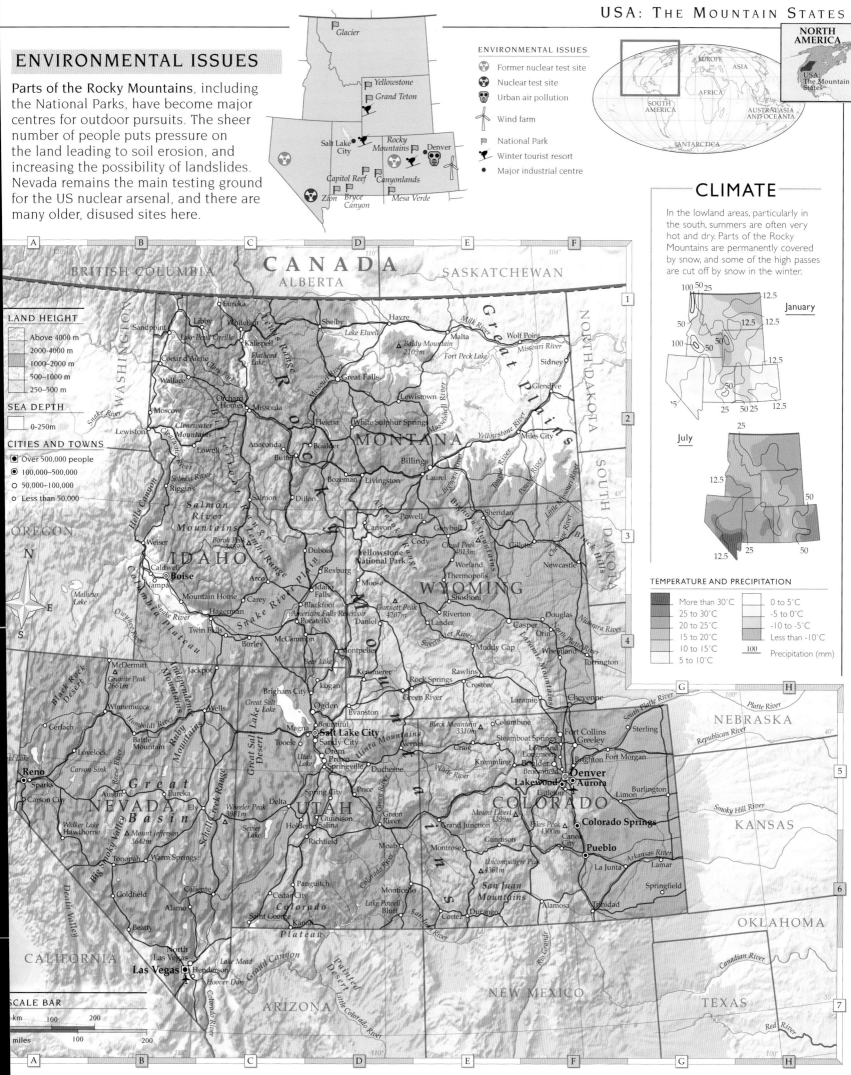

LAND HEIGHT

- Above 4000 m
- 2000–4000 m
- 1000–2000 m
- 500–1000 m
- 250–500 m

SEA DEPTH

- 0–250m

CITIES AND TOWNS

- Over 500,000 people
- 100,000–500,000
- 50,000–100,000
- Less than 50,000

SCALE BAR

47

USA: THE PACIFIC STATES

CALIFORNIA, OREGON, WASHINGTON

The earliest European visitors to the West Coast were fur-trappers and miners, but the Gold Rush of 1849 brought in the first major wave of settlers. Drawn by tales of the beautiful scenery, pleasant climate, and fertile valleys, more people arrived on the newly built railways. People from all over the world are still moving into this region, seeking jobs in the dynamic economy and the famous laid-back lifestyle.

INDUSTRY

The Pacific States are the centre of the high-tech computer industry with Silicon Valley between San Francisco and San Jose, and electronics industries growing in Portland and Seattle. Other major industries include research and development for the defence industry, film making in Los Angeles, food processing and lumbering. Tourism is well developed throughout the Pacific States.

STRUCTURE OF INDUSTRY

Primary 2%
Services 81%
Manufacturing 17%

INDUSTRY

✈ Aerospace	✕ Film industry
⚗ Chemicals	▭ High-tech
✿ Engineering	☢ Research and development
▤ Food processing	⛢ Tourism
◑ Iron and steel	
⚓ Shipbuilding	◉ Major industrial centre / area
⊺ Textiles	— Major road
⚘ Timber processing	

FARMING AND LAND USE

California's Central Valley and the river valleys of Washington and Oregon provide ideal conditions for a wide range of fruit and vegetables, including citrus fruit and grapes. Poultry farming is widespread in the northwest and there are many large cattle ranches. Millions of hectares of commercial forest are located in this region.

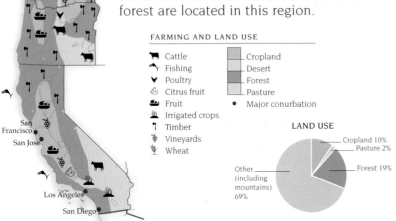

FARMING AND LAND USE

⛏ Cattle	▨ Cropland
➤ Fishing	▨ Desert
⋎ Poultry	▨ Forest
⚘ Citrus fruit	▨ Pasture
⚘ Fruit	● Major conurbation
⚶ Irrigated crops	
⟙ Timber	
⚘ Vineyards	
⚘ Wheat	

LAND USE

Cropland 10%
Pasture 2%
Forest 19%
Other (including mountains) 69%

ENVIRONMENTAL ISSUES

Some of the great national parks of the USA, including Yosemite and Sequoia, are found here. The immense numbers of visitors put great pressure on the landscape. Water is in short supply in large parts of California, and desertification, caused by over-intense farming methods, is a problem. Wind farms have been set up on the hills above the San Joaquin valley to provide alternative energy.

ENVIRONMENTAL ISSUES

⚑ National park	▨ Desert area
☻ Urban air pollution	▨ Risk of desertification
	▨ Severe risk of desertification
⚘ Wind farm	▨ Polluted rivers
	● Major industrial centre
✕ Risk of wild fire	

THE LANDSCAPE

The Coast and Cascade ranges run north–south through Oregon and Washington while further south, the high Sierra Nevada run along California's eastern fringes. Two broad valleys, the Sacramento and San Joaquin, are known as the Central Valley, and form a trough beneath the Sierra Nevada. The south is extremely dry – Death Valley is the hottest place in the entire USA.

Northern rain forest (B 2)

The ocean-facing side of the Olympic Mountains receives 3,600 mm of rain every year, supporting the only true temperate rainforest in the Northern Hemisphere.

Hells Canyon (D 3)

Hells Canyon is North America's deepest gorge. Running through part of Oregon, it was created as the Snake River cut down through the land.

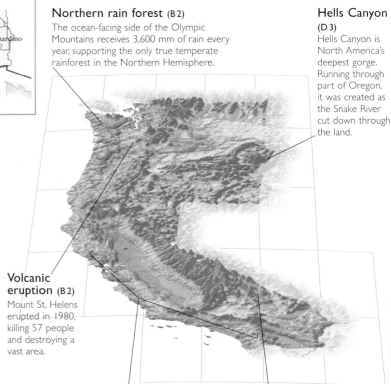

Volcanic eruption (B 2)

Mount St. Helens erupted in 1980, killing 57 people and destroying a vast area.

San Andreas Fault

The San Andreas Fault runs for 1,050 km underneath California. When both sides of the fault move at different rates, tremors and earthquakes result.

Hottest place (D 7)

In 1913, Death Valley set the record for the highest temperature ever recorded in the US, at 56.6°C.

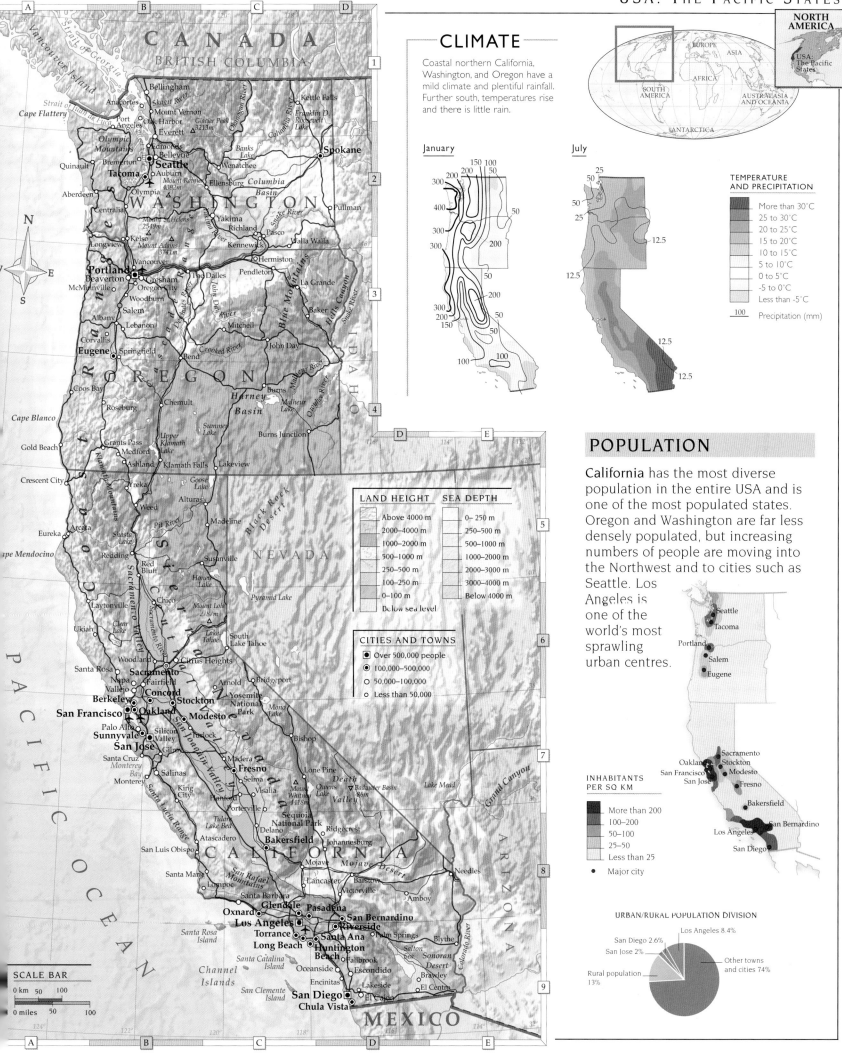

CLIMATE

Coastal northern California, Washington, and Oregon have a mild climate and plentiful rainfall. Further south, temperatures rise and there is little rain.

January

July

TEMPERATURE AND PRECIPITATION

- More than 30°C
- 25 to 30°C
- 20 to 25°C
- 15 to 20°C
- 10 to 15°C
- 5 to 10°C
- 0 to 5°C
- -5 to 0°C
- Less than -5°C

100 Precipitation (mm)

LAND HEIGHT

- Above 4000 m
- 2000–4000 m
- 1000–2000 m
- 500–1000 m
- 250–500 m
- 100–250 m
- 0–100 m
- Below sea level

SEA DEPTH

- 0– 250 m
- 250–500 m
- 500–1000 m
- 1000–2000 m
- 2000–3000 m
- 3000–4000 m
- Below 4000 m

CITIES AND TOWNS

- ● Over 500,000 people
- ◉ 100,000–500,000
- ○ 50,000–100,000
- ○ Less than 50,000

POPULATION

California has the most diverse population in the entire USA and is one of the most populated states. Oregon and Washington are far less densely populated, but increasing numbers of people are moving into the Northwest and to cities such as Seattle. Los Angeles is one of the world's most sprawling urban centres.

INHABITANTS PER SQ KM

- More than 200
- 100–200
- 50–100
- 25–50
- Less than 25
- ● Major city

URBAN/RURAL POPULATION DIVISION

- Los Angeles 8.4%
- San Diego 2.6%
- San Jose 2%
- Rural population 13%
- Other towns and cities 74%

SCALE BAR

0 km 50 100

0 miles 50 100

ALASKA

A **magnificent land** of mountains, forests and snowfields, with rich oil and mineral reserves, Alaska was purchased from Russia for $1 million in 1867. Almost 650,000 people live here, many drawn by the oil industry. Some of Alaska's native peoples like the Aleuts and Inupiaq still live by hunting and fishing.

ENVIRONMENTAL ISSUES

Much of northern Alaska is covered by permafrost (permanently frozen ground). The Trans-Alaska Pipeline, which brings oil from Prudhoe Bay to Valdez, was built above ground to stop the permafrost melting. A number of major oil spills have threatened Alaska's unique envrionment.

Exxon Valdez 1993

ENVIRONMENTAL ISSUES

- 🚢 Major oil spill
- – – – Oil pipeline
- 🛢 Oil wells
- ▨ Permafrost zone
- • Major town

INDUSTRY

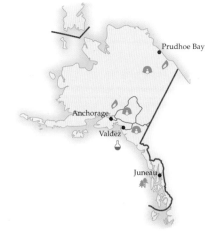

The Alaskan economy is dominated by the oil business. The oilfields of Alaska are of a similar size to those in the Persian Gulf. Minerals including gold are mined in the mountains, and paper products are exported to countries on the Pacific Rim.

INDUSTRY

- ⚗ Chemicals
- ⛏ Mining
- 🛢 Oil and gas
- 🏭 Timber processing
- ▣ Major industrial centre
- — Major road

FARMING AND LAND USE

Salmon are caught in great numbers in the waters of the north Pacific. Much of the state – more than 9 million hectares – is covered by forest which is commercially lumbered. Most food must be imported, although fruit is grown in hothouses near the larger cities.

FARMING AND LAND USE

- ➹ Fishing
- 🦐 Fruit
- ⼁ Timber
- Barren
- Forest
- Mountains
- Tundra
- • Major conurbation

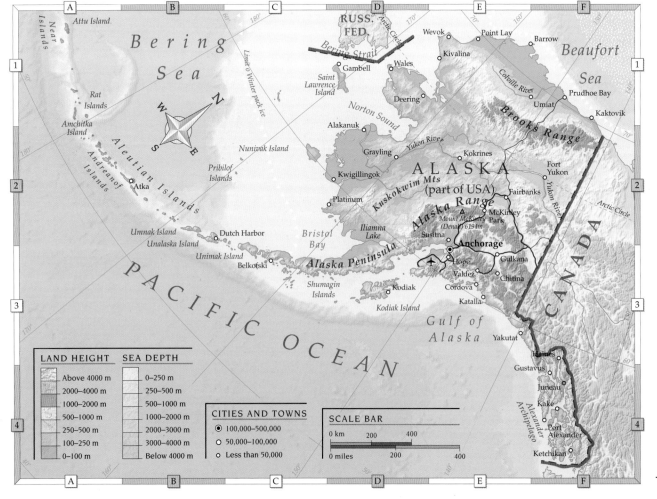

LAND HEIGHT
- Above 4000 m
- 2000–4000 m
- 1000–2000 m
- 500–1000 m
- 250–500 m
- 100–250 m
- 0–100 m

SEA DEPTH
- 0–250 m
- 250–500 m
- 500–1000 m
- 1000–2000 m
- 2000–3000 m
- 3000–4000 m
- Below 4000 m

CITIES AND TOWNS
- ◉ 100,000–500,000
- ○ 50,000–100,000
- ○ Less than 50,000

SCALE BAR
0 km   200   400
0 miles   200   400

CLIMATE

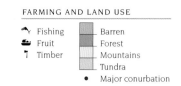

Parts of northern Alaska are frozen year-round and can be cut off entirely in the winter. Summers are milder – especially in the Aleutians.

January

July

TEMPERATURE AND PRECIPITATION
- More than 15°C
- 10 to 15°C
- 5 to 10°C
- 0 to 5°C
- -5 to 0°C
- -10 to -5°C
- -15 to -10°C
- Less than -15°C
- 100 Precipitation (mm)

HAWAII

Hawaii is the 50th US state. It lies far from the mainland in the middle of the Pacific Ocean. The island chain was formed by volcanoes, only one of which, Mauna Loa, remains active today. The islands' indigenous peoples are Polynesians, but continued immigration means that they now make up only 9% of the population.

INDUSTRY AND LAND USE

Tourism is the most important industry in Hawaii, accounting for one in every three jobs. The naval base at Pearl Harbor also provides jobs for numerous people. The many large plantations grow sugarcane, bananas and tropical fruit for export.

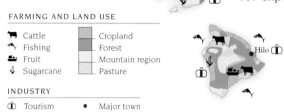

FARMING AND LAND USE

- Cattle
- Fishing
- Fruit
- Sugarcane
- Cropland
- Forest
- Mountain region
- Pasture

INDUSTRY

- Tourism
- Major town

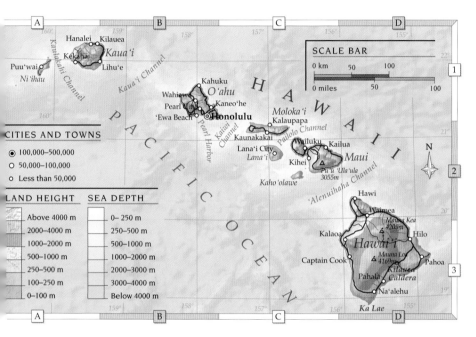

CITIES AND TOWNS
- ◉ 100,000–500,000
- ○ 50,000–100,000
- ○ Less than 50,000

LAND HEIGHT
- Above 4000 m
- 2000–4000 m
- 1000–2000 m
- 500–1000 m
- 250–500 m
- 100–250 m
- 0–100 m

SEA DEPTH
- 0– 250 m
- 250–500 m
- 500–1000 m
- 1000–2000 m
- 2000–3000 m
- 3000–4000 m
- Below 4000 m

ENVIRONMENTAL ISSUES

Climatic occurrences, combined with the growth of tourism, have an adverse effect on the indigenous flora and fauna. Eruptions from Mauna Loa are an accepted risk for the population.

ENVIRONMENTAL ISSUES

- Tourist resort
- Volcanic eruption
- Major town

Mauna Loa – 1984
Kilauea – 1983

UNITED STATES OVERSEAS TERRITORIES

America's overseas territories have traditionally been seen as strategically or economically important. In most cases, the local population has been given a say in deciding whether it wants to govern itself. A US commonwealth territory has a greater level of independence than a US unincorporated or external territory. The US has 13 overseas territories: the four largest are shown here.

AMERICAN SAMOA

American Samoa consists of five volcanic islands and two coral atolls in the south Pacific. The people are among the last true Polynesians.

PUERTO RICO

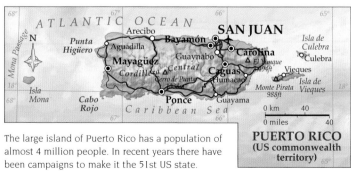

The large island of Puerto Rico has a population of almost 4 million people. In recent years there have been campaigns to make it the 51st US state.

GUAM

The US military base that covers one-third of the island makes Guam strategically important to the US. The Chamorro, the indigenous people, are in charge of political and social life.

US VIRGIN ISLANDS

There are 53 volcanic islands in the US Virgin Islands. Most people live on the main islands of St. John, St. Thomas and St. Croix, which has a vast oil refinery.

MEXICO

Mexico is a large country with a rich mixture of traditions and cultures. The ancient civilization of the Aztecs which flourished here was crushed by Spanish invaders in the 16th century. Spain ruled Mexico until its independence in 1836 and today, the country has the world's largest Spanish-speaking population. Mexico is mostly dry and mountainous, and farm land is limited, so the country has to import most of the basic foods it needs to feed its people.

FARMING AND LAND USE

Most of the land suitable for farming is planted with corn – a big part of the Mexican diet. Along the Gulf coast coffee, sugarcane and cotton are grown on plantations for export. Parts of the dry north are irrigated to grow cotton, but most of the land is taken up by large cattle ranches. Fishing, especially for shellfish such as lobster and shrimp is important in coastal areas.

FARMING AND LAND USE

- 🐂 Cattle
- 🐟 Fishing
- 🐑 Sheep
- 🍌 Bananas
- ☕ Coffee
- 🌽 Corn (maize)
- 🌿 Cotton
- 🍓 Fruit
- 🍇 Grapes
- 🦐 Shellfish
- ↓ Sugarcane
- 🌲 Timber

- Cropland
- Desert
- Forest
- Pasture
- Wetland
- • Major conurbation

LAND USE

Cropland 14%
Other 15%
Forest 29%
Pasture 42%

THE LANDSCAPE

Much of Mexico is made up of a high plateau. The climate there is very dry and varies between true desert in the north, and semi-desert further south. The plateau is separated from the coastal plains by two long, rugged mountain chains: the Eastern Sierra Madre and the Western Sierra Madre. Towards the south, the mountain ranges join, meeting in the region of high volcanic peaks that surround Mexico City.

Lower California (B 3)
This long and very dry peninsula, separates the Gulf of California from the Pacific Ocean. The Gulf was formed after the last Ice Age, when the sea rose to flood a major rift valley.

The Rio Grande (D 2)
This river flows from Colorado in the USA and forms much of Mexico's northern border. It crosses a vast arid area on its way to the Gulf of Mexico.

Earthquakes and volcanoes
Volcanic activity is common in Mexico. Popocatépetl (F 5) and Volcán El Chichónal (G 5) have erupted recently, and Mexico City was hit by a devastating earthquake in 1985

Western Sierra Madre (C 3).

Eastern Sierra Madre (D 5).

Yucatan Peninsula (H 4)
The Yucatan Peninsula is a low, wide tableland, formed by layers of limestone. Limestone absorbs water, so there are few rivers on the peninsula, and the tropical rainforests found there are fed mainly by streams and underground water.

POPULATION

Most of the north is sparsely populated due to the hot, dry climate and lack of cultivable farm land. As people have migrated from the countryside in search of work, the cities have grown dramatically; almost 75% of Mexicans now live in urban areas. Mexico City is home to almost a fifth of the population and is one of the world's largest cities.

INHABITANTS PER SQ KM

- More than 200
- 100–200
- 50–100
- Less than 50
- ■ Capital city
- ● Major city

URBAN/RURAL POPULATION DIVIDE

Mexico City 17.1%
Guadalajara 3.5%
Monterrey 3.1%
Other towns and cities 50.3%
Rural population 26%

ENVIRONMENTAL ISSUES

Fast, unplanned growth has led to poor sanitation and water supplies in Mexico City, while the wall of mountains which surround the city traps pollution from cars and factories, giving it some of the world's worst air pollution. Much of Mexico's tropical rainforest has been felled, leading to increased soil erosion. Land clearance further north is also causing desertification.

ENVIRONMENTAL ISSUES

- Risk of desertification
- Deforested areas
- Remaining tropical forests
- ⌇ Path of recent, devastating hurricane
- ● Major industrial city
- Volcanic eruption
- Urban air pollution
- Flooding

Emily 2005
Wilma 2005
Dean 2007
Mitch 1998
Nevado de Colima 1994
Guadalajara
Mexico City
Popocatépetl 1994
Volcán El Chichónal 1994

INDUSTRY

Oil and gas on the Gulf coast are the biggest source of income. Mexico is also rich in other minerals; it is the world's top silver producer. Manufacturing is centred around Mexico City and along the US border, where mainly foreign owned factories assemble products for export. Tourism is also very important to Mexico.

STRUCTURE OF INDUSTRY

- Primary 4%
- Services 70%
- Manufacturing 26%

INDUSTRY

- Car manufacture
- Electronics
- Engineering
- Food processing
- Iron & steel
- Oil refining
- Textiles
- Mining
- Oil and gas
- Tourism
- Major industrial centre / area
- Major road

CLIMATE

Northern Mexico and the peninsula of Lower California are dry, hot and largely desert. Towards the south, rainfall increases, especially in July. Moist, warm conditions allow rainforests to grow.

January

July

TEMPERATURE AND PRECIPITATION

- More than 30°C
- 25 to 30°C
- 20 to 25°C
- 15 to 20°C
- 10 to 15°C
- 5 to 10°C
- Less than 5°C
- 100 Precipitation (mm)

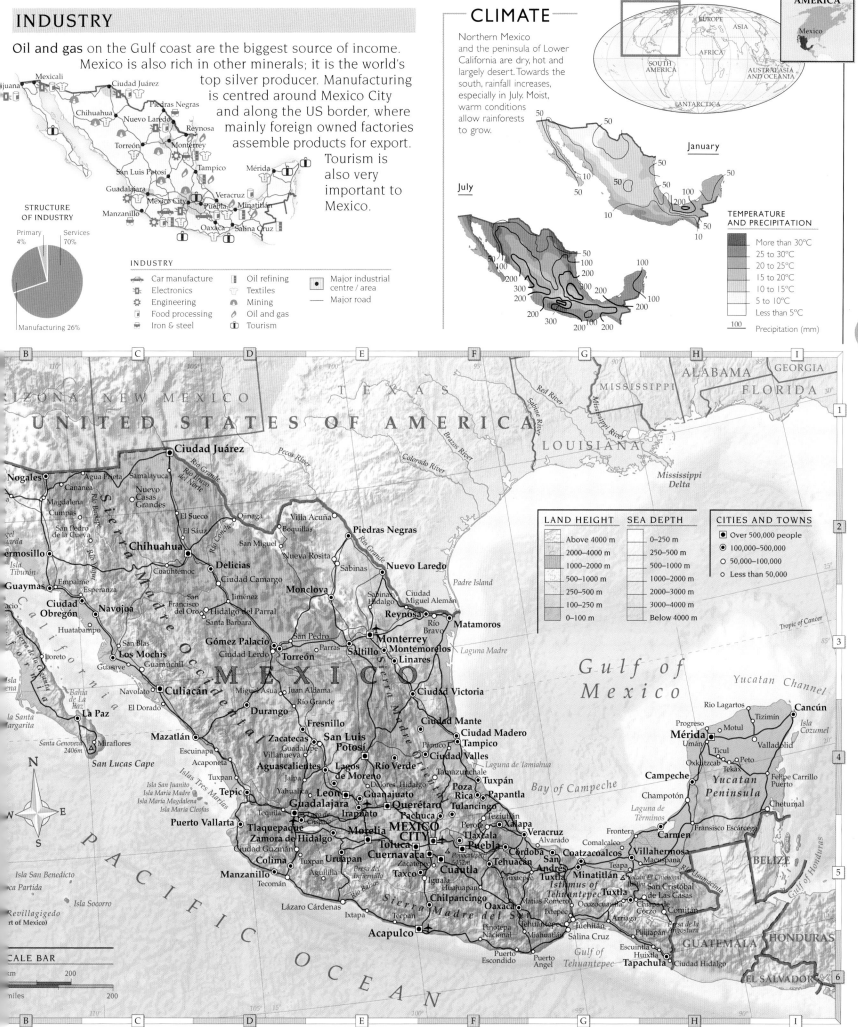

LAND HEIGHT
- Above 4000 m
- 2000–4000 m
- 1000–2000 m
- 500–1000 m
- 250–500 m
- 100–250 m
- 0–100 m

SEA DEPTH
- 0–250 m
- 250–500 m
- 500–1000 m
- 1000–2000 m
- 2000–3000 m
- 3000–4000 m
- Below 4000 m

CITIES AND TOWNS
- Over 500,000 people
- 100,000–500,000
- 50,000–100,000
- Less than 50,000

SCALE BAR

CENTRAL AMERICA

BELIZE, COSTA RICA, EL SALVADOR, GUATEMALA, HONDURAS, NICARAGUA, PANAMA

Central America lies on a narrow bridge of land which links North and South America. All the countries here, except Belize, were once governed by Spain. Today, most of their people are *mestizos* – a mix of the original Maya Indian inhabitants and Spanish settlers. The hot, steamy climate is ideal for growing tropical crops, such as coffee and bananas, which are exported worldwide.

FARMING AND LAND USE

About half of all the agricultural products grown here are exported. The Pacific coast has fertile, well-watered land suitable for growing cotton and sugarcane. In the central highlands are big coffee plantations, and ranches where beef cattle are raised. Bananas grow well along the humid Caribbean coastal plain, and shrimp and lobster are caught offshore.

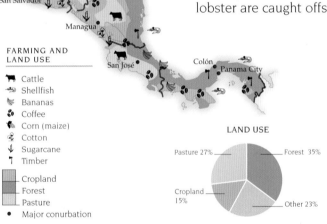

FARMING AND LAND USE

- 🐄 Cattle
- 🦐 Shellfish
- 🍌 Bananas
- ☕ Coffee
- 🌽 Corn (maize)
- Cotton
- Sugarcane
- Timber

Cropland
Forest
Pasture
• Major conurbation

LAND USE

Pasture 27%   Forest 35%

Cropland 15%   Other 23%

ENVIRONMENTAL ISSUES

Central America's rainforests are rapidly being cut down for timber and to make way for farmland and land for building. Over half of Guatemala's forests have been felled, mostly in the last 30 years. The situation is also bleak in Honduras, Costa Rica and Nicaragua. Central America has a line of volcanoes running through the region which are still active.

Mitch 1998
Volcán Tacaná 1986
Volcán de Fuego 1974
Felix 2007
Volcán de Izalco 1958
Volcán San Cristobal 2000
Volcán Cerro Negro 1995
Volcán Musaya 2001
Volcán Concepcion 1986
Volcán Rincon de la Vieja 1998
Volcán Arenal 1998, 2000

ENVIRONMENTAL ISSUES

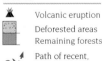

- 🌋 Volcanic eruption
- Deforested areas / Remaining forests
- Path of recent, devastating hurricane

POPULATION

Central America's people live mainly in the valleys of the central highlands or along the Pacific coastal plains. Despite the threat of volcanic eruptions and earthquakes, towns and cities developed in these areas because of the fertile volcanic soils found there. Around half the population still live in rural areas, mostly in small villages or remote settlements, but the cities have expanded rapidly and overcrowding has become a serious problem.

BELMOPAN
GUATEMALA CITY
TEGUCIGALPA
SAN SALVADOR
MANAGUA
SAN JOSÉ
PANAMA CITY

INHABITANTS PER SQ KM

- More than 50
- 25–50
- Less than 25
- ■ Capital city

URBAN/RURAL POPULATION DIVIDE

- Managua 2.2%
- Tegucigalpa 2%
- Guatemala City 2.4%
- Other towns and cities 43.4%
- Rural population 50%

THE LANDSCAPE

The Sierra Madre in the north and the Cordillera Central to the south form a mountainous ridge that stretches down most of Central America. Along the Pacific coast north of Panama is a belt of more than 40 active volcanoes. The mountains are broken by valleys and basins with large, fertile areas of rich, volcanic soil.

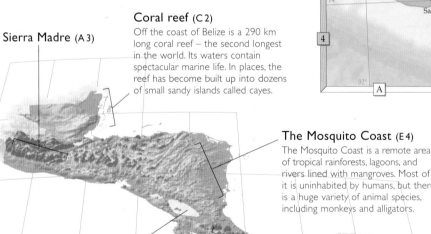

Sierra Madre (A 3)

Coral reef (C 2)
Off the coast of Belize is a 290 km long coral reef – the second longest in the world. Its waters contain spectacular marine life. In places, the reef has become built up into dozens of small sandy islands called cayes.

The Mosquito Coast (E 4)
The Mosquito Coast is a remote area of tropical rainforests, lagoons, and rivers lined with mangroves. Most of it is uninhabited by humans, but there is a huge variety of animal species, including monkeys and alligators.

Lake Nicaragua (E 5)
This large freshwater lake contains about 400 islands, some of which are active volancoes like Volcán Concepcion. The lake is also home to the world's only freshwater sharks.

Cordillera Central (G 6)

The Panama Canal (H 6)
The Panama Canal links the Atlantic and Pacific oceans along a distance of 82 km. Half of its route passes through Lake Gatún, a freshwater lake which acts as a reservoir for the canal, providing water to operate the locks.

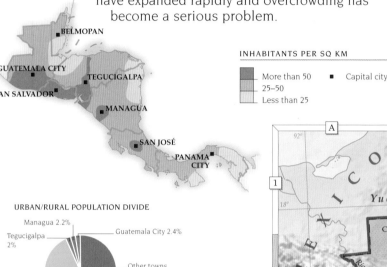

MEXICO
Yuca
Río Usumacinta
Barillas
Jacaltenango
GUA
Chajul
Huehuetenango
Nebaj
Volcán Tacaná 4093m
Santa Cruz del Quiché
San Marcos
Quezaltena
GUATEMALA CIT
Champerico
San J

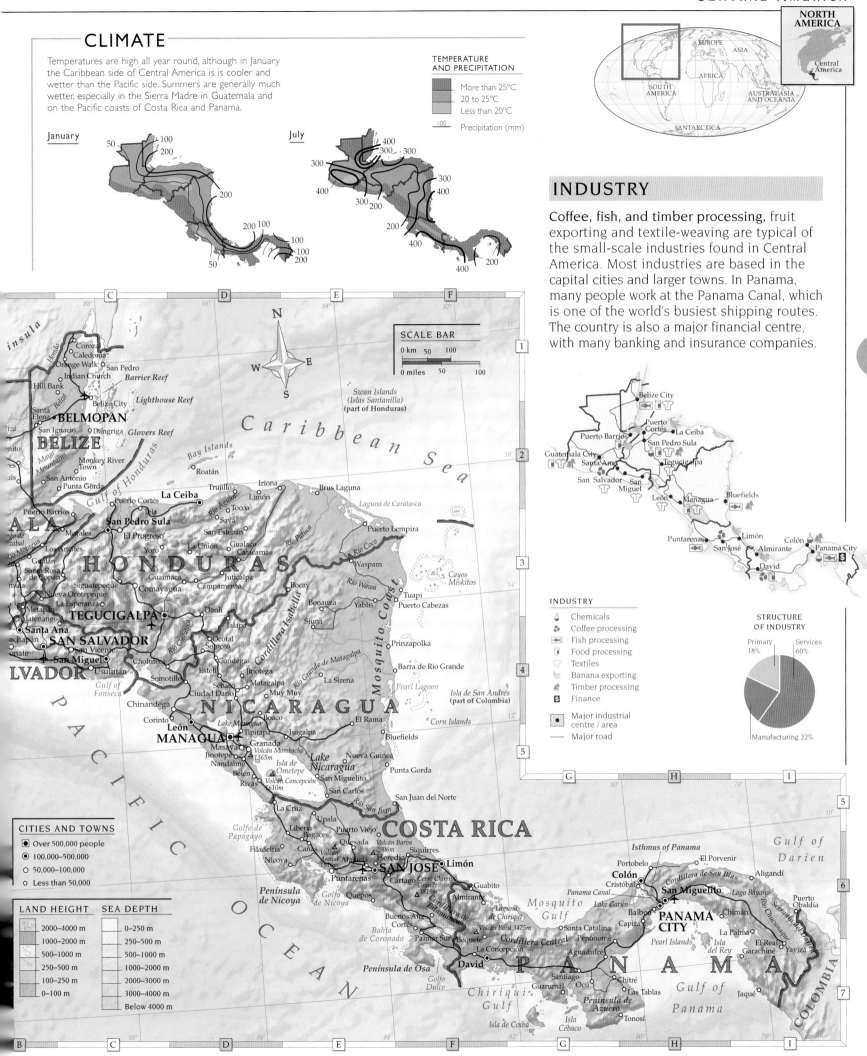

CLIMATE

Temperatures are high all year round, although in January the Caribbean side of Central America is is cooler and wetter than the Pacific side. Summers are generally much wetter, especially in the Sierra Madre in Guatemala and on the Pacific coasts of Costa Rica and Panama.

TEMPERATURE AND PRECIPITATION

More than 25°C
20 to 25°C
Less than 20°C
100 — Precipitation (mm)

January

July

NORTH AMERICA

Central America

EUROPE
ASIA
AFRICA
SOUTH AMERICA
AUSTRALASIA AND OCEANIA
ANTARCTICA

INDUSTRY

Coffee, fish, and timber processing, fruit exporting and textile-weaving are typical of the small-scale industries found in Central America. Most industries are based in the capital cities and larger towns. In Panama, many people work at the Panama Canal, which is one of the world's busiest shipping routes. The country is also a major financial centre, with many banking and insurance companies.

INDUSTRY

🜹 Chemicals
☕ Coffee processing
🐟 Fish processing
🍴 Food processing
👕 Textiles
🍌 Banana exporting
🌲 Timber processing
Ⓢ Finance
⊙ Major industrial centre / area
— Major road

STRUCTURE OF INDUSTRY

Primary 18%
Services 60%
Manufacturing 22%

SCALE BAR

0 km   50   100
0 miles   50   100

CITIES AND TOWNS

■ Over 500,000 people
◉ 100,000–500,000
◎ 50,000–100,000
○ Less than 50,000

LAND HEIGHT

2000–4000 m
1000–2000 m
500–1000 m
250–500 m
100–250 m
0–100 m

SEA DEPTH

0–250 m
250–500 m
500–1000 m
1000–2000 m
2000–3000 m
3000–4000 m
Below 4000 m

THE CARIBBEAN

The **Caribbean Sea** is enclosed by an arc of many hundreds of islands, islets and offshore reefs which reach from Florida in the USA round to Venezuela in South America. From 1492, Spain, France, Britain and the Netherlands claimed the islands as colonies. Most of the islands' original inhabitants were wiped out by disease and a wide mixture of peoples – of African, Asian and European descent – now make up the population. In 2010, a huge earthquake killed around 250,000 people in Haiti.

THE LANDSCAPE

The Bahamas
The Bahamas are low-lying, islands formed from limestone rock. Their coastlines are fringed by coral reefs, lagoons and mangrove swamps. Some of the bigger islands are covered by forests.

The islands are formed from two main mountain chains: the Greater Antilles, which are part of a chain running from west to east, and the Lesser Antilles, which run from north to south. The mountains are now almost submerged under the Atlantic Ocean and Caribbean Sea. Only the higher peaks reach above sea level to form islands.

Hispaniola (F 4)
Two countries, Haiti and the Dominican Republic occupy the island of Hispaniola. The land is mostly mountainous, broken by fertile valleys.

Cuba (C 3)
Cuba is the largest island in the Antilles. Its landscape is made up of wide, fertile plains with rugged hills and mountains in the southeast.

The Lesser Antilles
Most of these small volcanic islands have mountainous interiors. Barbados and Antigua & Barbuda are flatter, with some higher volcanic areas. Montserrat was evacuated in 1997, following volcanic eruptions on the island.

FARMING AND LAND USE

Agriculture is an important source of income, with over half of all produce exported. Many islands have fertile, well-watered land and large areas are set aside for commercial crops such as sugarcane, tobacco and coffee. Some islands rely heavily on a single crop; in Dominica, bananas provide over half the country's income. Cuba is one of the world's biggest sugar producers.

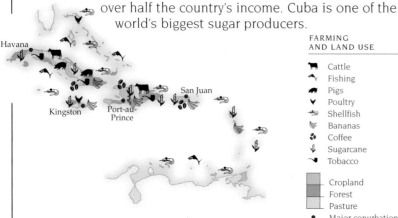

FARMING AND LAND USE

- 🐂 Cattle
- Fishing
- 🐖 Pigs
- Poultry
- Shellfish
- Bananas
- ☕ Coffee
- Sugarcane
- Tobacco

- Cropland
- Forest
- Pasture
- • Major conurbation

ENVIRONMENTAL ISSUES

The islands of the Caribbean are often under threat from hurricane storm systems which sweep in from the Atlantic Ocean between May and October. The winds can reach speeds of up to 300 km per hour, devastating everything that lies in their path and causing severe flooding. The storms themselves are enormous; a hurricane can extend outwards for 650 km from its calm centre, which is known as the 'eye'.

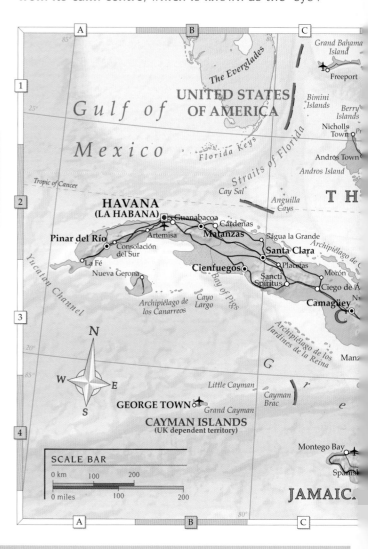

TOURISM

Tourism is thriving in the Caribbean, often bringing more income to the region than other, traditional industries. Long sandy beaches, clear, warm waters and the climate are the main attractions. In Cuba and the Dominican Republic, tourism is expanding at some of the fastest rates in North America. As hotel complexes and new roads and airports are developed, the environment is often damaged. Local people who work in the industry often receive little of the extra cash brought in by the tourists.

TOURISM

Major tourist destinations

NORTH AMERICA

The Caribbean

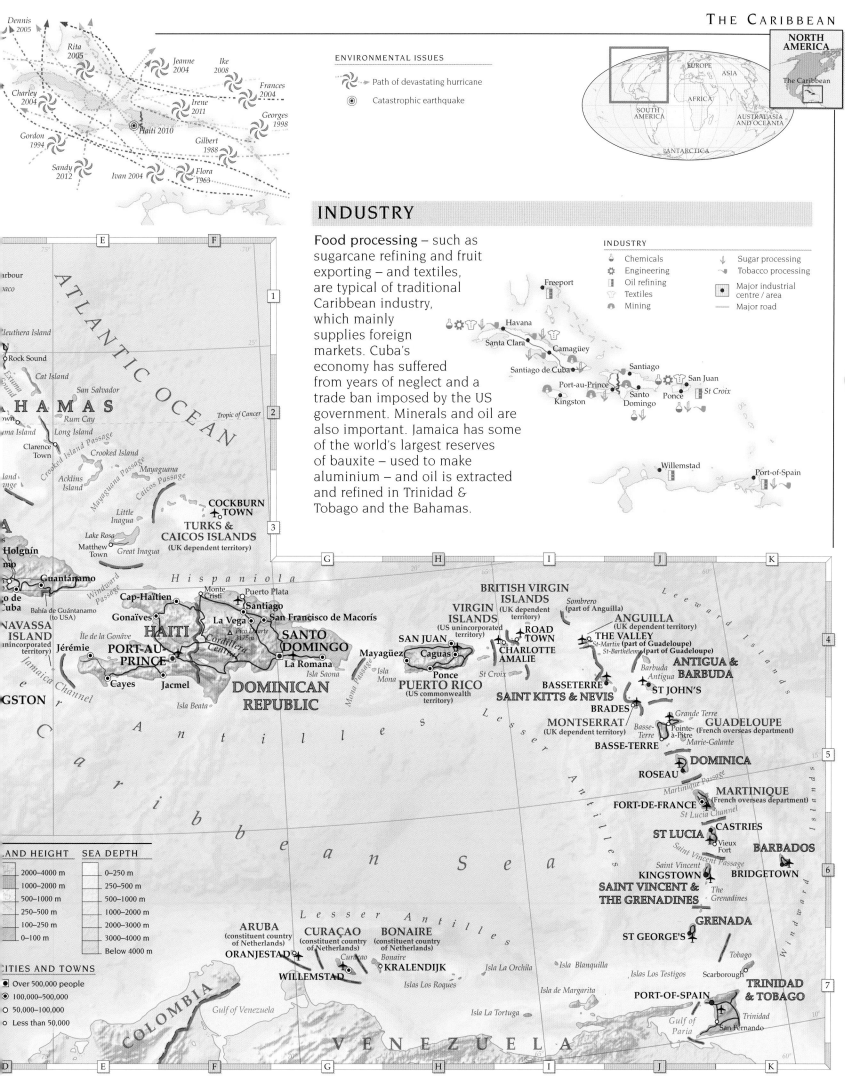

ENVIRONMENTAL ISSUES

Path of devastating hurricane

Catastrophic earthquake

Dennis 2005
Rita 2005
Jeanne 2004
Ike 2008
Frances 2004
Charley 2004
Irene 2011
Georges 1998
Gordon 1994
Haiti 2010
Gilbert 1988
Sandy 2012
Ivan 2004
Flora 1963

INDUSTRY

Food processing – such as sugarcane refining and fruit exporting – and textiles, are typical of traditional Caribbean industry, which mainly supplies foreign markets. Cuba's economy has suffered from years of neglect and a trade ban imposed by the US government. Minerals and oil are also important. Jamaica has some of the world's largest reserves of bauxite – used to make aluminium – and oil is extracted and refined in Trinidad & Tobago and the Bahamas.

INDUSTRY

Chemicals
Engineering
Oil refining
Textiles
Mining
Sugar processing
Tobacco processing
Major industrial centre / area
Major road

Freeport
Havana
Santa Clara
Camagüey
Santiago de Cuba
Santiago
San Juan
Port-au-Prince
St Croix
Kingston
Santo Domingo
Ponce
Willemstad
Port-of-Spain

ATLANTIC OCEAN

BAHAMAS

Eleuthera Island
Rock Sound
Cat Island
San Salvador
Rum Cay
Long Island
Clarence Town
Crooked Island
Mayaguana Passage
Acklins Island
Little Inagua
Lake Rosa
Matthew Town
Great Inagua
Mayaguana
Caicos Passage
Crooked Island Passage

Tropic of Cancer

COCKBURN TOWN
TURKS & CAICOS ISLANDS
(UK dependent territory)

Holguín
Guantánamo
Bahía de Guántanamo (to USA)
NAVASSA ISLAND
unincorporated territory
Jérémie
Cayes
Cap-Haïtien
Gonaïves
HAITI
PORT-AU-PRINCE
Jacmel
Île de la Gonâve
Monte Cristi
Santiago
La Vega
△ Pico Duarte 3175m
Cordillera Central
San Francisco de Macorís
SANTO DOMINGO
DOMINICAN REPUBLIC
La Romana
Isla Saona
Isla Beata
Puerto Plata

Hispaniola
Windward Passage
Jamaica Channel

KINGSTON

Mayagüez
Isla Mona
PUERTO RICO
(US commonwealth territory)
SAN JUAN
Caguas
Ponce
St Croix

Mona Passage

BRITISH VIRGIN ISLANDS
(UK dependent territory)
VIRGIN ISLANDS
(US unincorporated territory)
ROAD TOWN
CHARLOTTE AMALIE
Sombrero (part of Anguilla)
ANGUILLA
(UK dependent territory)
THE VALLEY
St-Martin (part of Guadeloupe)
St-Barthélemy (part of Guadeloupe)
ANTIGUA & BARBUDA
Barbuda
Antigua
ST JOHN'S
BASSETERRE
SAINT KITTS & NEVIS
BRADES
MONTSERRAT
(UK dependent territory)
Grande Terre
Basse-Terre
Pointe-à-Pitre
GUADELOUPE
(French overseas department)
BASSE-TERRE
Marie-Galante

Leeward Islands

Antilles

Lesser

DOMINICA
ROSEAU
Martinique Passage
MARTINIQUE
(French overseas department)
FORT-DE-FRANCE
St Lucia Channel
CASTRIES
ST LUCIA
Vieux Fort
Saint Vincent Passage
Saint Vincent
KINGSTOWN
The Grenadines
SAINT VINCENT & THE GRENADINES
BARBADOS
BRIDGETOWN

Windward Islands

Caribbean Sea

Lesser Antilles

ARUBA
(constituent country of Netherlands)
ORANJESTAD
CURAÇAO
(constituent country of Netherlands)
Curaçao
BONAIRE
(constituent country of Netherlands)
Bonaire
KRALENDIJK
WILLEMSTAD
Isla La Orchila
Isla Blanquilla
Islas Los Testigos
Scarborough
GRENADA
ST GEORGE'S
Tobago
TRINIDAD & TOBAGO
PORT-OF-SPAIN
Trinidad
San Fernando
Gulf of Paria

COLOMBIA
Gulf of Venezuela
Islas Los Roques
Isla de Margarita
Isla La Tortuga

VENEZUELA

LAND HEIGHT
2000–4000 m
1000–2000 m
500–1000 m
250–500 m
100–250 m
0–100 m

SEA DEPTH
0–250 m
250–500 m
500–1000 m
1000–2000 m
2000–3000 m
3000–4000 m
Below 4000 m

CITIES AND TOWNS
Over 500,000 people
100,000–500,000
50,000–100,000
Less than 50,000

CONTINENTAL SOUTH AMERICA

The towering peaks of the Andes stand high above the western side of South America. They act as a barrier to the sparsely inhabited interior of the continent which includes the dense rainforest of the Amazon Basin – one of the Earth's last great wildernesses. Most people live on South America's coastal fringes. Brazil is both the largest country, and the most populous. Over half the continent's land area and half its people are found there.

4,990 km
7,640 km

CROSS-SECTION ACROSS SOUTH AMERICA

Andes
Amazon River
Guiana Highlands
Mouths of the Amazon
Brazilian Highlands

W — 5,400 km — E

The high peaks of the Andes rise up from a narrow strip of land bordering the Pacific Ocean. East of the Andes, the land flattens into a broad, shallow basin into which the Amazon River flows. To the north are the older Guiana Highlands where rock has been eroded to form flat-topped 'table' mountains.

PHYSICAL SOUTH AMERICA

Ancient masses of rocks, like the Guiana and Brazilian highlands, which are known as shields, form the core of South America. The Andes are the solid backbone of the continent. They are relatively young, formed by collisions between different plates of the Earth's crust. The major rivers; the Paraná and the mighty Amazon flow in deep depressions to the east of the mountains.

ELEVATION

- Above 4000 m
- 2000–4000 m
- 1000–2000 m
- 500–1000 m
- 250–500 m
- 100–250 m
- 0–100 m
- Below sea level
- cross-section

SCALE 1:40,000,000

0 km 400 800
0 miles 400 800

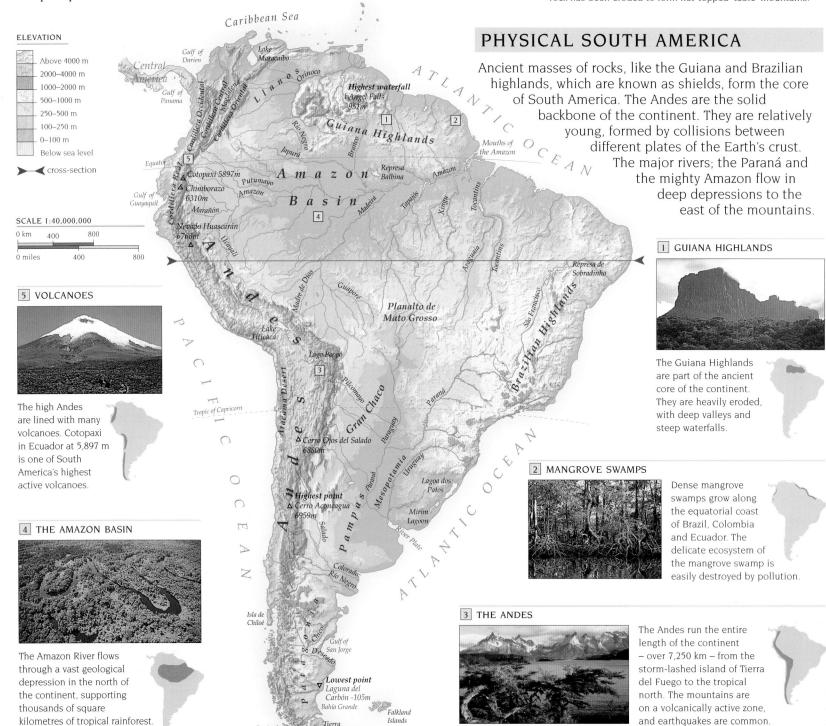

5 VOLCANOES

The high Andes are lined with many volcanoes. Cotopaxi in Ecuador at 5,897 m is one of South America's highest active volcanoes.

4 THE AMAZON BASIN

The Amazon River flows through a vast geological depression in the north of the continent, supporting thousands of square kilometres of tropical rainforest.

1 GUIANA HIGHLANDS

The Guiana Highlands are part of the ancient core of the continent. They are heavily eroded, with deep valleys and steep waterfalls.

2 MANGROVE SWAMPS

Dense mangrove swamps grow along the equatorial coast of Brazil, Colombia and Ecuador. The delicate ecosystem of the mangrove swamp is easily destroyed by pollution.

3 THE ANDES

The Andes run the entire length of the continent – over 7,250 km – from the storm-lashed island of Tierra del Fuego to the tropical north. The mountains are on a volcanically active zone, and earthquakes are common.

POLITICAL SOUTH AMERICA

In the 17th century, explorers from Spain and Portugal claimed most of South America for their rulers in Europe. Their influences are still strong today: Brazilians speak Portuguese, while much of the rest of the continent is Spanish-speaking. The small nations of the north, Surinam and Guyana, were Dutch and British colonies and French Guiana is a French overseas department. The mix of peoples is mainly European, native American and African. Some native peoples still live in the dense Amazon rainforest.

SOUTH AMERICA

BORDER DISPUTES

Many of South America's borders have been, or remain, disputed. Bolivia is landlocked as a result of a dispute with Chile in 1883, when it lost its lands bordering the Pacific Ocean.

TRANSPORT LINKS

The Pan American Highway is a vital transport link, running from the far south of the continent, northwards along the Pacific coast. Its route takes it through sparsely populated areas like the Atacama Desert.

SCALE 1:35,000,000

0 km   400   800

0 miles   400   800

POPULATION

Many South American countries have a similar pattern of population distribution. The largest numbers of people are found near the coasts. Migration to the coastal cities has led to rocketing population figures, and growing social problems. São Paulo is now one of the world's largest cities; its outskirts are fringed with sprawling, shantytown suburbs – known as *favelas*.

Largest city
SÃO PAULO
21.7 million people

POPULATION DENSITY
(People per sq km)

Below 5	10–14
5–9	15–19
	20–29
	Above 29

URBAN GROWTH

Urban growth has transformed São Paulo into a major population and industrial centre. Its rapid growth has created many problems, like traffic congestion, overcrowding, and inadequate sewerage.

POPULATION

Capital cities
- ◉ Above 500,000
- ◉ 100,000 to 500,000
- ● 50,000 to 100,000
- ● Below 50,000

Other cities
- ⊡ Above 500,000
- ○ 50,000 to 100,000

STANDARDS OF LIVING

There are many inequalities in living standards across South America. Argentina's economy has suffered during the regional recession but living standards are still above those of Guyana and Bolivia, which have weak economies, and are heavily reliant upon trade in raw materials. The booming black market drug trade increases crime and corruption.

STANDARD OF LIVING
(UN Human Development Index)

low   high   no data

Map labels

Caribbean Sea
Central America
ATLANTIC OCEAN
CARACAS
Lake Maracaibo
Orinoco
VENEZUELA
(Venezuelan territorial claim)
GEORGETOWN
GUYANA
PARAMARIBO
SURINAME
CAYENNE
French Guiana (to France)
BOGOTÁ
Magdalena
Rio Negro
Branco
COLOMBIA
(Surinamese territorial claims)
Equator
QUITO
ECUADOR
Putumayo
Amazon
Represa Balbina
Equator
Marañón
Amazon
Tocantins
Madeira
Tapajós
Ucayali
Xingu
Araguaia
Tocantins
PERU
Madre de Dios
B R A Z I L
Represa de Sobradinho
LIMA
São Francisco
BOLIVIA
BRASÍLIA
Lake Titicaca
LA PAZ
Lago Poopó
SUCRE
Pilcomayo
PARAGUAY
Pilcomayo
Paraguay
Paraná
São Paulo
Tropic of Capricorn
Tropic of Capricorn
ASUNCIÓN
PACIFIC OCEAN
Paraguay
Paraná
Uruguay
URUGUAY
A R G E N T I N A
C H I L E
Salado
SANTIAGO
BUENOS AIRES
MONTEVIDEO
River Plate
ATLANTIC OCEAN
Colorado
Rio Negro
Chico
Descado
Falkland Islands (to UK)

SOUTH AMERICAN GEOGRAPHY

Agriculture is still the most common form of employment in South America. Cattle and cash crops of coffee, cocoa and, in some places, coca for cocaine, provide the main sources of income. Brazil has the greatest range of industries, followed by Argentina, Venezuela and Chile. The large coastal cities such as Rio de Janeiro, Lima and Buenos Aires are where most of the jobs are found. This encourages people to migrate from the country to the city, in search of employment.

INDUSTRY

Brazil is the continent's leading industrial producer and São Paulo the major industrial city. Manufactured products include iron and steel, automobiles, chemicals, textiles, and meat and leather products from the continent's vast cattle herds. In the mountains of Bolivia and Colombia, coca plants are grown to make cocaine, which has created a black market for this illegal drug.

OIL AND GAS

Under the waters of Lake Maracaibo, Venezuela, lie some of South America's biggest oil reserves. Oil exploitation has brought great wealth to Venezuela. The money has helped the country to build new roads and develop other industries.

INDUSTRIAL CENTRE

São Paulo, Brazil, is the largest city in South America and a leading industrial centre. A wide range of goods is manufactured here, including automobiles, chemicals, textiles and electronic products. São Paulo is also a leading financial centre Hundreds of people flock to the city daily in search of work.

TRADE AND EXPORTS

The Chilean port of Valparaíso ships many different products out of South America. Trade is growing with Japan and other countries around the Pacific Ocean.

MINERAL RESOURCES

South America's mineral resources are highly localized. Few countries have both fossil fuels and metallic ores. The richest oilfields are in the north, especially in Venezuela. Coal, however, is scarce. When the Andes formed, heat helped create the many metallic minerals which are mined today.

MINERAL RESOURCES

- Bauxite
- Copper
- Iron
- Lead
- Silver
- Tin
- Oil/Gas field
- Coal field

COPPER MINES

Metallic mineral reserves are abundant in the Andes. Chuquicamata, northern Chile, is one of the world's largest copper mines.

ECONOMIC ACTIVITY

- ✈ Aerospace
- 🍺 Brewing
- 🚗 Car/vehicle manufacture
- ⚗ Chemicals
- Coal
- Electronics
- Engineering
- S Finance
- Fish processing
- Food processing
- Hi-tech industry
- Iron & steel
- △ Metal refining
- Narcotics
- Oil and gas
- Pharmaceuticals
- Printing & publishing
- Shipbuilding
- Textiles
- Timber processing
- Tobacco processing

GNI per capita (US$)

- Below 3,000
- 3,000-4,999
- 5,000-6,999
- 7,000-8,999
- 9,000-10,999
- Above 11,000
- • Industrial centre

Map labels

Caribbean Sea
Central America
Barranquilla
Cartagena
Maracaibo
Caracas
Valencia
Ciudad Guayana
Georgetown
Paramaribo
Barquisimeto
VENEZUELA
GUYANA
SURINAME
French Guiana (to France)
Medellín
Bogotá
Cali
COLOMBIA
Quito
ECUADOR
Guayaquil
Belém
ATLANTIC OCEAN
Amazon Basin
Manaus
Fortaleza
Natal
Recife
Chiclayo
Chimbote
PERU
BRAZIL
Maceió
Lima
Cusco
BOLIVIA
Salvador
Arequipa
La Paz
Santa Cruz
Sucre
Brasília
Arica
Iquique
Belo Horizonte
Chuquicamata
Antofagasta
PARAGUAY
Asunción
São Paulo
Rio de Janeiro
San Miguel de Tucumán
Corrientes
Curitiba
Córdoba
Mendoza
Santa Fe
Rosario
URUGUAY
Porto Alegre
Rio Grande
Valparaíso
Santiago
Talca
Concepción
Buenos Aires
Montevideo
ARGENTINA
Neuquén
Bahía Blanca
Valdivia
PACIFIC OCEAN
ATLANTIC OCEAN
Comodoro Rivadavia
Falkland Islands (to UK)
Punta Arenas
Cape Horn

CLIMATE

South America has four main climatic regions; tropical, arid, temperate, and the cold climate of the far south. The Amazon Basin, covered by massive rain forests, and the Guiana Highlands have a humid, tropical climate which allows vegetation to flourish. West of the Andes the climate tends to be very dry. Moist air flowing west from the Atlantic Ocean is prevented from reaching the shores of the Pacific Ocean by the Andes and rain falls before it can pass over the mountains. This creates arid deserts like the Atacama.

EXTREME WEATHER EVENTS

Symbols indicate climatic extremes

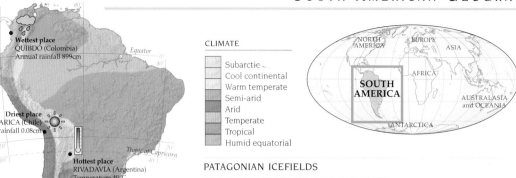

Wettest place
QUIBDO (Colombia)
Annual rainfall 899cm

Driest place
ARICA (Chile)
Annual rainfall 0.08cm

Hottest place
RIVADAVIA (Argentina)
Temperature 49°C

Coldest place
SARMIENTO (Argentina)
Temperature -33°C

Equator

Tropic of Capricorn

CLIMATE

Subarctic
Cool continental
Warm temperate
Semi-arid
Arid
Temperate
Tropical
Humid equatorial

NORTH AMERICA EUROPE ASIA AFRICA **SOUTH AMERICA** AUSTRALASIA and OCEANIA ANTARCTICA

PATAGONIAN ICEFIELDS

Towards the south of the continent, the climate becomes very cold. Large expanses of ice, forming glaciers are found in southern Patagonia and on islands such as Tierra del Fuego at the tip of South America.

LAND USE AND AGRICULTURE

Many plants now found throughout the world originated in South America, like the tomato, potato and cassava. Today, coffee, cocoa, rubber, soya beans, corn (maize), and sugarcane are widely cultivated, and grapes are grown in sheltered valleys in the Andes. Much of the Amazon Basin is covered by dense rainforest and is unsuitable for cultivation, although some farmers practise 'slash and burn' techniques to make land for crops and cattle farming, which destroy ancient forest.

COFFEE

South America, and Brazil in particular, is a major producer of coffee. The plants thrive in the rich red soils of southern Brazil and are grown on huge plantations on the mountain slopes.

LAND USE AND AGRICULTURE

- 🐂 Cattle
- 🐖 Pigs
- 🐑 Sheep
- 🍌 Bananas
- 🌽 Corn (Maize)
- 🍊 Citrus fruits
- 🌿 Coca
- 🌺 Cocoa
- ❀ Cotton
- ☕ Coffee
- 🎣 Fishing
- 🌴 Oil palms
- 🥜 Peanuts
- ◑◑ Rubber
- 🦐 Shellfish
- 🌱 Soya beans
- 🎋 Sugarcane
- 🍇 Vineyards
- 🌾 Wheat

Barren land
Cropland
Desert
Forest
Mountain region
Pasture
Wetland
● Major conurbation

Caribbean Sea

Barranquilla, Maracaibo, Caracas, Medellín, Bogotá, Cali, Lima

Central America

Llanos Orinoco, *Guiana Highlands*, *Rio Negro*, *Amazon Basin*, *Putumayo*, *Amazon*, *Marañón*, *Andes*, *Purus*, *Madeira*, *Tapajós*, *Xingu*, *Tocantins*, Manaus, Belém, Fortaleza, Recife, Salvador

São Francisco, *Brazilian Highlands*, Brasília, Belo Horizonte, Rio de Janeiro, São Paulo, Curitiba, Porto Alegre

Córdoba, Rosario, Santiago, Montevideo, Buenos Aires

Pilcomayo, *Gran Chaco*, *Paraguay*, *Paraná*, *Uruguay*, *Pampas*, *Colorado*, *Rio Negro*

Patagonia, *Gulf of San Jorge*, *Falkland Islands*, *Cape Horn*

PACIFIC OCEAN, *ATLANTIC OCEAN*

LOCAL MARKETS

At traditional markets such as this one in Ecuador, high in the Andes, local people trade fruit, vegetables and goods such as clothing, rugs and blankets. Some goods produced by Ecuadorean Indians are now exported world wide.

CATTLE

The vast plains of the Pampas, to the west of Buenos Aires, support large herds of cattle. Meat processing and canning is a major industry in Argentina, Paraguay and Uruguay.

NARCOTICS

Coca, grown in forest clearings in remote mountain areas, is used to make the drug cocaine. Government troops burn any coca plants they discover to discourage production.

NORTHERN SOUTH AMERICA

BRAZIL, COLOMBIA, ECUADOR, GUYANA, PERU,
SURINAME, VENEZUELA

High mountains, steamy rain forests and hot, grassy
plains cover much of northern South America. From
the 16th century, after the conquest of the Incas, the
western countries were ruled by Spain, while Brazil was
governed by Portugal, Guyana by Britain, and Suriname
by the Dutch. The more recent history of some of these
countries has included periods of civil war and military
rule. Most are still troubled by widespread poverty.

INDUSTRY

Important oil reserves are found in
Venezuela and parts of the Amazon
Basin; Venezuela is one of the world's
top oil producers. Brazil's cities have
a wide range of industries including
chemicals, clothes and shoes,
and textiles. Metallic minerals,
particularly iron ore, are mined
throughout the area and specially-built
industrial centres like Ciudad Guayana
have been developed to refine them.

STRUCTURE OF INDUSTRY

Primary 11%
Services 50%
Manufacturing 39%

INDUSTRY

- ✈ Aerospace
- ⚗ Chemicals
- ▣ Food processing
- 🚂 Iron & steel
- △ Metal refining
- ⛊ Textiles
- ⛏ Mining
- ▲ Oil
- ⛟ Timber processing
- ⛟ Tourism
- ▣ Major industrial centre / area
- — Major road

POPULATION

Most of the population lives in urban
areas. Many cities are extremely
overcrowded, with poor housing.
São Paulo in Brazil is one of
the world's fastest-growing
cities. The rainforests of
the interior and high Andes
are sparsely populated. The
few native American peoples
live in remote areas.

INHABITANTS PER SQ KM

- More than 200
- 100–200
- 50–100
- 10–50
- Less than 10
- ■ Capital city
- ● Major city

URBAN/RURAL POPULATION DIVIDE

Rio de Janeiro 4%
São Paulo 6.4%
Bogotá 2.6%
Rural population 21%
Other towns and cities 66%

FARMING AND LAND USE

The variety of climates means a wide range
of crops including sugarcane, cocoa and
bananas can be grown for export.
Coffee is the most important cash
crop; Brazil is the world's leading
coffee grower. Cattle are farmed
on the plains of Colombia,
Venezuela and southern Brazil.
Much of the good farmland is
owned by a few rich landowners,
and many peasant farmers do not
have enough land to make a living.

FARMING AND LAND USE

- 🐂 Cattle
- 🐟 Fishing
- 🐐 Goats
- 🐑 Sheep
- 🍌 Bananas
- Cocoa
- Cotton
- Coffee
- Rubber
- ⬇ Sugarcane
- ⅂ Timber
- Cropland
- Forest
- Mountain region
- Pasture
- Wetland
- ● Major conurbation

LAND USE

Cropland 6%
Other (including mountains) 15%
Pasture 23%
Forest 56%

THE LANDSCAPE

The Andes run down the western side of South
America. There are many volcanoes among their peaks,
and earthquakes are common. The tropical rainforests
surrounding the River Amazon take up most of western
Brazil. Huge, dry, flat grasslands called *llanos* cover
central Venezuela and part of eastern Colombia.

Angel Falls (D 2)
Venezuela's Angel Falls is the
world's highest waterfall. Twenty
times as high as Niagara Falls, it
drops 979 m from a spectacular
plateau deep in the Guiana Highlands.

River Amazon (D 4)
The Amazon is the longest
river in South America, and
the second longest in
the world. It flows over
6,516 km from the Peruvian
Andes to the coast of Brazil.
One-fifth of the world's fresh
water is carried by the river.

Andes (B 5)
The snow-capped
Andes are the
longest mountain
range on Earth.
They stretch
7,250 km down
the whole length
of South America.

Lake Titicaca (C 6)
South America's
largest lake is the
highest navigable
lake in the world
at 3,810 m above
sea level.
It lies across the
border between
Peru and Bolivia.

Pantanal (E 6)
This is the largest area of
wetlands in the world. It spreads
across 130,000 sq km of Brazil.
Many hundreds of plant and
animal species are found here.

Amazon rainforest (D 4)
The enormous rainforest
surrounding the River
Amazon and its tributaries
covers 6,500,000 sq km,
an area almost as big as
Australia. It is estimated
that at least half of all
known living species
are found in the forest.

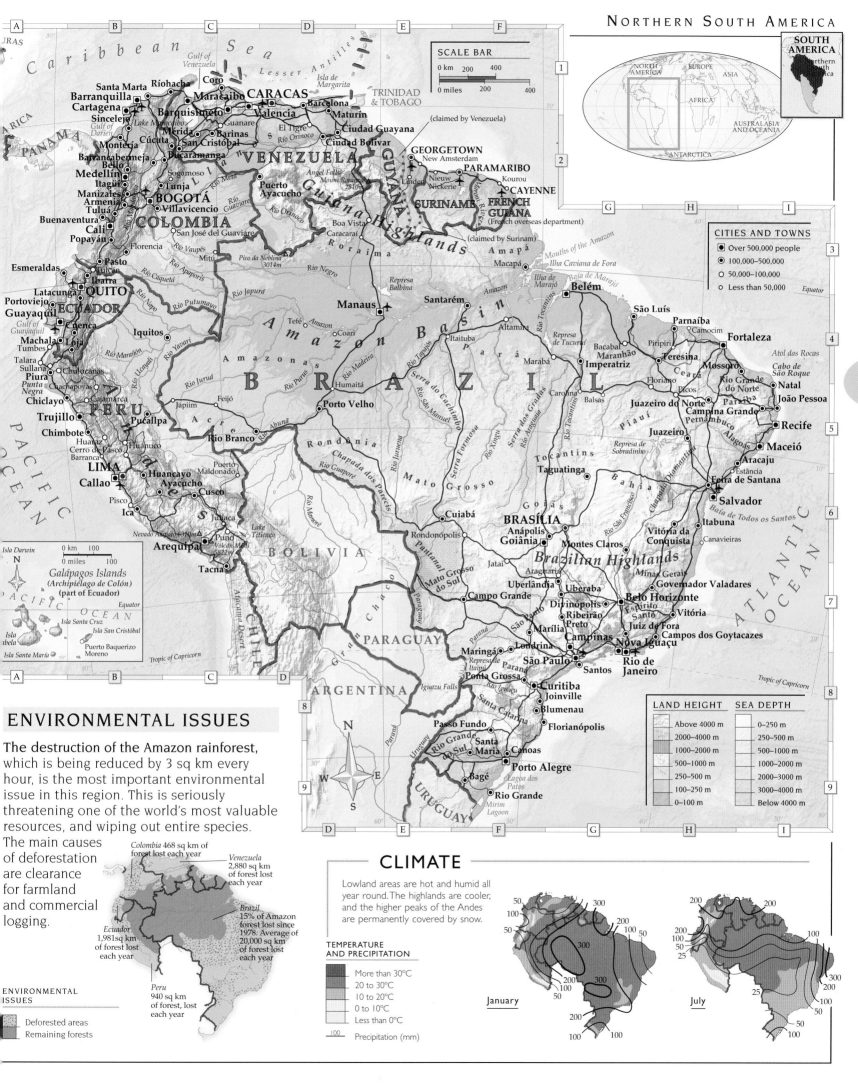

SOUTH AMERICA

SCALE BAR

0 km   200   400

0 miles   200   400

CITIES AND TOWNS
- ◼ Over 500,000 people
- ◉ 100,000–500,000
- ○ 50,000–100,000
- ∘ Less than 50,000

LAND HEIGHT
- Above 4000 m
- 2000–4000 m
- 1000–2000 m
- 500–1000 m
- 250–500 m
- 100–250 m
- 0–100 m

SEA DEPTH
- 0–250 m
- 250–500 m
- 500–1000 m
- 1000–2000 m
- 2000–3000 m
- 3000–4000 m
- Below 4000 m

Galápagos Islands
(Archipiélago de Colón)
(part of Ecuador)

0 km   100
0 miles   100

ENVIRONMENTAL ISSUES

The destruction of the Amazon rainforest, which is being reduced by 3 sq km every hour, is the most important environmental issue in this region. This is seriously threatening one of the world's most valuable resources, and wiping out entire species. The main causes of deforestation are clearance for farmland and commercial logging.

Colombia 468 sq km of forest lost each year

Venezuela 2,880 sq km of forest lost each year

Brazil 15% of Amazon forest lost since 1978. Average of 20,000 sq km of forest lost each year

Ecuador 1,981sq km of forest lost each year

Peru 940 sq km of forest, lost each year

ENVIRONMENTAL ISSUES
- Deforested areas
- Remaining forests

CLIMATE

Lowland areas are hot and humid all year round. The highlands are cooler, and the higher peaks of the Andes are permanently covered by snow.

TEMPERATURE AND PRECIPITATION
- More than 30°C
- 20 to 30°C
- 10 to 20°C
- 0 to 10°C
- Less than 0°C

—100— Precipitation (mm)

January

July

SOUTHERN SOUTH AMERICA

ARGENTINA, BOLIVIA, CHILE, PARAGUAY, URUGUAY

The southern half of South America forms a long, narrow cone, with landscapes ranging from barren desert in the west, to frozen glaciers in the far south. The whole area was governed by Spain until the early 19th century, and Spanish is still the main language spoken, although the few remaining native American groups use their own languages. Most people now live in vast cities such as Buenos Aires and Santiago.

INDUSTRY

Rich deposits of minerals – especially copper – in the Andes have led to the development of large metal refining industries in Chile. The capital cities, Buenos Aires and Santiago, are home to the widest range of industries and Argentina is an important producer of processed foods like canned beef. There are fewer industries in the south, although oil and gas are extracted in southern Argentina and Chile.

INDUSTRY

🚗 Car manufacture
⚗ Chemicals
▨ Food processing
△ Metal refining
⏛ Textiles
◊ Oil and gas
🌲 Timber processing

▣ Major industrial centre / area
— Major road

STRUCTURE OF INDUSTRY

Primary 10%
Services 55%
Manufacturing 35%

ENVIRONMENTAL ISSUES

Many of southern South America's rivers are polluted, particularly close to Buenos Aires. The Itaipú Dam on the Paraná River is the world's largest hydro-electric power project. Deforestation is a persistent problem in Bolivia, Paraguay and northern Argentina with 6,000 sq km cut down every year. Air quality in Buenos Aires and Santiago is poor, especially in Santiago which is surrounded by mountains, making it difficult for pollution to escape.

Río Loa
Itaipú Dam
Paraguay
Paraná
Río Salado
Río Carcarañá
Santiago
Buenos Aires
Río Bío Bío
Río Colorado

ENVIRONMENTAL ISSUES

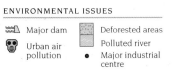

🌊 Major dam
👹 Urban air pollution
▨ Deforested areas
Polluted river
• Major industrial centre

POPULATION

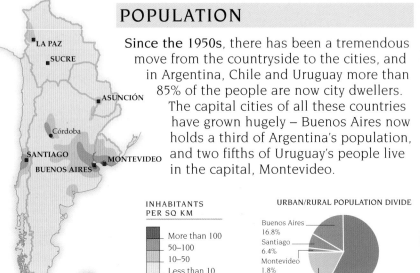

LA PAZ
SUCRE
ASUNCIÓN
Córdoba
SANTIAGO
BUENOS AIRES
MONTEVIDEO

Since the 1950s, there has been a tremendous move from the countryside to the cities, and in Argentina, Chile and Uruguay more than 85% of the people are now city dwellers. The capital cities of all these countries have grown hugely – Buenos Aires now holds a third of Argentina's population, and two fifths of Uruguay's people live in the capital, Montevideo.

INHABITANTS PER SQ KM

More than 100
50–100
10–50
Less than 10
■ Capital city
● Major city

URBAN/RURAL POPULATION DIVIDE

Buenos Aires 16.8%
Santiago 6.4%
Montevideo 1.8%
Rural population 17%
Other towns and cities 58%

THE LANDSCAPE

Southern South America's landscape varies from tropical forest and dry desert in the north, to sub-Antarctic conditions in the south. The towering Andes divide Chile from Argentina. East of the Andes lie forests and rolling grasslands. To the west is a thin coastal strip. The wet, windswept, freezing southern tip of the continent has volcanoes alongside glaciers and fjords.

Gran Chaco (C3)
This huge stretch of forest and grassland runs from Bolivia, through Paraguay and into Argentina. The south and east provide grazing for cattle.

The Paraná River (C4)
South America's second longest river is the Paraná. It stretches 4,000 km from the Brazilian Highlands, finally flowing into the River Plate near Buenos Aires in Argentina.

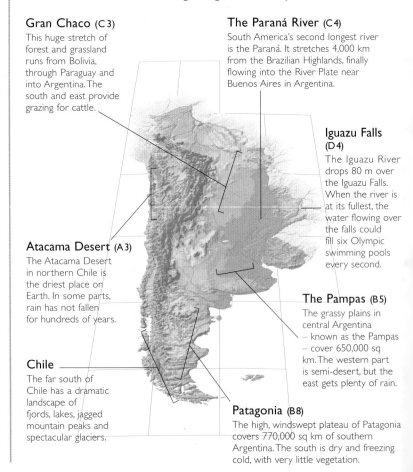

Iguazu Falls (D4)
The Iguazu River drops 80 m over the Iguazu Falls. When the river is at its fullest, the water flowing over the falls could fill six Olympic swimming pools every second.

Atacama Desert (A3)
The Atacama Desert in northern Chile is the driest place on Earth. In some parts, rain has not fallen for hundreds of years.

The Pampas (B5)
The grassy plains in central Argentina – known as the Pampas – cover 650,000 sq km. The western part is semi-desert, but the east gets plenty of rain.

Chile
The far south of Chile has a dramatic landscape of fjords, lakes, jagged mountain peaks and spectacular glaciers.

Patagonia (B8)
The high, windswept plateau of Patagonia covers 770,000 sq km of southern Argentina. The south is dry and freezing cold, with very little vegetation.

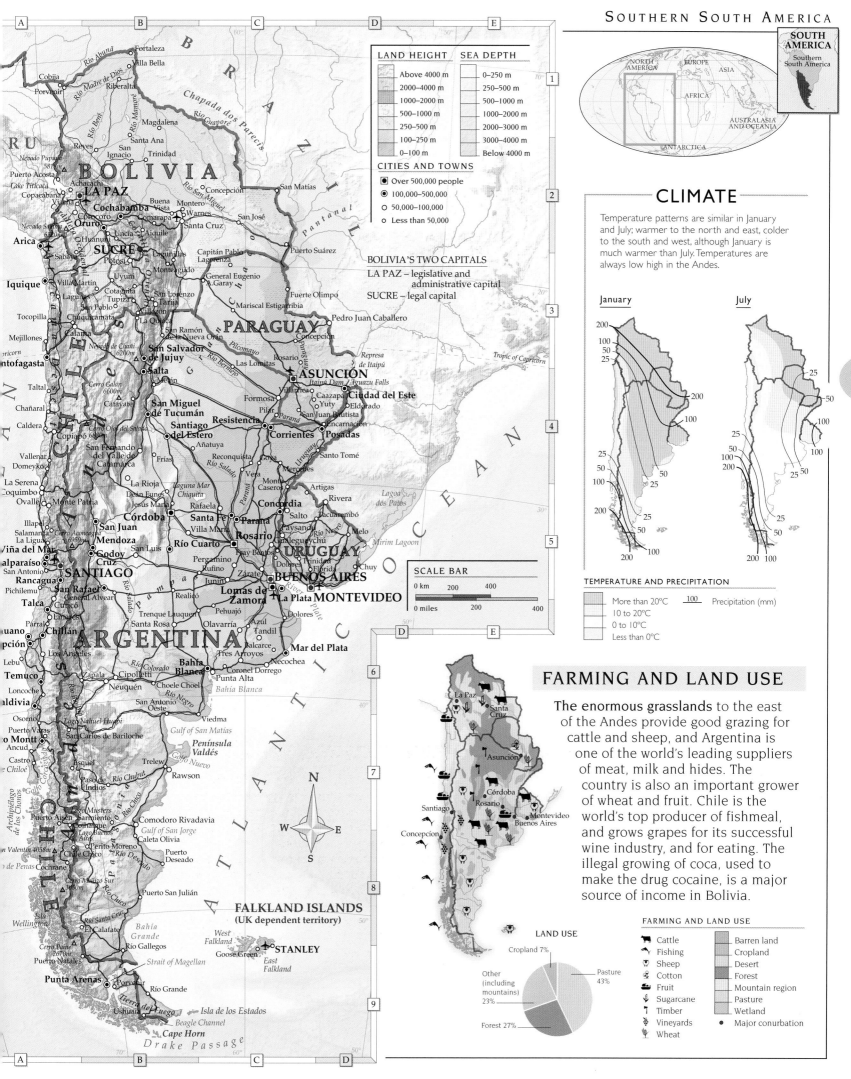

SOUTH
AMERICA
Southern
South America

Map labels

A B C D E

LAND HEIGHT — SEA DEPTH

LAND HEIGHT	SEA DEPTH
Above 4000 m	0–250 m
2000–4000 m	250–500 m
1000–2000 m	500–1000 m
500–1000 m	1000–2000 m
250–500 m	2000–3000 m
100–250 m	3000–4000 m
0–100 m	Below 4000 m

CITIES AND TOWNS

☐ Over 500,000 people
◉ 100,000–500,000
○ 50,000–100,000
∘ Less than 50,000

BOLIVIA'S TWO CAPITALS

LA PAZ – legislative and
administrative capital
SUCRE – legal capital

CLIMATE

Temperature patterns are similar in January
and July; warmer to the north and east, colder
to the south and west, although January is
much warmer than July. Temperatures are
always low high in the Andes.

January   July

TEMPERATURE AND PRECIPITATION

More than 20°C	100 Precipitation (mm)
10 to 20°C	
0 to 10°C	
Less than 0°C	

SCALE BAR
0 km   200   400
0 miles   200   400

FALKLAND ISLANDS
(UK dependent territory)

FARMING AND LAND USE

The enormous grasslands to the east
of the Andes provide good grazing for
cattle and sheep, and Argentina is
one of the world's leading suppliers
of meat, milk and hides. The
country is also an important grower
of wheat and fruit. Chile is the
world's top producer of fishmeal,
and grows grapes for its successful
wine industry, and for eating. The
illegal growing of coca, used to
make the drug cocaine, is a major
source of income in Bolivia.

LAND USE

Cropland 7%
Other
(including
mountains)
23%
Pasture
43%
Forest 27%

FARMING AND LAND USE

🐂 Cattle		Barren land
🐟 Fishing		Cropland
🐑 Sheep		Desert
Cotton		Forest
Fruit		Mountain region
Sugarcane		Pasture
Timber		Wetland
Vineyards		● Major conurbation
Wheat		

CONTINENTAL AFRICA

Africa is the second largest continent in the world. Its dramatic landscapes include arid deserts, humid rainforests, and the valleys of the east African rift – the place where humans first evolved. Today, there are 54 separate countries in Africa, and its people speak a rich variety of languages. The world's highest temperatures have been recorded in Africa's deserts.

7,260 km
7,623 km

CROSS-SECTION THROUGH AFRICA

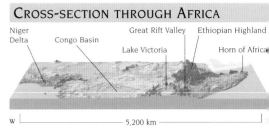

Niger Delta
Congo Basin
Lake Victoria
Great Rift Valley
Ethiopian Highland
Horn of Africa

W — 5,200 km —

In the west, the Niger River flows into the Atlantic Ocean through the swampy Niger Delta. Further east is the immense Congo Basin, where the Congo River winds its way through thick rainforests. In the east is the Great Rift Valley, and the Ethiopian Highlands. The Horn of Africa is Africa's most easterly point.

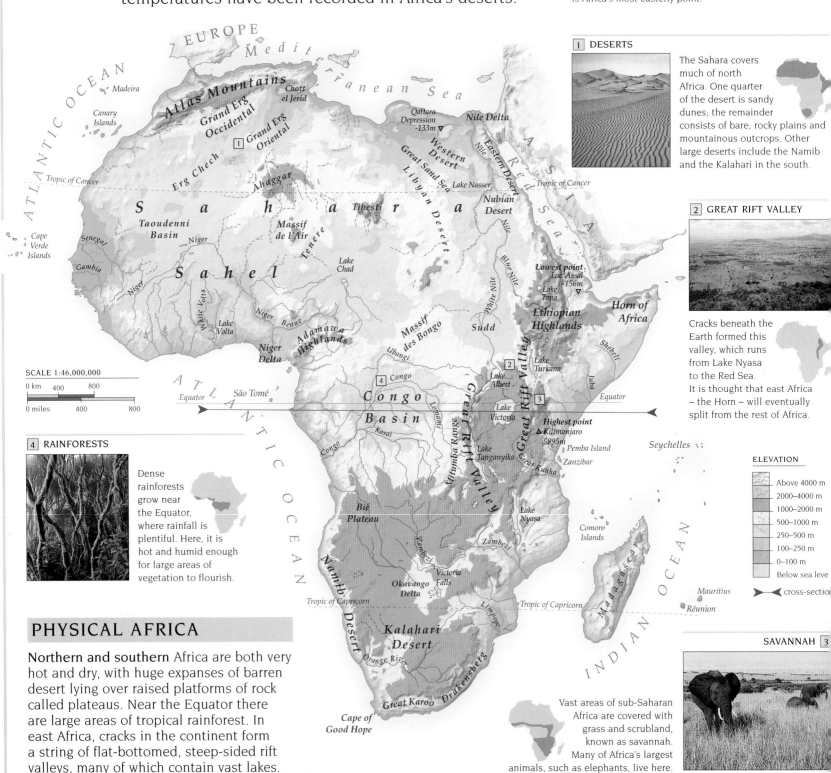

1 DESERTS

The Sahara covers much of north Africa. One quarter of the desert is sandy dunes; the remainder consists of bare, rocky plains and mountainous outcrops. Other large deserts include the Namib and the Kalahari in the south.

2 GREAT RIFT VALLEY

Cracks beneath the Earth formed this valley, which runs from Lake Nyasa to the Red Sea. It is thought that east Africa – the Horn – will eventually split from the rest of Africa.

4 RAINFORESTS

Dense rainforests grow near the Equator, where rainfall is plentiful. Here, it is hot and humid enough for large areas of vegetation to flourish.

ELEVATION

Above 4000 m
2000–4000 m
1000–2000 m
500–1000 m
250–500 m
100–250 m
0–100 m
Below sea leve

cross-sectio

PHYSICAL AFRICA

Northern and southern Africa are both very hot and dry, with huge expanses of barren desert lying over raised platforms of rock called plateaus. Near the Equator there are large areas of tropical rainforest. In east Africa, cracks in the continent form a string of flat-bottomed, steep-sided rift valleys, many of which contain vast lakes.

SAVANNAH 3

Vast areas of sub-Saharan Africa are covered with grass and scrubland, known as savannah. Many of Africa's largest animals, such as elephants, live here.

SCALE 1:46,000,000
0 km 400 800
0 miles 400 800

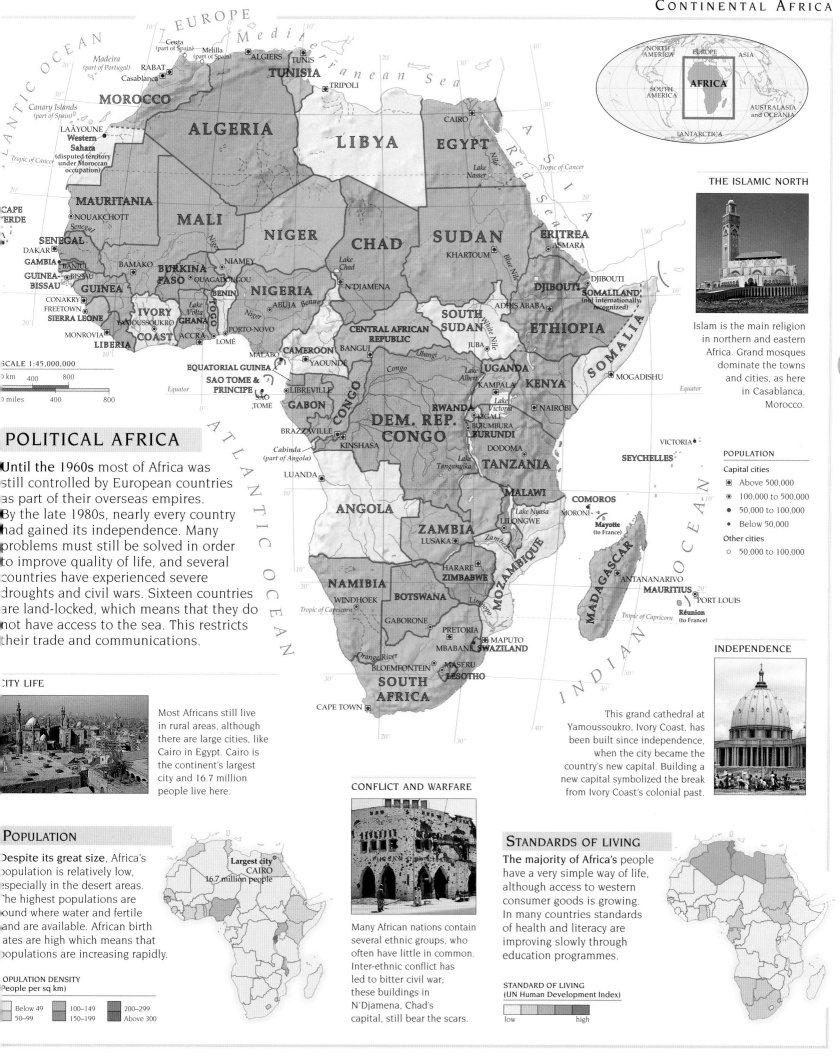

THE ISLAMIC NORTH

Islam is the main religion in northern and eastern Africa. Grand mosques dominate the towns and cities, as here in Casablanca, Morocco.

POLITICAL AFRICA

Until the 1960s most of Africa was still controlled by European countries as part of their overseas empires. By the late 1980s, nearly every country had gained its independence. Many problems must still be solved in order to improve quality of life, and several countries have experienced severe droughts and civil wars. Sixteen countries are land-locked, which means that they do not have access to the sea. This restricts their trade and communications.

POPULATION

Capital cities

◉ Above 500,000
◉ 100,000 to 500,000
● 50,000 to 100,000
● Below 50,000

Other cities

○ 50,000 to 100,000

INDEPENDENCE

This grand cathedral at Yamoussoukro, Ivory Coast, has been built since independence, when the city became the country's new capital. Building a new capital symbolized the break from Ivory Coast's colonial past.

CITY LIFE

Most Africans still live in rural areas, although there are large cities, like Cairo in Egypt. Cairo is the continent's largest city and 16.7 million people live here.

POPULATION

Despite its great size, Africa's population is relatively low, especially in the desert areas. The highest populations are found where water and fertile land are available. African birth rates are high which means that populations are increasing rapidly.

Largest city
CAIRO
16.7 million people

POPULATION DENSITY
People per sq km)

Below 49
50–99
100–149
150–199
200–299
Above 300

CONFLICT AND WARFARE

Many African nations contain several ethnic groups, who often have little in common. Inter-ethnic conflict has led to bitter civil war; these buildings in N'Djamena, Chad's capital, still bear the scars.

STANDARDS OF LIVING

The majority of Africa's people have a very simple way of life, although access to western consumer goods is growing. In many countries standards of health and literacy are improving slowly through education programmes.

STANDARD OF LIVING
(UN Human Development Index)

low   high

AFRICAN GEOGRAPHY

Africa's massive reserves of minerals, including oil, gold, copper and diamonds, are amongst the largest in the world. Mining is a very important industry for many countries, and has provided money for growth and development. Africa's wide range of environments means that many different types of crops can be grown. Rubber, bananas and oil palms are grown for export in the tropics, and east Africa is especially famous for its tea and coffee.

INDUSTRY

Most African industries are based on processing raw materials such as food crops or mineral ores. Some African countries depend on one product or crop for most of their income, but in many larger cities different industries are developing. Northern Africa, Nigeria, and South Africa have the widest range of industries.

INDUSTRY

- 🍶 Brewing
- 🚗 Car/vehicle manufacture
- ⚙ Cement
- ⚗ Chemicals
- ⛏ Coal
- ✿ Engineering
- ▣ Fish processing
- Ⓢ Finance
- ▣ Food processing
- 🚂 Iron & steel
- ⛏ Mining
- ◊ Oil and gas
- ✦ Pharmaceuticals
- ⚓ Shipbuilding
- ⍦ Textiles
- 🌲 Timber processing

GNP per capita (US$)
- Below 500
- 500-999
- 1,000-1,999
- 2,000-3,999
- 4,000-5,999
- Above 6,000
- • Industrial centre

MINERAL RESOURCES

The southern countries, in particular South Africa, have large reserves of diamonds, gold, uranium and copper. The large copper deposits in Dem. Rep. Congo and Zambia are known as the 'copper belt'. Oil and gas are extracted in Algeria, Angola, Egypt, Libya and Nigeria.

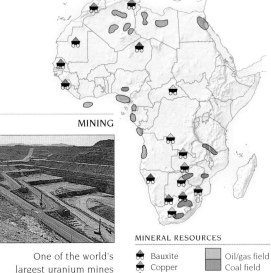

MINING

One of the world's largest uranium mines is at Rössing, Namibia. Uranium is used to fuel nuclear power stations. and is also mined in Niger and South Africa,

MINERAL RESOURCES
- ⛏ Bauxite
- ⛏ Copper
- ⛏ Diamonds
- ⛏ Iron
- ⛏ Phosphates
- ⛏ Gold
- ⛏ Uranium
- ▢ Oil/gas field
- ▢ Coal field

OIL AND GAS

In the desert wastes of Algeria, a drilling rig searches for new sources of oil in the rich north African oilfields. There are several large oil fields in the Niger delta, and north Africa.

FINANCE AND TRADE

Johannesburg, in South Africa, is home to many international banks. Wealth has been generated from the country's large mineral resources, such as diamonds

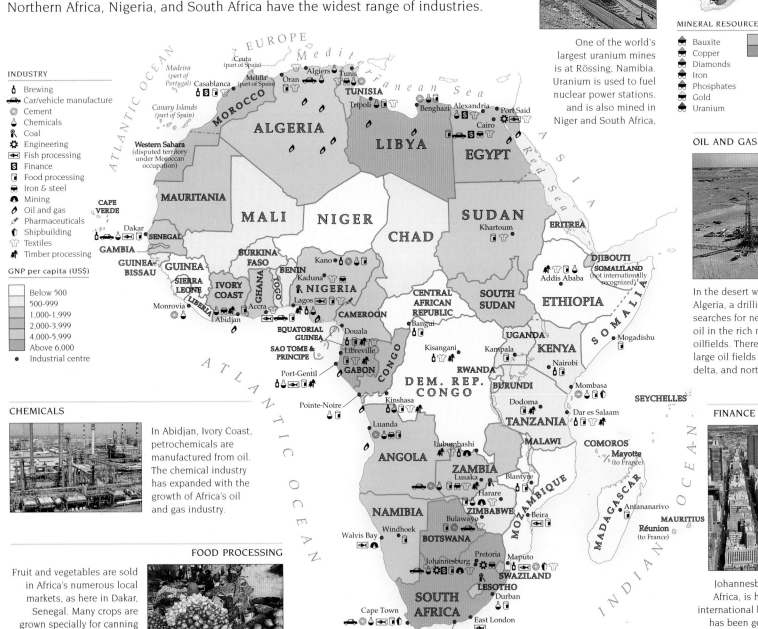

CHEMICALS

In Abidjan, Ivory Coast, petrochemicals are manufactured from oil. The chemical industry has expanded with the growth of Africa's oil and gas industry.

FOOD PROCESSING

Fruit and vegetables are sold in Africa's numerous local markets, as here in Dakar, Senegal. Many crops are grown specially for canning and export overseas and are known as 'cash crops.'

CLIMATE

Africa is the world's hottest continent: temperatures of more than 50°C have been recorded in the Sahara. The northern coast has a hot, dry climate with little rainfall. Further inland, the Sahara is extremely arid, with strong, dry winds. South of the Sahara is the Sahel, where cutting down trees for fuel has turned farmland into desert. Close to the Equator there is more rainfall, and huge rainforests can grow in western and central Africa. In the south, the climate is much drier, and drought is a problem.

EXTREME WEATHER EVENTS

Symbols indicate climatic extremes

Coldest place
IFRANE (Morocco)
Temperature -24°C

Hottest place
AL 'AZĪZĪYAH (Libya)
Temperature 58°C

Driest place
WADI HALFA (Sudan)
Annual rainfall <2.5mm

Wettest place
CAPE DEBUNDSHA (Cameroon)
Annual rainfall 10290mm

CLIMATE

- Warm temperate
- Mediterranean
- Semi-arid
- Arid
- Humid equatorial
- Tropical

THE ENCROACHING DESERT

Africa has three main desert areas: the Sahara in the north and the Namib and Kalahari deserts in the south. They are a mixture of sandy dunes and bare, rocky plateaus. At the desert's edges, low rainfall and land clearance is causing the deserts to expand into areas that were once grassland.

LAND USE AND AGRICULTURE

The quality of land and the amount of rainfall has a great impact on the type of farming. In the mountain regions of countries such as Rwanda, Uganda, and Kenya, tea and coffee are grown. In the north, there is not enough water to produce staple crops such as wheat for all the population, but 'cash crops' such as citrus fruits, dates and olives are grown for export. Sub-tropical west Africa grows peanuts, cocoa and coffee. In the southern part of the continent, South Africa grows many different crops: citrus fruits are grown for export, as well as grapes, which are used to make wine.

PASTORALISM

At the southern edge of the Sahara is a fragile region known as the Sahel. In this area shifting cultivation and nomadic herding are widely practised.

SUBSISTENCE AGRICULTURE

Although African countries produce a wide range of crops, in many cases people rely on a few basic crops, like cassava and yams, as a staple. The yam is a starchy root which is ground to make flour.

LAND USE AND AGRICULTURE

- Cattle
- Goats
- Sheep
- Bananas
- Cereals
- Citrus fruits
- Cocoa
- Cotton
- Coffee
- Dates
- Fishing
- Oil palms
- Olives
- Peanuts
- Rice
- Rubber
- Shellfish
- Sugarcane
- Tea
- Tobacco
- Vineyards
- Cropland
- Desert
- Forest
- Pasture
- Wetland
- Major conurbation

CASH CROPS

Kenya, Malawi, Tanzania and Zimbabwe are renowned for their teas. The leaves are picked by hand and dried. When mixed with boiling water, tea is enjoyed by over half the world's population.

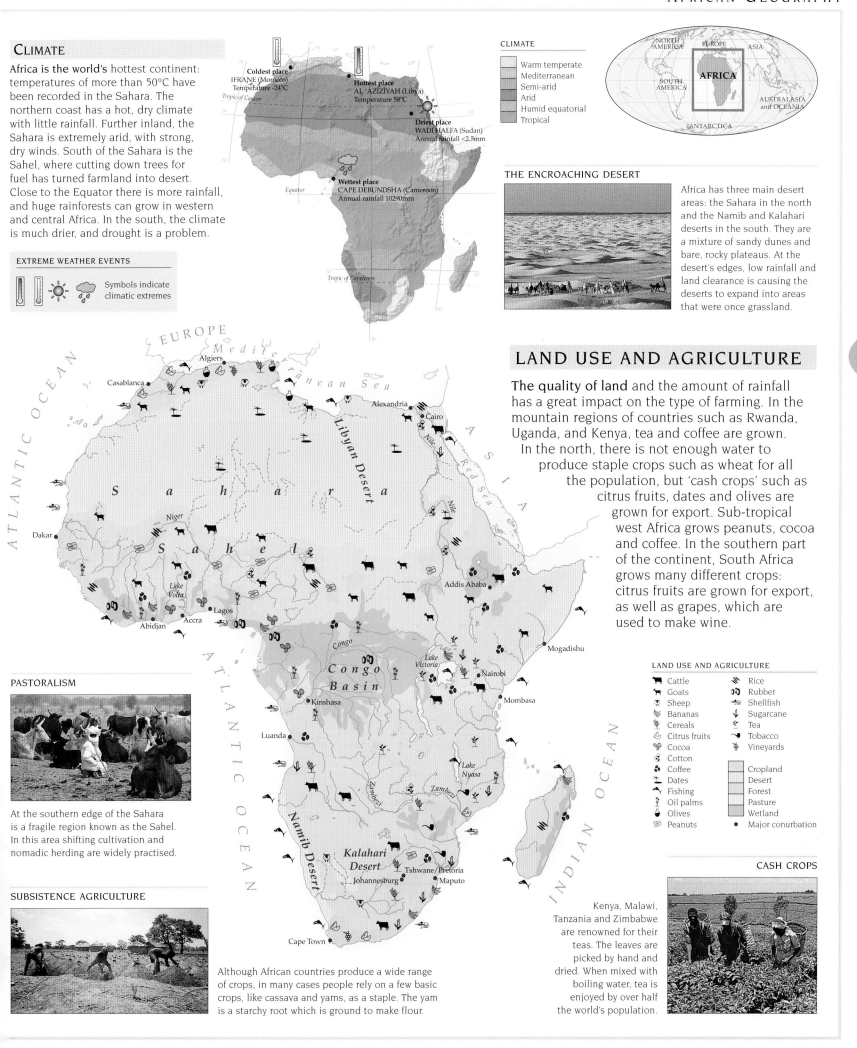

NORTH AFRICA

ALGERIA, EGYPT, LIBYA, MOROCCO, TUNISIA.

Sandwiched between the Mediterranean and the Sahara, North Africa has a history dating back to the dawn of civilization. 6,000 years ago, settlements were established along the banks of the River Nile, and since that time, waves of settlers, including Romans, Arabs and Turks have brought a mix of different cultures to the area. In the 19th century, Spain, France and Britain claimed colonies in the region, but today North Africa is independent, although Western Sahara is occupied by Morocco.

FARMING AND LAND USE

Most farming in North Africa is restricted to the fertile Mediterranean coastal strip, and the banks of the Nile where it relies heavily on irrigation. In spite of these seemingly inhospitable conditions, the region is a major producer of dates, which grow in desert oases, and of cork, made from the bark of the cork oak tree. A wide variety of other crops is also grown, including grapes, olives and cotton.

FARMING AND LAND USE

- Fishing
- Goats
- Sheep
- Citrus Fruits
- Cork
- Cotton
- Dates
- Olives
- Vineyards
- Cropland
- Desert
- Forest
- Pasture
- Major conurbation

CLIMATE

Most of north Africa is desert, and the climate is harsh. Rainfall is scarce, and drought is common. Temperatures are freezing at night, scorching by day and have been known to climb to over 50°C.

January

July

whole area has below 25mm rainfall

LAND USE

Forest 1%
Pasture 13%
Cropland 5%
Other (including desert) 81%

TEMPERATURE AND PRECIPITATION

- More than 35°C
- 30 to 35°C
- 25 to 30°C
- 20 to 25°C
- 15 to 20°C
- 10 to 15°C
- 5 to 10°C
- Less than 5°C

100 Precipitation (mm)

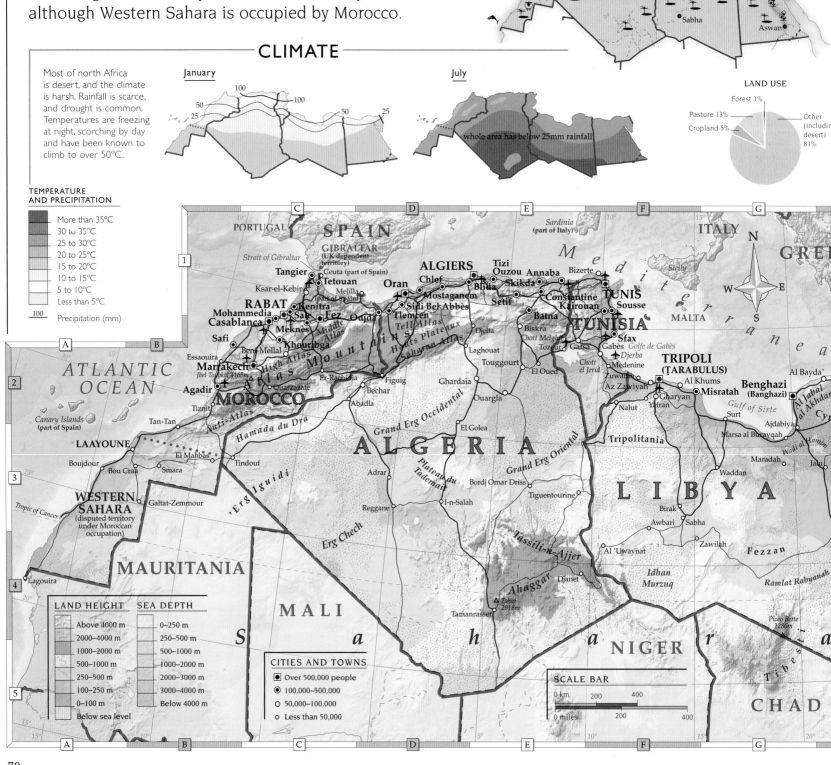

LAND HEIGHT
- Above 4000 m
- 2000–4000 m
- 1000–2000 m
- 500–1000 m
- 250–500 m
- 100–250 m
- 0–100 m
- Below sea level

SEA DEPTH
- 0–250 m
- 250–500 m
- 500–1000 m
- 1000–2000 m
- 2000–3000 m
- 3000–4000 m
- Below 4000 m

CITIES AND TOWNS
- Over 500,000 people
- 100,000–500,000
- 50,000–100,000
- Less than 50,000

SCALE BAR
0 km 200 400
0 miles 200 400

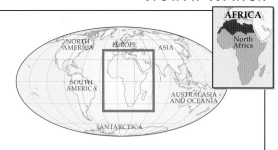

POPULATION

The majority of the population, and all of the big towns and cities, are found on the coastal plains, or along the banks of the Nile – about 99% of Egyptians live along the river. Egypt's capital, Cairo, is Africa's largest city, with over 11 million people. Western Sahara, and the southern portions of Egypt, Algeria and Libya are sparsely populated by Tuareg nomads who roam the Sahara.

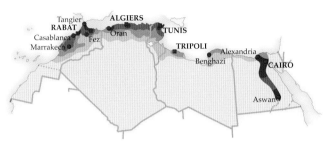

INHABITANTS PER SQ KM

- More than 200
- 100–200
- 50–100
- 10–50
- Less than 10
- ■ Capital city
- ● Major city

URBAN/RURAL POPULATION DIVIDE

- Alexandria 2.2%
- Cairo 4.5%
- Casablanca 2%
- Rural population 46%
- Other towns and cities 45.3%

THE LANDSCAPE

The parched rocks and endless sandy expanses of the Sahara occupy much of North Africa. The only major river here is the Nile, with a delta that extends into the Mediterranean Sea. The old, eroded Atlas Mountains are the highest mountain range.

Sand dunes
Winds blowing across the Sahara cause the sand to build up into dunes which can reach heights of up to 430 m.

Nile Delta (I2)
As the River Nile nears the Mediterranean, it separates into many small streams, which flow over a fertile triangle of land. Mud and rock carried by the river and deposited in the delta have formed new land.

Red Sea (J3)
The Red Sea may get its name from red algae that live on the sea floor and occasionally make the water appear red during algae blooms.

Atlas Mountains (C2)
The Atlas Mountains are made up of a number of different ranges – the Anti-Atlas, High Atlas, Middle Atlas, Tell Atlas and Saharan Atlas. They stretch some 2,250 km from the north of Tunisia to the Atlantic coast of Morocco.

Qattara Depression (I3)
In the northwest of Egypt is a huge desert depression 320 km long and 120 km wide. Its floor, part of which is 134 m below sea level, is covered with sand, brackish ponds and salt marshes.

The River Nile (I3)
The world's longest river flows 6,695 km to the Mediterranean Sea. The system of rivers and lakes that flow into the Nile drain some 2,850,000 sq km – about 10% of the entire African continent.

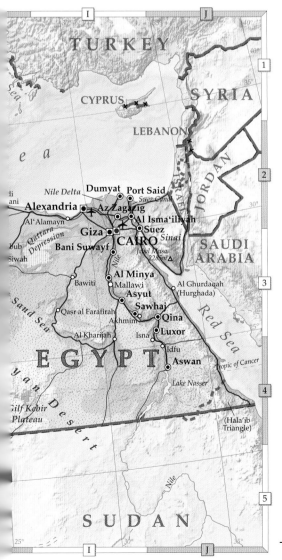

INDUSTRY

Oil and natural gas have brought wealth to the area, particularly to Libya, which has enough oil reserves to last into the middle of this century. Textile manufacture is widespread – North Africa is famous for its exotic cloths and rugs. Several large chemical refineries and steel plants have been established along the coast, especially in the major industrial cities like Alexandria and Cairo in Egypt.

STRUCTURE OF INDUSTRY

- Primary 16%
- Services 44%
- Manufacturing 40%

INDUSTRY

- ⚗ Chemicals
- 🍴 Food processing
- Iron and steel
- 👕 Textiles
- 🛢 Oil and gas
- 🏛 Tourism
- ▣ Major industrial centre / area
- — Major road

ENVIRONMENTAL ISSUES

Droughts, overgrazing and the stripping of vegetation for fuelwood and animal fodder have caused the Sahara to expand northwards. This has reduced the already limited amount of land available for farming. The risk of desertification is acute in many coastal areas. North Africa is very dry, and there are severe droughts periodically. Many of the larger cities like Alexandria and Cairo have very poor air quality.

ENVIRONMENTAL ISSUES

- 🥾 Drought
- 😷 Urban air pollution
- Existing desert
- Risk of desertification
- Severe risk of desertification
- Non-affected area
- ● Major industrial centre

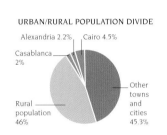

WEST AFRICA

BENIN, BURKINA FASO, CAMEROON, CENTRAL AFRICAN REPUBLIC, CHAD, EQUATORIAL
GUINEA, GAMBIA, GHANA, GUINEA, GUINEA-BISSAU, IVORY COAST, LIBERIA, MALI,
MAURITANIA, NIGER, NIGERIA, SAO TOME & PRINCIPE, SENEGAL, SIERRA LEONE, TOGO

West Africa's varied climate and agricultural and
mineral wealth have provided the foundation for
some of Africa's greatest civilizations, like those
of the Malinke and Asante people. The area remains
ethnically and culturally diverse today, as well
as densely populated; Nigeria is by far the most
populous country in Africa. A major outbreak of the
deadly Ebola virus in the region reached epidemic
proportions in 2014 and caused over 11,000 deaths.

INDUSTRY

Agricultural products still form the basis of most economies
in West Africa. Food processing is widespread – oil palms
and peanuts are processed for their valuable
vegetable oils. Oil
and gas are found
off the coast of
Ivory Coast and
around the Niger
delta, where a
large chemical
industry has
developed.

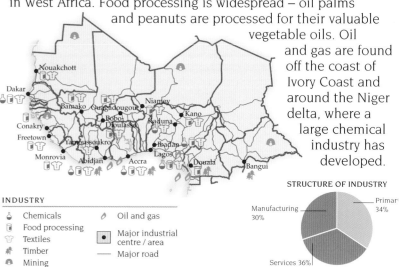

INDUSTRY

Chemicals	Oil and gas
Food processing	
Textiles	Major industrial centre / area
Timber	Major road
Mining	

STRUCTURE OF INDUSTRY

Primar 34%
Manufacturing 30%
Services 36%

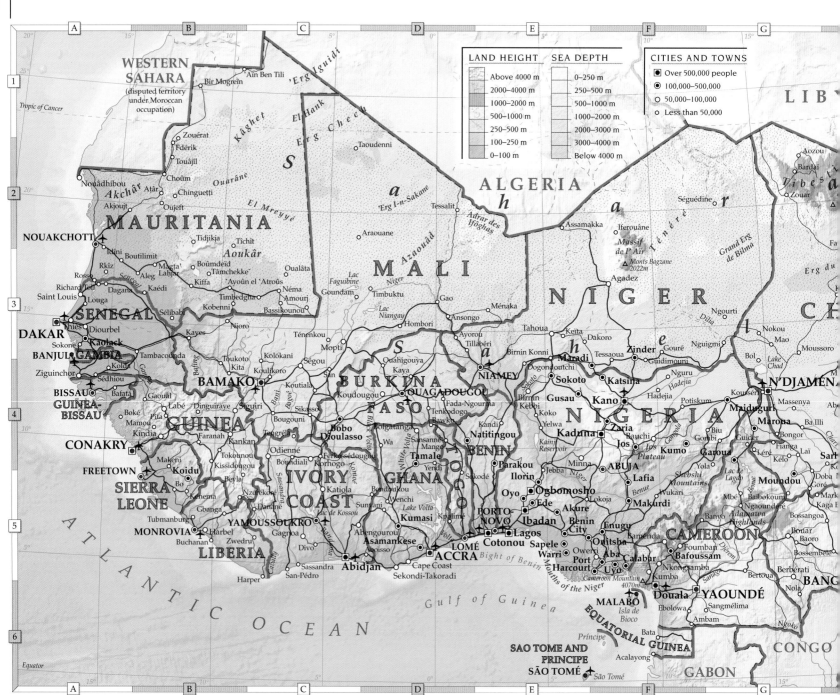

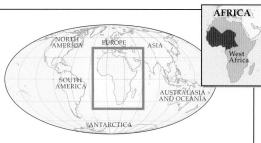

FARMING AND LAND USE

Well-watered land along the coast allows a wide variety of crops to be grown, including cocoa and oil palms, both of which provide important cash crops. In the drier north, goats and sheep are grazed, and subsistence crops such as yams, millet and cassava are grown.

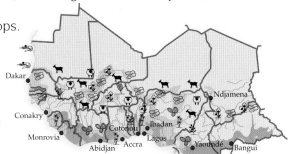

FARMING AND LAND USE

🐐 Goats	🦐 Peanuts	
🐑 Sheep		Cropland
🦪 Shellfish		Desert
🌿 Cassava		Forest
🌴 Cocoa		Pasture
🌾 Cotton		Wetland
🌾 Millet		
🌴 Oil palms	●	Major conurbation

LAND USE

Cropland 10%
Other (including desert) 48%
Pasture 26%
Forest 16 %

CLIMATE

The climate differs immensely from the hot desert north, through to the tropical rainforest south. July is the wet season, and rainfall is heavy in the south, while the desert areas remain dry throughout the year.

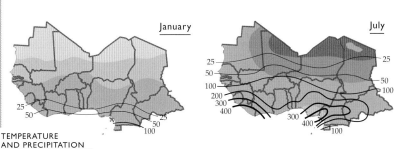

January

July

TEMPERATURE AND PRECIPITATION

	More than 35°C
	30 to 35°C
	25 to 30°C
	20 to 25°C
	Less than 20°C
100	Precipitation (mm)

ENVIRONMENTAL ISSUES

Persistent droughts are the main concerns in the north of the region. The problem is made worse by a shortage of wood needed for fuel, which leads to the cutting down of any available trees for fuelwood. In the tropical south, the timber industry is destroying much of the ancient forest. In 2007 huge floods affected almost all of the region.

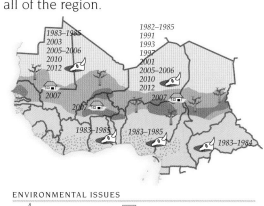

ENVIRONMENTAL ISSUES

🐟 Drought			Existing desert
🌳 Severe fuelwood shortage			Risk of desertification
			Severe risk of desertification
🏠 Flooding			Deforested area

POPULATION

Most of the population lives in the southern coastal regions. In the drier north, settlement becomes more sporadic, and nomadic tribespeople are best suited to live in the desert north. Nigeria is the most populated country in Africa and Lagos is one of the continent's larger cities, although West Africa's population remains mainly rural.

INHABITANTS PER SQ KM

	More than 200
	100–200
	50–100
	10–50
	Less than 10
■	Capital city
●	Major city

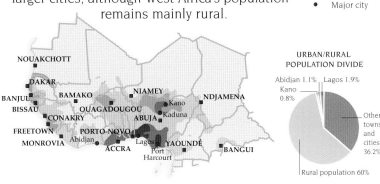

URBAN/RURAL POPULATION DIVIDE

Abidjan 1.1% Lagos 1.9%
Kano 0.8%
Other towns and cities 36.2%
Rural population 60%

THE LANDSCAPE

Large differences in rainfall from north to south have led to a varied landscape. The wet coastal regions contain tropical rainforest. To the north, savannah grasslands, arid Sahel scrubland and barren desert lie in successive bands. The Niger is one of the larger rivers and is unusual because it has two deltas; one at the sea, and one inland.

Sahel (E 3)
The band of semi-desert stretching from Senegal to Sudan along the southern boundary of the Sahara is called the Sahel. Frequent droughts in recent years, and excessive cutting of trees have meant that much of the Sahel is turning to desert.

Tibesti mountains (G 2)
These mountains in north-western Chad are a chain of extinct volcanoes which now form solitary peaks in the midst of the Sahara.

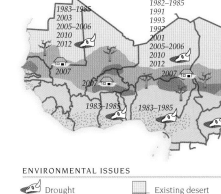

River Niger (D 3)
The River Niger is West Africa's longest river. When it reaches the sea, it flows through a vast delta of mud flats and mangrove swamps. Great oil deposits have been found here.

Adamawa Highlands (G 5)
This mountainous spine separates West Africa from the vast Congo Basin to the southeast.

EGYPT

Tropic of Cancer

Erdi

SUDAN

Birao

Ouanda
Djallé

SOUTH
SUDAN

Massif des
Bongo

CENTRAL AFRICAN
REPUBLIC

Bria
Djéma

Dembia
Obo

Bangassou
Bornu

Alindao

Mobaye

SCALE BAR

km 200 400

miles 200 400

DEM. REP. CONGO

Equator

EAST AFRICA

BURUNDI, DJIBOUTI, ERITREA, ETHIOPIA, KENYA, RWANDA, SOMALIA, SOUTH SUDAN, SUDAN, TANZANIA, UGANDA

Much of East Africa is covered by long grass, scrub and scattered trees, called savannah. This land is grazed by both domestic animals and a great variety of wild animals including lions, giraffes and elephants. The east of the region is known as the Horn of Africa, because it is shaped like an animal horn. Along with Sudan, the countries there have recently been devastated by civil wars, and periods of drought and famine. In contrast, Kenya in the south is more stable but still has to battle with corruption.

INDUSTRY

East Africa has few mineral resources, and industry is mainly based on processing raw materials. Coffee, tea, sugarcane and sisal, are harvested and processed before being exported. Textile production is widespread, but is only on a small scale. Tourism is increasingly important in Kenya and Tanzania; each year, many thousands of people visit the wildlife reserves there.

INDUSTRY

- ⚙ Cement manufacturing
- 🜃 Chemicals
- 🗌 Food processing
- 👕 Textiles
- 🏛 Tourism

- ▣ Major industrial centre / area
- — Major road

STRUCTURE OF INDUSTRY

Primary 38%
Services 44%
Manufacturing 18%

ENVIRONMENTAL ISSUES

Rapid population growth has created a need for increasing amounts of land for farming. This, as well as the need for fuelwood, has led to tree cover being stripped, allowing the soil to be washed or blown away. Over the past 30 years, eastern Africa has been stricken by many catastrophic droughts which have made desertification worse, and brought much human suffering.

ENVIRONMENTAL ISSUES

- 👟 Drought
- 🌲 Severe fuelwood shortage
- 🏠 Flooding
- ▨ Existing desert
- ▨ Risk of desertification
- ▨ Severe risk of desertification

FARMING AND LAND USE

Much of the north and east is too dry for farming, but in Sudan, cotton is grown on land irrigated by the River Nile. The Lake Victoria basin and rich volcanic soils of the highlands in Kenya, Uganda and Tanzania support staple food crops, and those grown for export, such as tea and coffee. Kenya also grows high-quality vegetables, like mangetout, and exports them by air to supermarkets abroad. Sheep, goats and cattle are herded on the savannah.

FARMING AND LAND USE

- 🐂 Cattle
- 🎣 Fishing
- 🐐 Goats
- 🐑 Sheep
- 🍌 Bananas
- ☕ Coffee
- ⚘ Cotton
- 🌴 Dates
- 🌿 Market gardening
- ⬇ Sugarcane
- 🌱 Sisal
- 🌿 Tea

- Cropland
- Desert
- Forest
- Pasture
- Wetland
- • Major conurbation

LAND USE

Cropland 9%
Pasture 40%
Other 26%
Forest 25%

THE LANDSCAPE

The south of East Africa is savannah grassland, broken by the rugged mountains – some of them active volcanoes – and large fresh and saltwater lakes that make up part of the Great Rift Valley. The River Nile has its source here, flowing through lakes Victoria, Kyoga and Albert as it takes much-needed water to the arid desert areas in the north.

Great Rift Valley (D 6) (D 4)
The Great Rift Valley is like a deep scar running 7,000 km from north to south through East Africa. It has been formed by the movements of two of the Earth's plates over millions of years. If these movements continue, East Africa may eventually become an island, separated by the ocean from the rest of the continent.

Sudd (B 4)
The north of Sudan is rocky desert, but in the south, the waters of the White Nile run into a swampy area called the Sudd where much of its water disperses and evaporates.

River Juba (E 5)
This river rises in the highlands of Ethiopia and flows some 1,200 km southwards to the Indian Ocean. It, and the River Shebeli, which joins it about 30 km from the coast, are the only permanent rivers in Somalia.

Lake Victoria (C 5)
Lake Victoria is Africa's largest lake and the second largest freshwater lake in the world. It lies on the Equator, between Kenya, Tanzania and Uganda, and covers 68,880 sq km. Its only outlet is the River Nile in the north.

Kilimanjaro (D 6)
This old volcano, made up of alternating layers of lava and ash, is Africa's highest mountain, rising to 5,895 m. Although it lies only three degrees from the Equator, its peak is permanently covered with snow.

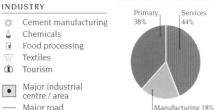

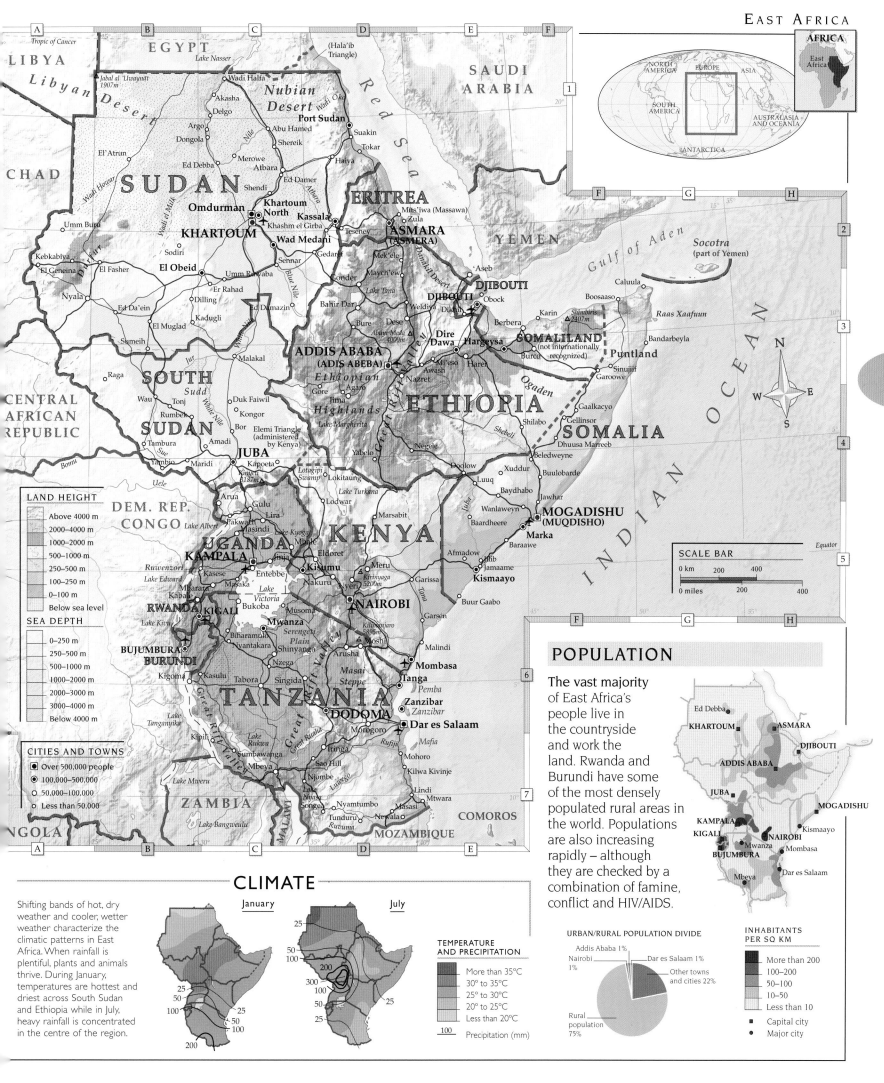

EAST AFRICA

AFRICA
East Africa

LAND HEIGHT
- Above 4000 m
- 2000–4000 m
- 1000–2000 m
- 500–1000 m
- 250–500 m
- 100–250 m
- 0–100 m
- Below sea level

SEA DEPTH
- 0–250 m
- 250–500 m
- 500–1000 m
- 1000–2000 m
- 2000–3000 m
- 3000–4000 m
- Below 4000 m

CITIES AND TOWNS
- ■ Over 500,000 people
- ◉ 100,000–500,000
- ◎ 50,000–100,000
- ○ Less than 50,000

SCALE BAR
0 km — 200 — 400
0 miles — 200 — 400

POPULATION

The vast majority of East Africa's people live in the countryside and work the land. Rwanda and Burundi have some of the most densely populated rural areas in the world. Populations are also increasing rapidly – although they are checked by a combination of famine, conflict and HIV/AIDS.

URBAN/RURAL POPULATION DIVIDE
- Addis Ababa 1%
- Nairobi 1%
- Dar es Salaam 1%
- Other towns and cities 22%
- Rural population 75%

INHABITANTS PER SQ KM
- More than 200
- 100–200
- 50–100
- 10–50
- Less than 10
- ■ Capital city
- ● Major city

CLIMATE

Shifting bands of hot, dry weather and cooler, wetter weather characterize the climatic patterns in East Africa. When rainfall is plentiful, plants and animals thrive. During January, temperatures are hottest and driest across South Sudan and Ethiopia while in July, heavy rainfall is concentrated in the centre of the region.

January

July

TEMPERATURE AND PRECIPITATION
- More than 35°C
- 30° to 35°C
- 25° to 30°C
- 20° to 25°C
- Less than 20°C
- Precipitation (mm)

SOUTHERN AFRICA

ANGOLA, BOTSWANA, COMOROS, CONGO, DEM. REP. CONGO, GABON, LESOTHO, MADAGASCAR, MALAWI, MOZAMBIQUE, NAMIBIA, SOUTH AFRICA, SWAZILAND, ZAMBIA, ZIMBABWE

Southern Africa contains the richest deposits of valuable minerals on the continent. South Africa is the wealthiest and most industrialized country in the region. Most of the surrounding countries rely on it for trade and work. Racial segregation under apartheid operated from 1948 until 1994, when South Africa held its first multiracial elections.

FARMING AND LAND USE

Most of southern Africa's farmers grow just enough food to feed their families, though much of the farmland is in the hands of a few wealthy landowners. In the tropical north, oil palms and rubber are grown on large commercial plantations. Fruits are cultivated in the south, and tea and coffee are important in the east. Cattle farming is widespread across the dry grasslands.

FARMING AND LAND USE

- Cattle
- Fishing
- Cocoa
- Coffee
- Cotton
- Fruit
- Maize
- Oil palms
- Rubber
- Tea
- Timber
- Vineyard

LAND USE

- Cropland
- Desert
- Forest
- Pasture
- Wetland
- Major conurbation

Cropland 5%
Other 17%
Pasture 38%
Forest 40%

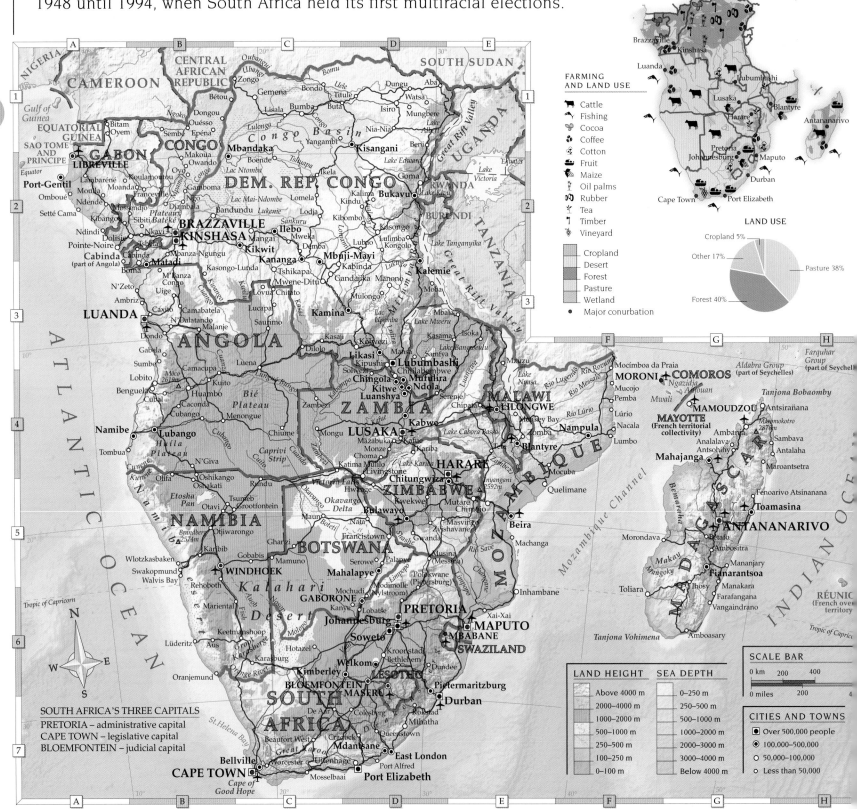

SOUTH AFRICA'S THREE CAPITALS
PRETORIA – administrative capital
CAPE TOWN – legislative capital
BLOEMFONTEIN – judicial capital

LAND HEIGHT

- Above 4000 m
- 2000–4000 m
- 1000–2000 m
- 500–1000 m
- 250–500 m
- 100–250 m
- 0–100 m

SEA DEPTH

- 0–250 m
- 250–500 m
- 500–1000 m
- 1000–2000 m
- 2000–3000 m
- 3000–4000 m
- Below 4000 m

SCALE BAR

CITIES AND TOWNS

- Over 500,000 people
- 100,000–500,000
- 50,000–100,000
- Less than 50,000

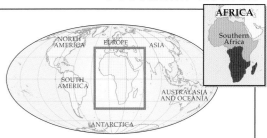

CLIMATE

During January, temperatures are highest in the Kalahari Desert and rainfall is plentiful in the centre of southern Africa. July is cooler and drier with rainfall concentrated in north Dem. Rep. Congo. The Atlantic coast of Namibia receives little rain all year round.

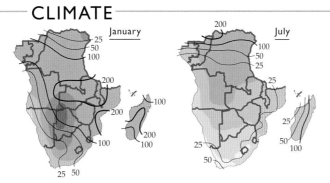

January

July

TEMPERATURE AND PRECIPITATION

- More than 35°C
- 30 to 35°C
- 25 to 30°C
- 20 to 25°C
- 15 to 20°C
- Less than 15°C
- —100— Precipitation (mm)

ENVIRONMENTAL ISSUES

The immense rain forests of the Congo Basin in the north remain relatively untouched, but deforestation is beginning to occur at their edges, with more forest due to be cleared in the future. Large parts of Madagascar have also been deforested. Further south, occasional drought and the clearing of bushlands for fuelwood can cause soil loss.

Congo Basin

1991–1992
1995
2000, 2005
1985
1989
1991–1992
2002, 2005, 2008
1982–1984, 1992
1997, 1998, 2001
2007–2008
1983–1985
1992–1993
2002–2003
2000
2007
1983
1985
2001
2004
2007

ENVIRONMENTAL ISSUES

- Drought
- Severe fuelwood shortage
- Flooding
- Existing desert
- Risk of desertification
- Severe risk of desertification
- Deforested area
- Remaining tropical forest

INDUSTRY

Southern Africa has extraordinary mineral resources. Angola has large deposits of oil, and diamonds are found in Angola, Botswana, Namibia, and South Africa. Copper is mined in the region known as the 'copper belt', that runs from Dem. Rep. Congo into Zambia. South Africa is the world's largest gold producer. Manufacturing, such as fruit canning and steel production, is most developed in South Africa.

Libreville
Kisangani
Brazzaville
Bukavu
Kinshasa
Luanda
Kolwezi
Lubumbashi
Ndola
Lusaka
Blantyre
Harare
Beira
Antananarivo
Bulawayo
Pretoria
Maputo
Johannesburg
Durban
Cape Town
Port Elizabeth

INDUSTRY

- Car manufacture
- Chemicals
- Engineering
- Food processing
- Iron & steel
- Metal refining
- Textiles
- Oil and gas
- Mining
- Timber processing
- Tourism
- Major industrial centre / area
- — Major road

STRUCTURE OF INDUSTRY

Primary 10%
Services 59%
Manufacturing 31%

THE LANDSCAPE

Southern Africa stretches from just north of the equator down to the southern tip of the continent. It is an area with an extremely varied climate and geography. In the north are the tropical rain forests of the Congo Basin, while arid desert covers much of the southwest. The eastern regions are mostly grasslands, with lush vegetation found on the tropical coast of Mozambique.

Victoria Falls (D 5)

On its way to the Indian Ocean, the Zambezi River plunges over a 128 m cliff into a narrow chasm. The resultant spray rises up to 490 m, and the thunder of the water can be heard up to 40 km away.

Madagascar (G 5)

The world's fourth largest island lies in isolation 250 km off the east coast of southern Africa. It became separated from the African continent 135 million years ago, and its plant and animal life are unique. The rich biodiversity of the rain forests is being threatened by lumbering for wood and timber.

Congo Basin (C 1)

The Congo River is Africa's second longest river, flowing in an arc through the dense tropical forests of the Congo Basin before emptying into the Atlantic Ocean.

Namib Desert (B 5)

The Namib is one of the world's driest deserts. The only water it receives is from mists that roll in from the sea. Where the desert meets the coast is known as the Skeleton Coast because of sailors who were shipwrecked and died there.

Okavango Delta (C 5)

The Okavango River terminates in the Kalahari Desert, forming a vast, swampy inland delta.

Drakensberg (D 4)

The Drakensberg are a chain of mountains that lie at the edge of a broad plateau that has tilted because of the movement of the Earth's plates. Rivers have carved through the high mountains, creating dramatic gorges and waterfalls.

POPULATION

The population is still mostly rural with two thirds of southern Africa's residents living in the countryside. Dense tropical rain forest in the north and arid desert in the southwest have kept habitation to a bare minimum. Malawi is the most densely populated country in the region.

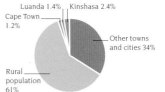

LIBREVILLE
Kisangani
BRAZZAVILLE
Bukavu
KINSHASA
LUANDA
Lobito
Lubumbashi
LILONGWE
LUSAKA
HARARE
Blantyre
WINDHOEK
Bulawayo
ANTANANARIVO
GABORONE
PRETORIA
Johannesburg
MAPUTO
BLOEMFONTEIN
MBABANE
MASERU
Durban
CAPE TOWN
Port Elizabeth

INHABITANTS PER SQ KM

- More than 100
- 50–100
- 10–50
- Less than 10
- ■ Capital city
- ● Major city

Luanda 1.4%
Kinshasa 2.4%
Cape Town 1.2%
Other towns and cities 34%
Rural population 61%

CONTINENTAL EUROPE

Europe is the world's second smallest continent, occupying the western tip of the vast Eurasian landmass. To the north and west are old highlands, with the high peaks of the Alps in the south. Most people live on the densely populated North European Plain, which runs from southern England, through northern France, across Germany into Russia.

CROSS-SECTION THROUGH EUROPE

Massif Central | British Isles | Alps | Great Hungarian Plain | Carpathian Mountains
Matterhorn

W ⊢————2,500 km————⊣ E

In the west, the land rises up from the Atlantic coast towards the Massif Central in France, and the high peaks of the Alps. Between the Alps and the Carpathian Mountains is the Great Hungarian Plain, where the River Danube flows on its way to the Black Sea.

PHYSICAL EUROPE

The ancient mountains of northwest Europe were scoured and smoothed by glaciers in the last Ice Age. The Alps are newer and more jagged – pushed up when Africa collided with Europe. In between is the North European Plain, where thick layers of fertile soils allow many different crops to be grown.

Novaya Zemlya
Arctic Circle
Iceland
Norwegian Sea
Ostrov Kolguyev
Barents Sea
Gora Narodnaya △ 1895m
Kölen
Kola Peninsula
White Sea
Scandinavia
Faroe Islands
Shetland Islands
Outer Hebrides
Gulf of Bothnia
Lake Onega
Northern Dvina
Galdhøpiggen 2469m
Lake Vaner
Lake Ladoga
Ben Nevis △ 1343m
Volga
North Sea
Ural Mountains
ASIA
British Isles
Ireland
Jutland
Baltic Sea
Western Dvina
North European Plain
Central Russian Upland
Volga Upland
English Channel
Thames
Elbe
Vistula
Pripet Marshes
Dnieper
Seine
Rhine
Ardennes
Loire
Danube
Volga
Bay of Biscay
Massif Central
Alps
Matterhorn △ 4478m
Carpathian Mountains
Gerlachovský Štít △ 2655m
Don
Lowest point ▽ Volga Delta -28m
Sea of Azov
Pyrenees
Mt Blanc 4807m
Rhône
Po
Apennines
Great Hungarian Plain
Crimea
Caucasus △ Highest point El'brus 5642m
Caspian Sea
Iberian Peninsula
Ebro
Corsica
Adriatic Sea
Dinaric Alps
Danube
Balkan Mountains
Black Sea
ASIA
Balearic Islands
Sardinia
Vesuvius 1171m
Tyrrhenian Sea
Sicily
Ionian Sea
Aegean Sea
Etna △ 3263m
Mediterranean Sea
Malta
Peloponnese
Crete
AFRICA

ELEVATION

- Above 4000 m
- 2000–4000 m
- 1000–2000 m
- 500–1000 m
- 250–500 m
- 100–250 m
- 0–100 m
- Below sea level
- ⋈ cross-section

SCALE 1:31,000,000

0 km   300   600

0 miles   300   600

1 THE FROZEN NORTH

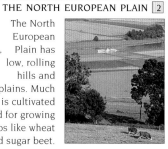

Europe's northern coastline stretches deep into the Arctic Circle. Here in Norway, icebergs drift into the deep, wide-bottomed fjords.

THE NORTH EUROPEAN PLAIN 2

The North European Plain has low, rolling hills and plains. Much of the area is cultivated and used for growing crops like wheat and sugar beet.

3 ANCIENT HIGHLANDS

Some of the world's oldest rocks are found in northwest Europe. Erosion by glaciers in the last Ice Age created smoothed hills such as the mountains of Wales.

4 THE ATLANTIC COAST

On Europe's Atlantic coast, the force of waves and winds has created striking landforms like this huge sand dune in southwest France.

THE ALPS 5

The Alps are Europe's major mountain chain. They formed about 65-million years ago. The Matterhorn is one of the most dramatic peaks.

POLITICAL EUROPE

Europe's population increased rapidly during the 18th and 19th centuries, following the Industrial Revolution. In the 20th century, Europe suffered a series of wars which redrew the political map. From 1989–1991, communist governments in eastern Europe and the former Soviet Union collapsed, as political reform swept through the countries behind the 'Iron Curtain'. In 2013, Croatia became the 28th country to join the European Union.

EUROPEAN UNION

- six original members, 1957
- nine further members, 1973 – 1995
- ten further members, 2004
- two further members, 2007
- one further member, 2013

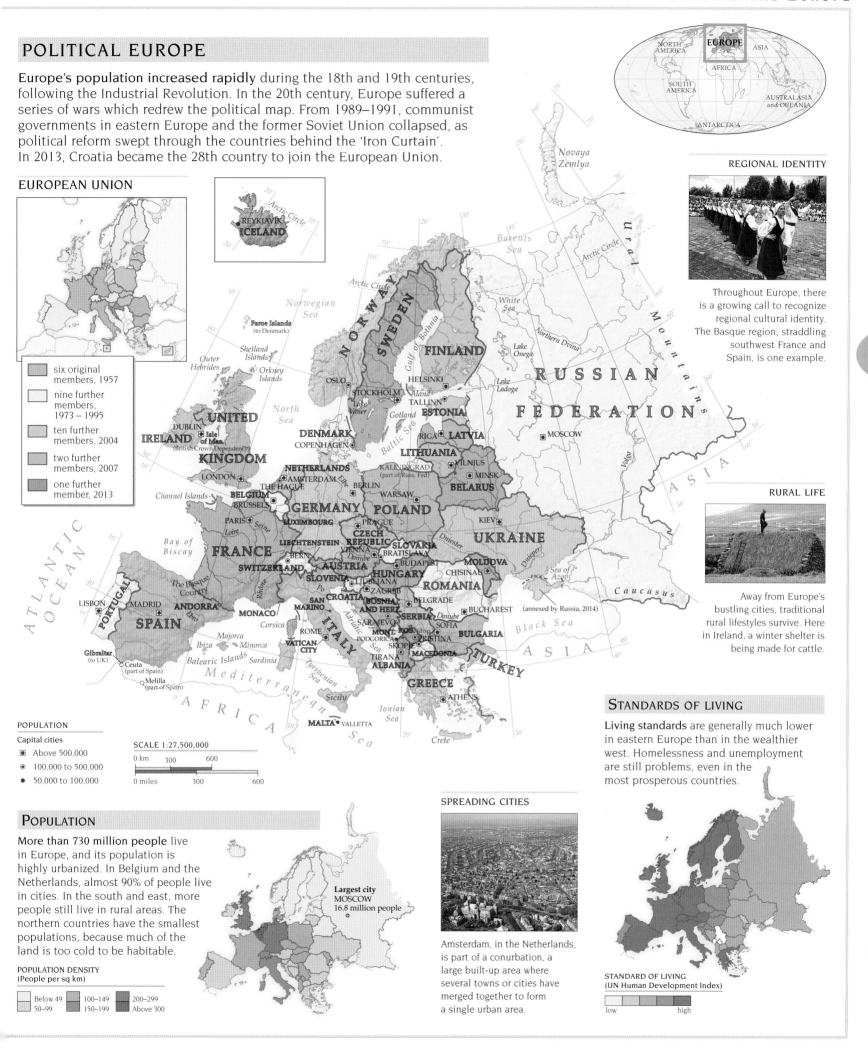

REGIONAL IDENTITY

Throughout Europe, there is a growing call to recognize regional cultural identity. The Basque region, straddling southwest France and Spain, is one example.

RURAL LIFE

Away from Europe's bustling cities, traditional rural lifestyles survive. Here in Ireland, a winter shelter is being made for cattle.

POPULATION

Capital cities
- ◉ Above 500,000
- ◉ 100,000 to 500,000
- ● 50,000 to 100,000

SCALE 1:27,500,000

0 km   300   600

0 miles   300   600

POPULATION

More than 730 million people live in Europe, and its population is highly urbanized. In Belgium and the Netherlands, almost 90% of people live in cities. In the south and east, more people still live in rural areas. The northern countries have the smallest populations, because much of the land is too cold to be habitable.

POPULATION DENSITY
(People per sq km)

- Below 49
- 50–99
- 100–149
- 150–199
- 200–299
- Above 300

Largest city
MOSCOW
16.8 million people

SPREADING CITIES

Amsterdam, in the Netherlands, is part of a conurbation, a large built-up area where several towns or cities have merged together to form a single urban area.

STANDARDS OF LIVING

Living standards are generally much lower in eastern Europe than in the wealthier west. Homelessness and unemployment are still problems, even in the most prosperous countries.

STANDARD OF LIVING
(UN Human Development Index)

low   high

EUROPEAN GEOGRAPHY

Europe is blessed with a temperate climate, ample mineral reserves, and good transport links. During the 18th and 19th centuries the continent was transformed, as new methods of production made industry and farming more efficient and productive. Today, in many countries, 'heavy' industries have been replaced by hi-tech and service industries. Agriculture is still important and many crops thrive on Europe's fertile plains.

INDUSTRY

Western Europe has some of the world's wealthiest countries. In countries such as France, Germany and the UK, traditional industries like iron and steel-making are now being replaced by light industries such as electronics, and services like finance and insurance. In Eastern Europe, industry was subsidized by the communist governments for years. Many factories are old fashioned and need investment to improve their equipment and production methods.

MINERAL RESOURCES

Europe has few sizeable reserves of metallic minerals; most were used up by industry during the 19th century. Oil, gas and coal are found in large quantities – gas in the North Sea and oil in the Volga basin. Coal, though abundant, is being steadily depleted.

MINERAL RESOURCES

- ⛏ Bauxite
- ⛏ Chromium
- ⛏ Copper
- ⛏ Iron
- ⛏ Manganese
- ⛏ Nickel
- ⛏ Uranium
- ▨ Oil/gas field
- ▨ Coal field

OIL AND GAS

Oil and gas reserves are plentiful in the Russian Federation. South of Rostov-on-Don, oil is pumped from the ground and piped to nearby refineries.

CAR MANUFACTURE

Germany is one of the world's largest and oldest manufacturer of cars. Companies like BMW, Mercedes-Benz and Volkswagen export cars across the world.

FINANCE

London, Frankfurt and Paris are among the most important financial centres in the world. Many banks and financial institutions have their headquarters here. At the London Stock Exchange, people buy and sell stocks and shares.

ECONOMIC ACTIVITY

- ✈ Aerospace
- 🚗 Car/vehicle manufacture
- ⚗ Chemicals
- Coal
- Defence
- Electronics
- Engineering
- Finance
- Food processing
- Hi-tech industry
- Iron & steel
- Oil and gas
- Printing & publishing
- Textiles
- Timber processing

GNI per capita (US$)

- Below 4,999
- 5,000-9,999
- 10,000-24,999
- 25,000-39,999
- 40,000-54,999
- Above 55,000
- • Industrial centre

CLIMATE

Europe's climate is temperate with few climatic extremes. In the far north, Europe extends into the Arctic Circle and the climate is so cold that in the winter, the Baltic Sea freezes over. Towards the Atlantic coast in the west, the climate becomes wetter and warmer because of a warm ocean current, known as the Gulf Stream. Countries such as Italy and Spain which border the Mediterranean Sea, have long, hot summers and low rainfall, which can sometimes lead to problems such as drought.

EXTREME WEATHER EVENTS

Symbols indicate climatic extremes

CLIMATE

- Tundra
- Subarctic
- Cool continental
- Temperate/humid
- Mediterranean
- Semi-arid

Coldest place
UST' SHCHUGOR (Russ. Fed.)
Temperature -55°C

Driest place
ASTRAKHAN' (Russ. Fed.)
Annual rainfall 160 mm

Hottest place
SEVILLE (Spain)
Temperature 50°C

Wettest place
CRKVICE (Montenegro)
Annual rainfall 4650 mm

THE MEDITERRANEAN CLIMATE

The mild, warm climate around the Mediterranean Sea allows olives, citrus fruits and grapes to thrive. Long, sunny days also help the fruits ripen. Grapes are harvested and crushed to make many different wines.

LAND USE AND AGRICULTURE

Europe's agricultural heart is the North European Plain, where fertile soils and ample rainfall mean that a variety of crops can be grown. Wheat is the main grain crop, and a wide range of fruit and vegetables are also grown. Dairy and beef cattle are raised for their milk and meat throughout Europe. In the south, the Mediterranean climate allows citrus fruits and olives to grow. Forests cover much of northern Scandinavia, while in the hills of the British Isles, sheep farming is common.

CROPLANDS

Many different crops are grown on the North European Plain. Sunflowers, wheat, and sugar beet – used to make sugar – are amongst the main crops grown there.

FISHING

The north Atlantic Ocean provides a rich marine harvest for fishermen. Today the cod, haddock and mackerel stocks have to be protected from over-fishing.

LAND USE AND AGRICULTURE

- Cattle
- Goats
- Pigs
- Reindeer
- Sheep
- Cereals
- Citrus fruits
- Fishing
- Fruit
- Olive oil
- Potatoes
- Root crops
- Shellfish
- Sunflowers
- Timber
- Vineyards

- Cropland
- Forest
- Ice cap
- Mountain region
- Pasture
- Tundra
- Wetland
- • Major conurbation

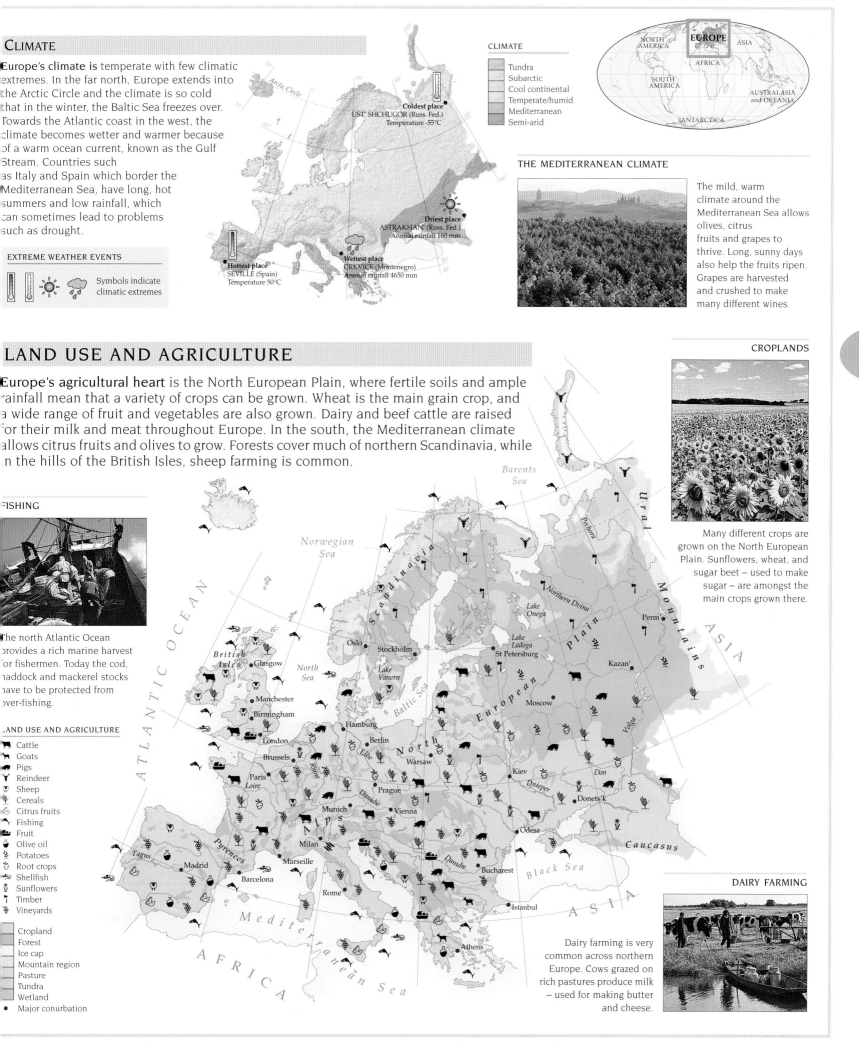

DAIRY FARMING

Dairy farming is very common across northern Europe. Cows grazed on rich pastures produce milk – used for making butter and cheese.

NORTHERN EUROPE

DENMARK, ESTONIA, FINLAND, ICELAND, LATVIA, LITHUANIA, NORWAY, SWEDEN

Denmark, Sweden and Norway are together known as Scandinavia. These countries, along with the North Atlantic island of Iceland, have similar languages and cultures. Finland has a very different language and a separate identity from its Scandinavian neighbours. Estonia, Latvia and Lithuania, known as the Baltic states, were part of the Soviet Union until 1989, when each became an independent country.

INDUSTRY

In Scandinavia, many natural resources are used in industry: timber for paper and furniture; iron ore for steel and cars; and fish and natural gas from the seas. Hydro-electric power is generated by water flowing down steep mountain slopes. The Baltic states still rely on Russia to supply their raw materials and energy.

INDUSTRY

- 🚗 Car manufacture
- 🔬 Chemicals
- ⚙ Engineering
- 🐟 Fish processing
- ⊣ Hydro-electric power
- Shipbuilding
- Timber processing
- Tourism

- ▪ Major industrial centre / area
- — Major road

STRUCTURE OF INDUSTRY

Primary 4%
Services 65%
Manufacturing 31%

POPULATION

The population is distributed mainly along the warmer and flatter southern and coastal areas. Population totals and densities are low for all of the countries, and Iceland has the lowest population density in Europe, with just three people per sq km. Many Scandinavians have holiday homes on the islands, along the lake shores, or in coastal areas.

INHABITANTS PER SQ KM

- More than 200
- 100–200
- 50–100
- Less than 50
- ■ Capital city
- ● Major city

URBAN/RURAL POPULATION DIVIDE

Copenhagen 3.4%   Stockholm 3.8%
Helsinki 3.3%
Other towns and cities 66.5%
Rural population 23%

FARMING AND LAND USE

Southern Denmark and Sweden are the most productive areas, with pig farming, dairy-farming and crops such as wheat, barley and potatoes. Sheep farming is important in southern Norway and Iceland. In the Baltic states, cereals, potatoes and sugar beet are the main crops and cattle graze on damp pasture.

FARMING AND LAND USE

- Cattle
- Fishing
- Pigs
- Sheep
- Cereals
- Root crops
- Timber

- Pasture
- Cropland
- Forest
- Ice cap
- Mountain region
- Tundra
- ● Major conurbation

LAND USE

Pasture 3%
Cropland 11%
Forest 49%
Other (including mountains) 37%

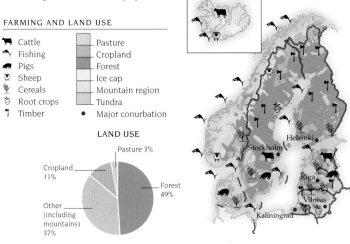

THE LANDSCAPE

The north and west of Scandinavia is extremely rugged and mountainous, with landscapes eroded by ice. In the south of Scandinavia the land is flatter, with fertile soils deposited by glaciers. Much of Finland, Norway and Sweden is covered by dense forests. The Baltic states are much lower, with rounded hills and many lakes and marshes.

The land of ice and fire.
Iceland is one of the world's most active volcanic areas. There are about 200 volcanoes on the island, along with bubbling hot springs, mud-holes, and geysers which spurt boiling water and steam high into the air.

Fjords
Norway has many fjords: deep, wide valleys carved by glaciers, drowned by seawater when the ice melted at the end of the last Ice Age.

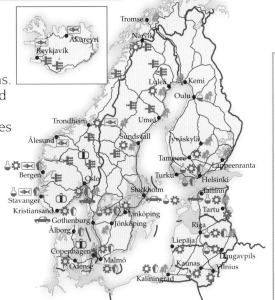

Baltic Sea (D 7)
Ships from Finland, Sweden and the Baltic states use the Baltic Sea as their route to the north Atlantic Ocean. In winter, much of the sea is frozen.

Glacial lakes
Finland and Sweden have many thousands of lakes. During the last Ice Age, glaciers scoured hollows which filled with water when the ice melted.

Courland Spit (D 7
This wide sandspit runs 100 km along the Balti of Lithuania and the Ru enclave of Kaliningrad. It encloses a huge lago

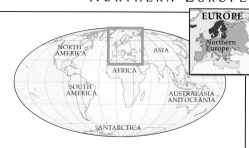

EUROPE
Northern Europe

Vatnajökull 1996
Surtsey 1963

Stockholm
Helsinki
Tallinn
Riga
Copenhagen

ENVIRONMENTAL ISSUES

Major dams

Urban air pollution

Volcanic eruption

Wind farm

Geothermal power

Affected by acid rain
Sea pollution

● **Major industrial centre**

CLIMATE

Warm ocean currents flowing north along the coasts of Norway and Iceland make the climate mild and wet. Away from the sea, the climate is generally colder, and drier.

January

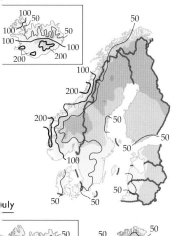

100
50
100
50
100
200
200
100
50
200
50
50

July

50
100
50
100
100
100
200
100
100
100
100
100

TEMPERATURE AND PRECIPITATION

More than 15°C	0 to -5°C
10 to 15°C	-5 to -10°C
5 to 10°C	-10 to -15°C
0 to 5°C	Less than -15°C

100 Precipitation (mm)

ENVIRONMENTAL ISSUES

Northern Europe has been badly affected by industrial pollution from other parts of Europe. Polluted air moves north, and mixes with the rain to create acid rain. This poisons forests and lakes, destroying the plants and animals living in them. Renewable energy plays a major role in this region, hydro-electric, geothermal and wind power are all exploited.

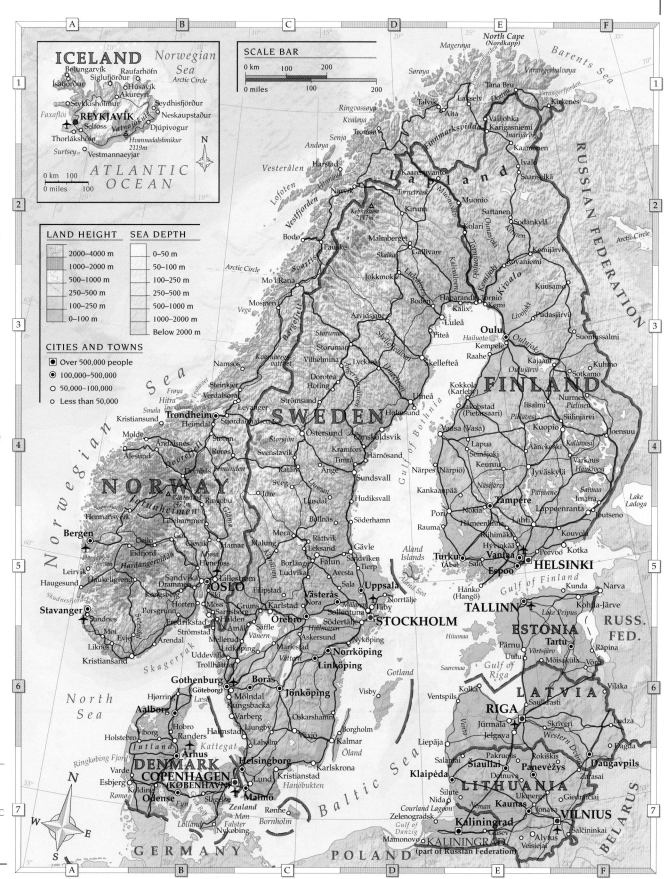

ICELAND

Norwegian Sea

Bolungarvík
Siglufjörður
Raufarhöfn
Ísafjörður
Húsavík
Akureyri
Stykkishólmur
Seydhisfjörður
Faxaflói
REYKJAVÍK
Neskaupstaður
Selfoss
Djúpivogur
Thorlákshöfn
Hvannadalshnúkur 2119m
Surtsey
Vestmannaeyjar

ATLANTIC OCEAN

Arctic Circle

SCALE BAR

0 km 100 200
0 miles 100 200

LAND HEIGHT

2000–4000 m
1000–2000 m
500–1000 m
250–500 m
100–250 m
0–100 m

SEA DEPTH

0–50 m
50–100 m
100–250 m
250–500 m
500–1000 m
1000–2000 m
Below 2000 m

CITIES AND TOWNS

■ Over 500,000 people
◉ 100,000–500,000
○ 50,000–100,000
○ Less than 50,000

NORWAY

SWEDEN

FINLAND

DENMARK

ESTONIA

LATVIA

LITHUANIA

RUSSIAN FEDERATION

Lapland

North Cape (Nordkapp)
Barents Sea

Kirkenes
Varangerfjorden
Tana Bru
Valljohka
Lakselv
Alta
Talvik
Karigasniemi
Inarijärvi
Kaamanen
Ivalo
Saariselkä
Kebnekaise 2117m
Kiruna
Muonio
Kolari
Sattanen
Sodankylä
Malmberget
Gällivare
Jokkmokk
Kemijärvi
Rovaniemi
Boden
Haparanda
Tornio
Kalix
Kemi
Luleå
Piteå
Oulu
Skellefteå
Raahe
Kokkola (Karleby)
Kajaani
Kuhmo
Sotkamo
Suomussalmi
Pudasjärvi

Arctic Circle

Mo I Rana
Mosjøen
Namsos
Vilhelmina
Dorotea
Lycksele
Hoting
Strömsund
Vaasa (Vasa)
Jakobstad (Pietarsaari)
Nurmes
Pielinen
Iisalmi
Siilinjärvi
Kuopio
Joensuu
Varkaus
Haukivesi
Jyväskylä
Äänekoski
Keuruu
Saimaa
Imatra
Lappeenranta
Tampere
Nokia
Riihimäki
Hyvinkää
Vantaa
HELSINKI
Espoo
Turku (Åbo)
Porvoo
Kotka
Kouvola
Lahti
Hämeenlinna
Pori
Rauma
Kankaanpää
Närpes (Närpiö)
Lapua
Seinäjoki
Näsijärvi
Päijänne

Trondheim
Heimdal
Steinkjer
Verdalsøra
Levanger
Stjørdalshalsen
Kristiansund
Molde
Åndalsnes
Ålesund
Dombås
Røros
Østersund
Strömsund
Storuman
Kramfors
Timrå
Härnösand
Örnsköldsvik
Ånge
Svenstavik
Sundsvall
Hudiksvall
Bollnäs
Söderhamn

Bergen
Hermansverk
Glittertind 2472m
Jotunheimen
Ringebu
Lillehammer
Hamar
Mora
Rättvik
Leksand
Falun
Gävle
Sandviken
Tierp
Osilo
Gjøvik
Eidfjord
Honefoss
Malung
Borlänge
Ludvika
Avesta
Sala
Uppsala
Norrtälje
Haugesund
Drammen
OSLO
Filipstad
Västerås
Nora
Täby
Sollentuna
STOCKHOLM
Stavanger
Sandnes
Horten
Moss
Grums
Karlstad
Örebro
Hjälmaren
Södertälje
Nyköping
Leirvik
Kongsberg
Ski
Sarpsborg
Halden
Åmål
Säffle
Askersund
Norrköping
Moi
Evje
Arendal
Fredrikstad
Strömstad
Mellerud
Lidköping
Mariestad
Vättern
Linköping
Liknes
Kristiansand
Uddevalla
Trollhättan
Vänern
Gothenburg (Göteborg)
Borås
Jönköping
Visby
Gotland

North Sea

Skagerrak

Hjørring
Mölndal
Kungsbacka
Varberg
Oskarshamn
Borgholm
Aalborg
Holstebro
Viborg
Hobro
Randers
Halmstad
Ljungby
Laholm
Växjö
Kalmar
Öland
Jutland
Kattegat
Helsingborg
Karlskrona
COPENHAGEN (KØBENHAVN)
Lund
Kristianstad
Malmö
Hanöbukten
Varde
Esbjerg
Kolding
Odense
Slagelse
Zealand
Rønne
Bornholm
Nykøbing
Falster
Lolland
Møn

Baltic Sea

GERMANY

POLAND

RIGA
Jūrmala
Jelgava
Saulkrasti
Valmiera
Ventspils
Kolka
Liepāja
Klaipėda
Šiauliai
Panevėžys
Daugavpils
LITHUANIA
Kaunas
VILNIUS
Kaliningrad
(part of Russian Federation)

TALLINN
ESTONIA
Tartu
Pärnu
Gulf of Riga
Saaremaa
Hiiumaa
Lake Peipus
Narva
Kohtla-Järve

Gulf of Finland

Åland Islands

Gulf of Bothnia

Lake Ladoga

RUSS. FED.

BELARUS

THE LOW COUNTRIES

BELGIUM, LUXEMBOURG, NETHERLANDS

Belgium, Luxembourg and the Netherlands are called the Low Countries because most of their land is flat and low-lying. Much of the Netherlands lies below sea level, and over hundreds of years the Dutch have built dykes and dams to prevent flooding, and have pumped water off large areas of land to reclaim them from the sea. The Low Countries are Europe's most densely populated countries, but most of their people have a high living standard.

ENVIRONMENTAL ISSUES

Huge land reclamation projects in the Netherlands, such as the IJsselmeer project, have created some new land for agricultural use, and also for houses, roads and open spaces. However, because of this work, sea-level rise is a major threat to large parts of the Netherlands.

ENVIRONMENTAL ISSUES

- Urban air pollution
- Built-up areas
- Reclaimed land
- Polluted river
- Major industrial centre

CLIMATE

The Low Countries share a similar climate, with mild winters and warm summers. Only in the upland Ardennes region does rainfall increase and temperatures decrease.

January

Less than 50

July

Less than 50

100

100

TEMPERATURE AND PRECIPITATION

- More than 15°C
- 10 to 15°C
- 5 to 10°C
- 0 to 5°C
- Less than 0°C

100 Precipitation (mm)

NETHERLANDS' TWO CAPITALS
AMSTERDAM - capital
THE HAGUE - seat of government

LAND HEIGHT
- 500–1000 m
- 250–500 m
- 100–250 m
- 0–100 m
- Below sea level

SEA DEPTH
- 0–100 m

CITIES AND TOWNS
- Over 500,000 people
- 100,000–500,000
- 50,000–100,000
- Less than 50,000

SCALE BAR

0 km   25   50

0 miles   25   50

Map labels: West Frisian Islands (Waddeneilanden), Schiermonnikoog, Ameland, Terschelling, Eemshaven, Ferwert, Dokkum, Loppersum, Bedum, Delfzijl, Appingedam, Vlieland, Waddenzee, Menaldum, Winsum, Zuidhorn, Groningen, Hoogezand-Sappemeer, Texel, Harlingen, Leeuwarden, Leek, Haren, Winschoten, Drachten, Roden, Veendam, Vlagtwedde, Sneek, Heerenveen, Zuidlaren, Assen, Stadskanaal, Den Helder, Wolvega, Beilen, Borger, Odoorn, Emmen, Schagen, Emmeloord, Steenwijk, Hoogeveen, Klazienaveen, Coevorden, Bergen, Opmeer, Heerhugowaard, IJsselmeer, Staphorst, Meppel, Dedemsvaart, Heiloo, Alkmaar, Hoorn, IJsselmuiden, Ommen, Hardenberg, Heemskerk, Castricum, Purmerend, Broek-in-Waterland, Lelystad, Zwolle, Den Ham, Tubbergen, Velsen-Noord, Zaandam, Wezep, Hattem, Heerde, Wierden, Almelo, Oene, Oldenzaal, NETHERLANDS, Haarlem, Almere, Zeewolde, Oldebroek, Raalte, Rijssen, Borne, AMSTERDAM, Amstelveen, Blaricum, Nunspeet, Ermelo, Deventer, Hengelo, Enschede, Hillegom, Aalsmeer, Hilversum, Tjerkerk, Vaassen, Goor, Lochem, Haaksbergen, Noordwijk aan Zee, Sassenheim, Lisse, Uithoorn, Baarn, Apeldoorn, Voorst, Gorssel, Needle, Eibergen, THE HAGUE ('S-GRAVENHAGE), Leiden, Alphen aan den Rijn, De Bilt, Amersfoort, Lunteren, Brummen, Dieren, Lichtenvoorde, Winterswijk, Zoetermeer, Nieuwegein, Zeist, Veenendaal, Ede, Oosterbeek, Arnhem, Duiven, Zevenaar, Aalten, 's-Gravenzande, Delft, Gouda, Vianen, Wijk bij Duurstede, Bemmel, Ulft, Vlaardingen, Capelle aan den IJssel, Geldermalsen, Nijmegen, Rotterdam, Barendrecht, Gorinchem, Groesbeek, Goeree, Hellevoetsluis, Woudrichem, Wijchen, Gennep, Overflakkee, Dordrecht, Werkendam, Bosmalen, Oss, Grave, Cuijk, Schouwen, Middelharnis, Raamsdonksveer, Vlijmen, 's-Hertogenbosch, Sint-Michielsgestel, Boxmeer, Zierikzee, Zevenbergen, Oosterhout, Schijndel, Nieuw-Bergen, Noord-Beveland, Tholen, Roosendaal, Breda, Tilburg, Oirschot, Helmond, Horst, Middelburg, Goes, Kapelle, Zundert, Best, Baarle-Hertog, Eindhoven, Deurne, Vlissingen, Zuid-Beveland, Essen, Kalmthout, Brecht, Veldhoven, Eersel, Someren, Venlo, Zeebrugge, Knokke-Heist, Oostburg, Terneuzen, Stabroek, Kapellen, Turnhout, Bergeyk, Valkenswaard, Tegelen, Nederweert, Reuver, Blankenberge, Assenede, Axel, Hulst, Beveren, Schoten, Lommel, Mol, Weert, Beesel, Roermond, Ostend (Oostende), Middelkerke, Eeklo, Sint-Niklaas, Oostakker, Willebroek, Duffel, Geel, Balen, Kinrooi, Posterholt, Koksijde, Beernem, Aalter, Laarne, Zele, Mechelen, Tremelo, Herselt, Beringen, Maaseik, Echt, Veurne, Torhout, Deinze, Roeselare, Melle, Aalst, Haacht, Zonhoven, Peer, Bree, Susteren, Sittard, Flanders, Ghent (Gent), Izegem, Gavere, Wemmel, Vilvoorde, Leuven, Herk-de-Stad, Diepenbeek, Hasselt, Genk, Geleen, Heerlen, Kerkrade, Poperinge, Ieper, Izegem, BRUSSELS (BRUSSEL/BRUXELLES), Schaerbeek, Tervuren, Tienen, Landen, Tongeren, Bilzen, Riemst, Maastricht, Simpelveld, Kortrijk, Zwevegem, Sint-Pieters-Leeuw, Halle, Overijse, Wavre, Waremme, Oupeye, Rijsden, Vaals, Mouscron, Denderleeuw, Ath, Enghien, Ottignies, Louvain-la-Neuve, Seraing, Herstal, Liège, Eupen, Verviers, Tournai, Leuze-en-Hainaut, Braine-le-Comte, Gembloux, Eghezée, Amay, Huy, Péruwelz, Mons, Binche, La Louvière, Namur, Andenne, Ciney, Malmédy, Jemappes, Anderlues, Châtelet, Charleroi, Gerpinnes, Marche-en-Famenne, Couvin, Thuin, Jerquelinnes, Walcourt, Ciney, Ourthe, Weiswampach, Sambre, Dinant, Rochefort, Bastogne, Hosingen, Recogne, Neufchâteau, Semois, Sûre, Diekirch, Mosel, Ettelbrück, LUXEMBOURG, Grevenmacher, Etalle, Arlon, Alzette, LUXEMBOURG, Aubange, Pétange, Differdange, Esch-sur-Alzette, Dudelange, FRANCE, Fagne, Ardennes, Hautes Fagnes, Botrange 694m, GERMANY, Rhine (Rhein), Bergse Maas, Waal, Nieder Rijn, Lek, IJssel, North Sea

POPULATION

More than 27 million people live in the Low Countries and nine out of every ten people live in a town or city. The largest urban area – known as the *Randstad Holland* – is in the Netherlands. It runs in an unbroken line from Rotterdam in the south, to Amsterdam in the west. Even most rural areas in the Low Countries are densely populated.

INHABITANTS PER SQ KM

- More than 200
- 100–200
- 50–100
- 0–50
- ■ Capital city
- ● Major city

URBAN/RURAL POPULATION DIVIDE

Amsterdam 2.8%   Brussels 3.9%
Rotterdam 2.3%
Rural population 8%
Other towns and cities 83%

INDUSTRY

The Low Countries are an important centre for the hi-tech and electronics industries. Good transport links to the rest of Europe allow them to sell their products in other countries. The built-up area stretching from Amsterdam in the Netherlands to Antwerp in Belgium has the greatest number of factories. Luxembourg is also an important banking centre; many international banks have their headquarters in its capital city.

STRUCTURE OF INDUSTRY

Primary 2%
Services 73%
Manufacturing 25%

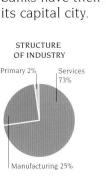

INDUSTRY

- ✈ Aerospace
- 🚗 Car manufacture
- ♨ Chemicals
- ✿ Engineering
- ✎ Pharmaceuticals
- 👕 Textiles
- Ⓢ Finance
- 🖳 High-tech industry
- ⚓ Tourism
- ▣ Major industrial centre / area
- — Major road

FARMING AND LAND USE

The Low Countries' fertile soils and flat plains provide excellent conditions for farming. The main crops grown are barley, potatoes, and flax for making linen. In the Netherlands, much farmland is used for dairy-farming. The country is also famous for growing flowers, which are exported around the world. Flowers and vegetables are grown either in open fields or in enormous greenhouses, which allow production all year round.

FARMING AND LAND USE

- 🐄 Cattle
- 🐖 Pigs
- 🌾 Cereals
- ✾ Flax
- ⚘ Flowers
- 🌿 Market gardening
- 🌱 Sugar beet
- Pasture
- Cropland
- Forest
- Wetland
- ● Major conurbation

LAND USE

Forest 16%
Other (including urban) 29%
Cropland 29%
Pasture 26%

THE LANDSCAPE

The Low Countries are largely flat and low-lying. The ancient hills of the Ardennes, in the far southeast, are the only higher region. They rise to heights of more than 500 m. Two major rivers – the Meuse and the Rhine – flow across the Low Countries to their mouths in the North Sea. At the coast, the River Rhine deposits large quantities of sediment to form a delta.

Polders

In the Netherlands, land has been reclaimed from the sea since the Middle Ages by building dykes and drainage ditches. These areas of land are called polders. They are very fertile.

The River Rhine (E4)

The River Rhine erodes and carries large amounts of sediment along its course. When it reaches the Netherlands it divides into three rivers. As they approach the North Sea, the rivers slow down, depositing the sediment to form a delta.

Low-lying Netherlands

Over two-thirds of the Netherlands lies at or below sea level. This makes flooding a constant threat in coastal areas.

Flanders (B6)

The plains of Flanders in western Belgium have fertile soils which were deposited by glaciers during the last Ice Age. They provide excellent land for growing crops.

Heathlands

The heathlands on the Dutch-Belgian border have thin, sandy soils. The only plants which grow well here are heathers and gorse.

The Ardennes (D8)

The hills of the Ardennes were formed over 300 million years ago. They have many deep valleys, which have been eroded by rivers like the Meuse.

THE BRITISH ISLES

IRELAND, UNITED KINGDOM

The British Isles lie off the northwest coast of mainland Europe. They are made up of two large islands and over 5,000 smaller ones. Politically, the region is divided into two countries: the United Kingdom – England, Wales, Scotland and Northern Ireland – and Ireland. In 2014, Scotland held a referendum on independence in which 55.3% of voters elected to remain a part of the United Kingdom.

THE LANDSCAPE

Low rolling hills, high moorlands, and small fields with high hedges are all typical of the British Isles. Ireland is known as the Emerald Isle, because heavy rainfall gives it a lush, green appearance. Scotland and Wales are mountainous; the rocks forming the mountains there are some of the oldest in the world.

Indented coastlines

The west coast of the British Isles faces the Atlantic Ocean, and over 3,000 km of open sea to the North American continent. Storms and high waves constantly batter the hard, rocky coastline, giving it a jagged outline.

Ben Nevis (C 4)

This mountain is the highest point in the British Isles. It is 1,343 m above sea level.

The Lake District (D 5)

The Lake District National Park has England's highest peak, Scafell Pike, at 978 m (E4), its deepest lake, Wast Water (80 m), and its largest lake, Windermere (16 km long).

The Pennines (D 6)

The Pennines are a chain of high hills, topped by moorland. They run for over 400 km, and are known as the 'backbone of England'.

The Burren (A 6)

The Burren is a large area of limestone rock in the west of Ireland. Its flat surfaces are known as limestone 'pavements'. There are also many caves and sinkholes in the area.

Rias

Rias are river valleys that have been drowned by rising sea levels. The southern coast of southwest England has many good examples.

The Fens (E 6)

This is the flattest area in England. Much of the land here has been reclaimed from the sea.

FARMING AND LAND USE

The English lowlands and the wide, flat stretches of land in East Anglia are the agricultural heartland of the United Kingdom. The country is no longer self-sufficient in food, but wheat, potatoes and other vegetables, and fruits, are widely grown. In Ireland, and in central and southern England, dairy and beef cattle feed off grassy pastures. In the hilly and mountainous areas, sheep farming is more usual.

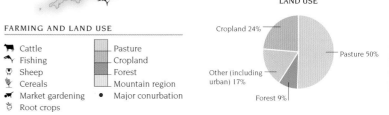

FARMING AND LAND USE

- 🐄 Cattle
- Fishing
- 🐑 Sheep
- Cereals
- Market gardening
- Root crops
- Pasture
- Cropland
- Forest
- Mountain region
- • Major conurbation

LAND USE

Cropland 24%
Pasture 50%
Other (including urban) 17%
Forest 9%

INDUSTRY

The United Kingdom's traditional industries, such as coal mining, steel-making, and textiles, have declined in recent years. Today, newer industries make cars, chemicals, electronic and hi-tech goods. Service industries, especially banking and insurance, have grown in importance. The country's hugely valuable North Sea oil and gas fields are expected to remain in production until around 2050.

INDUSTRY

- ✈ Aerospace
- 🚗 Car manufacture
- Chemicals
- ✿ Engineering
- Textiles
- $ Finance
- Hi-tech industry
- Tourism
- ▣ Major industrial centre / area
- — Major road

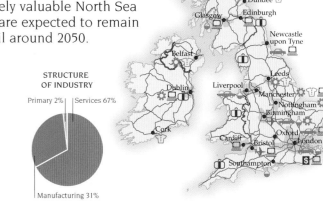

STRUCTURE OF INDUSTRY

Primary 2%
Services 67%
Manufacturing 31%

POPULATION

The United Kingdom is densely populated, with most of the people living in urban areas. The southeast is the most crowded part of the country. The Scottish Highlands are less populated today than they were 200 years ago. Ireland is still mainly rural, with many Irish people making their living from farming.

URBAN/RURAL POPULATION DIVIDE

Birmingham 1.6%
London 11.4%
Glasgow 1%
Rural population 12%
Other towns and cities 74%

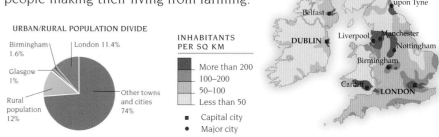

INHABITANTS PER SQ KM

- More than 200
- 100–200
- 50–100
- Less than 50
- ▪ Capital city
- • Major city

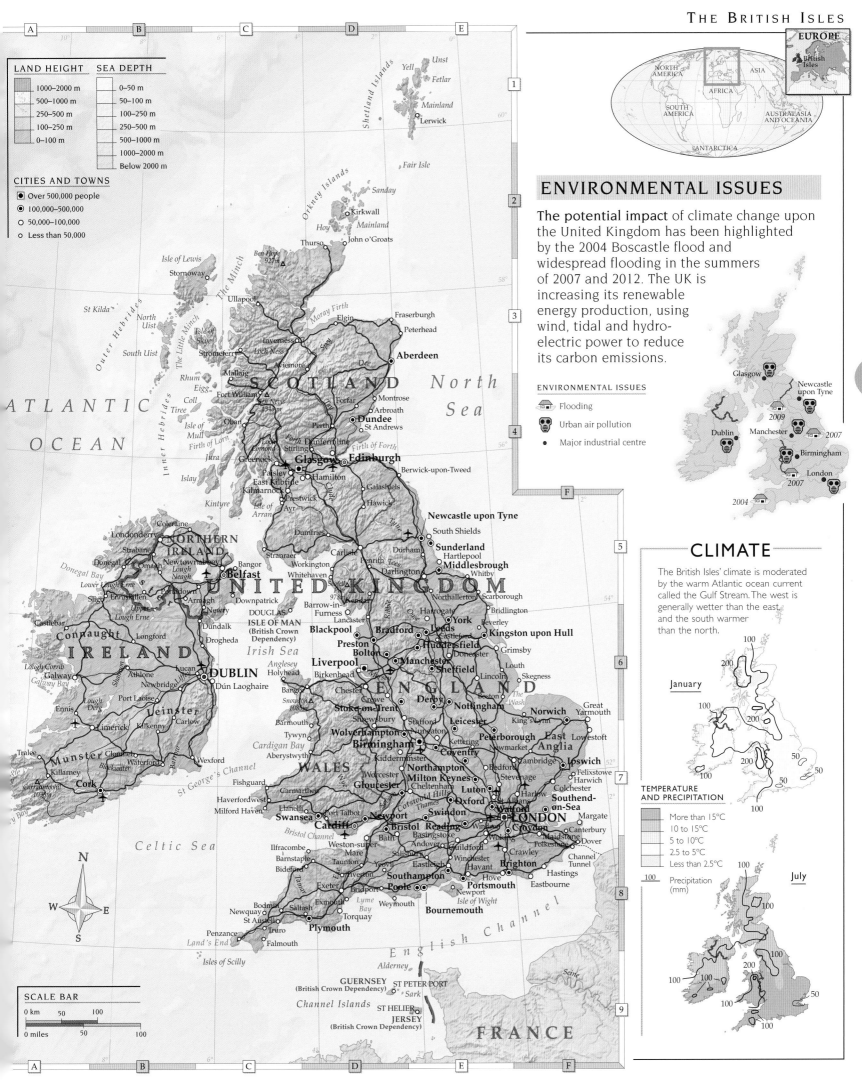

LAND HEIGHT
- 1000–2000 m
- 500–1000 m
- 250–500 m
- 100–250 m
- 0–100 m

SEA DEPTH
- 0–50 m
- 50–100 m
- 100–250 m
- 250–500 m
- 500–1000 m
- 1000–2000 m
- Below 2000 m

CITIES AND TOWNS
- ◉ Over 500,000 people
- ● 100,000–500,000
- ○ 50,000–100,000
- ∘ Less than 50,000

EUROPE

British Isles

NORTH AMERICA   ASIA

AFRICA

SOUTH AMERICA   AUSTRALASIA AND OCEANIA

ANTARCTICA

ENVIRONMENTAL ISSUES

The potential impact of climate change upon the United Kingdom has been highlighted by the 2004 Boscastle flood and widespread flooding in the summers of 2007 and 2012. The UK is increasing its renewable energy production, using wind, tidal and hydro-electric power to reduce its carbon emissions.

ENVIRONMENTAL ISSUES
- Flooding
- Urban air pollution
- Major industrial centre

Glasgow

Newcastle upon Tyne

2009

Dublin   Manchester   2007

2007   Birmingham

2004   London

CLIMATE

The British Isles' climate is moderated by the warm Atlantic ocean current called the Gulf Stream. The west is generally wetter than the east, and the south warmer than the north.

January

July

TEMPERATURE AND PRECIPITATION
- More than 15°C
- 10 to 15°C
- 5 to 10°C
- 2.5 to 5°C
- Less than 2.5°C

100 Precipitation (mm)

SCALE BAR
0 km   50   100

0 miles   50   100

87

IRELAND

IRELAND, NORTHERN IRELAND

Ireland faces the north Atlantic Ocean and is one of the remotest parts of the European Union. Since 1921 the island has been divided into two separate states: Northern Ireland, which is part of the United Kingdom, and Ireland, which has its own government in Dublin. The eastern side of the island has more people and industry. In the west, traditional ways of life based on farming remain strong and the native Irish language is still spoken by some people.

INDUSTRY

Ireland has few mineral resources, around 8% of its electricity is produced by burning peat. In the last 20 years the European Union has given money to help the Irish economy and many new factories have been set up, mainly in the area around Dublin. Hi-tech industries expanded rapidly, as a result of low set-up costs and tax benefits.

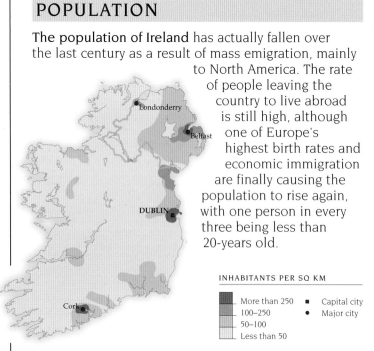

INDUSTRY

✈ Aerospace	▭ Hi-tech industry
♂ Brewing	⊕ Tourism
♀ Chemicals	
⚙ Engineering	▢ Major industrial centre / area
▯ Food processing	— Major road
⍦ Textiles	

POPULATION

The population of Ireland has actually fallen over the last century as a result of mass emigration, mainly to North America. The rate of people leaving the country to live abroad is still high, although one of Europe's highest birth rates and economic immigration are finally causing the population to rise again, with one person in every three being less than 20-years old.

INHABITANTS PER SQ KM

■ More than 250	■ Capital city
▨ 100–250	● Major city
▧ 50–100	
☐ Less than 50	

FARMING AND LAND USE

Potatoes were once the traditional staple food of the Irish; potatoes and cereals flourish in the drier east. The climate is too wet for many types of crop, particularly in the west, where the soils are thin and the land is mostly used for sheep grazing. In bog areas a type of soil called peat is cut from the ground and dried to be burned as fuel.

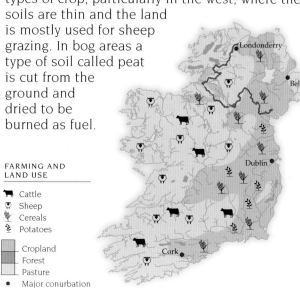

FARMING AND LAND USE

🐄 Cattle	
🐑 Sheep	
⍦ Cereals	
⚘ Potatoes	
▨ Cropland	
▦ Forest	
☐ Pasture	
● Major conurbation	

THE LANDSCAPE

Ireland's mountains are nearly all close to the sea. They form a ring of high ground – broken in only a few places – encircling a lower lying plain which fills the central areas. Hundreds of lakes, large areas of bogland and low, grassy hills cover this central plain. The west coast follows an extremely irregular line, with many long bays and headlands.

High cliffs (C2)
The cliffs of Donegal are some of the highest in Europe. Slieve League has been half cut away by sea erosion, so that the cliff rises vertically, all the way up from the shore to its 670 m summit.

Lakes made by glaciers
The central plain is covered with lakes of many different sizes. Most of these lakes were formed by huge blocks of ice which remained lying around as the last Ice Age came to an end, slowly melting over hundreds of years to leave sunken pits in the land surface.

Flooded river valleys (A6)
Dingle Bay extends deep inland. Rising seas have flooded the old river valley. Bays formed when the sea floods a river valley are known as rias.

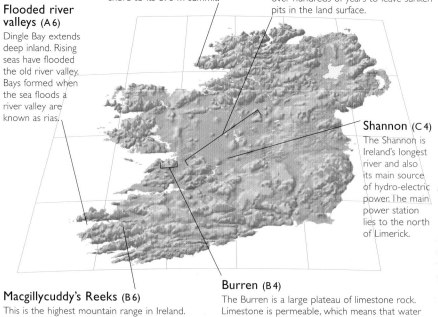

Shannon (C4)
The Shannon is Ireland's longest river and also its main source of hydro-electric power. The main power station lies to the north of Limerick.

Macgillycuddy's Reeks (B6)
This is the highest mountain range in Ireland. The jagged peaks and steep-sided valleys were cut from the highly resistant rocks by glacial erosion, during the last Ice Age.

Burren (B4)
The Burren is a large plateau of limestone rock. Limestone is permeable, which means that water sinks below the surface and flows underground. The bare rock is visible at the surface in many places, where it is called a limestone pavement.

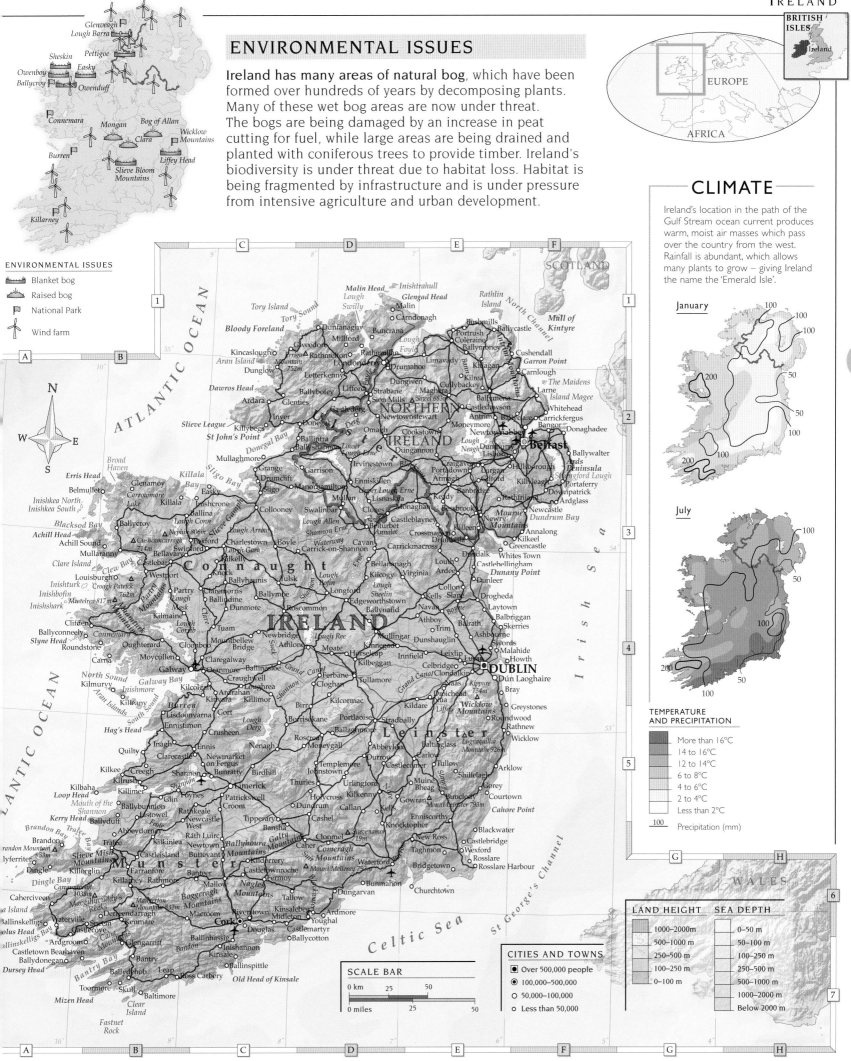

ENVIRONMENTAL ISSUES

Ireland has many areas of natural bog, which have been formed over hundreds of years by decomposing plants. Many of these wet bog areas are now under threat. The bogs are being damaged by an increase in peat cutting for fuel, while large areas are being drained and planted with coniferous trees to provide timber. Ireland's biodiversity is under threat due to habitat loss. Habitat is being fragmented by infrastructure and is under pressure from intensive agriculture and urban development.

BRITISH ISLES
Ireland
EUROPE
AFRICA

ENVIRONMENTAL ISSUES
- Blanket bog
- Raised bog
- National Park
- Wind farm

CLIMATE

Ireland's location in the path of the Gulf Stream ocean current produces warm, moist air masses which pass over the country from the west. Rainfall is abundant, which allows many plants to grow – giving Ireland the name the 'Emerald Isle'.

January

July

TEMPERATURE AND PRECIPITATION
- More than 16°C
- 14 to 16°C
- 12 to 14°C
- 6 to 8°C
- 4 to 6°C
- 2 to 4°C
- Less than 2°C
- 100 Precipitation (mm)

CITIES AND TOWNS
- Over 500,000 people
- 100,000–500,000
- 50,000–100,000
- Less than 50,000

SCALE BAR
0 km 25 50
0 miles 25 50

LAND HEIGHT
- 1000–2000m
- 500–1000 m
- 250–500 m
- 100–250 m
- 0–100 m

SEA DEPTH
- 0–50 m
- 50–100 m
- 100–250 m
- 250–500 m
- 500–1000 m
- 1000–2000 m
- Below 2000 m

SCOTLAND

Scotland occupies the northern third of Britain and has three main regions: the northern highlands and islands, the Southern Uplands and, between these two mountain areas, the central lowlands, where around three quarters of the population live and work. Scotland was once an independent country and, after nearly 300 years of union with England, has regained its own parliament, with certain autonomous powers. In 2014, Scotland held a vote on independence and decided to remain a part of the UK.

INDUSTRY

A century ago, the area around the River Clyde was one of the great industrial regions of the world. The old heavy industries have since declined and been replaced by hi-tech and electronics industries, earning the area the name of 'Silicon Glen'. North Sea oil has brought many jobs and attracted new, oil-based industries such as chemicals and plastics production to the east coast.

INDUSTRY

✈ Aerospace	◊ Oil and gas
♦ Brewing	▢ Hi-tech industry
⚗ Chemicals	▦ Printing and publishing
✿ Engineering	⬡ Tourism
▨ Fish processing	
▤ Food processing	◼ Major industrial centre / area
⏚ Textiles	— Major road

ENVIRONMENTAL ISSUES

Over recent years dependence on coal-fired and nuclear powered electricity generation has decreased in favour of more sustainable and environmentally friendly methods. In particular, due to its favourable landscape and climate, Scotland has seen a significant rise in the number of large-scale wind farms, although these also attract criticism from environmental groups.

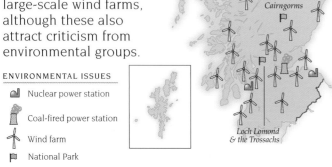

Cairngorms

Loch Lomond & the Trossachs

ENVIRONMENTAL ISSUES

◔	Nuclear power station
⛁	Coal-fired power station
⟑	Wind farm
⚑	National Park

FARMING AND LAND USE

The eastern side of Scotland has a drier climate than the west and is suitable for growing cereal crops and vegetables. Most of the mountain areas are too wet and barren for arable farming and are put to a variety of uses, which include sheep and deer farming, game-keeping, forestry, tourism and recreation. Scottish fishermen currently land about two-thirds of all the fish caught by the UK.

FARMING AND LAND USE

⬂	Cattle
⬈	Deer
⟍	Fishing
⬆	Sheep
⬇	Cereals
⬀	Root crops
⬁	Timber
▓	Cropland
▒	Forest
░	Mountains
▤	Pasture
•	Major conurbation

THE LANDSCAPE

Much of Scotland is rugged and mountainous. During the last Ice Age, around 18,000 years ago, glaciers and great sheets of ice attacked Scotland's hard, ancient rocks, leaving behind a landscape of high moorlands and steep-sided mountains separated by deep valleys, often filled by lakes known as lochs.

Glen Mor (D 3)

Glen Mor is a deep valley which runs right across Scotland. It marks a major line of rock fracture, known as a fault. Much of the fault line is filled by Loch Ness (D 3) and Loch Linnhe (C 4).

Grampians (D 4)

The Grampians are Britain's largest and highest mountain region. They include the spectacular Cairngorm range (E 3) and, to the west, Ben Nevis (D 4), the highest point in the British Isles, at 1,343 m.

Hebrides (A 2), (B 6)

The Inner and Outer Hebrides comprise several large islands and hundreds of small ones. Many of these were formed following the last Ice Age, as the sea level rose, cutting off parts of the mountainous landscape from the mainland.

Firth of Forth (E 5)

The Firth of Forth is one of several great sea inlets, known as firths, along the Scottish coast. They include the Firths of Clyde (D 6), Tay (F 5) and Moray (E 3).

Lochs (D 5)

The many sea lochs (fjords) of the west coast were formed as the sea level rose after the last Ice Age, flooding the deep valleys that had been cut by glaciers. The sea lochs cause the coast to follow a highly irregular line.

Rannoch Moor (D 5)

Rannoch Moor is the largest wild moorland in Scotland. A great ice sheet covered the area during the last Ice Age, leaving behind a vast expanse of bleak, bare ground, pitted with small depressions.

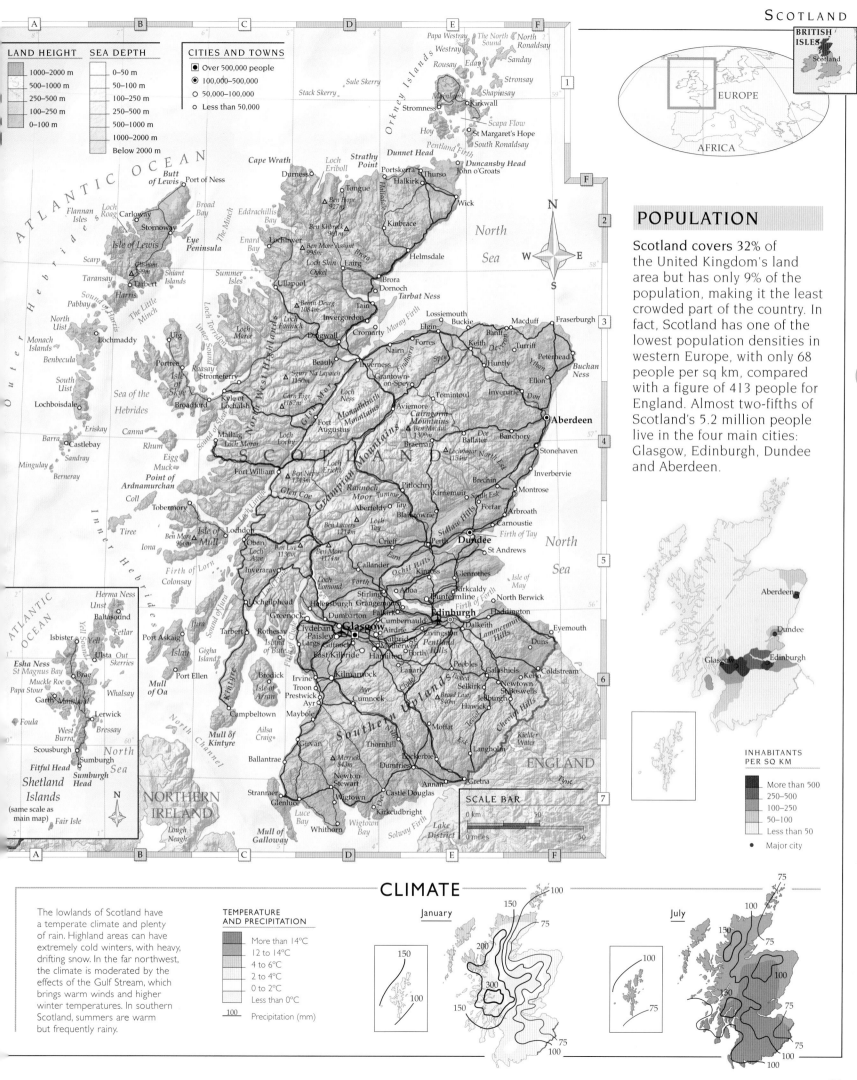

BRITISH ISLES

EUROPE

AFRICA

LAND HEIGHT
- 1000–2000 m
- 500–1000 m
- 250–500 m
- 100–250 m
- 0–100 m

SEA DEPTH
- 0–50 m
- 50–100 m
- 100–250 m
- 250–500 m
- 500–1000 m
- 1000–2000 m
- Below 2000 m

CITIES AND TOWNS
- ■ Over 500,000 people
- ⬤ 100,000–500,000
- ◯ 50,000–100,000
- ○ Less than 50,000

POPULATION

Scotland covers 32% of the United Kingdom's land area but has only 9% of the population, making it the least crowded part of the country. In fact, Scotland has one of the lowest population densities in western Europe, with only 68 people per sq km, compared with a figure of 413 people for England. Almost two-fifths of Scotland's 5.2 million people live in the four main cities: Glasgow, Edinburgh, Dundee and Aberdeen.

INHABITANTS PER SQ KM
- More than 500
- 250–500
- 100–250
- 50–100
- Less than 50
- ● Major city

CLIMATE

The lowlands of Scotland have a temperate climate and plenty of rain. Highland areas can have extremely cold winters, with heavy, drifting snow. In the far northwest, the climate is moderated by the effects of the Gulf Stream, which brings warm winds and higher winter temperatures. In southern Scotland, summers are warm but frequently rainy.

TEMPERATURE AND PRECIPITATION
- More than 14°C
- 12 to 14°C
- 4 to 6°C
- 2 to 4°C
- 0 to 2°C
- Less than 0°C
- 100 Precipitation (mm)

January

July

NORTHERN ENGLAND & WALES

The **Industrial Revolution** of the 18th and 19th centuries began in northern England, exploiting rich local resources to begin a new era of mass production. Today, these industries have declined, but despite a number of difficult years, northern England is becoming more prosperous again. Similarly, south Wales was once a major coal-mining and heavy industrial area but this has largely been replaced by new service industries. The magnificent scenery throughout this region attracts many tourists and outdoor enthusiasts.

INDUSTRY

Traditional industries such as iron and steel, coal-mining and textiles have been in decline for many years. More recently, the type of industries have changed to light engineering and hi-tech industries, producing microchips and computers, together with service industries such as insurance and retailing, printing and publishing. Tourism is important; large numbers of people visit the area's stunning national parks each year.

INDUSTRY

✈ Aerospace	⚗ Pharmaceuticals
♨ Brewing	⚓ Shipbuilding
🚗 Car manufacture	👕 Textiles
⚙ Ceramics	🛢 Oil refining
⚗ Chemicals	💻 Hi-tech industry
⚙ Engineering	📖 Printing and publishing
🐟 Fish processing	⚓ Tourism
🍴 Food processing	
🚂 Iron & steel	▪ Major industrial centre / area
△ Metal refining	— Major road

ENVIRONMENTAL ISSUES

Some of the UK's most dramatic scenery is found in this area, and national parks have long been established to protect the environment. These parks have proved so popular that in some places tourists are in danger of destroying the environment. Coal-fired power stations in the region power the large cities, but recently there has been an increase in renewable energy production.

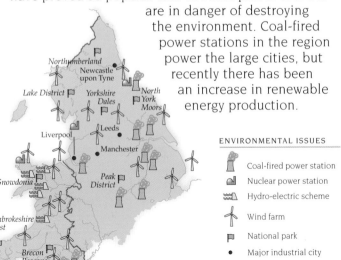

ENVIRONMENTAL ISSUES

🏭	Coal-fired power station
⬛	Nuclear power station
〰	Hydro-electric scheme
🌀	Wind farm
⚑	National park
•	Major industrial city

FARMING AND LAND USE

The eastern lowlands have an ideal climate for arable crops, while oats and potatoes grow in the north and west. The southwest is used mainly for grazing cattle and sheep, which also graze rough in the upland areas of the Pennines and Wales. Forestry is increasingly important in mountain areas.

FARMING AND LAND USE

🐄	Cattle
🐑	Sheep
🌾	Cereals
🌱	Market gardening
🍓	Root crops
	Cropland
	Forest
	Pasture
•	Major conurbation

THE LANDSCAPE

The Pennines form the backbone of northern England. Likewise, the Cambrian Mountains, including the spectacular landscape of Snowdonia, run the length of central Wales. To the east, the Aire and Ouse rivers have cut a broad flood plain between the Pennines and the North York Moors, while in the far northwest, Cumbria's Lake District has many long, deep lakes, which were formed during the last Ice Age.

Limestone pavements
Bare 'pavements' of weathered limestone are also known as karst scenery. They have a block-like appearance, with deep cracks between the blocks that have been dissolved by rainwater.

Spurn Head (F 4)
Spurn Head is a long sand bar (called a spit) at the mouth of the Humber estuary. It was formed by waves which deposited sand across the mouth of the bay. Constant erosion has often made Spurn Head almost inaccessible from the mainland.

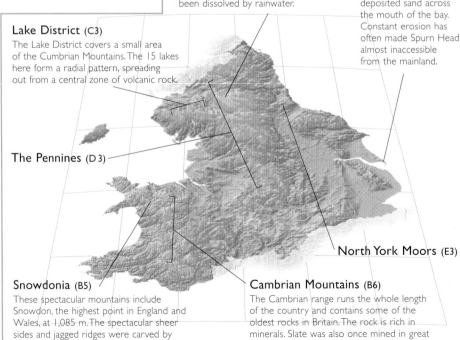

Lake District (C3)
The Lake District covers a small area of the Cumbrian Mountains. The 15 lakes here form a radial pattern, spreading out from a central zone of volcanic rock.

The Pennines (D 3)

North York Moors (E3)

Snowdonia (B5)
These spectacular mountains include Snowdon, the highest point in England and Wales, at 1,085 m. The spectacular sheer sides and jagged ridges were carved by glaciers during the last Ice Age.

Cambrian Mountains (B6)
The Cambrian range runs the whole length of the country and contains some of the oldest rocks in Britain. The rock is rich in minerals. Slate was also once mined in great quantities in northern and central areas.

POPULATION

The cities of Liverpool, Manchester, Leeds and Bradford have spread out to form great conurbations. In the West Midlands, large populations grew up in and around the industrial cities of Coventry and Birmingham. The northeastern coast from Middlesbrough to Newcastle upon Tyne is also densely populated. The area around Newport, Cardiff and Swansea is home to more than 60% of the population of Wales. Upland regions are sparsely populated.

INHABITANTS PER SQ KM

- More than 500
- 250–500
- 100–250
- 50–100
- Less than 50
- ● Major city

CLIMATE

Northern England tends to be cooler and wetter than the south, especially in the summer months. High rainfall totals are recorded in the upland areas of the west. The east, in the 'rainshadow' of the Pennines, is drier.

January

July

TEMPERATURE AND PRECIPITATION

- More than 16°C
- 14 to 16°C
- 12 to 14°C
- 4 to 6°C
- 2 to 4°C
- Less than 2°C
- 100 Precipitation (mm)

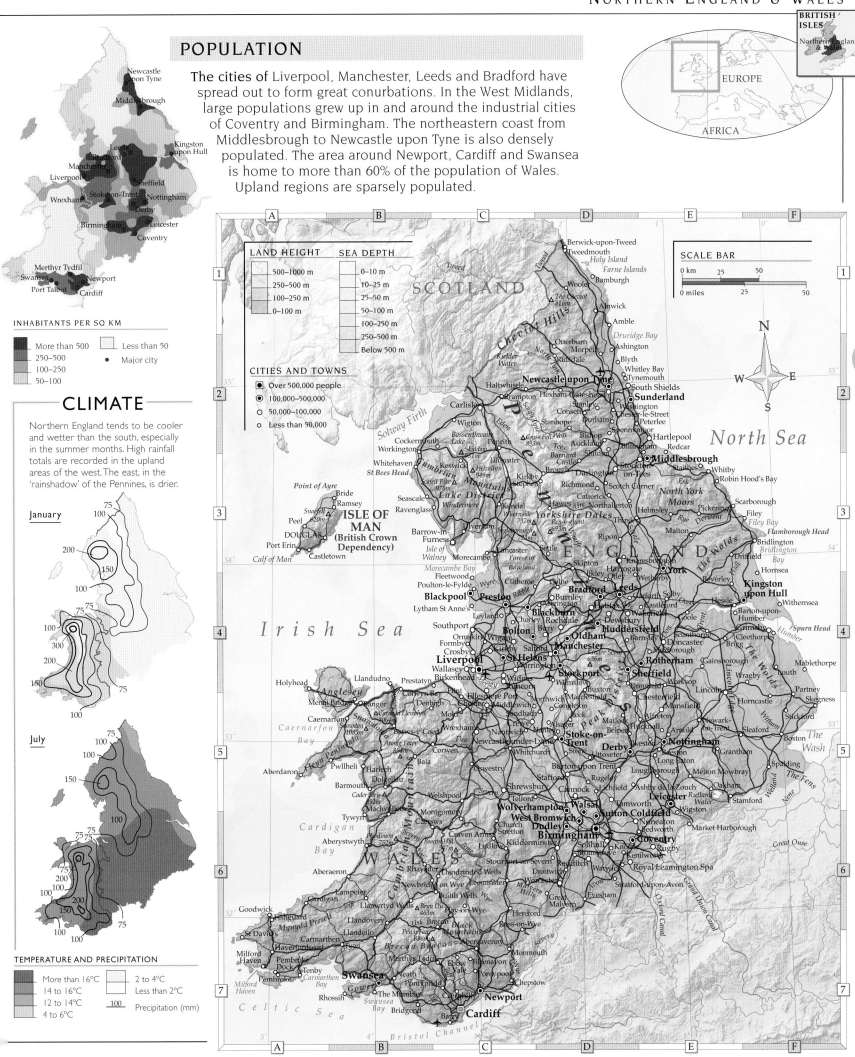

LAND HEIGHT

- 500–1000 m
- 250–500 m
- 100–250 m
- 0–100 m

SEA DEPTH

- 0–10 m
- 10–25 m
- 25–50 m
- 50–100 m
- 100–250 m
- 250–500 m
- Below 500 m

CITIES AND TOWNS

- ▣ Over 500,000 people
- ◉ 100,000–500,000
- ◎ 50,000–100,000
- ○ Less than 50,000

SCALE BAR

0 km 25 50

0 miles 25 50

SOUTHERN ENGLAND

The southern counties of England, and particularly Greater London, are the most densely populated part of the British Isles. There are more industries and more jobs here than anywhere else in the UK. In contrast, the counties of the far west and east are much less heavily populated and more rural, although towns in the eastern counties have been growing rapidly since the 1980s. Following the completion of the Channel Tunnel, the UK has had a direct rail link to Europe.

INDUSTRY

London is one of the world's top financial centres and is also a leading centre for other service industries including insurance, the media and publishing. Many car manufacturers are based in southern England, though the numbers of people employed have greatly decreased. Several cities, including Cambridge and Swindon, are centres for hi-tech industry. Thousands of tourists visit the historic and cultural centres in southern England every year.

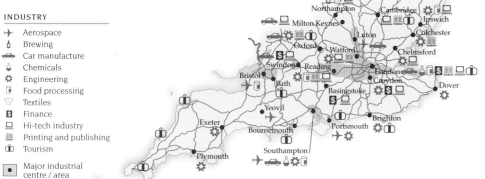

INDUSTRY

- ✈ Aerospace
- 🍺 Brewing
- 🚗 Car manufacture
- 🧪 Chemicals
- ⚙ Engineering
- 🍲 Food processing
- 👕 Textiles
- S Finance
- 💻 Hi-tech industry
- 🖨 Printing and publishing
- 🏛 Tourism
- ▪ Major industrial centre / area
- — Major road

ENVIRONMENTAL ISSUES

The large and growing population of southern England has increased pressure for the development of 'green belt' land, designed to protect the countryside surrounding large cities. A perceived shortage of airport capacity in the southeast of England means that either Heathrow or Gatwick airports will be recommended for expansion over the next 15 years.

ENVIRONMENTAL ISSUES

- Nuclear power station
- 'Green belt' areas
- National Park
- Wind farm
- ● Major town/city

FARMING AND LAND USE

Fertile soils and reliable rainfall mean that a wide range of crops can be grown in southern England. Large arable farms growing wheat and barley are found in the flat eastern counties, and a great variety of soft and orchard fruits and vegetables are grown in market gardens in the far southeast. Beef and dairy cattle and large flocks of sheep are grazed throughout the south.

FARMING AND LAND USE

- Cattle
- Fishing
- Sheep
- Cereals
- Market gardening
- Cropland
- Forest
- Pasture
- ● Major conurbation

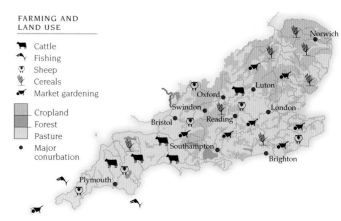

THE LANDSCAPE

The landscape of southern England is very varied. Cornwall in the far west has craggy hills, and a jagged coastline shaped by the Atlantic Ocean. The Cotswolds and the North and South Downs are gentle hills, while towards the east, the land becomes flatter. Near the east coast, low-lying areas are occasionally prone to flooding.

Chalk hills The rounded hills of the Chilterns (F 3) are made from chalk. Because chalk is a porous rock, water quickly seeps through it, so few rivers can be seen in chalk areas.

The Broads (H 2)
The Broads in Norfolk are a series of wide waterways flowing across flat meadows. The channels were cut by peat cutters and are not 'natural'. They then flooded, forming shallow inland lakes.

Steep cliffs
The coasts of north Devon and Cornwall are battered by great waves from the Atlantic Ocean. The force of the waves weakens the rock at the foot of the cliffs, causing them to be 'undercut'. The top layer of rock breaks off and the cliffs recede.

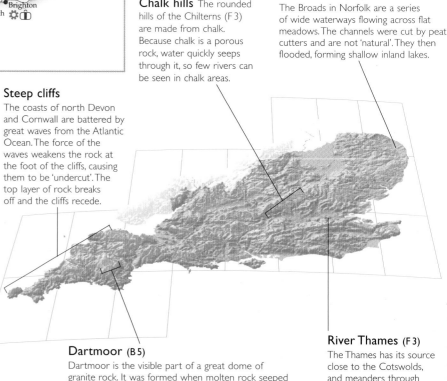

Dartmoor (B 5)
Dartmoor is the visible part of a great dome of granite rock. It was formed when molten rock seeped into and cooled in the Earth's crust. Because granite is so hard it erodes very slowly, so outcrops of rock known as *tors* can be seen all over Dartmoor.

River Thames (F 3)
The Thames has its source close to the Cotswolds, and meanders through Oxford and London before reaching the North Sea in a wide estuary.

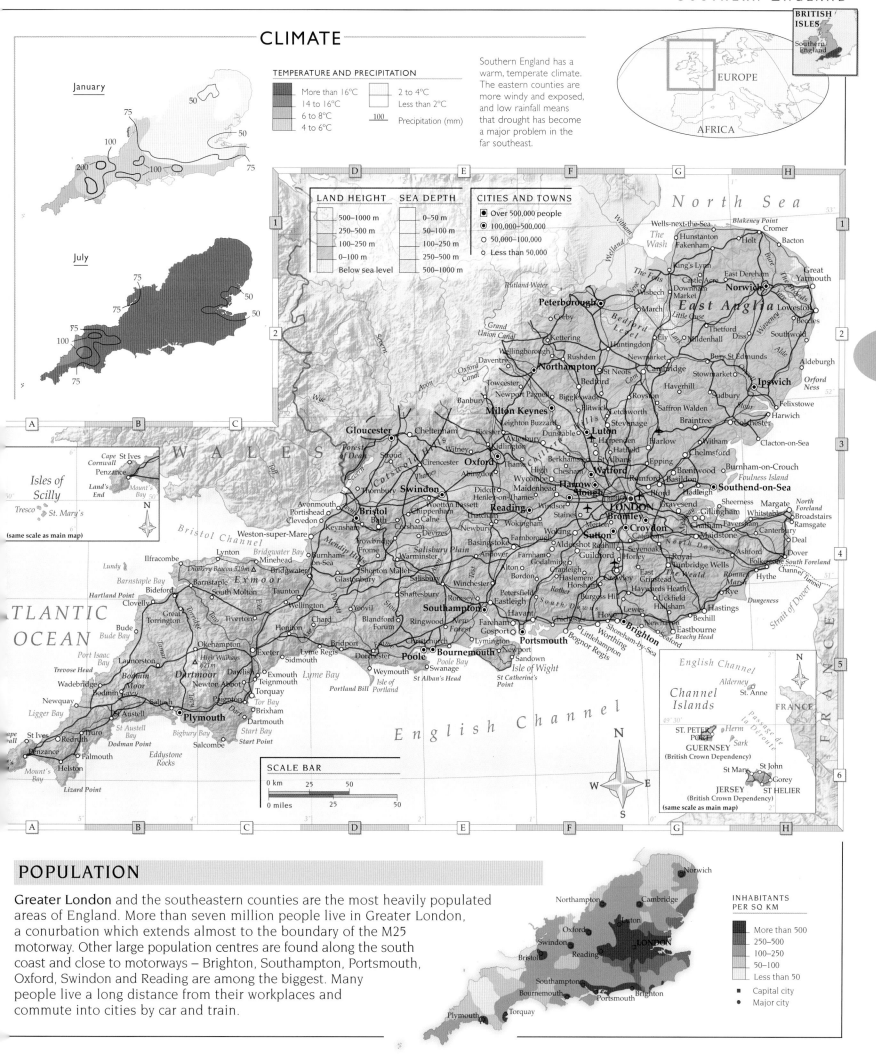

CLIMATE

TEMPERATURE AND PRECIPITATION

More than 16°C
14 to 16°C
6 to 8°C
4 to 6°C
2 to 4°C
Less than 2°C

100 — Precipitation (mm)

Southern England has a warm, temperate climate. The eastern counties are more windy and exposed, and low rainfall means that drought has become a major problem in the far southeast.

January

July

LAND HEIGHT
500–1000 m
250–500 m
100–250 m
0–100 m
Below sea level

SEA DEPTH
0–50 m
50–100 m
100–250 m
250–500 m
500–1000 m

CITIES AND TOWNS
● Over 500,000 people
◉ 100,000–500,000
○ 50,000–100,000
○ Less than 50,000

POPULATION

Greater London and the southeastern counties are the most heavily populated areas of England. More than seven million people live in Greater London, a conurbation which extends almost to the boundary of the M25 motorway. Other large population centres are found along the south coast and close to motorways – Brighton, Southampton, Portsmouth, Oxford, Swindon and Reading are among the biggest. Many people live a long distance from their workplaces and commute into cities by car and train.

INHABITANTS PER SQ KM
More than 500
250–500
100–250
50–100
Less than 50
■ Capital city
● Major city

95

FRANCE

ANDORRA, FRANCE, MONACO

France has helped to shape the history and culture of Europe for centuries. Today, as a founder-member of the European Union, France is a keen supporter of the eventual political and economic integration of Europe's different countries. France is Western Europe's leading farming nation, and one of the world's top industrial powers. Its cultural attractions and scenery draw tourists from around the world.

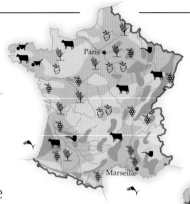

FARMING AND LAND USE

France is able to produce a variety of crops because of its rich soils and mild climate. Wheat is grown in many parts of the north, along with potatoes and other vegetables. Fields of maize and sunflowers and fruit orchards, are found in the south, while grapes for the famous wine industry are grown across the country. Beef and dairy cattle are grazed on low-lying pasture.

FARMING AND LAND USE

- 🐄 Cattle
- 🎣 Fishing
- 🌾 Cereals
- 🐂 Market gardening
- 🌱 Root crops
- 🍂 Tobacco
- 🍇 Vineyards

- Pasture
- Cropland
- Forest
- Mountain region
- Wetland
- ● Major conurbation

LAND USE

Cropland 35%
Other (including urban) 18%
Forest 27%
Pasture 20%

THE LANDSCAPE

The north and west of France is made up of mainly flat, grassy plains or low hills. Wooded mountains line the country's borders in the south and east, and much of central France is taken up by the Massif Central, an enormous plateau, cut by deep river valleys and scattered with extinct volcanoes. Three major rivers, the Loire, Seine and Garonne drain the lowland basins.

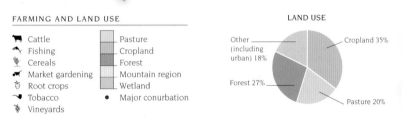

Paris Basin
The Paris Basin is a saucer-shaped hollow made up of layers of hard and soft rock, covered with very fertile soils. It runs across about 100,000 sq km of northern France.

Alps (E 5)
The western end of the European Alpine mountain chain stretches into southeast France. The French Alps can be crossed by several passes, which give access to Italy and Switzerland.

Normandy
The coast of Normandy is lined with high chalk cliffs.

INDUSTRY

France is one of the world's top manufacturing nations, with a variety of both traditional and hi-tech industries. Cars, machinery and electronic products are exported worldwide, along with luxury goods such as perfumes, fashions and fine wines. Extensive use of nuclear power has allowed France to become the world's largest net exporter of electricity.

STRUCTURE OF INDUSTRY

Primary 3% | Services 73%
Manufacturing 24%

INDUSTRY

- ✈ Aerospace
- 🚗 Car manufacture
- ⚗ Chemicals
- ⚙ Engineering
- 👕 Textiles
- 💻 Hi-tech industry
- 💼 Tourism

- ▣ Major industrial centre / area
- — Major road

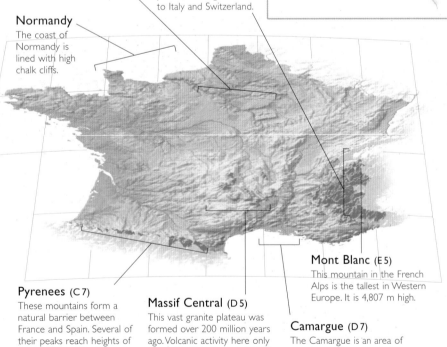

Pyrenees (C 7)
These mountains form a natural barrier between France and Spain. Several of their peaks reach heights of over 3,000 m. The Pyrenees are difficult to cross, due to their height, and because they have few low passes.

Massif Central (D 5)
This vast granite plateau was formed over 200 million years ago. Volcanic activity here only stopped within the last 10,000 years and the region's rounded hills are the worn down remains of volcanic mountains.

Camargue (D 7)
The Camargue is an area of marshes, pastures, sand dunes and salt flats at the mouth of the River Rhône. Rare animal and plant species are found there.

Mont Blanc (E 5)
This mountain in the French Alps is the tallest in Western Europe. It is 4,807 m high.

POPULATION

In the past 50 years, most people have moved from the countryside into urban areas. Paris and its suburbs, the industrial cities, and the Côte d'Azur in the southeast are the most economically developed parts of France and now have the biggest populations.

URBAN/RURAL POPULATION DIVIDE

Paris 16%
Lyon 2.2%
Marseille 2.2%
Rural population 24%
Other towns and cities 55.6%

INHABITANTS PER SQ KM

- More than 200
- 100–200
- 50–100
- Less than 50

- ■ Capital city
- ● Major city

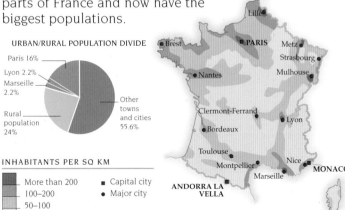

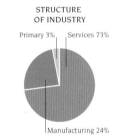

EUROPE

France

ENVIRONMENTAL ISSUES

Many of France's coastal areas have been polluted by industry and tourism. A summer heatwave in 2003 severeley affected France, with temperatures of up to 40°C contributing to the deaths of an estimated 15,000 people. France's reliance on nuclear energy – over 75% of its electricity is generated by nuclear power – means that it suffers less from the pollution caused by burning fossil fuels than many other countries in Europe.

NORTH AMERICA
ASIA
AFRICA
SOUTH AMERICA
AUSTRALASIA AND OCEANIA
ANTARCTICA

ENVIRONMENTAL ISSUES

- Nuclear power station
- Sea pollution
- Polluted rivers
- Major industrial centre

Lille
Seine
Paris
Loire
Saône
Lyon
Bordeaux
Garonne
Rhône
Marseille

CLIMATE

In winter, the coldest areas of France are the mountains of the Massif Central, and the Alps. Summers are hottest on the Mediterranean coast.

TEMPERATURE AND PRECIPITATION

- More than 20°C
- 15 to 20°C
- 10 to 15°C
- 5 to 10°C
- 0 to 5°C
- 0 to -5°C
- Less than -5°C

100 Precipitation (mm)

January

100 100 100 100 50 50 100 50 100 100 100 100 100

July

50 50 100 100 50 100 100 50 50 50 100 100 50

Main map

SCALE BAR
0 km 50 100
0 miles 50 100

UNITED KINGDOM

English Channel

GUERNSEY (British Crown Dependency)
Channel Islands
JERSEY (British Crown Dependency)

Ouessant
Brest
Alderney
Cherbourg
Fécamp
Baie de la Seine
le Havre
Bayeux
Caen
Coutances
Lisieux
Rouen
Barentin
Dieppe
Abbeville
Albert
Arras
Doullens
Amiens
Picardy (Picardie)
Beauvais
Oise
Louviers
Évreux
Senlis
Pontoise
Compiègne
Laon
St-Quentin
Hirson
Charleville-Mézières
Sedan
Thionville
Metz
Hagondange
Verdun
Bar-le-Duc
Châlons-en-Champagne
Reims
Château-Thierry
PARIS
Argenteuil
Nanterre
Créteil
Versailles
Antony
Melun
Fontainebleau
Nemours
Chartres
Alençon
Mortagne
Channel Tunnel
Strait of Dover
Dunkerque
Boulogne-sur-Mer
le Portel
Berck-Plage
St-Omer
Tourcoing
Lille
Roubaix
Valenciennes
Cambrai
Artois
BELGIUM
Ardennes
LUXEMBOURG
GERMANY
Rhine
Moselle
Lorraine
Nancy
Toul
Épinal
St-Dié
Alsace
Haguenau
Saverne
Schiltigheim
Strasbourg
Sélestat
Colmar
Mulhouse
St-Louis
Belfort
Montbéliard
Audincourt
Besançon
Franche-Comté
Vosges
Jura
SWITZERLAND
Lake Geneva
Thonon-les-Bains
Mont Blanc 4807m
Annecy
Chambéry
Savoie
Aix-les-Bains
Bourg-en-Bresse
Mâcon
Villefranche
Lyon
Villeurbanne
Vienne
St-Étienne
St-Chamond
Dauphiné
Grenoble
Voiron
St-Égrève
Briançon
Gap
ITALY
Po
Turin

Brittany (Bretagne)
Morlaix
Plérin
St-Brieuc
Dinan
St-Malo
Granville
Avranches
Fougères
Laval
Vitré
Quimper
Concarneau
Quimperlé
Pontivy
Loudéac
Rennes
le Mans
Maine
Sarthe
la Flèche
Angers
Saumur
Touraine
Tours
Blois
Orléans
Vendôme
Châteaudun
Orléanais
Olivet
Montargis
Sens
Auxerre
Troyes
Chaumont
Langres
Côte d'Or
Dijon
Burgundy (Bourgogne)
Beaune
Dôle
Chalon-sur-Saône
Lons-le-Saunier
St-Claude
Pontarlier

Hennebont
Auray
Lorient
Vannes
Redon
St-Nazaire
Rezé
Nantes
Anjou
Cholet
Thouars
Challans
les Herbiers
la Roche-sur-Yon
les Sables-d'Olonne
Fontenay-le-Comte
Belle Île
Île d'Yeu
Île de Ré
la Rochelle
Île d'Oléron
Niort
Poitiers
Poitou
Châtellerault
Châteauroux
Berry
Bourges
Vierzon
Nevers
Nivernais
Moulins
Digoin
Bourbonnais
Montluçon
Guéret
Marche
Vichy
Roanne
Thiers
Tarare
Ambérieu-en-Bugey

Bay of Biscay

Saintes
Cognac
Royan
Charente
Angoulême
Angoumois
Limoges
Limousin
Ussel
Clermont-Ferrand
Riom
Issoire
Puy de Sancy 1885m
Auvergne
St-Flour
Aurillac
Mauriac
Tulle
Périgueux
Brive-la-Gaillarde
le Puy
Mende
Privas
Valence
Montélimar
Ardèche
Drôme
Bollène
Orange
Durance
Digne
Gap
Briançon
Col du Mont Cenis 2083m

Médoc
Lesparre
Mérignac
Pessac
Bordeaux
Libourne
Bergerac
Dordogne
Isle
Dordogne
Figeac
Cahors
Rodez
Aveyron
Albi
Carmaux
Gaillac
Graulhet
Tarn
Castres
Arcachon
la Teste
Marmande
Houeilles
Agen
Moissac
Montauban
Castelsarrasin
Aquitaine
Garonne
Lot
Lot

Mont-de-Marsan
Dax
Anglet
Biarritz
Bayonne
Orthez
Pau
Lourdes
Tarbes
St-Gaudens
Auch
Armagnac
Gascony (Gascogne)
Toulouse
Montauban
Castelnaudary
Carcassonne
Pamiers
Foix
Limoux
Narbonne
Tarn
Languedoc
Nîmes
Béziers
Agde
Sète
Frontignan
Montpellier
Arles
Camargue
Martigues
Salon-de-Provence
Aix-en-Provence
Marseille
Aubagne
la Ciotat
Six-Fours-les-Plages
la Seyne-sur-mer
Toulon
Hyères
Îles d'Hyères
Roussillon
Perpignan
Gulf of Lion

Provence
Nice
MONACO
Antibes
Cannes
le Cannet
Côte d'Azur
Ligurian Sea

SPAIN
ANDORRA LA VELLA
ANDORRA
Pyrenees
Ebro

Gulf of Gascony

LAND HEIGHT
- Above 4000 m
- 2000–4000 m
- 1000–2000 m
- 500–1000 m
- 250–500 m
- 100–250 m
- 0–100 m

SEA DEPTH
- 0–50 m
- 50–100 m
- 100–250 m
- 250–500 m
- 500–1000 m
- 1000–2000 m
- Below 2000 m

CITIES AND TOWNS
- Over 500,000 people
- 100,000–500,000
- 50,000–100,000
- Less than 50,000

FRANCE

Golfe de St-Malo
Normandy (Normandie)
Île-de-France
Champagne
Marne
Vosges
Nivernais
Morvan
Jura
Loire
Creuse
Vienne
Bourbonnais
Massif Central
Gascony
Roussillon

Corsica inset

Ligurian Sea
Bastia
Corsica (Corse)
Monte Cinto 2706m
Ajaccio
Sartène
Bonifacio
Strait of Bonifacio
Sardinia (Sardegna) (part of Italy)
Scale: same as main map
Mediterranean Sea
Tyrrhenian Sea
Monte Incudine 2136m

Corsica (Corse)
Bastia
Monte Cinto 2706m

SPAIN AND PORTUGAL

PORTUGAL, SPAIN

Spain and Portugal occupy the Iberian Peninsula, which is cut off from the rest of Europe by the Pyrenees. Over the centuries, Iberia has been invaded and settled by many different peoples. The Moors, who arrived from North Africa in the 8th century, ruled much of Spain for almost 800 years and their influence can still be seen in Spanish culture. Portugal has modernized it's economy since joining the European Union, and both countries have changed their currencies to the euro.

INDUSTRY

Madrid, Barcelona and the northern ports are Spain's industrial centres. Here, iron ore from Spanish mines is used to make steel, and factories produce cars, machinery and chemicals. Portugal exports textiles, clothing and footwear, along with fish such as sardines and tuna, caught off the Atlantic coast. In both countries, tourism is very important to the economy.

STRUCTURE OF INDUSTRY

Primary 4%
Services 67%
Manufacturing 29%

INDUSTRY

✈ Aerospace	⊺ Textiles
🚗 Car manufacture	⬧ Mining
⚗ Chemicals	⌂ Tourism
⚙ Engineering	▦ Publishing
▤ Fish processing	
⚓ Shipbuilding	■ Major industrial centre / area
⚒ Steel	— Major road

POPULATION

In the first half of the 20th century, most Spaniards lived in villages or small towns, scattered around the country. Today, tourism and industry have drawn most of the population to the cities and coastal areas. Most Portuguese live in cities, but one third still live in rural areas along the coast or in the river valleys.

URBAN/RURAL POPULATION DIVIDE

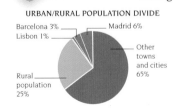

Barcelona 3%
Madrid 6%
Lisbon 1%
Other towns and cities 65%
Rural population 25%

INHABITANTS PER SQ KM

■ More than 200	■ Capital city
100–200	● Major city
50–100	
Less than 50	

FARMING AND LAND USE

Cereals, especially wheat and barley, are Iberia's chief crops. In the dry south of Spain, the land is irrigated to grow citrus fruits, especially oranges, and vegetables. In both countries, olive trees and vineyards occupy large areas of land; olive oil and wine are important exports. Cork oak trees from Iberia's forests supply 80% of the world's cork.

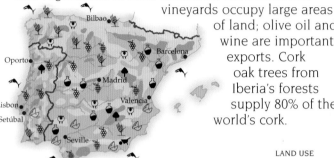

FARMING AND LAND USE

⌐ Fishing	♠ Cork
🐑 Sheep	
🌾 Cereals	▦ Pasture
🍊 Citrus fruit	▦ Cropland
⚒ Market gardening	▦ Forest
◉ Olive oil	▦ Mountain region
🍇 Vineyards	● Major conurbation

LAND USE

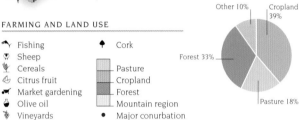

Other 10%
Cropland 39%
Forest 33%
Pasture 18%

THE LANDSCAPE

Most of inland Spain is taken up by the Meseta, a dry, almost treeless plateau surrounded by steep mountain ranges. The only lowlands, apart from narrow strips along the Mediterranean coast, are the valleys of the Ebro, Tagus, Guadiana and Guadalquivir rivers. Portugal's coast is lined by wide plains. Inland, the River Tagus divides the country in two. To the north the land is hilly and wooded; to the south it is low-lying and drier.

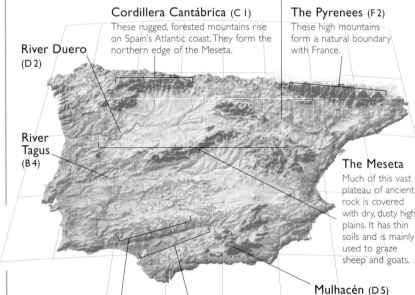

Westward-flowing rivers
The Duero, Tagus and Guadalquivir rivers flow across the Meseta on their courses to the Atlantic Ocean.

River Ebro (E 2)
The River Ebro carries vital irrigation water to Spain's northeastern plains before flowing into the Mediterranean Sea.

Cordillera Cantábrica (C 1)
These rugged, forested mountains rise on Spain's Atlantic coast. They form the northern edge of the Meseta.

The Pyrenees (F 2)
These high mountains form a natural boundary with France.

River Duero (D 2)

River Tagus (B 4)

The Meseta
Much of this vast plateau of ancient rock is covered with dry, dusty high plains. It has thin soils and is mainly used to graze sheep and goats.

Sierra Morena (C 5)
The southern end of the Meseta is marked by this low range of mountains.

Guadalquivir Basin (C 5)
The River Guadalquivir has deposited layers of rich soil called alluvium on its flood plain, making this one of Spain's most fertile regions.

Mulhacén (D 5)
Mulhacén, in the snow-capped Sierra Nevada range in southern Spain, is 3,481 m high. It is Iberia's tallest mountain.

ENVIRONMENTAL ISSUES

Soil erosion – where the top layer of soil has been worn away by wind and rain – has affected much of the Iberian Peninsula. This is caused by farming, combined with drought and deforestation. In Spain, a national tree-planting scheme has been started to combat this problem. Industrial and tourist development along the Mediterranean coast of Spain, and in the Balearic Islands, has damaged natural habitats on both land and sea.

ENVIRONMENTAL ISSUES

- Major oil spill
- Overbuilding
- Soil degradation
- Severe soil degradation
- Polluted rivers
- Sea pollution

CLIMATE

Northern Spain is wetter and cooler than the south. On the central plateau, summers are very hot and dry, and winters often freezing. The north of Portugal is cooled by winds blowing off the Atlantic Ocean. The south is warmer, with dry, mild winters.

TEMPERATURE AND PRECIPITATION

- More than 25°C
- 20 to 25°C
- 15 to 20°C
- 10 to 15°C
- 5 to 10°C
- 0 to 5°C
- 0 to -5°C
- -5 to -10°C
- Less than -10°C

100 — Precipitation (mm)

January

July

EUROPE

LAND HEIGHT
- 2000–4000 m
- 1000–2000 m
- 500–1000 m
- 250–500 m
- 100–250 m
- 0–100 m

SEA DEPTH
- 0–250 m
- 250–500 m
- 500–1000 m
- 1000–2000 m
- 2000–3000 m
- 3000–4000 m
- Below 4000 m

CITIES AND TOWNS
- Over 500,000 people
- 100,000–500,000
- 50,000–100,000
- Less than 50,000

SCALE BAR

0 km   50   100

0 miles   50   100

GERMANY AND THE ALPINE STATES

AUSTRIA, GERMANY, LIECHTENSTEIN, SLOVENIA, SWITZERLAND

Germany lies at the heart of Europe and is the biggest industrial power in the continent. In 1945, Germany was divided into two separate countries, East and West Germany, which were reunited in 1990. To the south, the snow-capped peaks of the Alps, Europe's highest mountains, tower over the Alpine states – Switzerland, Austria, Liechtenstein and the former Yugoslavian state of Slovenia.

INDUSTRY

Germany is a leading manufacturer of cars, chemicals, machinery and transport equipment. Switzerland and Liechtenstein, with few raw materials, make high-value products such as watches and pharmaceuticals, and provide services such as banking. The Alpine states are a popular tourist location all year round.

INDUSTRY

✈ Aerospace
🚗 Car manufacture
🧪 Chemicals
⚙ Engineering
🏭 Iron & steel
⚓ Shipbuilding
💊 Pharmaceuticals
$ Finance
🖥 Hi-tech industry
🏛 Tourism

▣ Major industrial centre / area
— Major road

STRUCTURE OF INDUSTRY

Primary 1% | Services 68%
Manufacturing 31%

POPULATION

Western and central Germany are the most densely populated areas in this region – particularly in and around the Rhine and Ruhr valleys, where there are many industries. In the south, the steep slopes of the Alps and permanent snow cover on the higher peaks means that most large towns and cities are in scattered lowland areas.

INHABITANTS PER SQ KM

■ More than 200
■ 100–200
■ 50–100
■ Less than 50

■ Capital city
● Major city

URBAN/RURAL POPULATION DIVIDE

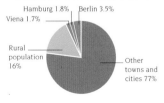

Hamburg 1.8% | Berlin 3.5%
Viena 1.7%
Rural population 16%
Other towns and cities 77%

FARMING AND LAND USE

Germany produces three-quarters of its own food. Crop farming is widespread, with cereals and root crops grown in flat, fertile areas. Cattle and pig farming supplies meat and dairy products. Across the Alps, the mountains limit farming, although vines are grown on the warmer, south-facing slopes. The rich pastures of the lower slopes are used to graze beef and dairy cattle.

FARMING AND LAND USE

🐄 Cattle
🐖 Pigs
🌾 Cereals
🥔 Root crops
🍇 Vineyards

Pasture
Cropland
Forest
Mountain region
● Major conurbation

LAND USE

Forest 33% | Other (including mountains) 20%
Pasture 18% | Cropland 29%

THE LANDSCAPE

To the north, flat plains and heathlands surround the North Sea coast. Further south are Germany's central uplands, which are lower and older than the jagged peaks of the Alps, which began to form about 65 million years ago. From its source in the Black Forest, the River Danube flows eastward across Germany and Austria on its course to the Black Sea. The other major river, the Rhine, flows northward.

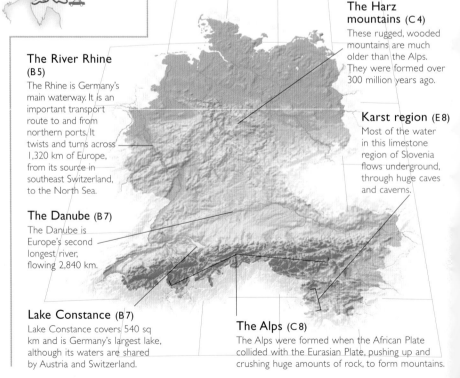

The Harz mountains (C 4)
These rugged, wooded mountains are much older than the Alps. They were formed over 300 million years ago.

The River Rhine (B 5)
The Rhine is Germany's main waterway. It is an important transport route to and from northern ports. It twists and turns across 1,320 km of Europe, from its source in southeast Switzerland, to the North Sea.

Karst region (E 8)
Most of the water in this limestone region of Slovenia flows underground, through huge caves and caverns.

The Danube (B 7)
The Danube is Europe's second longest river, flowing 2,840 km.

Lake Constance (B 7)
Lake Constance covers 540 sq km and is Germany's largest lake, although its waters are shared by Austria and Switzerland.

The Alps (C 8)
The Alps were formed when the African Plate collided with the Eurasian Plate, pushing up and crushing huge amounts of rock, to form mountains.

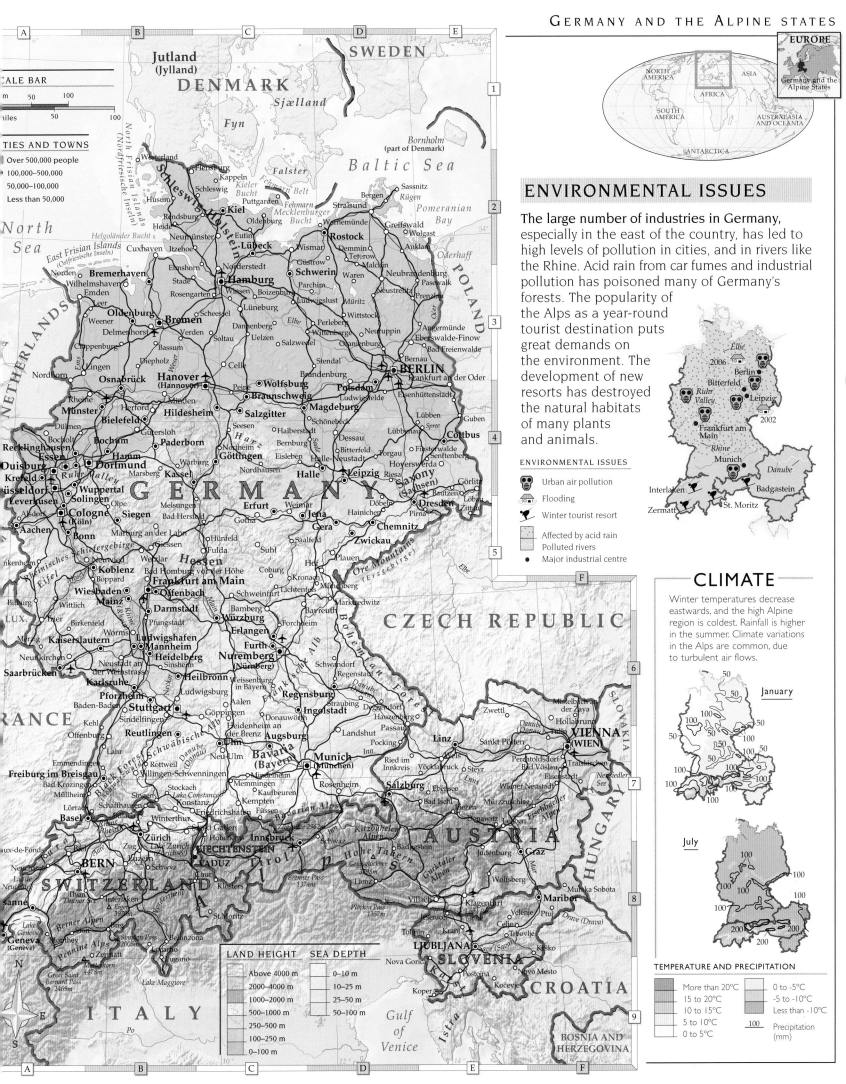

ENVIRONMENTAL ISSUES

The large number of industries in Germany, especially in the east of the country, has led to high levels of pollution in cities, and in rivers like the Rhine. Acid rain from car fumes and industrial pollution has poisoned many of Germany's forests. The popularity of the Alps as a year-round tourist destination puts great demands on the environment. The development of new resorts has destroyed the natural habitats of many plants and animals.

ENVIRONMENTAL ISSUES

- Urban air pollution
- Flooding
- Winter tourist resort
- Affected by acid rain
- Polluted rivers
- Major industrial centre

CLIMATE

Winter temperatures decrease eastwards, and the high Alpine region is coldest. Rainfall is higher in the summer. Climate variations in the Alps are common, due to turbulent air flows.

January

July

TEMPERATURE AND PRECIPITATION

More than 20°C	0 to -5°C
15 to 20°C	-5 to -10°C
10 to 15°C	Less than -10°C
5 to 10°C	
0 to 5°C	100 Precipitation (mm)

LAND HEIGHT

- Above 4000 m
- 2000–4000 m
- 1000–2000 m
- 500–1000 m
- 250–500 m
- 100–250 m
- 0–100 m

SEA DEPTH

- 0–10 m
- 10–25 m
- 25–50 m
- 50–100 m

CITIES AND TOWNS

- Over 500,000 people
- 100,000–500,000
- 50,000–100,000
- Less than 50,000

ITALY

ITALY, SAN MARINO, VATICAN CITY

Italy has played an important role in Europe since the Romans based their mighty empire here over 2,000 years ago. The famous boot shape divides into two very different halves. Northern Italy has a varied range of industries and agriculture. Beautiful cities like Venice, Florence, and Rome draw tourists from all over the world. Southern Italy is poorer and less developed than the north, with a hotter, drier climate and less productive land.

THE LANDSCAPE

Italy is a peninsula jutting south from mainland Europe into the Mediterranean Sea. In northern and central Italy the land is mainly mountainous. Most of the flat land is in the Po Valley and along the eastern coast. Italy lies within an earthquake zone, which makes the land unstable, and there are also a number of active volcanoes.

Italian lakes
Great lakes like Garda (B3) and Como (B2) fill several south-facing valleys once occupied by glaciers.

The Dolomites (D 2)
These high mountains are part of the same range as the Alps. They were formed 65 million years ago.

Po Valley (C 2)
The basin of the River Po has the best soils in Italy. Rich alluvium is washed from the mountains by the river to form a wide plain.

The Apennines (C 4)
This mountain range forms the 'backbone' of Italy, dividing the rocky west coast from the flatter, sandy east coast.

Earthquakes
The southern Apennines, as well as coastal areas of southwestern Italy, often experience earthquakes and mudslides.

Tyrrhenian Sea (C 6)
This sea, which divides the Italian mainland from Sardinia, is gradually filling with sediment from the rivers which flow into it.

Sardinia
The island of Sardinia is made from very old rocks which were thrust up to form mountains.

Sicily
Sicily is the largest island in the Mediterranean. It has a famous active volcano called Mount Etna, and often experiences earthquakes

Gulf of Taranto (F 7)
During earthquakes, great blocks of land have broken away and sunk into the sea, forming the Gulf's square shape.

FARMING AND LAND USE

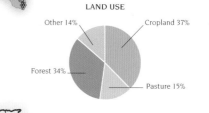

The Po Valley is a broad, flat plain in the north of Italy. It contains the most fertile land in the country, and wheat and rice are the main cereal crops grown here. Grapes for wine are grown everywhere in Italy. In much of the south, the land must be irrigated to support crops. Where there is enough water, citrus fruits, olives, and many kinds of tomatoes are grown.

LAND USE

Other 14%
Cropland 37%
Forest 34%
Pasture 15%

FARMING AND LAND USE

- Cattle
- Pigs
- Sheep
- Cereals
- Citrus fruits
- Olive oil
- Rice
- Vineyards
- Pasture
- Cropland
- Forest
- Mountain region
- Major conurbation

INDUSTRY

Italian industry is located mainly in the north. Design is extremely important to Italians and they are proud of the elegant designs of their furniture, clothes and shoes. Though many firms are small, they are very efficient. Italy has few mineral resources so it needs to import raw materials to make cars, engines and other hi-tech products.

INDUSTRY

- Car manufacture
- Chemicals
- Iron & steel
- Textiles
- Finance
- Hi-tech industry
- Tourism
- Major industrial centre / area
- Major road

STRUCTURE OF INDUSTRY

Primary 3%
Services 66%
Manufacturing 31%

POPULATION

Most of Italy's population lives in the north, mainly in and around the Po Valley, which is home to over 25 million people. Most people here have a high standard of living. Southern Italy is much more rural; towns are smaller and life is often much harder.

URBAN/RURAL POPULATION DIVIDE

Milan 2.2%
Rome 4.4%
Naples 1.7%
Rural population 33%
Other towns and cities 58.7%

INHABITANTS PER SQ KM

- More than 200
- 100–200
- 50–100
- 0–50
- Capital city
- Major city

EUROPE

ENVIRONMENTAL ISSUES

Sewage and chemical by-products from industry have polluted the Mediterranean and Adriatic seas. Southern Italy is subject to natural dangers like volcanoes, earthquakes and mudslides. Mount Etna is one of the most active volcanoes in the world.

ENVIRONMENTAL ISSUES

- ◎ Catastrophic earthquakes
- 😷 Urban air pollution
- ▨ Affected by acid rain
- ▨ Sea pollution
- ▨ Severe sea pollution
- ● Major industrial centre

CLIMATE

The Alpine north has cold winters, often with snow. Further south, temperatures are higher. Sicily has Italy's highest temperatures, due to warm African winds.

January

July

TEMPERATURE AND PRECIPITATION

- More than 25°C
- 20 to 25°C
- 15 to 20°C
- 10 to 15°C
- 5 to 10°C
- 0 to 5°C
- 0 to -5°C
- -5 to -10°C
- Less than -10°C

—100— Precipitation (mm)

SCALE BAR

0 km   40   80

0 miles   40   80

CITIES AND TOWNS

- ▣ Over 500,000 people
- ◉ 100,000–500,000
- ○ 50,000–100,000
- ∘ Less than 50,000

LAND HEIGHT

- Above 4000 m
- 2000–4000 m
- 1000–2000 m
- 500–1000 m
- 250–500 m
- 100–250 m
- 0–100 m

SEA DEPTH

- 0–50 m
- 50–100 m
- 100–250 m
- 250–500 m
- 500–1000 m
- 1000–2000 m
- Below 2000 m

103

CENTRAL EUROPE

CZECH REPUBLIC, HUNGARY, POLAND, SLOVAKIA

Central Europe has been invaded many times throughout history. The countries have changed shape frequently as their borders have shifted backwards and forwards. From the end of the Second World War until 1989, they were ruled by communist governments, which were supported by the Soviet Union. In 1993, the state of Czechoslovakia voted to split into two separate nations, called the Czech Republic and Slovakia.

INDUSTRY

Brown coal, or lignite, is central Europe's main fuel, and one of Poland's major exports. A variety of minerals are mined in the mountains of the Czech Republic and Slovakia. Hungary has a wide range of industries producing vehicles, metals, and chemicals, as well as textiles and electrical goods. The Czech Republic is famous for its breweries and glass-making.

STRUCTURE OF INDUSTRY

Primary 3%
Services 65%
Manufacturing 32%

INDUSTRY

- 🜛 Brewing
- 🚗 Car manufacture
- ⚗ Chemicals
- ✦ Engineering
- ▣ Food processing
- ⚒ Iron & steel
- ⛏ Coal mining
- ▣ Major industrial centre / area
- — Major road

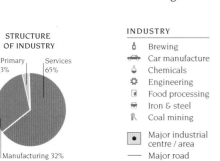

ENVIRONMENTAL ISSUES

The growth of heavy industries that took place under communist rule has caused terrible environmental pollution in some places. Hungary's oil and Poland's brown coal have a high sulphur content. Burning these fuels to produce electricity causes air pollution, and the sulphur dioxide produced combines with moisture in the air, leading to acid rain.

ENVIRONMENTAL ISSUES

- ☁ Severe industrial pollution
- ⌂ Flooding
- 😷 Urban air pollution
- Affected by acid rain
- Polluted rivers
- ● Major industrial centre

FARMING AND LAND USE

Central Europe's main crops are cereals such as maize, wheat and rye, along with sugar beet and potatoes. In Hungary, sweet peppers grow, helped by the warm summers and mild winters. They are used to make paprika. Grapes are also grown, to make wine. Large areas of the plains of Hungary and Poland are used for rearing pigs and cattle. Trees for timber grow in the mountains of Slovakia and the Czech Republic.

FARMING AND LAND USE

- 🐂 Cattle
- 🐖 Pigs
- 🌾 Cereals
- Root crops
- 🥔 Potatoes
- Timber
- Vineyards
- Pasture
- Cropland
- Forest
- ● Major conurbation

LAND USE

Other 11%
Cropland 47%
Forest 29%
Pasture 13%

THE LANDSCAPE

The high Carpathian Mountains sweep across northern Slovakia. The lower Sudeten Mountains lie on the border of the Czech Republic and Poland. Together, these mountains form a barrier which divides the Great Hungarian Plain and the River Danube basin in the south from Poland and the vast rolling lowlands of the North European Plain.

Pomerania (C 2)
This is a sandy coastal area with lakes formed by glaciers. It stretches west from the River Vistula to just beyond the German border.

River Vistula (F 4)
Poland's largest river is the Vistula. It flows northwards, passing through the capital, Warsaw, on its way to the Baltic Sea.

North European Plain

Hot springs
The Sudeten mountains (C5) are famous for their hot mineral springs. These occur where water heated deep within the Earth's crust finds its way to the surface along fractures in the rock.

River Danube (D 7)
The River Danube forms the border between Slovakia and Hungary for over 162 km. It then turns south to flow across the Great Hungarian Plain.

Great Hungarian Plain (E 8)
This huge plain covers almost half of Hungary's land area. It is a mixture of farmland and steppe.

Tatra Mountains (E 6)
The Tatra Mountains are a small range at the northern end of the Carpathian Mountains. They include Gerlachovsky Stít, which is Central Europe's highest point at 2,655 m.

POPULATION

Most people in central Europe live in low-lying areas, for example, along the River Vistula in Poland, and in the lowlands of the Czech Republic. In mountainous Slovakia, many people still live in rural towns and villages. The industrial areas and capital cities have the highest population densities.

URBAN/RURAL POPULATION DIVIDE

Warsaw 2.6%   Budapest 2.7%
Prague 1.7%

Other towns and cities 59%

Rural population 34%

EUROPE
Central Europe

NORTH AMERICA   ASIA
AFRICA
SOUTH AMERICA   AUSTRALASIA AND OCEANIA
ANTARCTICA

INHABITANTS PER SQ KM

- More than 200
- 100–200
- 50–100
- Less than 50
- ■ Capital city
- ● Major city

CLIMATE

The Carpathian Mountains are both the coldest and the wettest part of central Europe. Temperatures plunge below zero across the whole region during winter. In summer, eastern Hungary is the hottest place.

January

July

TEMPERATURE AND PRECIPITATION

- More than 20°C
- 15 to 20°C
- 10 to 15°C
- 5 to 10°C
- 0 to 5°C
- 0 to -5°C
- Less than -5°C
- 100 Precipitation (mm)

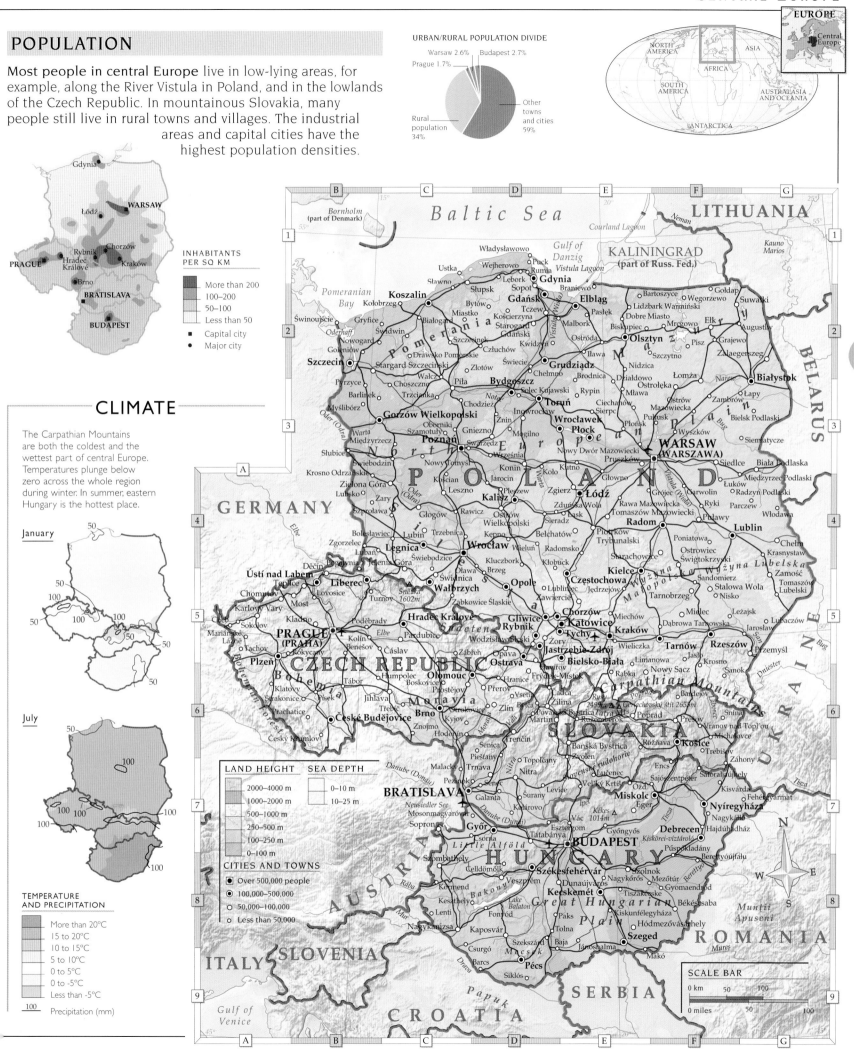

LAND HEIGHT
- 2000–4000 m
- 1000–2000 m
- 500–1000 m
- 250–500 m
- 100–250 m
- 0–100 m

SEA DEPTH
- 0–10 m
- 10–25 m

CITIES AND TOWNS
- ● Over 500,000 people
- ◉ 100,000–500,000
- ◎ 50,000–100,000
- ○ Less than 50,000

SCALE BAR

0 km   50   100
0 miles   50   100

SOUTHEAST EUROPE

ALBANIA, BOSNIA AND HERZEGOVINA, BULGARIA, CROATIA, GREECE, KOSOVO, MACEDONIA, MONTENEGRO, SERBIA

Southeast Europe extends inland from the coasts of the Aegean, Adriatic and Black seas. Ancient Greece was the birthplace of European civilization. Albania and Bulgaria were ruled by communists for over 50 years, until the early 1990s. The rest of the region was part of a communist union of states called Yugoslavia. The collapse of this union in 1991 led to a civil war, after which seven separate countries emerged.

THE LANDSCAPE

Southeast Europe is largely mountainous, with ranges running from northwest to southeast. The Dinaric Alps run parallel to the Dalmatian coast, and the Pindus Mountains continue this line into Greece. In the Aegean Sea, the drowned peaks of an old mountain chain form thousands of islands.

Earthquakes
Bulgaria, Greece, and Macedonia lie in earthquake zones. Major earthquakes have hit the Ionian Islands in 1953, and Macedonia in 1963.

Great Hungarian Plain (D 1)
The Vojvodina region of Serbia is the southern part of the Great Hungarian Plain. The plain is flat and fertile soils allow grain crops like corn and wheat to be grown.

Dinaric Alps (C 2)

Balkan Mountains (F 3)
The mountains form a spur running east to west through Bulgaria and separate the two main rivers, the Danube and the Maritsa.

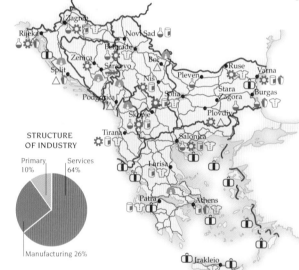

STRUCTURE OF INDUSTRY
Primary 10%
Services 64%
Manufacturing 26%

Dalmatian coast (B 2)
The Dalmatian coast has many long, narrow islands near the shore. These were formed as the Adriatic Sea flooded the river valleys which ran parallel to the coast.

Greek Islands

The Peloponnese (E 6)
The Peloponnese is a mountainous peninsula linked to the Greek mainland only by a narrow strip of land, only 6 km wide, called the Isthmus of Corinth.

Greek Islands
There are two groups of Greek Islands, the Ionian Islands to the west of mainland Greece, and the more numerous islands to the east in the Aegean Sea.

FARMING AND LAND USE

Cereals like wheat, and fruits, vegetables and grapes are grown in the fertile north of the region. The band of mountains across southeast Europe is used mainly for grazing sheep and goats. Further south, and in coastal areas, the warm Mediterranean climate is ideal for growing grapes, olives and tobacco.

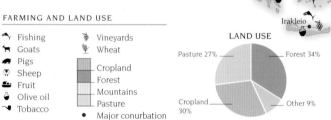

FARMING AND LAND USE

- Fishing
- Goats
- Pigs
- Sheep
- Fruit
- Olive oil
- Tobacco
- Vineyards
- Wheat
- Cropland
- Forest
- Mountains
- Pasture
- Major conurbation

LAND USE

Pasture 27%
Forest 34%
Cropland 30%
Other 9%

INDUSTRY

Mainland Greece and the many islands in the Aegean Sea are centres of a thriving tourist trade, while tourism on the Black Sea coast continues to grow. The Dalmatian coast's growing tourist industry is recovering after the civil war in former Yugoslavia disrupted it, and other industries. Heavy industries like chemicals, engineering and shipbuilding remain an important source of income in Bulgaria.

INDUSTRY

- Car manufacture
- Chemicals
- Engineering
- Food processing
- Metal refining
- Shipbuilding
- Textiles
- Mining
- Tourism
- Major industrial centre / area
- Major road

POPULATION

Greece's population is two thirds urban; over 35% live in the capital, Athens and in Salonica. In Bulgaria, most people live in cities. About half of Albania's and Macedonia's people are still rural. Since the civil war, the different ethnic groups in Bosnia and Herzegovina, Montenegro, Serbia and Croatia have lived apart from one another.

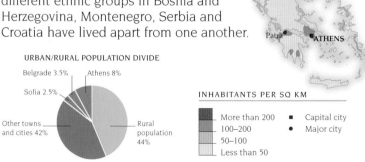

URBAN/RURAL POPULATION DIVIDE
Belgrade 3.5%
Athens 8%
Sofia 2.5%
Other towns and cities 42%
Rural population 44%

INHABITANTS PER SQ KM
- More than 200
- 100–200
- 50–100
- Less than 50
- Capital city
- Major city

CLIMATE

Southeastern Europe's climate varies from north to south. Continental climates are found in the north; winters are cold and dry, while towards the south, winters are milder and summers much hotter. Europe's wettest place is found in the mountains in Bosnia and Herzegovina.

January

July

TEMPERATURE AND PRECIPITATION

More than 25°C
20 to 25°C
15 to 20°C
10 to 15°C
5 to 10°C
0 to 5°C
0 to -5°C
Less than -5°C

100 Precipitation (mm)

EUROPE

NORTH AMERICA
SOUTH AMERICA
ASIA
AFRICA
AUSTRALASIA AND OCEANIA
ANTARCTICA

Southeast Europe

SCALE BAR

0 km   50   100
0 miles   50   100

CITIES AND TOWNS

⦾ Over 500,000 people
⊙ 100,000–500,000
○ 50,000–100,000
· Less than 50,000

ENVIRONMENTAL ISSUES

Emissions from industry and traffic fumes have polluted the air in Athens and Zagreb. In Athens, smog from vehicle exhausts can be severe as it gets trapped in the city's natural basin. The situation is made worse because many residents drive, rather than use public transport. Earthquakes are possible; Macedonia's capital city, Skopje, was badly hit in 1963.

Zagreb
Belgrade
Danube
Skopje 1963
Sofia
Salonica 1978
Athens

ENVIRONMENTAL ISSUES

◉ Catastrophic earthquake
👥 Urban air pollution
✠ Risk of wild fire
  Sea pollution
  Severe sea pollution
  Polluted river
· Major town

LAND HEIGHT

2000–4000 m
1000–2000 m
500–1000 m
250–500 m
100–250 m
0–100 m

SEA DEPTH

0–50 m
50–100 m
100–250 m
250–500 m
500–1000 m
1000–2000 m
Below 2000 m

EASTERN EUROPE

BELARUS, MOLDOVA, ROMANIA, UKRAINE

Much of Eastern Europe, which extends north from the River Danube and the Black Sea, is covered by open grasslands called steppe. Ukraine, Moldova and Belarus were all part of the former Soviet Union, until they became independent in 1991. Romania joined the European Union in 2007. In 2014, Russia drew international condemnation for annexing the Ukrainian territory of Crimea.

INDUSTRY

In Ukraine, most industry is based around the country's mineral reserves. The Donbass region has Europe's largest coalfield and is an important centre for iron and steel production. Belarus's main industries are chemicals, machine building and food-processing. Romania's manufacturing industries are growing, with the help of foreign investment.

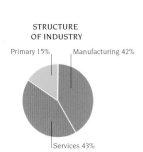

STRUCTURE OF INDUSTRY
Primary 15%
Manufacturing 42%
Services 43%

INDUSTRY
- ✈ Aerospace
- 🚗 Car manufacture
- ♨ Chemicals
- ⚙ Engineering
- Food processing
- Iron & steel
- 👕 Textiles
- Coal
- Mining
- Oil and gas
- 🛆 Tourism
- ⊡ Major industrial centre / area
- — Major road

FARMING AND LAND USE

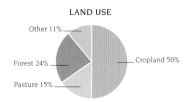

The black soils found across much of Ukraine are very fertile and the country is a big producer of cereals, sugar beet, and sunflowers, which are grown for their oil. In Moldova and southern Romania, the warm summers are ideal for growing grapes for wine, along with sunflowers and a variety of vegetables. Cattle and pigs are farmed throughout Eastern Europe.

LAND USE
Other 11%
Forest 24%
Pasture 15%
Cropland 50%

FARMING AND LAND USE
- 🐄 Cattle
- 🐖 Pigs
- 🐑 Sheep
- Root crops
- Sunflowers
- Vineyards
- Wheat
- Cropland
- Forest
- Pasture
- Wetland
- • Major conurbation

POPULATION

Many Romanians still live in rural areas, although Bucharest, the capital, is home to six times as many people as the next largest city. In Ukraine, two-thirds of the population live in cities such as those in the Donbass industrial area. Most of Belarus's people are city dwellers. Moldova is the most rural country in Eastern Europe; over half live in the countryside.

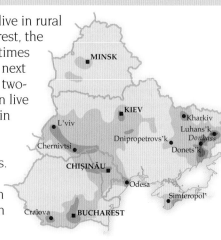

URBAN/RURAL POPULATION DIVIDE
Bucharest 2.3% Kiev 3.1%
Minsk 2.1%
Rural population 36%
Other towns and cities 56.5%

INHABITANTS PER SQ KM
- More than 200
- 100–200
- 50–100
- Less than 50
- ■ Capital city
- • Major city

THE LANDSCAPE

Flat or rolling grasslands, marshes and river flood plains cover almost all of Ukraine and Belarus. The Carpathian Mountains cross the southwestern corner of Ukraine and continue in a large arc-shaped chain of high peaks at the heart of Romania. Along the southern part of this chain, the Carpathians are called the Transylvanian Alps.

Pripet Marshes (C 3)
The Pripet Marshes in Belarus and Ukraine form the largest area of marshland in Europe.

The steppes
The steppes are great, wide grasslands which are found across eastern Europe and central Asia. Over 70% of the Ukrainian landscape is steppe. Little rain falls throughout the steppes.

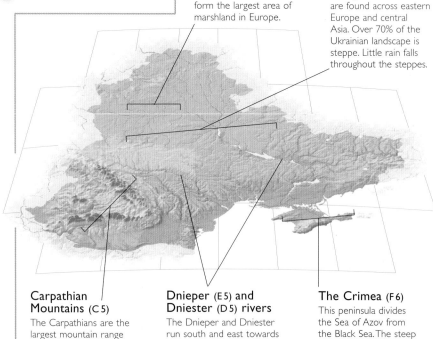

Carpathian Mountains (C 5)
The Carpathians are the largest mountain range in Eastern Europe. They are a rich source of timber and minerals.

Dnieper (E 5) and Dniester (D 5) rivers
The Dnieper and Dniester run south and east towards the Black Sea. They flow slowly across huge areas of low-lying land.

The Crimea (F 6)
This peninsula divides the Sea of Azov from the Black Sea. The steep mountains of Kryms'ki Hory run along the southeastern coast of the Crimea.

CLIMATE

January

July

The climate is continental, with warm, dry summers and very cold, dry winters. Temperatures are higher along the fringes of the Black Sea, while the Carpathian Mountains are colder and wetter all year round.

EUROPE
Eastern Europe

NORTH AMERICA
SOUTH AMERICA
AFRICA
ASIA
AUSTRALASIA AND OCEANIA
ANTARCTICA

TEMPERATURE AND PRECIPITATION

More than 20°C
15 to 20°C
10 to 15°C
5 to 10°C
0 to 5°C
0 to -5°C
Less than -5°C

100 Precipitation (mm)

Less than 50

50

Less than 50

50

50

50

50

50

100

100

50

50

100

ENVIRONMENTAL ISSUES

The worst nuclear accident in history happened at Chornobyl' nuclear power station in northern Ukraine in 1986. Around 70% of the nuclear fallout was received by Belarus, contaminating its farmland, forests and water supplies. Four million Ukrainians still live in dangerously radioactive areas.

ENVIRONMENTAL ISSUES

Destroyed nuclear reactor
Levels of nuclear fallout
Very high
High
Moderate
Urban air pollution
Flooding
Polluted river
Sea pollution
Major industrial centre

Minsk
Chornobyl' Kiev Kharkiv
Dnipropetrovs'k Donets'k
Dnieper
Arad Târgu Mures Volganeft-139 2007
2005
Bucharest

LAND HEIGHT

2000–4000 m
1000–2000 m
500–1000 m
250–500 m
100–250 m
0–100 m

SEA DEPTH

0–50 m
50–100 m
100–250 m
250–500 m
500–1000 m
1000–2000 m
Below 2000 m

CITIES AND TOWNS

Over 500,000 people
100,000–500,000
50,000–100,000
Less than 50,000

LATVIA

LITHUANIA

RUSSIAN FEDERATION

Bihosava
Drysa
Navapolatsk/Novopolotsk
Polatsk/Polotsk
Haradok
Vitsyebsk/Vitebsk
Western Dvina
Bacheykava
Hlybokaye
Lyepyel'
Bahushewsk
Chashniki
Myadzyel
Dnieper
Orsha
Barysaw/Borisov
Horki
Maladzyechna
Zhodzina
MINSK
Mahilyow/Mogilev
Lida
Minskaya Wzvyshsha
Byarezina
Kastsyukovichy
Shchuchyn
Asipovichy
Hrodna/Grodno
Vawkavysk
BELARUS
Babruysk/Bobruysk
Zhlobin
Baranavichy/Baranovichi
Slutsk
Svyetlahorsk/Svetlogorsk
Byelaruskaye Hrada
Salihorsk
Drahichyn
Yasyel'da
Luninyets
Homyel'/Gomel
Pinsk
Mazyr
Psich
Brest
Kobryn
Pripet
Pripet
Marshes
Narowlya
Makrany
Bug
Pripet
Horyn
Shchors
Chornobyl'
Mukhuv
POLAND
Kovel'
Styr
Sarny
Sluch
Olevs'k
Korosten
Kiev Reservoir
Chernihiv
Konotop
RUSSIAN FEDERATION
Volodymyr-Volyns'kyy
Dubno
Luts'k
Rivne
KIEV (KYYIV)
Fastiv
Nizhyn
Romny
Sumy
Okhtyrka
Vistula (Wisła)
Wyżyna Lubelska
Zhovkva
Zhytomyr
Bila Tserkva
Kantsi'ske Vodoskhovyshche
Pryluky
Lubny
Kharkiv
Kup"yans'k
L'viv
UKRAINE
Khmel'nyts'kyy
Dnieper Lowland
Poltava
Starobil's'k
Tatra Mountains
Sambir
Ternopil'
Cherkasy
Kremenchuk
Kreminna
Rubizhne
Stryy
Vinnytsya
Zvenyhorodka
Kremenchuk Reservoir
Slov"yans'k
Kramators'k
Syeverodonets'k
Lysychans'k
Ivano-Frankivs'k
Podil's'ka Vysochyna
Haysyn
Oleksandriya
Dniprodzerzhyns'ke Vodoskhovyshche
Kostyantynivka
Stakhanov
Luhans'k
SLOVAKIA
Uzhhorod
Mukacheve
Kamyanets'-Podil's'kyy
Uman
Novomoskovs'k
Pavlohrad
Horlivka
Khust
Chernivtsi
Pervomays'k
Dniprodzerzhyns'k
Dnipropetrovs'k
Krasnyy Luch
Hora Hoverla 2061m
Dniester
Transnistria
Kotovs'k
Kirovohrad
Zhovti Vody
Donets'k
Makiyivka
HUNGARY
Satu Mare
Botoșani
Bălți
Novyy Buh
Kryvyy Rih
Zaporizhzhya
Volnovakha
Pridniprovs'k Buh
Nikopol'
Orikhiv
Novoazovs'k
Baia Mare
Suceava
Iași
MOLDOVA
Dniprorudne
Mariupol'
Gulf of Taganrog
Yeya
Zalău
Bistrița
Piatra Neamț
Roman
CHIŞINĂU
Mykolayiv
Berdyans'k
Great Hungarian Plain
Oradea
Transylvania
Cluj-Napoca
Târgu Mureş
Turda
Bacău
Vaslui
Tighina (Bendery)
Tiraspol
Melitopol'
Sea of Azov
Muntii Apuseni
Bârlad
Kherson
Heniches'k
RUSSIAN FEDERATION
Arad
ROMANIA
Alba Iulia
Medias
Miercurea-Ciuc
Sfântu Gheorghe
Focșani
Basarabeasca
Kakhovs'ke Vodoskhovyshche
Dniprorudne
Armyans'k
Timișoara
Hunedoara
Deva
Sibiu
Brașov
Buzău
Galați
Camu
Artsyz
Lacul Shahany
Illichivs'k
Dzhankoy
Kerch
Kuban'
Lugoj
Vârful 2544m
Reșița
Transylvanian Alps
Brăila
Izmayil
Karkinits'ka Zatoka
Zatoka Syvash
Mureș
Târgu Jiu
Râmnicu Vâlcea
Pitești
Ploiești
Târgoviște
Tulcea
Lacul Razim
Crimea
Yevpatoriya
Simferopol'
Feodosiya
Kerch Strait
Caucasus
Drobeta-Turnu Severin
Strehaia
Slatina
Wallachia
Lacul Sinoie
Sevastopol'
Krym. Hory
Yalta
(annexed by Russia, 2014)
SERBIA
Craiova
Caracal
BUCHAREST (BUCUREŞTI)
Giurgiu
Constanța
Danube (Dunărea)
Ialomița
Black Sea
GEORGIA
Veliki Morava
Danube (Dunăre)
Olt
BULGARIA

N
W E
S

SCALE BAR

0 km 50 100
0 miles 50 100

EUROPEAN RUSSIA

RUSSIAN FEDERATION

European Russia is separated from the Asiatic part of the Russian Federation by the Ural Mountains. It is home to two-thirds of the country's population. Russia was the largest and most powerful republic of the communist Soviet Union, which collapsed in 1991. Though new businesses were set up when communism ended, many old state industries closed down, causing unemployment and further hardship for many people.

INDUSTRY

European Russia is rich in natural resources. Minerals are mined on the Kola Peninsula, and in the Urals, while dense forests are felled and processed in many of the larger northern cities. The Volga basin is one of Europe's largest sources of oil and gas. Moscow, and the cities near the Volga are centres of skilled labour for a wide range of manufacturing industries like cars, chemicals and heavy engineering and steel production.

INDUSTRY

🚗	Car manufacture	⬧	Oil & gas
🧴	Chemicals	🔥	Timber processing
⚙	Engineering	▣	Major industrial centre/area
🚂	Iron & steel	—	Major road
👕	Textiles		
⛏	Mining		

FARMING AND LAND USE

Russia's best farmland lies within this region. Big crops of wheat, barley and oats, potatoes and sunflowers are produced in the fertile black soil which forms a thick band across the country to the south of Moscow. The far north is cold and frozen, with bare mountains and tundra making cultivation impossible. Further south there are extensive forests, and rough pastures used for herding and hunting.

FARMING AND LAND USE

🐄	Cattle		Barren land
🎣	Fishing		Cropland
🐖	Pigs		Forest
🦌	Reindeer		Mountain region
🐑	Sheep		Pasture
🌾	Cereals		Tundra
🌱	Root crops		Wetland
🌻	Sunflowers	•	Major conurbation
🌲	Timber		

POPULATION

Three-quarters of European Russia's people live in towns and cities, most in a broad band stretching south from Saint Petersburg to Moscow, and eastwards to the Urals. The capital, Moscow, and Saint Petersburg are very crowded cities. Living conditions there are cramped, with two families often sharing one flat. The southeast is also heavily populated. Over 12 million people live in the cities and towns which line the banks of the River Volga.

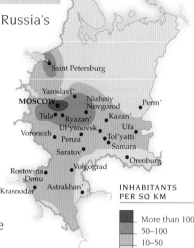

INHABITANTS PER SQ KM

▨	More than 100
▨	50–100
▨	10–50
▨	Less than 10
■	Capital city
●	Major city

THE LANDSCAPE

European Russia lies on the North European Plain, a huge, rolling lowland with wide river basins. The northern half of the plain, which was once covered by glaciers, has many lakes and swamps. The River Volga drains much of the plain as it flows south to the Caspian Sea. The Caucasus and Ural mountains form natural boundaries in the south and east.

Northern European Russia (C 3)
Northern European Russia reaches into the Arctic Circle. It is a region of pine and birch forests, marshes and tundra. There are also tens of thousands of lakes, including the biggest in Europe, Ladoga, which covers about 17,700 sq km.

Ural Mountains (E 5)
The Ural Mountains run from north to south, stretching almost 4,020 km.

Lake Ladoga (B 4)

Valdai Hills (A 5)
The Valdai Hills are a high, swampy region of the North European Plain. Two of Europe's biggest rivers, the Volga and the Western Dvina, have their sources here.

Caucasus (A 9)
This massive barrier of mountains stretches from the Black Sea to the Caspian Sea. It includes El'brus, the highest peak in Europe, at 5,642 m.

Caspian Sea (C 9)

River Volga (C 7)
The River Volga flows for 3,688 km, making it Europe's longest river and Russia's most important inland waterway. It is used for transport and to generate hydro-electric power.

The North European Plain (C 4)
The North European Plain sweeps west from the Ural Mountains, all the way to the River Rhine in Germany. In European Russia it includes a number of hill ranges, such as the Volga Uplands and the Central Russian Upland.

ENVIRONMENTAL ISSUES

The many factories in European Russia have caused widespread pollution, Dzerzhinsk is said to be the most polluted town on earth. Several of Russia's older nuclear power stations have been declared unsafe, but are yet to be shut down. Waste from these power stations, as well as from nuclear submarines, has for many years been dumped in the Barents Sea and off Novaya Zemlya.

ENVIRONMENTAL ISSUES

- Nuclear waste dump site
- Nuclear power station
- Urban air pollution
- Polluted rivers
- Sea pollution
- • Major industrial centre

CLIMATE

Winters are extremely cold and dry; temperatures plunge well below zero in the north and east. Summer brings much warmer and wetter weather, especially in the south, while along the northern coast, it remains relatively cold. Rainfall is highest in the Caucasus.

January

July

TEMPERATURE AND PRECIPITATION

- More than 20°C
- 15 to 20°C
- 10 to 15°C
- 5 to 10°C
- 0 to 5°C
- 0 to -5°C
- -5 to -10°C
- -10 to -15°C
- Less than -15°C

100 — Precipitation (mm)

CITIES AND TOWNS
- ■ Over 500,000 people
- ● 100,000–500,000
- ○ 50,000–100,000
- ○ Less than 50,000

LAND HEIGHT / SEA DEPTH

LAND HEIGHT	SEA DEPTH
Above 4000 m	0–50 m
2000–4000 m	50–100 m
1000–2000 m	100–250 m
500–1000 m	250–500 m
250–500 m	500–1000 m
100–250 m	1000–2000 m
0–100 m	Below 2000 m
Below sea level	

SCALE BAR

0 km 100 200

0 miles 100 200

THE MEDITERRANEAN

The Mediterranean Sea separates Europe from Africa. It stretches more than 4,000 km from east to west and is almost completely enclosed by land. Many great civilizations, including the Greek and Roman empires grew up around the Mediterranean. It has been a crossroads of international trade routes for many centuries. More than 100 million people live in the 28 countries which border the sea and their numbers are increased by the large crowds of tourists who regularly visit the area.

ENVIRONMENTAL ISSUES

Sea pollution is widespread in the Mediterranean, especially near the large coastal resorts where raw sewage and industrial effluent is pumped out to sea and often ends up on the beaches. Oil refining and oil spills have also furthered pollution.

ENVIRONMENTAL
ISSUES

⬭ Oil spill

◻ Mild sea pollution
◼ Severe sea pollution

THE LANDSCAPE

The Mediterranean Sea would be an enormous lake if it were not for the Strait of Gibraltar, a narrow opening only 13 km wide, which joins it to the Atlantic Ocean. The Mediterranean lies over the boundary of two continental plates. Where they meet, earthquakes and volcanoes are common.

Strait of Gibraltar

Sandy beaches
The Mediterranean coasts are bordered by several thousand miles of sandy beaches.

Shallow shelves
The area of sea off the coast of Tunisia and also the Adriatic sea, are shallower than the rest of the Mediterranean.

Greek islands
Greece has thousands of islands which lie both in the Mediterranean and in the smaller Aegean Sea. Some of them are the remains of old volcanoes which have left black sand on the beaches.

Suez Canal
The Suez Canal links the Mediterranean to the Gulf of Suez and the Red Sea. Before it was built, ships had to sail around the whole of Africa to reach Asia.

Atlas Mountains
The rugged Atlas Mountains run through most of Morocco and Algeria. They form a barrier between the Mediterranean coast and the Sahara which lies south of them.

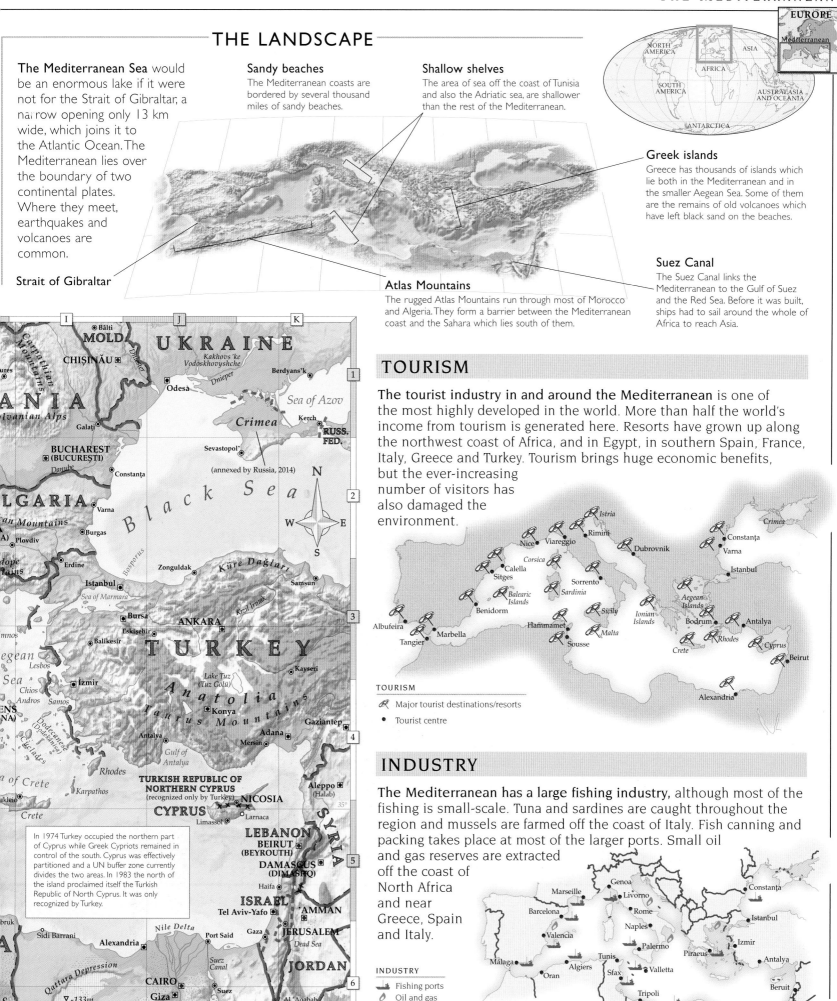

TOURISM

The tourist industry in and around the Mediterranean is one of the most highly developed in the world. More than half the world's income from tourism is generated here. Resorts have grown up along the northwest coast of Africa, and in Egypt, in southern Spain, France, Italy, Greece and Turkey. Tourism brings huge economic benefits, but the ever-increasing number of visitors has also damaged the environment.

TOURISM
- Major tourist destinations/resorts
- Tourist centre

INDUSTRY

The Mediterranean has a large fishing industry, although most of the fishing is small-scale. Tuna and sardines are caught throughout the region and mussels are farmed off the coast of Italy. Fish canning and packing takes place at most of the larger ports. Small oil and gas reserves are extracted off the coast of North Africa and near Greece, Spain and Italy.

INDUSTRY
- Fishing ports
- Oil and gas
- Major city

In 1974 Turkey occupied the northern part of Cyprus while Greek Cypriots remained in control of the south. Cyprus was effectively partitioned and a UN buffer zone currently divides the two areas. In 1983 the north of the island proclaimed itself the Turkish Republic of North Cyprus. It was only recognized by Turkey.

CONTINENTAL ASIA

Asia is the world's largest continent, and has the greatest range of physical extremes. Some of the highest, lowest, and coldest places on Earth are found in Asia: Mount Everest in the Himalayas is the highest, the Dead Sea in the west is the lowest, and the frozen wastes of northern Siberia are among the coldest. More people live in Asia than on any other continent – 1.3 billion of them in China, and 1.2 billion in India.

6,500 km

9,700 km

CROSS-SECTION THROUGH ASIA

Persian Gulf   Iranian   Plateau of Tibet   Yellow River
Arabian   Plateau   Mouth of   Taiwan
Peninsula   Himalayas   the Ganges

W   7,800 km   E

The Arabian Peninsula and the mountainous Iranian Plateau are divided by the Persian Gulf, fed by the Tigris and Euphrates rivers. Further east, the land begins to rise, the mountains spreading north to the Plateau of Tibet, and south to the Himalayas. The plains to the south of the Himalayas are drained by the Indus and Ganges, and to the east of the Plateau of Tibet by the Yellow River.

PHYSICAL ASIA

Northern Asia is made up of old mountains and ancient, stable plateaus. The jagged Himalayan mountains dominate the central part of the continent, along with the Plateau of Tibet, which stretches north into China. In Southeast Asia, there are many islands. Volcanoes and earthquakes are common, and some of the islands are volcanically-formed.

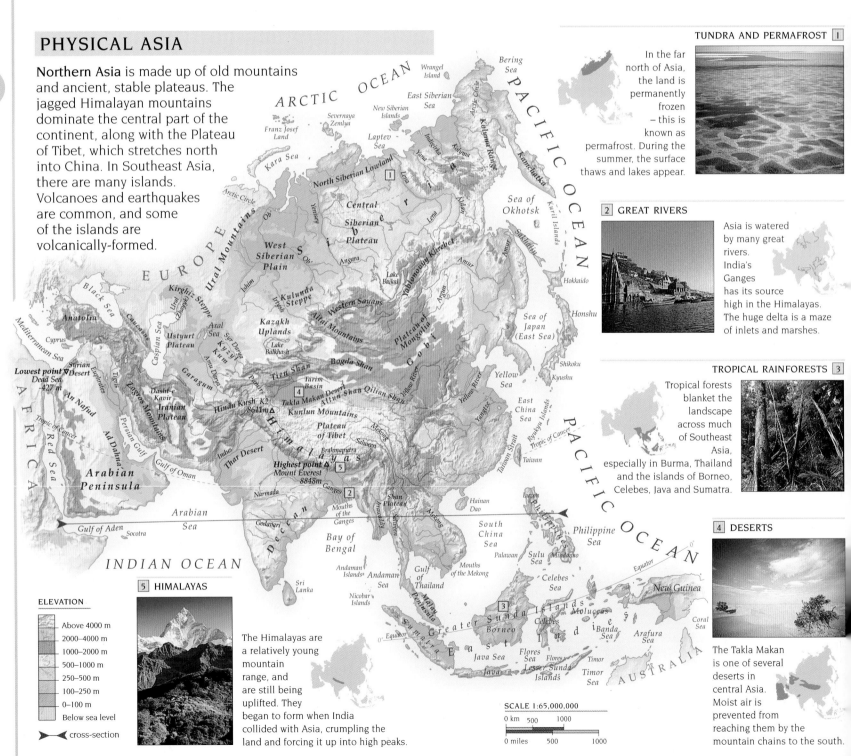

TUNDRA AND PERMAFROST   1

In the far north of Asia, the land is permanently frozen – this is known as permafrost. During the summer, the surface thaws and lakes appear.

2   GREAT RIVERS

Asia is watered by many great rivers. India's Ganges has its source high in the Himalayas. The huge delta is a maze of inlets and marshes.

TROPICAL RAINFORESTS   3

Tropical forests blanket the landscape across much of Southeast Asia, especially in Burma, Thailand and the islands of Borneo, Celebes, Java and Sumatra.

4   DESERTS

The Takla Makan is one of several deserts in central Asia. Moist air is prevented from reaching them by the mountain chains to the south.

5   HIMALAYAS

ELEVATION

- Above 4000 m
- 2000–4000 m
- 1000–2000 m
- 500–1000 m
- 250–500 m
- 100–250 m
- 0–100 m
- Below sea level

cross-section

The Himalayas are a relatively young mountain range, and are still being uplifted. They began to form when India collided with Asia, crumpling the land and forcing it up into high peaks.

SCALE 1:65,000,000

0 km   500   1000

0 miles   500   1000

POLITICAL ASIA

Asia is a continent of many contrasts: in its lands, its peoples and its traditions. The break up of the Soviet Union, which once stretched south from Russia to Iran, produced the new central Asian republics of Kazakhstan, Kyrgyzstan, Tajikistan, Turkmenistan and Uzbekistan. The countries in southwest Asia are mainly Muslim, and include monarchies, republics and theocracies. India is the world's largest democracy, while China is a communist power regaining its economic influence in the world.

POPULATION

Capital cities	● 50,000 to 100,000
◙ Above 500,000	• Below 50,000
◎ 100,000 to 500,000	

COMMUNISM

China and North Korea have been governed by strict communist governments since the late 1940s.
In 1991, people in the Soviet Union rejected communism, and elected the first non-communist government for almost 70 years.

NEW REPUBLICS

Registan Square in Samarqand, Uzbekistan, dates from the 14th century. During the Soviet era, the Islamic faith and culture in Central Asia were actively suppressed.

TERRITORIAL CONFLICT

Territorial conflicts between the Jewish state of Israel and its Arab neighbours have caused continuing unrest since 1948.

SCALE 1:58,000,000

0 km   500   1000

0 miles   500   1000

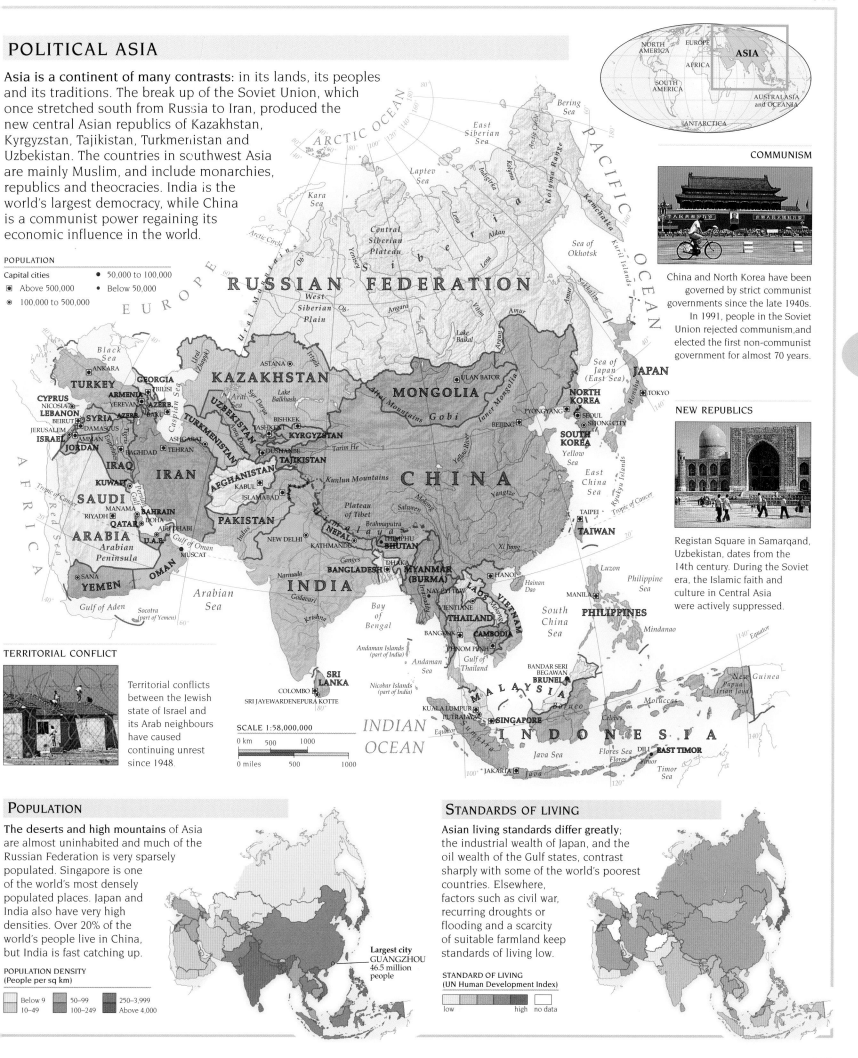

POPULATION

The deserts and high mountains of Asia are almost uninhabited and much of the Russian Federation is very sparsely populated. Singapore is one of the world's most densely populated places. Japan and India also have very high densities. Over 20% of the world's people live in China, but India is fast catching up.

Largest city
GUANGZHOU
46.5 million
people

POPULATION DENSITY
(People per sq km)

Below 9	50–99	250–3,999
10–49	100–249	Above 4,000

STANDARDS OF LIVING

Asian living standards differ greatly; the industrial wealth of Japan, and the oil wealth of the Gulf states, contrast sharply with some of the world's poorest countries. Elsewhere, factors such as civil war, recurring droughts or flooding and a scarcity of suitable farmland keep standards of living low.

STANDARD OF LIVING
(UN Human Development Index)

low   high   no data

Asian Geography

Asia's forbidding mountain ranges, barren deserts, and fertile plains have affected the way in which people settled the continent. Intensive agriculture is found in the more fertile areas, and the largest concentrations of people grew up near fertile land and close to great rivers. Asia's mineral wealth has brought people to the more inhospitable parts of the continent: the deserts of southwest Asia for oil, and frozen Siberia for oil, gas and minerals.

Mineral resources

Over half of the world's oil and gas reserves are in Asia, most importantly around the Persian Gulf and in western Siberia. Coal in Siberia and China has provided power for steel industries. Metallic minerals are also abundant: tin in Southeast Asia, and platinum and nickel in Siberia.

MINERAL RESOURCES

- Chromium
- Tin
- Nickel
- Iron
- Platinum
- Gold
- Lead
- Oil/gas field
- Coal field

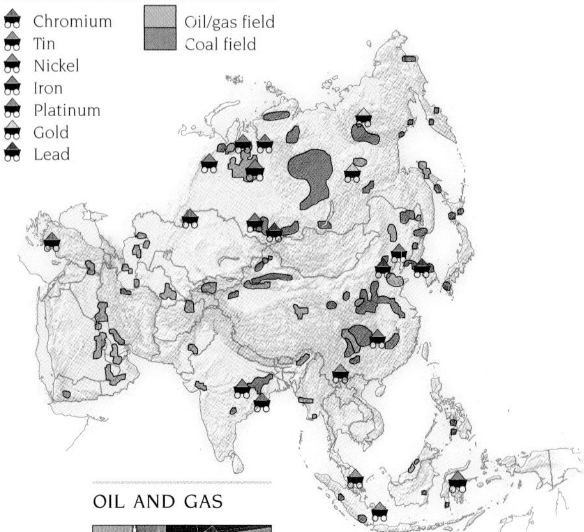

Industry

Many people in Asia still rely on agriculture as a source of income, and some countries have very few industries. Heavy industry dominates eastern China and Russia, but Japan is the most industrially productive country. In recent years, booming 'tiger' economies have developed in countries such as Taiwan, that border the Pacific Ocean.

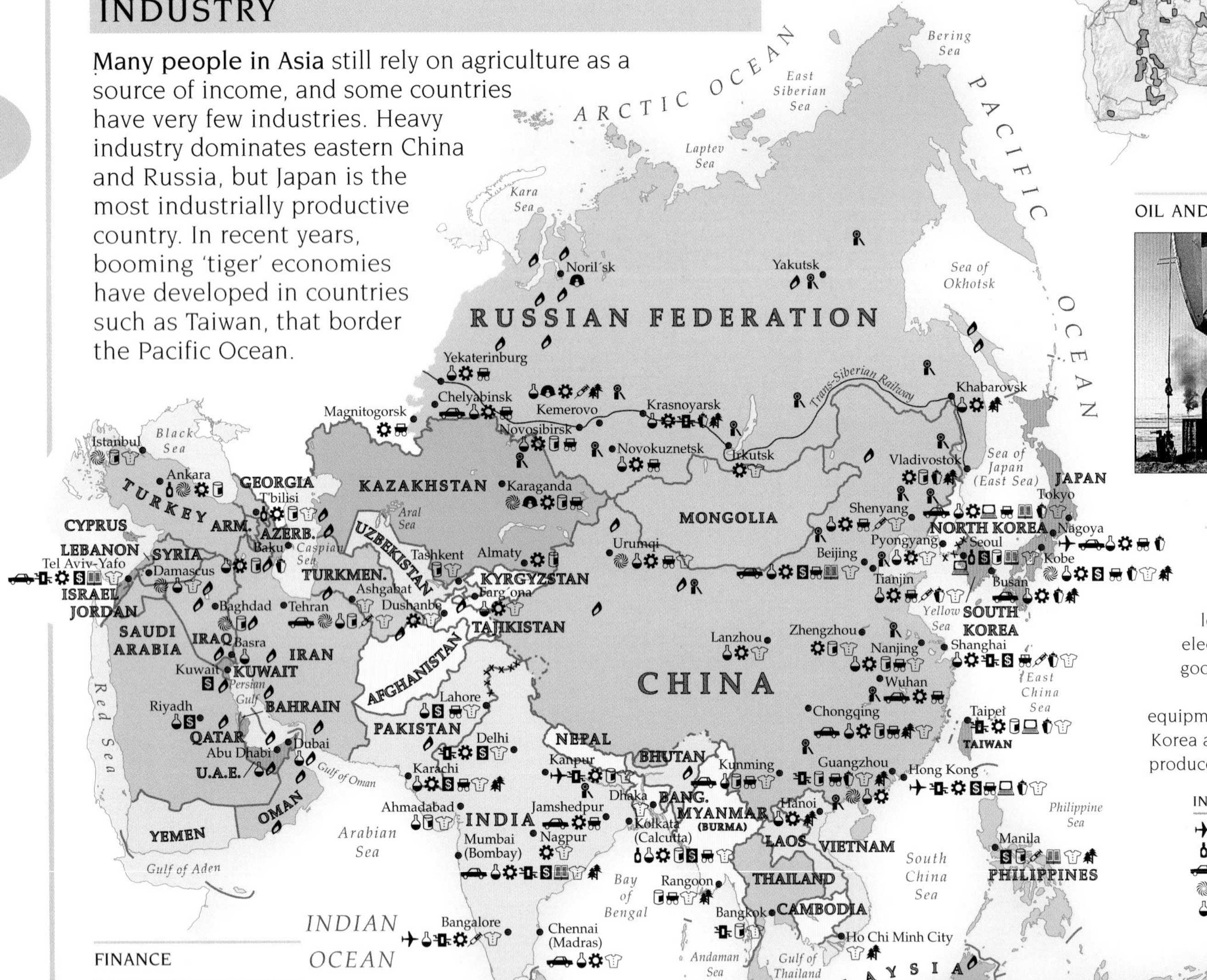

INDUSTRY

- Aerospace
- Brewing
- Car/vehicle manufacture
- Cement
- Chemicals
- Coal
- Electronics
- Engineering
- Finance
- Food processing
- Hi-tech industry
- Iron & steel
- Mining
- Oil & gas
- Pharmaceuticals
- Printing & publishing
- Shipbuilding
- Textiles
- Timber processing

GNI per capita (US$)

- Below 999
- 1,000-1,999
- 2,000-4,999
- 5,000-9,999
- 10,000-19,999
- Above 20,000
- Industrial centre

OIL AND GAS

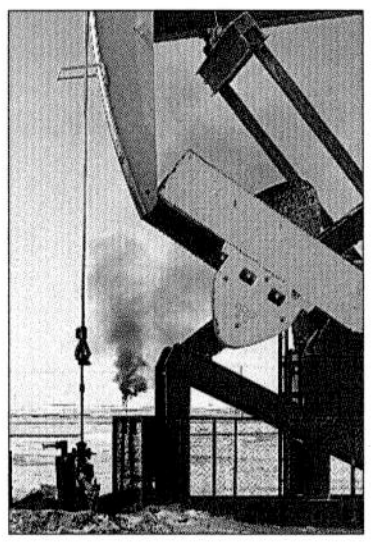

The discovery of oil in The Gulf has generated enormous wealth, and produced rapid industrial and social change in countries such as Saudi Arabia, U.A.E. and Kuwait that control the oil supplies.

HIGH-TECH INDUSTRIES

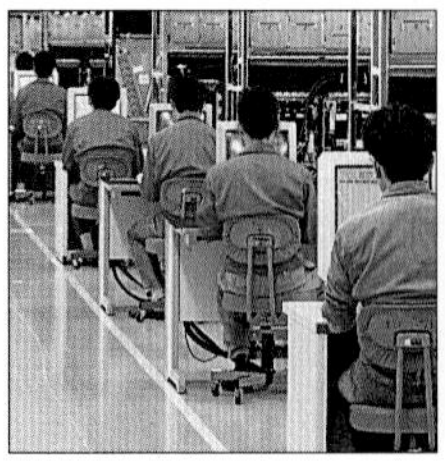

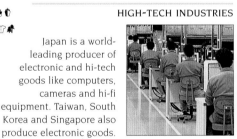

Japan is a world-leading producer of electronic and hi-tech goods like computers, cameras and hi-fi equipment. Taiwan, South Korea and Singapore also produce electronic goods.

FINANCE

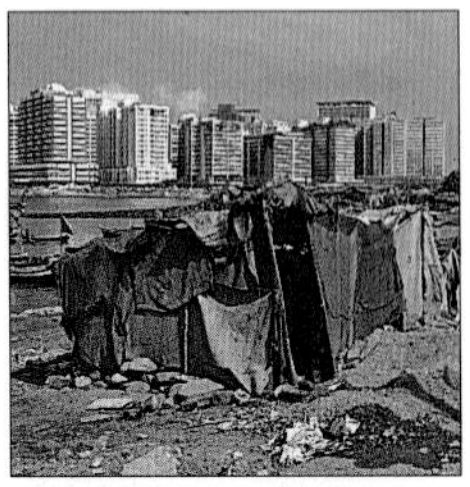

Mumbai (Bombay) is India's leading industrial city and has a thriving stock market. Modern office blocks stand close to sprawling slums.

INDUSTRIAL COMPLEXES

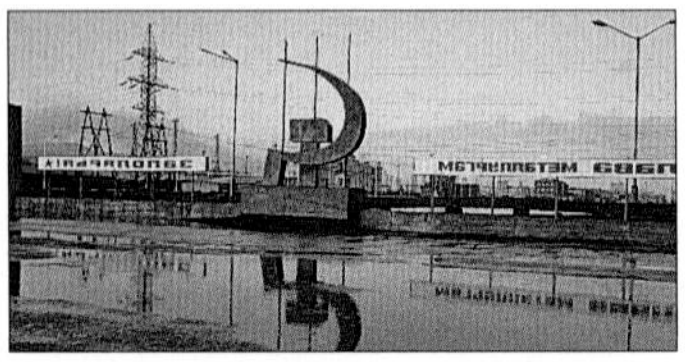

Noril'sk is one of several Soviet-era industrial complexes built in Russia. It is a processing center for the rich mineral reserves found nearby.

TRADITIONAL INDUSTRIES

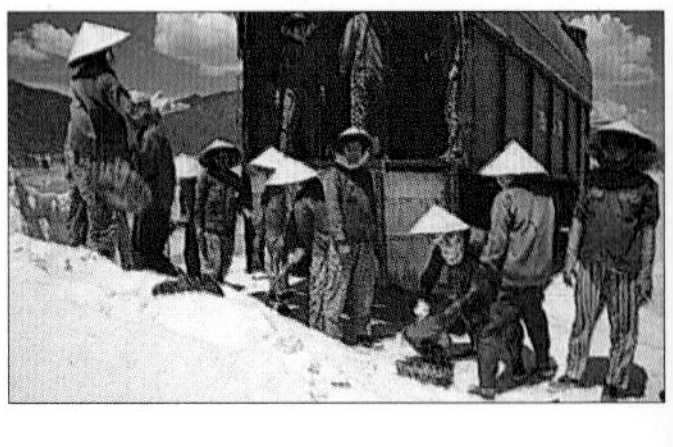

Traditional industries and methods of working are still important to less industrialized nations. Here in Vietnam, seawater has been evaporated by the sun, and the salt is collected for market.

CLIMATE

Most of Asia has a continental climate, apart from coastal areas. Without the moderating effects of the ocean, temperatures can soar during the day and plummet at night, while rainfall is generally low – producing several large deserts. Temperatures as low as –68°C have been recorded in the frozen wastes of Siberia, while the islands in southeast Asia have tropical climates. Southern and eastern Asia are also affected by a seasonal wind called the monsoon. This originates in the Indian Ocean and brings heavy rainfall and high winds, often devastating small coastal and low-lying villages and towns.

Coldest place
VERKHOYANSK (Russ. Fed.)
Temperature -68°C

Hottest place
TIRAT TSVI (Israel)
Temperature 54°C

Driest place
ADEN (Yemen)
Annual rainfall 4.6 cm

Wettest place
CHERRAPUNJI (India)
Annual rainfall 1143cm

CLIMATE

- Tundra
- Subarctic
- Cool continental
- Warm temperate
- Mediterranean
- Semi-arid
- Arid
- Humid equatorial
- Tropical
- Hot humid

EXTREME WEATHER EVENTS

Symbols indicate climatic extremes

RAINFORESTS

The tropical climate across the islands of southeast Asia produces warm, humid conditions in which rainforests flourish. Each island provides a slightly different habitat, so the animals and plants that have evolved on one island may be very different to those on the next.

LAND USE AND AGRICULTURE

Large expanses of Asia are uncultivated because the soil is too poor, or the climate is too cold or dry for crops to grow. The Plateau of Tibet, much of Siberia and the Arabian Peninsula have limited agriculture. Some of the most fertile land is found in eastern China and India, where rice is a staple. Elsewhere, cash crops are grown for profit, such as dates in southwest Asia; rubber in Southeast Asia; tea in India, China and Sri Lanka; and coconuts throughout the island archipelago of Southeast Asia.

LAND USE AND AGRICULTURE

- Cattle
- Goats
- Pigs
- Sheep
- Cereals
- Coconuts
- Corn (maize)
- Cotton
- Dates
- Fishing
- Fruit
- Jute
- Peanuts
- Rice
- Root crops
- Rubber
- Shellfish
- Sugarcane
- Soya beans
- Tea
- Timber

- Mountains
- Cropland
- Desert
- Forest
- Pasture
- Wetland
- ● Major conurbation

RICE

China is the world's largest producer of rice, which is grown in muddy fields called paddy fields. Water buffaloes are used to plough the ground before planting.

COTTON

Uzbekistan is the world's fifth largest producer of cotton. Water has been diverted from nearby rivers to water the crops, which has led to the drying up of the Aral Sea.

DATES

Dates have been cultivated on the Arabian Peninsula since ancient times. They are an important cash crop, grown for export in dry sandy areas where few other crops can grow.

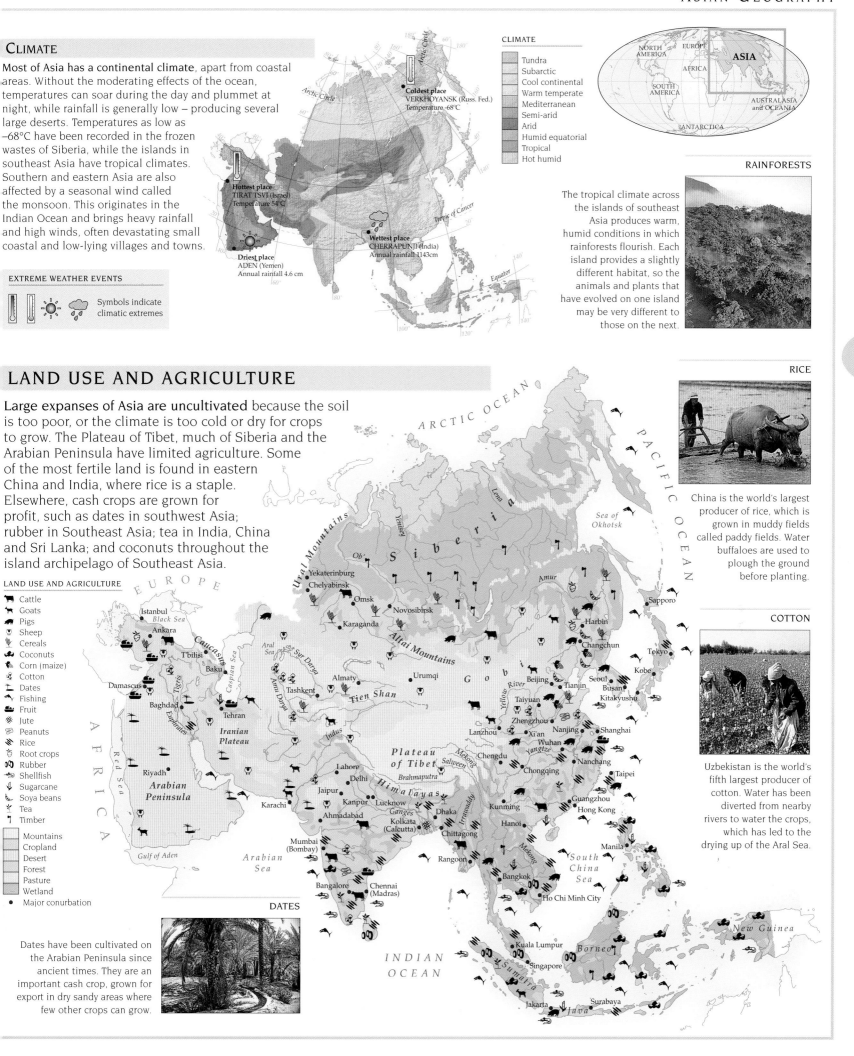

RUSSIA AND KAZAKHSTAN

Russia lies partly in Europe, but mostly in Asia. The land to the east of the Ural Mountains is called Siberia. This immense stretch of grasslands, thick, evergreen forest and tundra is crossed by giant rivers. Vast areas of Siberia are almost untouched by human activity, yet in the industrial regions set up under communism (1922–1991), air, water and soil are heavily polluted with harmful substances. Along with the former Soviet state of Kazakhstan, Siberia is rich in a huge variety of minerals.

INDUSTRY

The discovery of gold in the 19th century opened Siberia up to economic and industrial development. Later, vast reserves of oil, coal and gas were found, especially in the west, which is now the main centre for oil extraction. Gold and diamonds are mined in the east. In Kazakhstan, mining and other industries are growing, with the help of foreign investors.

STRUCTURE OF INDUSTRY

Primary 5%
Services 60%
Manufacturing 35%

INDUSTRY

- Car manufacture
- Chemicals
- Engineering
- Iron & steel
- Textiles
- Diamonds
- Mining
- Oil and gas
- Timber manufacturing
- Major industrial centre / area
- Major road

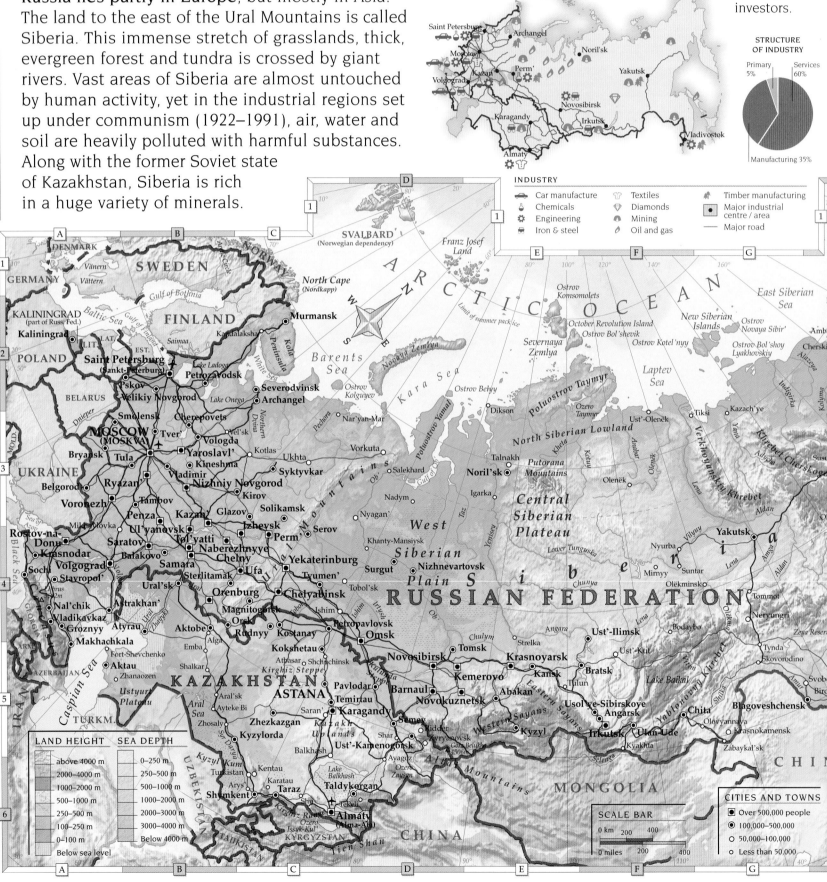

LAND HEIGHT
- above 4000 m
- 2000–4000 m
- 1000–2000 m
- 500–1000 m
- 250–500 m
- 100–250 m
- 0–100 m
- Below sea level

SEA DEPTH
- 0–250 m
- 250–500 m
- 500–1000 m
- 1000–2000 m
- 2000–3000 m
- 3000–4000 m
- Below 4000 m

SCALE BAR
0 km 200 400
0 miles 200 400

CITIES AND TOWNS
- Over 500,000 people
- 100,000–500,000
- 50,000–100,000
- Less than 50,000

THE LANDSCAPE

East of the Ural Mountains lies the West Siberian Plain – the world's biggest area of flat ground. The plain gradually rises to the Central Siberian Plateau, and then again to highlands in the southeast. Great coniferous forests called *taiga* stretch across most of this land. The far north of Siberia extends into the Arctic Circle. There, the landscape is made up of frozen plains called tundra. Much of Kazakhstan is covered by huge rolling grasslands, or steppe; in the south are arid sandy deserts.

Tundra and *taiga*

Stubby birch trees, dwarf bushes, moss and lichen huddle close to the ground in the frozen tundra wastes of northern Russia. They lie between the permanent ice and snow of the Arctic, and the thick *taiga* forests which cover an area greater than the Amazon rainforest.

The Caspian Sea (A 5)

The Caspian Sea covers 371,000 sq km and is the world's largest expanse of inland water. It is fed by the Volga and Ural rivers, which flow in from the plains of the north.

West Siberian Plain (D 4)

This vast, flat expanse is covered with a network of marshes and streams. The Ob' river, which winds its way north across the plains, is frozen for up to half the year.

Lake Baikal (F 5)

Lake Baikal is the deepest lake in the world, and the largest freshwater one – it is more than 1.6 km deep, and covers 32,500 sq km. It is fed by 336 rivers and contains around 20% of all the fresh water in the world.

CLIMATE

Russia and Kazakhstan have strongly continental climates, and their distance away from seas and oceans means that temperatures fluctuate wildly, both daily and seasonally. Temperatures in eastern Siberia have been known to reach -68°C.

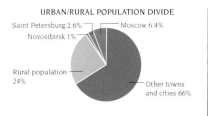

January

July

TEMPERATURE AND PRECIPITATION

- More than 30°C
- 25 to 30°C
- 20 to 25°C
- 15 to 20°C
- 10 to 15°C
- 5 to 10°C
- 0 to 5°C
- 0 to -5°C
- -5 to -10°C
- -10 to -15°C
- Less than -15°C

— 100 — Precipitation (mm)

FARMING AND LAND USE

Siberia's harsh climate has restricted farming to the south, where there are a few areas warm enough to grow cereal crops, such as wheat and oats, and to raise cattle on the small pockets of pasture. The rest of the region is used for hunting, herding reindeer, and forestry – the *taiga* forests contain the world's biggest timber reserves. In Kazakhstan, big herds of cattle, goats and sheep are raised for wool and meat, and wheat is cultivated in the fertile north.

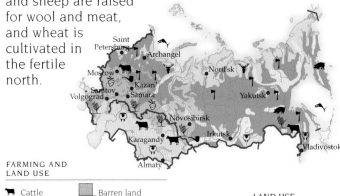

FARMING AND LAND USE

- 🐂 Cattle
- 🐟 Fishing
- 🐷 Pigs
- Reindeer
- 🐑 Sheep
- Root crops
- Timber
- Tobacco
- Wheat

- Barren land
- Cropland
- Desert
- Forest
- Mountains
- Pasture
- Tundra
- Wetland
- ● Major conurbation

LAND USE

Cropland 9%
Pasture 14%
Forest 41%
Other (including mountains) 36%

POPULATION

Siberia has some of the world's largest areas of uninhabited land – the bitingly cold climate and harsh living conditions have kept the population small. The industrial cities in the west hold the most people. Despite its huge size, Kazakhstan has only 16 million people; just over half live in urban areas.

INHABITANTS PER SQ KM

- More than 100
- 50–100
- 10–50
- Less than 10
- ■ Capital city
- ● Major city

URBAN/RURAL POPULATION DIVIDE

Saint Petersburg 2.6%
Moscow 6.4%
Novosibirsk 1%
Rural population 24%
Other towns and cities 66%

ENVIRONMENTAL ISSUES

Decades of industrial development during the communist regime brought new industries to undeveloped parts of the region, like Siberia. This industrial development has now led to environmental degradation on a massive scale and river, air and land pollution in Russia is among the worst in the world.

ENVIRONMENTAL ISSUES

- Urban air pollution
- Polluted rivers
- Sea pollution
- ● Major industrial centre

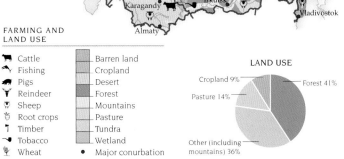

TURKEY AND THE CAUCASUS

ARMENIA, AZERBAIJAN, GEORGIA, TURKEY

Turkey and the Caucasus lie partly in Europe, partly in Asia. Turkey has a long Islamic tradition, and although the country is now a secular (non-religious) one, most Turks are Muslims. Turkey is becoming more industrialized, although one third of its workforce is still employed in agriculture. The countries of the Caucasus were under Russian rule for 70 years, until 1991. They are home to more than 50 different ethnic groups.

INDUSTRY

Turkey has a wide range of industries, including tourism and growing trade links with Europe. Azerbaijan has large oil reserves and is able to export oil. The other states use imported fuel and hydro-electric power generated by their rushing rivers. Georgia produces industrial machinery and chemicals. Armenia's economy is recovering from the conflict with Azerbaijan.

FARMING AND LAND USE

With its warm climate and good soils, Turkey is able to produce all of its own food. Cattle and goats are kept on the central plateau. Along the Mediterranean coast, farmers grow olives, figs, grapes and peaches. Hazelnuts are cultivated along the shores of the Black Sea. Across the Caucasus, the limited fertile land is used to grow wine grapes, tobacco and cotton.

FARMING AND LAND USE

- 🐄 Livestock
- 🐟 Fishing
- ⚘ Cotton
- 🍓 Fruit
- 🌰 Hazelnuts
- 🍠 Root crops
- 🍂 Tobacco
- 🍇 Vineyards

- ▢ Pasture
- ▢ Cropland
- ▢ Forest
- ● Major conurbation

LAND USE

Other 31% — Cropland 34%
Forest 15%
Pasture 20%

INDUSTRY

- 🚗 Car manufacture
- ◎ Cement manufacturing
- 🜇 Chemicals
- ⚙ Engineering
- ▤ Food processing
- 👕 Textiles
- ⚓ Oil field
- ⚓ Tourism
- ▣ Major industrial centre / area
- — Major road

STRUCTURE OF INDUSTRY

Primary 12% — Services 57%
Manufacturing 31%

THE LANDSCAPE

A huge semi-arid plateau called Anatolia runs across the centre of Turkey. It is rimmed by several mountain ranges along the Black Sea coast, and the steep Taurus Mountains in the south. A narrow strip of lowland separates the Caucasus and the Lesser Caucasus mountains in the northeast.

Anatolia
Anatolia has large areas of soft limestone rock. Over a long period of time, layers of rock have been worn away by water to produce strange landscapes with caves, and tall, isolated rock pinnacles.

Caucasus Mountains (H1)

Lesser Caucasus (H2)

Earthquakes
In 1988, 25,000 people were killed in an earthquake in the west of Armenia.

Between two continents
The city of Istanbul (B2) in Turkey is divided in two by a narrow channel of water called the Bosporus. One part of the city is in Europe, the other in Asia. The two parts are linked by bridges.

Taurus Mountains (D5)
The Taurus Mountains were formed around 60 to 65 million years ago. Weathering has formed caves and deep gorges.

Lake Van (H4)
Lake Van is one of the shallow salt lakes found in Anatolia. Salt lakes develop in hot, dry areas where large quantities of water evaporate, leaving behind salty deposits.

POPULATION

Over 75% of Turks live in large towns or cities, mostly in the western half of the country. The eastern and southeastern parts of Anatolia are home to the Kurdish people. The Caucasian republics became more industrialized under Russian rule, and today, two thirds of their people live in urban places.

ENVIRONMENTAL ISSUES

Turkey has built many large dams to use water from rivers – especially the Euphrates – to irrigate its farmland. Syria and Iraq, which lie downstream, have opposed the dams, because they will have less water flowing into their countries. The safety of old-style nuclear plants such as Metsamor in Armenia has caused concern.

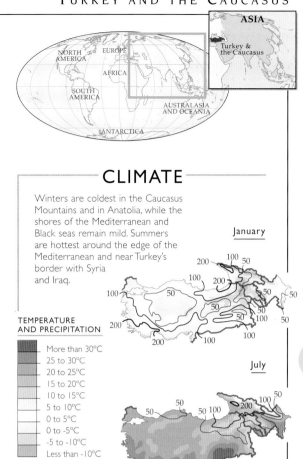

ASIA
Turkey & the Caucasus

CLIMATE

Winters are coldest in the Caucasus Mountains and in Anatolia, while the shores of the Mediterranean and Black seas remain mild. Summers are hottest around the edge of the Mediterranean and near Turkey's border with Syria and Iraq.

January

July

TEMPERATURE AND PRECIPITATION

- More than 30°C
- 25 to 30°C
- 20 to 25°C
- 15 to 20°C
- 10 to 15°C
- 5 to 10°C
- 0 to 5°C
- 0 to -5°C
- -5 to -10°C
- Less than -10°C

100 —— Precipitation (mm)

URBAN/RURAL POPULATION DIVIDE

Istanbul 10%
Ankara 3.7%
Izmir 2.5%
Other towns and cities 55.8%
Rural population 28%

INHABITANTS PER SQ KM

- More than 200
- 100–200
- 50–100
- Less than 50
- ■ Capital city
- ● Major city

ENVIRONMENTAL ISSUES

- ◎ Earthquake zone
- 〰 Major dam
- ⌂ Unstable nuclear power station
- ☻ Urban air pollution
- Sea pollution
- ● Major industrial centre

SCALE BAR

0 km 75 150
0 miles 75 150

CITIES AND TOWNS
- ■ Over 500,000 people
- ◉ 100,000–500,000
- ◎ 50,000–100,000
- ○ Less than 50,000

LAND HEIGHT	SEA DEPTH
Above 4000 m	0–50 m
2000–4000 m	50–100 m
1000–2000 m	100–250 m
500–1000 m	250–500 m
250–500 m	500–1000 m
100–250 m	1000–2000 m
0–100 m	Below 2000 m
Below sea level	

SOUTHWEST ASIA

BAHRAIN, IRAN, IRAQ, ISRAEL, JORDAN, KUWAIT, LEBANON, OMAN, QATAR, SAUDI ARABIA, SYRIA, UNITED ARAB EMIRATES, YEMEN

Most of southwest Asia is barren desert, yet the world's first cities developed here, over 5,000 years ago. It was also the birthplace of three major religions: Islam, Judaism and Christianity. In recent years, the discovery of oil has brought great wealth to much of the region, but it has been torn by internal conflicts and wars between neighbouring countries. Most people here are Muslims, although Israel is the world's only Jewish state.

INDUSTRY

Oil has made the previously poor Arab states very wealthy. Oil and natural gas continue to be the main source of income for many of the countries here, although other industries are being developed to support their economies when these resources run out. Iran is famous for its carpets, which are woven from wool or silk.

INDUSTRY

- ⚙ Cement manufacturing
- 🍴 Food processing
- 🏭 Iron and steel
- 🛢 Oil refining
- 👕 Textiles
- ⬦ Oil and gas
- Ⓢ Finance

- ▪ Major industrial centre / area
- — Major road

STRUCTURE OF INDUSTRY

Primary 10%
Services 49%
Manufacturing 41%

FARMING AND LAND USE

The best farmland is found along the Mediterranean coast, and in the fertile valleys of the Tigris, Euphrates and Jordan rivers. Wheat is the main cereal crop, and cotton, dates, citrus and orchard fruits are grown for export. Elsewhere, modern irrigation techniques have created patches of fertile land in the desert. Dates, wheat and coffee are cultivated in the oases and along the Persian Gulf coast.

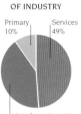
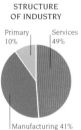

LAND USE

Forest 2%
Pasture 45%
Other (including desert) 47%
Cropland 6%

FARMING AND LAND USE

- 🐐 Goats
- 🎣 Fishing
- 🐑 Sheep
- 🍊 Citrus fruits
- ☕ Coffee
- 🌿 Cotton
- 🌴 Dates
- 🍇 Fruit
- 🍃 Tobacco
- 🌾 Wheat

- ▢ Cropland
- ▢ Desert
- ▢ Forest
- ▢ Pasture
- ▢ Wetland
- • Major conurbation

ENVIRONMENTAL ISSUES

Water shortages are common because of the hot, dry climate and the lack of rivers. Desalination plants convert sea water into fresh water, and are found along the Red Sea and Gulf coasts. Lack of water also makes the risk of desertification greater. Iran has had many catastrophic earthquakes; in 2003 an earthquake in Bam killed 26,000 people.

ENVIRONMENTAL ISSUES

- 🚰 Area with many desalination plants
- ◉ Catastrophic earthquake
- ☠ Urban air pollution

- ▢ Existing desert
- ▢ Risk of desertification
- ▢ Sea pollution
- • Major industrial centre

THE LANDSCAPE

Great desert plateaus, both sandy and rocky, cover much of southwest Asia. On the enormous Arabian Peninsula, which covers an area almost the size of India, narrow, sandy plains along the Red Sea and south coast rise to dry mountains. In the centre is a vast, high plateau that slopes gently down to the flat shores of the Persian Gulf. The mountainous areas of Iran experience frequent earthquakes.

Wadis

Valleys or riverbeds, called *wadis*, are found in the Saudi Arabian desert. Usually they are dry, but after heavy rains, they are briefly filled by fast flowing rivers.

Syrian Desert (B 2)

The Syrian Desert extends from the Jordan valley in the west, to the fertile plains of the Tigris and Euphrates rivers in the east. It is mainly a rocky desert, as the sand has been swept away by winds and occasional heavy rainstorms.

Oases

Oases are areas within a desert where water is available for plants, and human use. They are usually formed when a fault, or split, in the rock allows water to come to the surface. Oases can be no bigger than a few palm trees, or cover several hundred sq km.

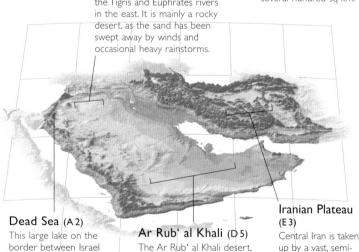

Dead Sea (A 2)

This large lake on the border between Israel and Jordan is the lowest point on the Earth's surface – its shores lie 427 m below sea level. It is also the world's saltiest body of water, and can support no life forms.

Ar Rub' al Khali (D 5)

The Ar Rub' al Khali desert, also known as the 'Empty Quarter', is the largest uninterrupted stretch of sand on Earth. It covers some 650,000 sq km and is one of the world's driest and most hostile deserts.

Iranian Plateau (E 3)

Central Iran is taken up by a vast, semi-arid plateau, which rises steeply from the coastal lowlands bordering the Persian Gulf. It is ringed by the high Zagros and Elburz mountains.

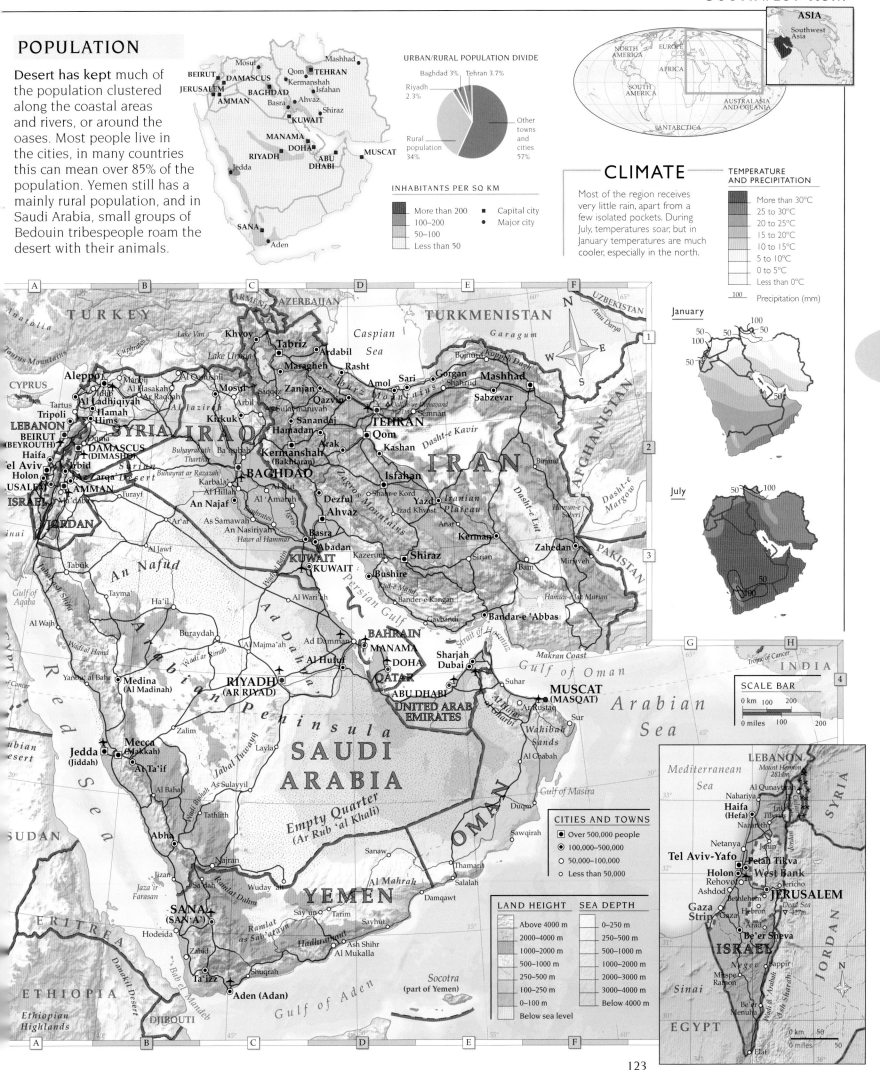

POPULATION

Desert has kept much of the population clustered along the coastal areas and rivers, or around the oases. Most people live in the cities, in many countries this can mean over 85% of the population. Yemen still has a mainly rural population, and in Saudi Arabia, small groups of Bedouin tribespeople roam the desert with their animals.

ASIA
Southwest Asia

URBAN/RURAL POPULATION DIVIDE

Baghdad 3% Tehran 3.7%
Riyadh 2.3%
Rural population 34%
Other towns and cities 57%

INHABITANTS PER SQ KM

More than 200
100–200
50–100
Less than 50

■ Capital city
● Major city

CLIMATE

Most of the region receives very little rain, apart from a few isolated pockets. During July, temperatures soar, but in January temperatures are much cooler, especially in the north.

TEMPERATURE AND PRECIPITATION

More than 30°C
25 to 30°C
20 to 25°C
15 to 20°C
10 to 15°C
5 to 10°C
0 to 5°C
Less than 0°C

100 Precipitation (mm)

January

July

CITIES AND TOWNS

● Over 500,000 people
◉ 100,000–500,000
○ 50,000–100,000
○ Less than 50,000

SCALE BAR

0 km 100 200
0 miles 100 200

LAND HEIGHT	SEA DEPTH
Above 4000 m	0–250 m
2000–4000 m	250–500 m
1000–2000 m	500–1000 m
500–1000 m	1000–2000 m
250–500 m	2000–3000 m
100–250 m	3000–4000 m
0–100 m	Below 4000 m
Below sea level	

CENTRAL ASIA

AFGHANISTAN, KYRGYZSTAN, TAJIKISTAN, TURKMENISTAN, UZBEKISTAN

Central Asia is a land of hot, dry deserts and high, rugged mountains. It lies on the ancient Silk Road, an important trade route between China and Europe for over 400 years, until the 15th century. All of the countries here, apart from Afghanistan, were part of the Soviet Union from the 1920s, until 1991, when they gained independence. Since then, their people have re-established their local languages and Islamic faith, all of which were restricted under Russian rule.

INDUSTRY

Fossil fuels, especially coal, natural gas and oil, are extracted and processed throughout Central Asia. Agriculture supplies the raw materials for many industries, including food and textile processing, and the manufacture of leather goods and clothing. The region is famous for its colourful traditional carpets, hand-woven from the wool of the Karakul sheep. The Fergana Valley, southeast of Tashkent, is the main industrial area.

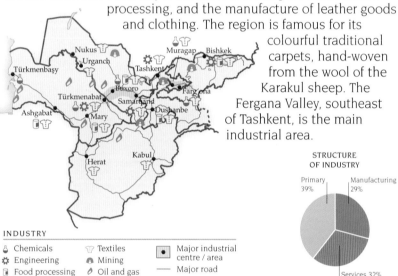

INDUSTRY
- ⚗ Chemicals
- ⚙ Engineering
- ▣ Food processing
- ⊺ Textiles
- ⛏ Mining
- ⬦ Oil and gas
- ■ Major industrial centre / area
- — Major road

STRUCTURE OF INDUSTRY
- Primary 39%
- Manufacturing 29%
- Services 32%

POPULATION

The peoples of Central Asia are mostly rural farmers, living in the river valleys and in oases. There are few large cities. A few still lead a traditional nomadic lifestyle, moving from place to place with their animals, in search of new pastures. Large areas of Afghanistan, the western deserts and the mountain regions in the east, are virtually uninhabited.

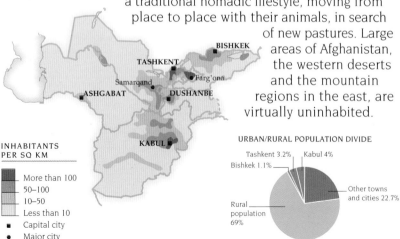

INHABITANTS PER SQ KM
- More than 100
- 50–100
- 10–50
- Less than 10
- ■ Capital city
- ● Major city

URBAN/RURAL POPULATION DIVIDE
- Tashkent 3.2%
- Kabul 4%
- Bishkek 1.1%
- Other towns and cities 22.7%
- Rural population 69%

FARMING AND LAND USE

Farming is concentrated around the fertile river valleys in the east, like the Fergana Valley. A variety of cereals, and fruits, including peaches, melons and apricots, are grown. In drier areas, animal breeding is important, with goats, sheep and cattle supplying wool, meat and hides. Big crops of cotton, which is a major export, are produced on land irrigated by the Amu Darya river.

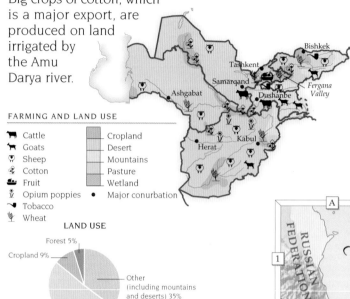

FARMING AND LAND USE
- 🐄 Cattle
- 🐐 Goats
- 🐑 Sheep
- ✿ Cotton
- 🍈 Fruit
- 🌸 Opium poppies
- 🌿 Tobacco
- 🌾 Wheat
- Cropland
- Desert
- Mountains
- Pasture
- Wetland
- ● Major conurbation

LAND USE
- Forest 5%
- Cropland 9%
- Pasture 51%
- Other (including mountains and deserts) 35%

THE LANDSCAPE

Two of the world's great deserts, the Garagum and the Kyzyl Kum, cover much of the western portion of Central Asia. In the east, a belt of high mountain ranges – the Hindu Kush, the Tien Shan and the Pamirs – tower above the land. Few rivers cross the deserts, apart from the Amu Darya, which flows from the Pamirs to the shrinking Aral Sea.

The Aral Sea (D 1)
The Aral Sea was once the fourth largest lake in the world, but it has shrunk by 90% since 1960. Diversion of its water for irrigation has made the lake shallower, so its waters evaporate faster.

Garagum (D 3)
The sandy desert of the Garagum occupies over 70% of Turkmenistan. Its surface consists of wind-sculpted dunes and depressions. Human settlement is limited to the desert's fringes.

Tien Shan (H 2)

Fergana Valley (G 3)
Stresses and strains in the Earth created the Fergana Valley, a deep depression encircled by high mountains. The valley's fertile soils are irrigated by water from the Syr Darya river, and underground sources.

Amu Darya river (E 3)

Hindu Kush (G 4)

Pamirs (G 4)
The Pamirs lie mainly in Tajikistan. Their highest point, at 7,495 m, is Qullai Ismoili Somoni, previously known as Communism Peak because it was the highest peak in the former Soviet Union.

ENVIRONMENTAL ISSUES

Central Asia is a very dry area, and desertification is a constant threat, especially in Afghanistan. Severe urban and industrial air pollution is a legacy from the communist era, when heavy industries were established in the countries here. Efforts to stabilise the shrinking Aral Sea have met with some success in the northern section.

ENVIRONMENTAL ISSUES

🙂 Urban air pollution

Existing desert
Risk of desertification
Severe risk of desertification
Polluted river
Sea pollution

● Major industrial centre

CLIMATE

Central Asia's climate is strongly inflenced by its position deep within Asia, far from the moderating effects of the oceans. Winters are cold, summers are very hot everywhere. Rainfall is virtually non-existent all year round.

ASIA
Central Asia

January — Less than 50mm precipitation

July — Less than 50mm precipitation

TEMPERATURE AND PRECIPITATION

More than 30°C
25 to 30°C
5 to 10°C
0 to 5°C
Less than 0°C

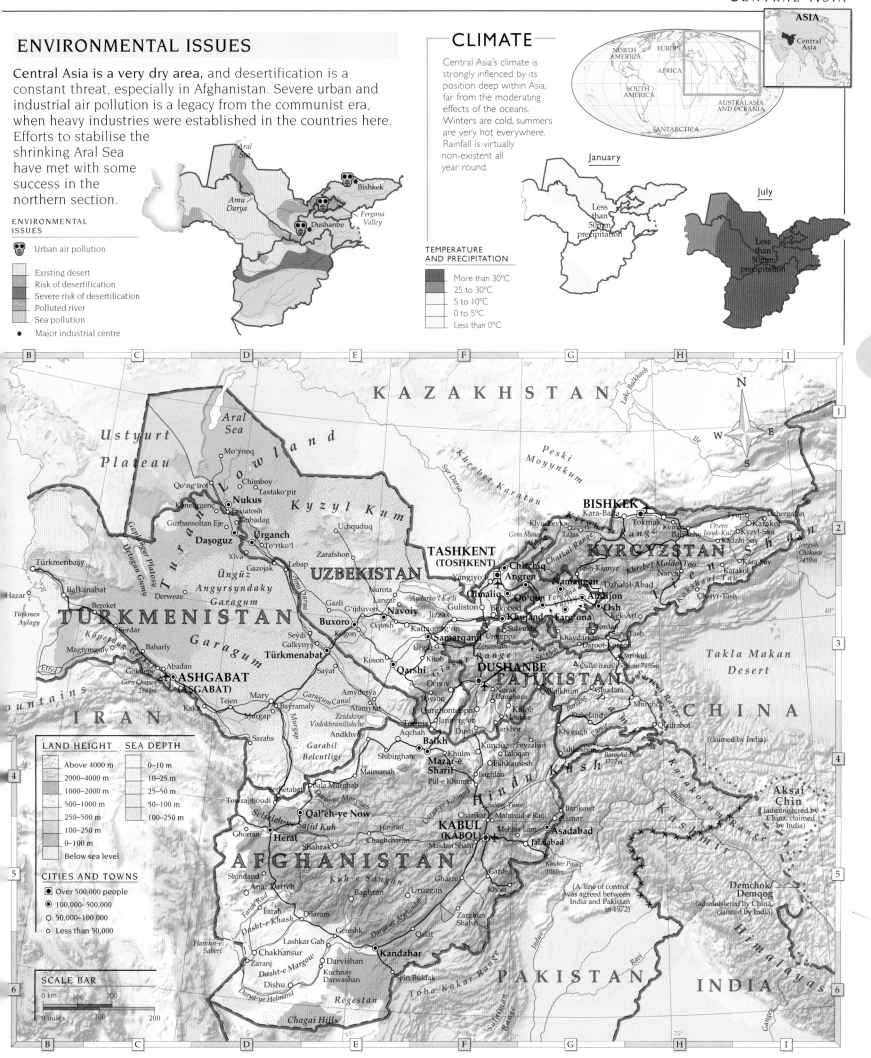

LAND HEIGHT
- Above 4000 m
- 2000–4000 m
- 1000–2000 m
- 500–1000 m
- 250–500 m
- 100–250 m
- 0–100 m
- Below sea level

SEA DEPTH
- 0–10 m
- 10–25 m
- 25–50 m
- 50–100 m
- 100–250 m

CITIES AND TOWNS
- ■ Over 500,000 people
- ◉ 100,000–500,000
- ◎ 50,000–100,000
- ○ Less than 50,000

SCALE BAR
0 km   100   200
0 miles   100   200

SOUTH ASIA

BANGLADESH, BHUTAN, INDIA, NEPAL, PAKISTAN, SRI LANKA

South Asia is a land of many contrasts. Its landscape ranges from the mighty peaks of the Himalayas in the north, through vast plains and arid desert, to tropical forests and palm-fringed beaches in the south. More than one-fifth of the world's people live here, and a long history of foreign invasions has left a mosaic of hugely different cultures, religions and traditions, and thousands of languages and dialects.

INDUSTRY

Industry has expanded in India in recent years, and in the cities a variety of goods are produced and processed, including cars, aeroplanes, chemicals, food and drink. Service industries such as tourism and banking are also growing. Elsewhere, small-scale cottage industries serve the needs of local people, but many products, mainly silk and cotton textiles, clothing, leather and jewellery, are also exported.

STRUCTURE
OF INDUSTRY

Primary 23%
Services 49%
Manufacturing 28%

INDUSTRY

- ✈ Aerospace
- 🚗 Car manufacture
- ⚗ Chemicals
- 📠 Electronics
- ⚙ Engineering
- 🗎 Food processing
- 🏭 Iron and steel
- 👕 Textiles
- 🅜 Mining
- 💻 High-tech industry
- Ⓢ Finance
- 🛈 Tourism
- ▪ Major industrial centre / area
- — Major road

POPULATION

Most of South Asia's people live in villages scattered across the fertile river floodplains, in mountain valleys or along the coasts, but increasing numbers are migrating to the cities in search of work. Overcrowding is a serious problem in both rural and urban areas; in many cities, thousands of people are forced to live in slums, or on the streets.

INHABITANTS
PER SQ KM

- More than 200
- 100–200
- 50–100
- Less than 50
- ▪ Capital city
- ● Major city

URBAN/RURAL POPULATION DIVIDE

Kolkata 1% Mumbai 1.2%
Delhi 0.8%
Other towns and cities 23%
Rural population 74%

FARMING AND LAND USE

Over 60% of the population is involved in agriculture, but most farms are small, and produce only enough food to feed one family. Grains are the staple food crops – rice in the wetter parts of the east and west, corn and millet on the Deccan plateau, and wheat in the north. Groundnuts are widely grown as a source of cooking oil. Cash crops include tea, which is grown on plantations, and jute.

FARMING AND LAND USE

- 🐄 Cattle
- Fishing
- 🐐 Goats
- Cereals
- Groundnuts
- Jute
- Rice
- Tea
- Cropland
- Desert
- Forest
- Pasture
- Wetland
- ● Major conurbation

LAND USE

Pasture 5%
Forest 21%
Other 24%
Cropland 50%

THE LANDSCAPE

A massive, towering wall of snow-capped mountains stretches in an arc across the north, isolating South Asia from the rest of the continent. The huge floodplains and deltas of the Indus, Ganges and Brahmaputra rivers separate the mountains from the rest of the peninsula: a great rolling plateau, bordered on either side by coastal hills called the Eastern and Western Ghats.

Himalayas (E 2)
The Himalayas are the highest mountain system in the world. They were formed about 40 million years ago when two of the Earth's plates collided, thrusting up huge masses of land.

Mount Everest (F 3)
The northern ranges of the Himalayas average 7,000 m in height. They include the highest point on Earth, Mount Everest on the Nepal–China border, which soars to 8,848 m.

Thar Desert (C 3)
The border between India and Pakistan runs through the arid, sandy Thar Desert.

Western Ghats (C 5)
The Western Ghats run continuously along the Arabian Sea coast, while the lower Eastern Ghats are interrupted by rivers that follow the gentle slope of the Deccan plateau and flow across broad lowlands into the Bay of Bengal. This is one of the wettest regions in the world.

Eastern Ghats (E 5)

Deccan plateau (D 5)
This giant plateau makes up most of central and southern India. Its volcanic rock has been deeply cut by rivers such as the Krishna, creating stepped valleys called *traps*.

Bangladesh (G 3)
Much of Bangladesh lies in an enormous delta formed by the Brahmaputra and Ganges rivers. During the summer monsoon, the rivers become swollen by the torrential rains – and meltwater from the Himalayas – and the delta floods. Over the years, millions of people have drowned or been made homeless by heavy flooding.

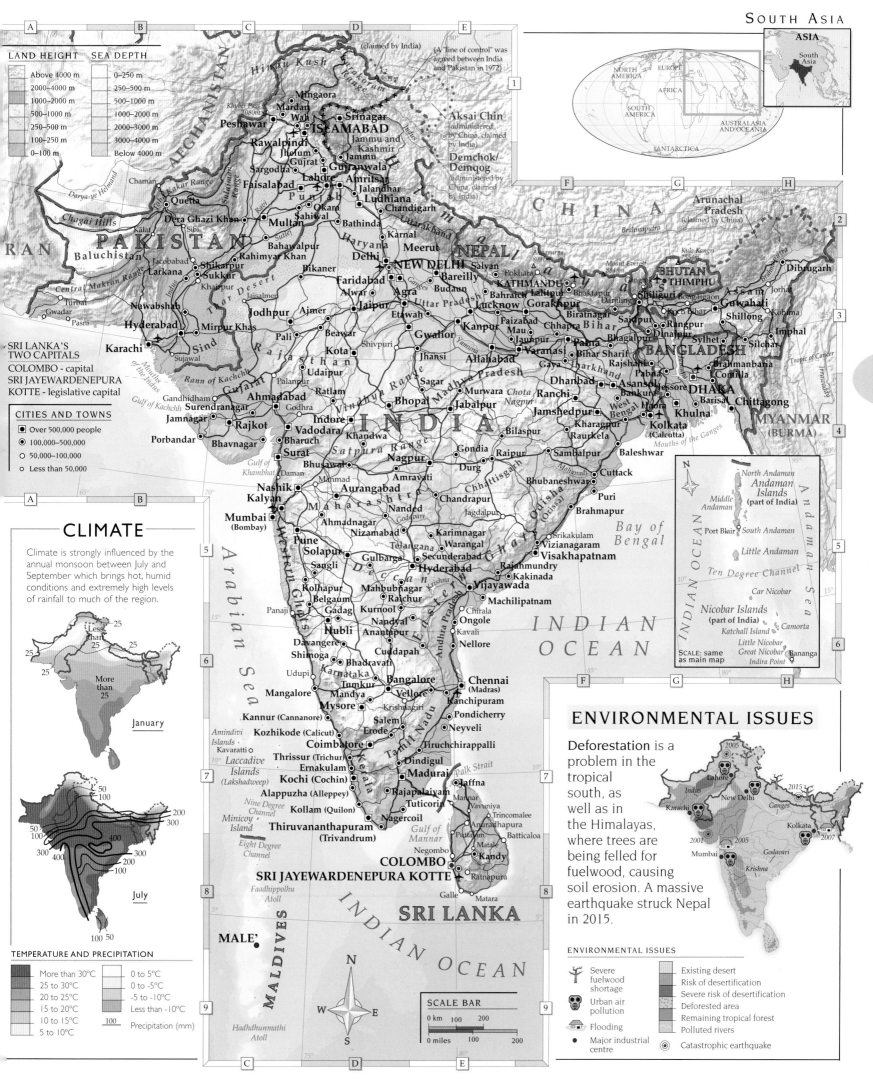

ASIA

South Asia

(claimed by India)

(A "line of control" was agreed between India and Pakistan in 1972)

LAND HEIGHT
- Above 4000 m
- 2000–4000 m
- 1000–2000 m
- 500–1000 m
- 250–500 m
- 100–250 m
- 0–100 m

SEA DEPTH
- 0–250 m
- 250–500 m
- 500–1000 m
- 1000–2000 m
- 2000–3000 m
- 3000–4000 m
- Below 4000 m

SRI LANKA'S
TWO CAPITALS

COLOMBO - capital
SRI JAYEWARDENEPURA
KOTTE - legislative capital

CITIES AND TOWNS
- ■ Over 500,000 people
- ● 100,000–500,000
- ○ 50,000–100,000
- ○ Less than 50,000

CLIMATE

Climate is strongly influenced by the annual monsoon between July and September which brings hot, humid conditions and extremely high levels of rainfall to much of the region.

January

July

TEMPERATURE AND PRECIPITATION
- More than 30°C
- 25 to 30°C
- 20 to 25°C
- 15 to 20°C
- 10 to 15°C
- 5 to 10°C
- 0 to 5°C
- 0 to -5°C
- -5 to -10°C
- Less than -10°C
- 100 Precipitation (mm)

SCALE BAR
0 km 100 200
0 miles 100 200

ENVIRONMENTAL ISSUES

Deforestation is a problem in the tropical south, as well as in the Himalayas, where trees are being felled for fuelwood, causing soil erosion. A massive earthquake struck Nepal in 2015.

ENVIRONMENTAL ISSUES
- Severe fuelwood shortage
- Urban air pollution
- Flooding
- Major industrial centre
- Existing desert
- Risk of desertification
- Severe risk of desertification
- Deforested area
- Remaining tropical forest
- Polluted rivers
- Catastrophic earthquake

SCALE: same as main map

127

EAST ASIA

CHINA, MONGOLIA, TAIWAN

China is the world's fourth largest country and its most populous – over 1.3 billion people live there. Under its communist government, which came to power in 1949, China has become a major industrial nation, but most of its people still live and work on the land, as they have for thousands of years. Taiwan also has a booming economy and exports its products around the world. Mongolia is a vast, remote country with a small population, many of whom are nomads.

INDUSTRY

Chemicals, iron and steel, engineering and textiles are the main industries in China's east coast cities, and in industrial centres like Shenyang. Shanghai, Hong Kong and Beijing are also important financial centres. In the interior, large deposits of coal support the heavy industries in major cities such as Chengdu and Wuhan. Taiwan specializes in textiles and shoe manufacture, along with electronic goods. Mongolia's economy is mainly agricultural.

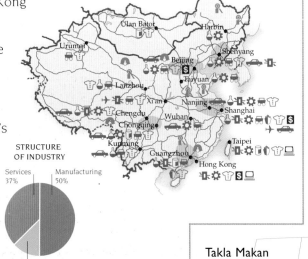

INDUSTRY

✈ Aerospace	⛴ Shipbuilding
🚗 Car manufacture	👕 Textiles
⚗ Chemicals	⛏ Coal
🔌 Electronics	⚒ Mining
💻 Electronic goods	$ Finance
⚙ Engineering	
🍴 Food processing	▪ Major industrial centre / area
🚂 Iron & steel	— Major road

STRUCTURE OF INDUSTRY

Services 37%
Manufacturing 50%
Primary 13%

POPULATION

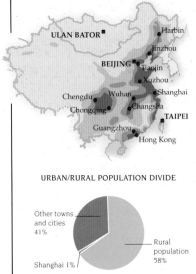

URBAN/RURAL POPULATION DIVIDE

Most of China's people live in the eastern part of the country, where the climate, landscape and soils are most favourable. Chinese cities are home to over 690 million people, surpassing the rural population for the first time in 2011. Taiwan's lowlands are very densely populated. In Mongolia, one third of the people live in the countryside.

Other towns and cities 41%
Rural population 58%
Shanghai 1%

INHABITANTS PER SQ KM

▨ More than 200	▪ Capital city
▨ 100–200	● Major city
▨ 50–100	
☐ Less than 50	

FARMING AND LAND USE

FARMING AND LAND USE

⌐ Fishing	⚘ Tea
🐖 Pigs	☘ Tobacco
🐑 Sheep	🌾 Wheat
🌽 Corn (maize)	
🌿 Cotton	☐ Cropland
🍎 Fruit	☐ Desert
🌾 Rice	☐ Forest
🫘 Soya beans	☐ Mountain region
🌾 Sugarcane	☐ Pasture
	● Major conurbation

Despite its size, about 90% of China is unsuitable for farming. Either the soils and climate are poor, or the landscape is too mountainous. In the north and west, most farmers make their living by herding animals. On the fertile eastern plains, soya beans, wheat, corn and cotton are grown. Further south, rice becomes the main crop, and pigs are raised in large numbers.

LAND USE

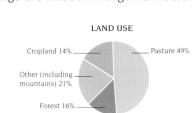

Cropland 14%
Pasture 49%
Other (including mountains) 21%
Forest 16%

THE LANDSCAPE

China's landscape divides into three areas. The vast Plateau of Tibet in the southwest is the highest and largest plateau on Earth. It contains both dry deserts and pockets of pasture surrounded by high mountains. Northwest China has dry highlands. The great plains of eastern China were formed from soils deposited by rivers like the Yellow River over thousands of years. Most of Mongolia is dry, grassland steppe and cold, arid desert.

Tien Shan mountains (B 2)

The Tien Shan, or 'Heavenly Mountains' reach heights of 7,443 m. They surround fields of permanent ice and spectacular glaciers.

Gobi (E 2) and Takla Makan (B 3) deserts

The arid landscapes of the Gobi and Takla Makan deserts are made up of bare rock surfaces and huge areas of shifting sand dunes. They are hot in summer, but unlike most other deserts, are extremely cold in winter.

Takla Makan Desert

'The Roof of the World'

The cold, remote Plateau of Tibet (C 4) averages 4,000 m in height. Many of China's great rivers have their sources here. The world's highest human settlement, a town called Wenquan, is found in the east of the plateau. It lies 5,099 m above sea level.

The Yellow River (E 3)

The Yellow River (Huang He) is the world's muddiest river, carrying hundreds of lorry loads of sediment to the sea every minute. The river has burst its banks many times throughout history, causing enormous damage and claiming millions of human lives.

A handmade landscape

In the farming areas of eastern and southern China, terraces have been carved into the hillsides to make them flat enough to grow rice and other crops. This method of farming has been used for over 7,000 years.

ENVIRONMENTAL ISSUES

China is now the world's largest emitter of greenhouse gases. Its rapid economic growth has had a huge impact upon the environment. The Yangtze and Yellow Rivers are badly polluted. Urbanization is increasing, with over 150 cities in China having populations above 1 million. The Three Gorges Dam is the largest hydro-electric project in the world.

ENVIRONMENTAL ISSUES

Polluted river
Sea pollution
Major dam
Urban air pollution
Industrial city
Catastrophic earthquake

Shenyang
Beijing
Yellow River
Xi'an
2008
Three Gorges Dam
Guangzhou
Shanghai
Yangtze
Hong Kong

CLIMATE

Two air masses control climate; one cold and dry from Siberia, and one moist and warm from the Pacific. Winters are long and cold away from the coast – especially on the Plateau of Tibet.

ASIA
East Asia

NORTH AMERICA
EUROPE
AFRICA
SOUTH AMERICA
AUSTRALASIA AND OCEANIA
ANTARCTICA

TEMPERATURE AND PRECIPITATION

More than 30°C
20 to 30°C
10 to 20°C
0 to 10°C
0 to -10°C
-10 to -20°C
Less than -20°C

100 Precipitation (mm)

January

July

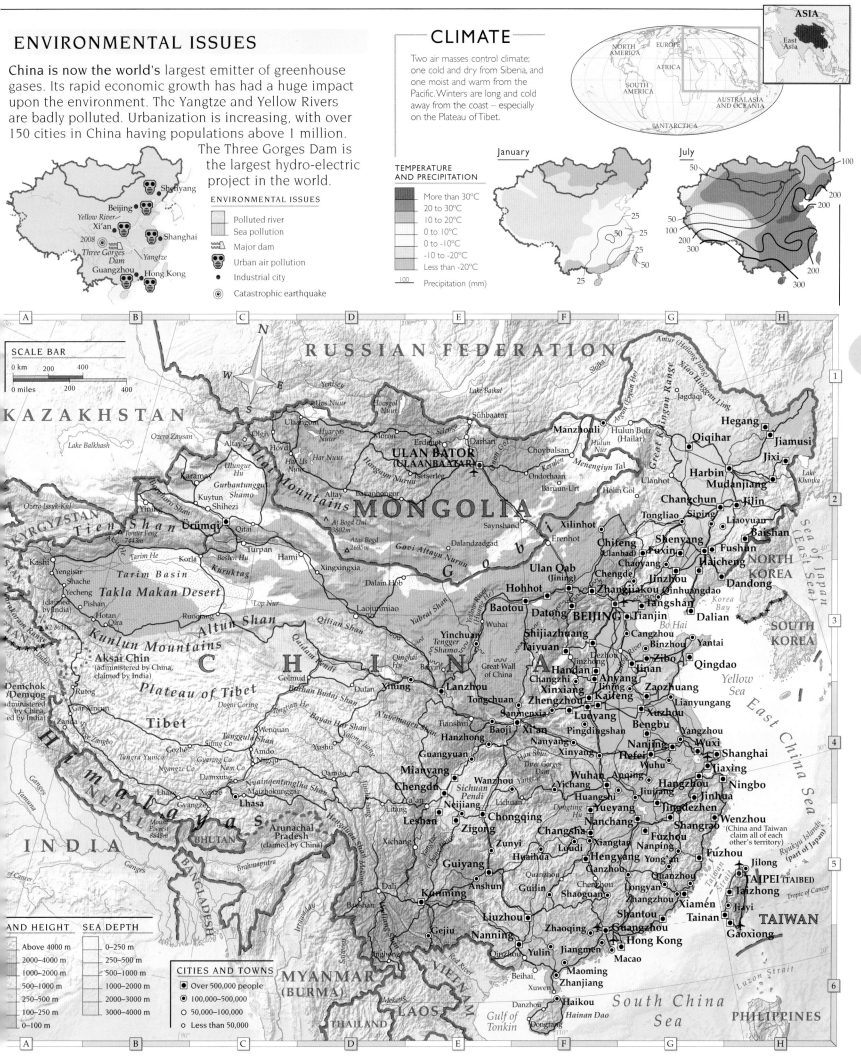

SCALE BAR
0 km 200 400
0 miles 200 400

RUSSIAN FEDERATION

KAZAKHSTAN

KYRGYZSTAN

MONGOLIA

ULAN BATOR (ULAANBAATAR)

Gobi

CHINA

Tien Shan
Tarim Basin
Takla Makan Desert
Kunlun Mountains
Altun Shan
Plateau of Tibet
Tibet
Himalayas
Mount Everest 8848m

NEPAL
BHUTAN
INDIA
BANGLADESH

Arunachal Pradesh (claimed by China)

NORTH KOREA
SOUTH KOREA

BEIJING
Tianjin

Yellow Sea
East China Sea

Shanghai

TAIPEI (TAIBEI)
TAIWAN

MYANMAR (BURMA)
LAOS
THAILAND
VIETNAM

South China Sea
Gulf of Tonkin
Hainan Dao

PHILIPPINES

LAND HEIGHT
Above 4000 m
2000–4000 m
1000–2000 m
500–1000 m
250–500 m
100–250 m
0–100 m

SEA DEPTH
0–250 m
250–500 m
500–1000 m
1000–2000 m
2000–3000 m
3000–4000 m

CITIES AND TOWNS
Over 500,000 people
100,000–500,000
50,000–100,000
Less than 50,000

SOUTHEAST ASIA

BRUNEI, CAMBODIA, EAST TIMOR, INDONESIA, LAOS, MALAYSIA, MYANMAR (BURMA), PHILIPPINES, SINGAPORE, THAILAND, VIETNAM

Southeast Asia is made up of a mainland area and many thousands of tropical islands. The region has great natural wealth and has recently undergone rapid industrial growth. Some countries, especially Singapore and Malaysia, have become prosperous, but Laos and Cambodia remain poor, and are still recovering from years of terrible warfare.

ENVIRONMENTAL ISSUES

In Myanmar (Burma), Malaysia and Indonesia, rainforests are being cut down faster than they can grow back. On 26th of December, 2004 a tsunami devastated the west of the region, it is estimated that over 225,000 people died around the Indian Ocean.

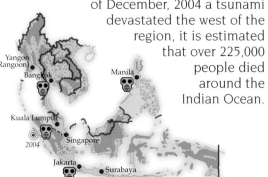

POPULATION

On the mainland, the population is concentrated in the river valleys, plateaus or plains. Upland areas are inhabited by small groups of hill peoples. Most people still live in rural areas, but the cities are growing fast. In Indonesia and the Philippines, the population is unevenly distributed. Some islands, such as Java, are densely settled; others are barely occupied.

INHABITANTS PER SQ KM
- More than 200
- 100–200
- 50–100
- Less than 50
- ■ Capital city
- ● Major city

URBAN/RURAL POPULATION DIVIDE

Bangkok 1.2%
Jakarta 1.5%
Manilla 1.8%
Rural population 37%
Other towns and cities 58.5%

INDUSTRY

Industries based on the processing of raw materials, like metallic minerals, timber, oil and gas and agricultural produce, are important here, but manufacturing has grown dramatically in recent years. Many foreign firms, attracted by low labour costs, have invested in the region. Malaysia and Singapore are major producers of electronic goods like disk drives for computers.

STRUCTURE OF INDUSTRY

Primary 19%
Services 45%
Manufacturing 36%

INDUSTRY
- 🧪 Chemicals
- ⚙ Engineering
- 🍴 Food processing
- 👕 Textiles
- ⛏ Mining
- 🛢 Oil and gas
- 🌲 Timber
- S Finance
- 💻 Hi-tech
- 🏨 Tourism
- ▣ Major industrial centre / area
- — Major road

THE LANDSCAPE

On the mainland, a belt of mountain ranges, cloaked in thick forest, runs north–south. The mountains are cut through by the wide valleys of five great rivers. On their route to the sea, these rivers have deposited sediment, forming immense, fertile flood plains and deltas. To the southeast of the mainland lies a huge arc of over 20,000 mountainous, volcanic islands.

Borneo (D 7)
Borneo is the world's third-largest island, with a total area of 757,050 sq km. Lying on the Equator and in the path of two monsoons, the island is hot, and one of the wettest places on Earth. The landscape contains thickly-forested central highlands and swampy lowlands.

Asian Tsunami (A6)
On December 26th, 2004 the second largest earthquake ever recorded occured under the sea off the west coast of Sumatra. This triggered a huge Tsunami wave, up to 30 m high in places, that devastated coastal communities causing the deaths of over 225,000 people in eleven countries.

Philippines (E 4)
The Philippines' 7,000 islands are mountainous and volcanic with narrow coastal plains.

Papua (Irian Jaya) (I 7)
Papua is a province of Indonesia. Its dense rainforests are some of the last unexplored areas on Earth and are inhabited by many rare plant and animal species.

Volcanoes
Indonesia is the most active volcanic region in the world; Java alone has over 50 active volcanoes out of the country's total of more than 220.

Indonesia (C 7)
Indonesia is an archipelago of 13,677 islands, scattered over almost 5,000 km. The islands lie on the boundary between two of the Earth's tectonic plates and frequently experience earthquakes.

SCALE BAR
0 km 200 400
0 miles 200

FARMING AND LAND USE

The staple crop here is rice, which grows in low-lying flooded fields called paddies, or on terraces cut into the hillsides. Sugarcane, coconuts, bananas and pineapples are widely grown as cash crops, and Malaysia produces 25% of the world's rubber. Freshwater and marine fish are caught in large quantities; fish is one of the main foods in this region.

FARMING AND LAND USE

- Cattle
- Fishing
- Pigs
- Shellfish
- Coconuts
- Fruit
- Rice
- Rubber
- Sugarcane
- Timber
- Cropland
- Forest
- Pasture
- Wetland
- Major conurbation

LAND USE

Pasture 4%
Cropland 21%
Forest 51%
Other 24%

ASIA
Southeast Asia

CLIMATE

Southeast Asia's climate is strongly affected by the monsoon, which brings warm, humid air and high rainfall to mainland Southeast Asia during July, and to maritime southeast Asia during January.

January

July

TEMPERATURE AND PRECIPITATION
- More than 30°C
- 20 to 30°C
- 10 to 20°C
- Less than 10°C
- 100 Precipitation (mm)

LAND HEIGHT
- Above 4000 m
- 2000–4000 m
- 1000–2000 m
- 500–1000 m
- 250–500 m
- 100–250 m
- 0–100 m

SEA DEPTH
- 0–250 m
- 250–500 m
- 500–1000 m
- 1000–2000 m
- 2000–3000 m
- 3000–4000 m
- Below 4000 m

CITIES AND TOWNS
- Over 500,000 people
- 100,000–500,000
- 50,000–100,000
- Less than 50,000

MALAYSIA'S TWO CAPITALS
KUALA LUMPUR - capital
PUTRAJAYA - administrative capital

JAPAN AND KOREA

JAPAN, NORTH KOREA, SOUTH KOREA

Japan is a curved chain of over 4,000 islands in the Pacific Ocean. To the west, Korea juts out from northern China. Japan has few natural resources but it has become one of the world's most successful industrial nations due to investment in new technology and a highly efficient workforce. North Korea is a communist state with limited contact with the outside world, while South Korea is a democracy with major international trade links.

FARMING AND LAND USE

Modern farming methods allow Japan to grow much of its own food, despite a shortage of farmland. Rice is the main crop grown throughout the region. Japan has a large fishing fleet; the Japanese eat more fish than any other nation. In North Korea, farming is controlled by the government.

FARMING AND LAND USE

- 🐄 Cattle
- 🐟 Fishing
- 🐖 Pigs
- 🍎 Fruit
- 〰 Rice
- 🫘 Soya beans
- 🌿 Tea
- 🍂 Tobacco
- ▦ Cropland
- ▦ Forest
- ▦ Pasture
- ● Major conurbation

LAND USE

Pasture 1%
Cropland 16%
Other (including mountains) 18%
Forest 65%

POPULATION

Most of Japan's 128 million people live in crowded cities on the coasts of the four main islands. The Kanto Plain around Tokyo is Japan's biggest area of flat land, and the most populous part of the country. In South Korea, a quarter of the population lives in the capital, Seoul. Most North Koreans live on the coastal plains.

URBAN/RURAL POPULATION DIVIDE

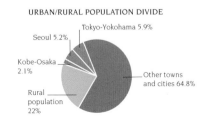

Tokyo-Yokohama 5.9%
Seoul 5.2%
Kobe-Osaka 2.1%
Rural population 22%
Other towns and cities 64.8%

INHABITANTS PER SQ KM

- ▦ More than 200
- ▦ 100–200
- ▦ 50–100
- ▦ Less than 50
- ■ Capital city
- ● Major city

THE LANDSCAPE

Most of Japan is covered by forested mountains and hills, among which are many short, fast-flowing rivers and small lakes. Only about a quarter of the land is suitable for building and farming and new land has been created by cutting back hillsides and reclaiming land from the sea. North and South Korea are mostly mountainous, with some coastal plains.

Hokkaido, Honshu, Shikoku and Kyushu

Japan's four main islands were formed when two giant plates making up the Earth's crust collided, making their edges buckle upwards.

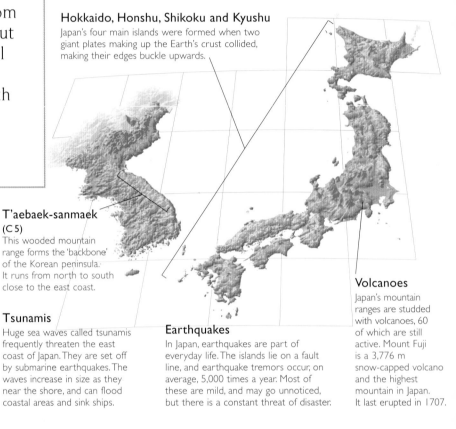

T'aebaek-sanmaek (C 5)

This wooded mountain range forms the 'backbone' of the Korean peninsula. It runs from north to south close to the east coast.

Tsunamis

Huge sea waves called tsunamis frequently threaten the east coast of Japan. They are set off by submarine earthquakes. The waves increase in size as they near the shore, and can flood coastal areas and sink ships.

Earthquakes

In Japan, earthquakes are part of everyday life. The islands lie on a fault line, and earthquake tremors occur, on average, 5,000 times a year. Most of these are mild, and may go unnoticed, but there is a constant threat of disaster.

Volcanoes

Japan's mountain ranges are studded with volcanoes, 60 of which are still active. Mount Fuji is a 3,776 m snow-capped volcano and the highest mountain in Japan. It last erupted in 1707.

INDUSTRY

Japan is a world leader in hi-tech electronic goods like computers, televisions and cameras, as well as cars. South Korea also has a thriving economy. It produces ships, cars, hi-tech goods, shoes and clothes for worldwide export. Both countries have to import most of their raw materials and energy. North Korea has little trade with other countries, but it is rich in minerals such as coal and silver.

STRUCTURE OF INDUSTRY

Primary 2%
Services 70%
Manufacturing 28%

INDUSTRY

- 🚗 Car manufacture
- ⚗ Chemicals
- ⚙ Engineering
- 🍲 Food processing
- ⚒ Iron & steel
- ⚓ Shipbuilding
- 👕 Textiles
- ⛏ Mining
- $ Finance
- 💻 Hi-tech
- ☢ Research & Development
- ▣ Major industrial centre / area
- — Major road

ENVIRONMENTAL ISSUES

Industrial pollution from Korea and China has produced acid rain. Air pollution in cities has led to many people routinely wearing masks. Following the devastating 2011 tsunami and subsequent radiation leak at Fukushima, Japan closed all of its 22 nuclear power stations.

ENVIRONMENTAL ISSUES

- ⊙ Catastrophic earthquake
- Urban air pollution
- Affected by acid rain
- Site of nuclear accident
- • Major industrial area

Sea of Japan / East Sea

Tohoku 2011
1999/2011
Seoul
Tokyo
Kobe 1995
Osaka

CLIMATE

Korea has hot summers and dry, very cold winters, especially in the north, where snow is common. In Japan, winters are less cold than on the Asian mainland; summers are hot, wet and humid.

January

200
50
100
100
Less than 50
100

July

50
200
100
100

TEMPERATURE AND PRECIPITATION

More than 20°C	0 to 5°C
15 to 20°C	0 to -5°C
10 to 15°C	Less than -5°C
5 to 10°C	

100 Precipitation (mm)

ASIA
Japan and Korea

NORTH AMERICA
EUROPE
AFRICA
SOUTH AMERICA
AUSTRALASIA AND OCEANIA
ANTARCTICA

SCALE BAR

0 km 100 200
0 miles 100 200

C H I N A

RUSS. FED.

Hoeryong
Najin
Paektu-san 2750m
Ch'ongjin
Hyesan
Kilchu
Huch'ang
Kimch'aek
Kanggye
Ch'osan
Pukch'ong
Huich'on
Sinp'o
Namsan-ni
Hamhung
Sinuiju
Anju
East Korea Bay
Chongju
Yonghung
-inmi-do
-rea
Kosong
Namp'o
PYONGYANG
Sariwon
Sokcho
Changyon
NORTH KOREA
Wonsan
Haeju Kaesong
Chuncheon
Ongjin
Gangneung
-nyeong-do
Wonju
Donghae
Incheon
SEOUL (SOUL)
Suwon
Yellow Sea
Cheonan
Chungju
SEJONG CITY
Daejeon
Andong
SOUTH KOREA
Gunsan
Daegu
Pohang
Namwon
Masan
Ulsan
Gwangju
Busan
Suncheon
Geogeum-do
Mokpo
Namhae-do
Tsushima
Kyushu
km 200
miles 200
Osumi-shoto
ast China
Sea
Amami-gunto
Naze
Amami-o-shima
Ryukyu Islands (part of Japan)
Okinawa
Naha
Jeju Strait
Jeju-do
East China Sea
enkaku-shoto
Okinawa-shoto
Philippine Sea
Ishigaki-jima
Iriomote-jima

NORTH KOREA

(North and South Korea have been divided by a ceasefire agreement since 1953)

Sea of Japan / East Sea

Liancourt Rocks (under South Korean control)

Oki-shoto
Dogo
Dozen

Matsue
Tottori
Yonago
Chugoku-sanchi
Gotsu
Hamada
Okayama
Himeji
Kobe
Masuda
Kurashiki
Takamatsu
Nagato
Hiroshima
Kure
Tokushima
Yamaguchi
Iwakuni
Niihama
Hofu
Matsuyama
Shimonoseki
Ube
Kochi
Kitakyushu
Iyo-nada
Shikoku
Fukuoka
Oita
Kurume
Saga
Nakamura
Omuta
Sukumo
Sasebo
Kumamoto
Bungo-suido
Nobeoka
Nagasaki
Yatsushiro
Amakusa-nada
Kyushu
Miyazaki
Satsuma-Sendai
Miyakonojo
Koshikijima-retto
Kagoshima
Shibushi-wan

Hokkaido

Wakkanai
La Pérouse Strait
Sea of Okhotsk
Rebun-to
Rishiri-to
Monbetsu
Abashiri
Kuril Islands
(administered by Russian Federation, claimed by Japan)
Nayoro
Shibetsu
Kitami
Nemuro
Asahikawa
Asahi-dake 2290m
Takikawa
Akkeshi
Obihiro
Kushiro
Otaru
Ebetsu
Horoshiri-dake 2052m
Sapporo
Chitose
Iwanai
Tomakomai
Noboribetsu
Muroran
Uchiura-wan
Okushiri-to
Hakodate
Tsugaru-kaikyo

Aomori
Goshogawara
Hachinohe
Kuji
Hirosaki
Odate
Miyako
Noshiro
Iwate
Gojome
Morioka
Akita
Yokote
Kesennuma
Honjo
Shinjo
Shizugawa
Sakata
Shingo
Furukawa
Tsuruoka
Ishinomaki
Sendai
Sendai-wan
Honshu
Yamagata
Soma
Niigata
Fukushima
Haramachi
Sado
Koriyama
Inawashiro-ko
Nagaoka
Sukagawa
Iwaki
Joetsu
Utsunomiya
Hitachi
Itoigawa
Takaoka
Maebashi
Oyama
Mito
Kanazawa
Toyama
Nagano
Kawagoe
Kasumiga-ura
Kanto Plain
Komatsu
Matsumoto
Choshi
Hida-sanmyaku
Fukui
TOKYO
Chiba
Kofu
Kawasaki
Nakatsugawa
Mount Fuji 3776m
Yokohama
Gifu
Boso-hanto
Tsuruga
Shizuoka
Izu-hanto
Ogaki
Nagoya
Suruga-wan
O-shima
Toyota
Okazaki
Wakasa-wan
Biwa-ko
Nii-jima
Otsu
Hamamatsu
Kozu-shima
Otsu
Kyoto
Tsu
Ise-wan
Mikura-jima
Harima-nada
Ise
Miyako-jima
Awaji-shima
Osaka
Owase
Wakayama
Gobo
Izu-shoto
Kii-suido
Shingu
Tanabe
Tosa-wan
Kii-sanchi

PACIFIC OCEAN

JAPAN

LAND HEIGHT

2000–4000 m	
1000–2000 m	
500–1000 m	
250–500 m	
100–250 m	
0–100 m	

SEA DEPTH

0–250 m	
250–500 m	
500–1000 m	
1000–2000 m	
2000–3000 m	
3000–4000 m	
Below 4000 m	

CITIES AND TOWNS

- ■ Over 500,000 people
- ◉ 100,000–500,000
- ○ 50,000–100,000
- ∘ Less than 50,000

SOUTH KOREA'S TWO CAPITALS

SEOUL - capital
SEJONG CITY - administrative capital

AUSTRALASIA & OCEANIA

Micronesia is one of the Pacific's island nations, consisting of a group of volcanic islands, low-lying coral reefs and lagoons. Many of the smaller Pacific islands are only a few metres above sea level.

Australasia and Oceania encompasses the ancient land mass of Australia, the islands of New Zealand, and the scattering of thousands of small islands that stretch out into the Pacific Ocean. Indigenous peoples of the South Pacific, such as the Aborigines, Maoris, Polynesians, Micronesians and Melanesians, inhabit the region. In Australia and New Zealand, they live alongside people of European origin who settled in the 18th century, and more recent arrivals from East and Southeast Asia.

LAND USE AND AGRICULTURE

Much of the centre of Australia is a dry, barren desert and unsuitable for agriculture. At its fringes, sheep farming is practised, and Australia and New Zealand alike are massive producers of wool and lamb. The Pacific islands export many exotic fruits and crops – especially oil palms and coconut palms. Oil from the palms is processed and sold, as well as the fruits themselves. Small-scale fishing is common, but larger scale operations are run by foreign fishing fleets, especially the Japanese, who fish tuna from the deeper waters of the Pacific.

SHEEP FARMING

New Zealand and Australia are the world's biggest producers of wool. In New Zealand, sheep outnumber people by 12 to 1.

POPULATION

Capital cities
- ◙ Above 500,000
- ◉ 100,000 to 500,000
- ● 50,000 to 100,000
- • Below 50,000

State capitals
- ◙ Above 500,000
- ◉ 100,000 to 500,000
- ○ 50,000 to 100,000

BORDERS

- full international border
- indication of maritime country extent
- indication of maritime dependent territory extent
- state border

COCONUTS

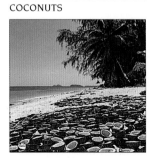

Coconuts are grown throughout the islands of the Pacific, and the white flesh is dried in the sun to produce copra. Copra is a valuable export crop for many islands.

LAND USE AND AGRICULTURE

Cattle	Vineyards
Sheep	Wheat
Coconuts	Cropland
Coffee	Desert
Fishing	Forest
Fruit	Mountain region
Shellfish	Pasture
Sugarcane	• Major conurbation
Timber	

MINERAL RESOURCES

Mineral resources are not widespread, but where they are found, it is in great abundance. Most of the small Pacific islands have no mineral resources, but Australia has enormous reserves of bauxite and iron ore, and also sizeable reserves of gold and zinc. Copper is found in Papua New Guinea, and New Caledonia has large nickel reserves. There are ample supplies of fossil fuels and although coal is plentiful in eastern Australia, oil and gas are found only in isolated pockets around Australia's coast.

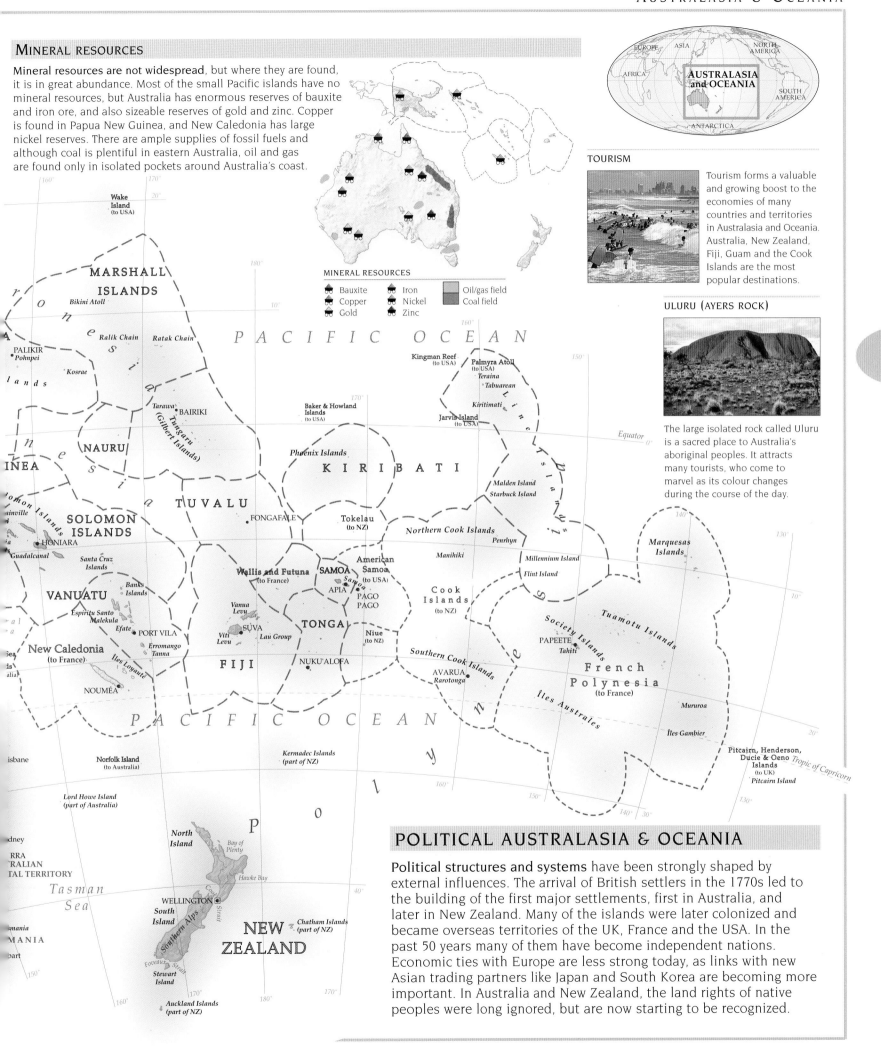

MINERAL RESOURCES

- Bauxite
- Copper
- Gold
- Iron
- Nickel
- Zinc
- Oil/gas field
- Coal field

TOURISM

Tourism forms a valuable and growing boost to the economies of many countries and territories in Australasia and Oceania. Australia, New Zealand, Fiji, Guam and the Cook Islands are the most popular destinations.

ULURU (AYERS ROCK)

The large isolated rock called Uluru is a sacred place to Australia's aboriginal peoples. It attracts many tourists, who come to marvel as its colour changes during the course of the day.

POLITICAL AUSTRALASIA & OCEANIA

Political structures and systems have been strongly shaped by external influences. The arrival of British settlers in the 1770s led to the building of the first major settlements, first in Australia, and later in New Zealand. Many of the islands were later colonized and became overseas territories of the UK, France and the USA. In the past 50 years many of them have become independent nations. Economic ties with Europe are less strong today, as links with new Asian trading partners like Japan and South Korea are becoming more important. In Australia and New Zealand, the land rights of native peoples were long ignored, but are now starting to be recognized.

AUSTRALIA

Australia is the world's sixth-largest country, and also the smallest, flattest continent, with the lowest rainfall. Most Australians are of European, mainly British, origin. However, since 1945 almost six million settlers from more than 170 countries have made Australia their home. The Aboriginal peoples, now only a tiny minority, were the first inhabitants. Recently, there have been several moves to restore their ancient lands.

INDUSTRY

Australia has one of the world's biggest mining industries. Bauxite, coal, copper, gold and iron ore are mined and exported, especially to Japan. In the cities, service industries, particularly tourism, are growing fast; Australia's sunshine and dramatic scenery are attracting an increasing number of overseas visitors.

STRUCTURE OF INDUSTRY

Primary 3%
Services 67%
Manufacturing 30%

INDUSTRY

⚗	Brewing	⛏	Mining
🚗	Car manufacture	⚗	Oil and gas
⚗	Chemicals	⛴	Tourism
⚡	Electronics		
⚙	Engineering	▪	Major industrial centre / area
🍱	Food processing		
⚒	Coal	—	Major road

Darwin
Nhulunbuy
Tennant Creek
Mount Isa
Alice Springs
Kalgoorlie
Broken Hill
Perth
Albany
Cairns
Townsville
Brisbane
Adelaide
Newcastle
Sydney
Melbourne
Hobart

POPULATION

Despite its vast size, Australia is sparsely populated. The desert 'outback', which covers most of the interior, is too dry and barren to support many people. About 85% of the population live in the cities and towns on the east and southeast coasts, and around Perth in the west.

INHABITANTS PER SQ KM

- More than 50
- 10–50
- 1–10
- Less than 1
- ▪ Capital city
- ● Major city

Darwin
Cairns
Mount Isa
Alice Springs
Townsville
Brisbane
Perth
Newcastle
Adelaide
Sydney
Melbourne
CANBERRA
Hobart

URBAN/RURAL POPULATION DIVIDE

Sydney 17.8%
Melbourne 16%
Brisbane 7.7%
Other towns and cities 43.5%
Rural population 15%

FARMING AND LAND USE

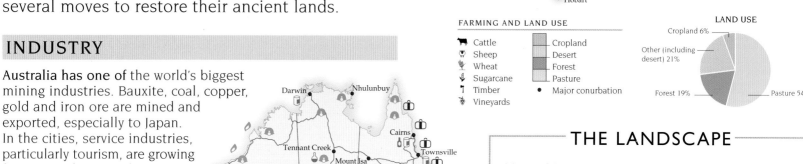

Away from the coasts, much of the land is too dry for agriculture. Fields of sugarcane grow close to the east coast, and grapes for the thriving wine industry are cultivated in the south and west, along with wheat. Vast numbers of cattle and sheep are raised for their meat and wool – both of which are major exports. They are grazed in the desert, on huge farms called 'stations', and in more fertile areas.

Darwin
Townsville
Brisbane
Perth
Adelaide
Sydney
Canberra
Melbourne
Hobart

FARMING AND LAND USE

🐄	Cattle		Cropland
🐑	Sheep		Desert
🌾	Wheat		Forest
🎋	Sugarcane		Pasture
🌲	Timber	●	Major conurbation
🍇	Vineyards		

LAND USE

Cropland 6%
Other (including desert) 21%
Forest 19%
Pasture 54%

THE LANDSCAPE

Most of Australia is dry, flat and barren; all of the wetter, fertile land is found along its coastline. Huge sun-baked deserts, fringed by semi-arid plains of scrub and grassland cover most of the west and centre of the country. In the east, the land rises to the highlands of the Great Dividing Range, which run the whole length of the east coast. The tropical north coast has rainforests and mangrove swamps.

Blue Mountains (G 6)

The Blue Mountains lie towards the southern end of the Great Dividing Range. They get their name from the blue haze of oil droplets given off by the eucalyptus trees covering their slopes.

Great Barrier Reef (G 2)

This spectacular coral reef, which stretches for over 2,000 km off the coast of Queensland, is the largest living structure on Earth. The reef has built up over millions of years and its waters are home to thousands of different species of coral and marine animals.

Uluru (Ayers Rock) (D 4)

Uluru is an enormous block of red sandstone, standing almost in the middle of Australia. It is the world's biggest free-standing rock – 9.4 km around the base, and 867 m high. It is the summit of a sandstone hill that is buried beneath the sands of the desert.

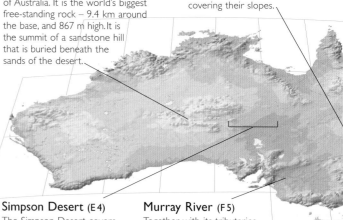

Simpson Desert (E 4)

The Simpson Desert covers around 130,000 sq km. It contains long, parallel lines of sand dunes and is scattered with large salt pans and salt lakes, which were created when old rivers evaporated. They are now fed by the seasonal rains.

Murray River (F 5)

Together with its tributaries, the Murray River is Australia's main river system. It winds slowly westwards for more than 2,500 km from the Great Dividing Range to the Indian Ocean. It is fed by snow from mountains in the far southeast.

Great Dividing Range (H 5)

These highlands separate the desert regions from the fertile eastern plains. Rivers and streams have eroded them, creating deep valleys and gorges.

ENVIRONMENTAL ISSUES

Australia's dry climate and low rainfall make it susceptible to desertification. Between 2001 and 2007, southeast Australia experienced one of its worst droughts on record. The Murray-Darling basin, one of Australia's most productive agricultural regions, was very badly affected. During the dry season, vegetation becomes tinder-dry, and bush fires are common, burning huge tracts of land.

2001–2007

ENVIRONMENTAL
ISSUES

- Area at risk from bushfires
- Drought
- Existing desert
- Risk of desertification
- Severe risk of desertification

CLIMATE

Much of Australia's climate is continental, and temperatures soar during the day and fall rapidly at night. The climate is also arid and very little rain falls, apart from in the summer months when the north is affected by tropical storms.

January

July

TEMPERATURE AND PRECIPITATION

- More than 35°C
- 30 to 35°C
- 25 to 30°C
- 20 to 25°C
- 15 to 20°C
- 10 to 15°C
- 5 to 10°C
- Less than 5°C
- 100 Precipitation (mm)

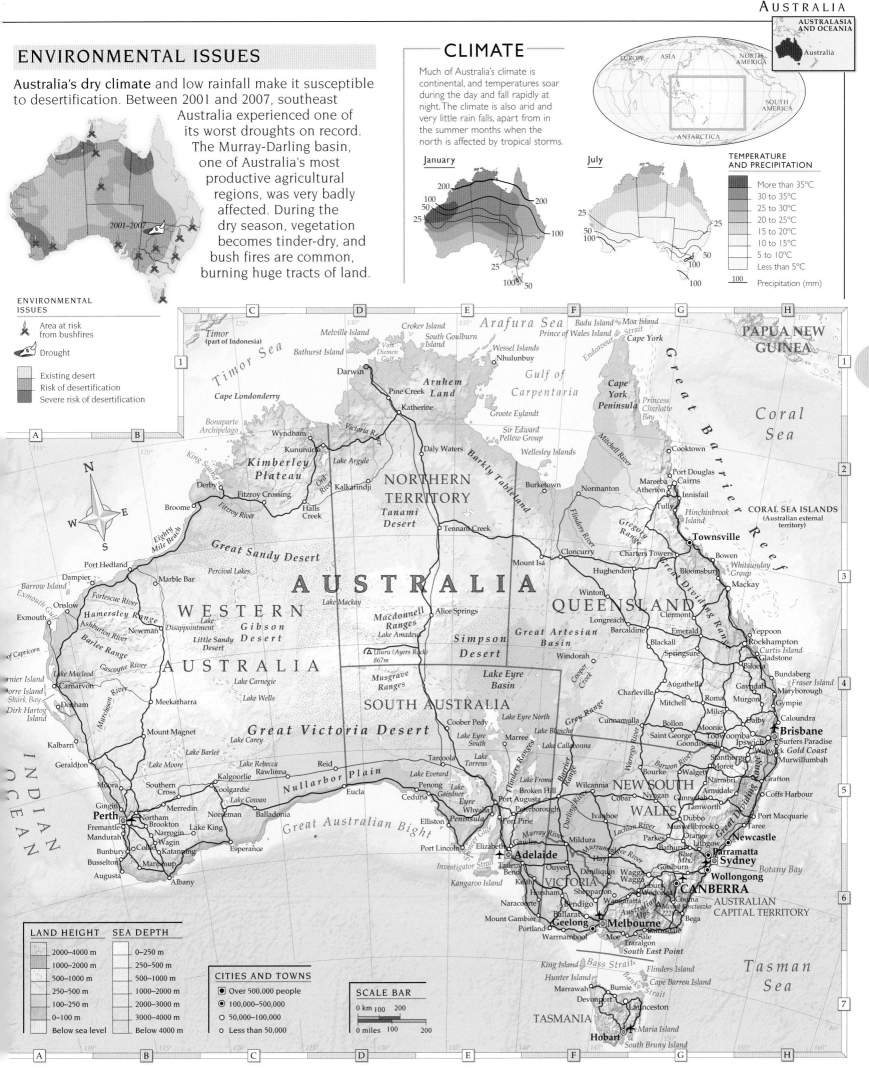

LAND HEIGHT
- 2000–4000 m
- 1000–2000 m
- 500–1000 m
- 250–500 m
- 100–250 m
- 0–100 m
- Below sea level

SEA DEPTH
- 0–250 m
- 250–500 m
- 500–1000 m
- 1000–2000 m
- 2000–3000 m
- 3000–4000 m
- Below 4000 m

CITIES AND TOWNS
- Over 500,000 people
- 100,000–500,000
- 50,000–100,000
- Less than 50,000

SCALE BAR
0 km 100 200
0 miles 100 200

NEW ZEALAND

New Zealand is one of the most remote populated places in the world. The first people to settle on the islands were the Maori, a Polynesian people. When European settlers arrived during the 19th century, the Maori became a minority, and now only make up about 8% of the population. With a small population and rich natural resources, New Zealand's people have high living standards. The country's magnificent rugged scenery is popular with tourists.

INDUSTRY

Hi-tech industries such as electronics and computing are growing in the major cities of Auckland and Wellington, although agricultural products such as meat, wool and milk are still among New Zealand's major exports, and large pine forests supply wood for paper pulp and timber. The exciting scenery and varied climate draw tourists from all over the world, especially for walking and adventure holidays.

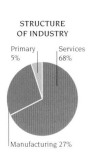

STRUCTURE OF INDUSTRY

Primary 5%
Services 68%
Manufacturing 27%

INDUSTRY

- 🜍 Chemicals
- ⚡ Electronics
- ⚙ Engineering
- ⊟ Fish processing
- ▯ Food processing
- ⛴ Iron and steel
- ⚘ Textiles
- ♣ Timber
- ⚰ Tourism

- ▣ Major industrial centre / area
- — Major road

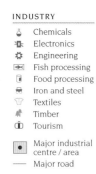

POPULATION

Most of the population is descended from European settlers, although immigrants from Asia and from the Pacific islands are increasing. About one-third of New Zealand's 4 million people live in Auckland on North Island, which also has the largest Polynesian population of any city in the Pacific. Elsewhere, the population is clustered along the coasts, where the land is lower.

URBAN/RURAL POPULATION DIVIDE

Auckland 30.7%
Other towns and cities 36.8%
Wellington 9.3%
Christchurch 9.2%
Rural population 14%

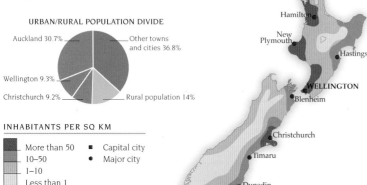

INHABITANTS PER SQ KM

- ▨ More than 50
- ▧ 10–50
- ▩ 1–10
- ▢ Less than 1

- ■ Capital city
- • Major city

ENVIRONMENTAL ISSUES

New Zealand is one of the world's least polluted countries – largely due to its low population and lack of heavy industries, although air quality is occasionally poor in Auckland and Christchurch. Environment-friendly geothermal energy is tapped to make electricity in the volcanic region of North Island. Recently, logging companies have begun to exploit the rich forest reserves, although this has been widely opposed.

ENVIRONMENTAL ISSUES

- ⛭ Geothermal power generation
- ⊙ Logging activity
- ☠ Urban air pollution
- • Major industrial centre
- ⊚ Catastrophic earthquake

THE LANDSCAPE

Two large, mountainous islands form New Zealand's main land areas. A large crack or fault – the Alpine Fault, in the west of South Island – is the boundary between two plates in the Earth's crust. Land either side of the fault tends to move, causing earthquakes. Volcanoes, many of them still active, are also found, on both islands. South Island has many high peaks, several more than 3,000 m high.

Geysers and boiling mud
Geysers occur when hot volcanic rocks come into contact with underground water. The water boils and turns to steam forcing the water above it to burst through the Earth's surface into the air. There are many geysers and boiling mud pools in the areas around Rotorua and Taupo.

Northland (C 1)
This is a tropical region in the far northwest. Many of the inlets are fringed by mangrove swamps.

Mount Taranaki (C 4)
The dormant volcano of Mount Taranaki lies on New Zealand's North Island. It rises to a height of 2,518 m.

Probable location of Alpine Fault

Lake Taupo (D 3)
New Zealand's largest lake, Lake Taupo, covers 606 sq km of North Island. It lies in the crater of an extinct volcano

Southern Alps
New Zealand's Southern Alps stretch more than 483 km down the backbone of South Island. They were formed by the collision of the Indo-Australian and Pacific plates. Heavy snowfalls here, brought by westerly winds, feed the Fox Glacier which moves at a speed of 0.5–4.5 m a day.

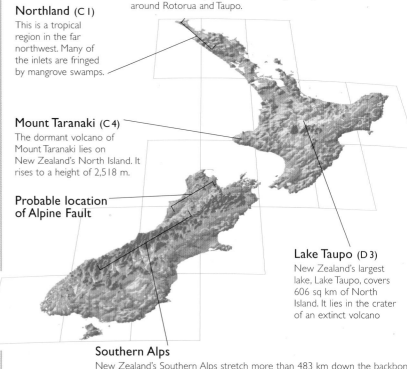

FARMING AND LAND USE

Large areas of rich, sweet grasslands have made New Zealand one of the world's top areas for rearing sheep. There are around 12 sheep for every person, grazing alongside about ten million cattle. Fruits, including apples, strawberries, oranges, peaches, and the famous kiwi fruit, are cultivated, particularly on South Island, and are exported throughout the world. Fish caught off the Pacific coast are another important source of income.

LAND USE

Other 8%
Cropland 14%
Forest 28%
Pasture 50%

FARMING AND LAND USE

- 🐂 Cattle
- ⚓ Fishing
- 🐑 Sheep
- 🍎 Fruit
- 🌲 Timber
- 🌾 Wheat

- Cropland
- Forest
- Mountains
- Pasture
- • Major conurbation

CLIMATE

North Island has a generally warm climate which becomes tropical – hotter and more humid – towards the far north. South Island is cooler and wetter. There may be heavy snowfall in winter, particularly in the highlands, and many mountains are permanently snow-capped

TEMPERATURE AND PRECIPITATION

- More than 15°C
- 10 to 15°C
- 5 to 10°C
- 0 to 5°C
- 0 to -5°C
- Less than -5°C
- 100 Precipitation (mm)

January

July

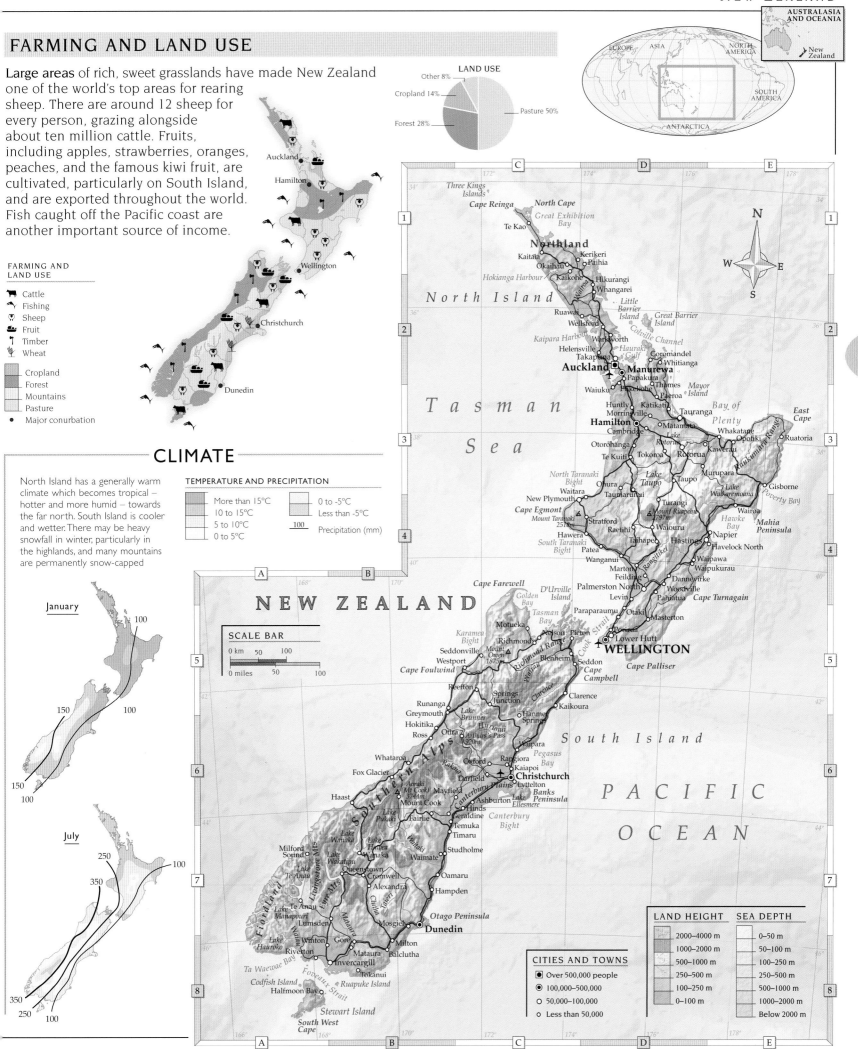

NEW ZEALAND

SCALE BAR
0 km   50   100
0 miles   50   100

CITIES AND TOWNS
- ■ Over 500,000 people
- ◉ 100,000–500,000
- ○ 50,000–100,000
- ○ Less than 50,000

LAND HEIGHT
- 2000–4000 m
- 1000–2000 m
- 500–1000 m
- 250–500 m
- 100–250 m
- 0–100 m

SEA DEPTH
- 0–50 m
- 50–100 m
- 100–250 m
- 250–500 m
- 500–1000 m
- 1000–2000 m
- Below 2000 m

SOUTHWEST PACIFIC

The many thousands of islands in the Pacific Ocean are scattered across an enormous area. The original inhabitants, the Polynesians, Melanesians and Micronesians, settled the islands following the last Ice Age. In the 1700s Europeans arrived. They colonized all of the Pacific islands, introducing their culture, languages and religion. Today, many, though not all, of the islands have become independent. Their economies are simple, based largely on fishing and agriculture. Many are increasingly relying on their beautiful scenery and tropical climates to attract tourists and give a valuable boost to their economies.

LANDSCAPE

Most of the Pacific islands are extremely small, the largest land mass is the half of the island of New Guinea occupied by Papua New Guinea. The edges of the Indo-Australian and Pacific plates meet on the western edge of the area, leading to much volcanic and earthquake activity. Many of the islands are coral atolls, originally formed by volcanic activity, and some are no more than a few metres above sea level.

New Guinea (A2)
A mountainous spine runs through the centre of the island, separating the northern coast from the dense forests and mangroves found in the south.

Pacific Ocean
The Pacific Ocean is the Earth's oldest and deepest ocean. Its name means peaceful, though it is far from being so; the highest wave ever recorded on open ocean – 34 m – occurred during a hurricane in the Pacific.

Kavachi
Kavachi is a submarine volcano lying off the coast of New Georgia, in the Solomon Islands. It still erupts every few years.

Ring of Fire
The 'Ring of Fire' is the term used to describe the string of volcanoes which surround the entire Pacific Ocean and erupt frequently because of intense stress and movement from within the Earth. The ring crosses the south Pacific, running between Vanuatu and New Caledonia, along the edge of the Solomon Islands, and between New Britain and New Guinea.

Sea trenches
Deep trenches mark the sea floor boundary where the Indo-Australian plate 'dives' under the Pacific plate.

Coral atolls
Volcanic activity in the Pacific has led to the creation of many islands. These islands become fringed with a ring of coral. When the islands subside beneath the sea once again, only the circle of coral is left, forming an atoll.

INDUSTRY

Today, **the main industry** for many of the Pacific islands is tourism. Food processing and small-scale textile industries are also common on many islands.

INDUSTRY
- 🍺 Brewing
- Food processing
- Textiles
- 🌲 Timber processing
- ⛏ Mining
- Tourism

- Major industrial centre
- — Major road

FARMING AND LAND USE

Most farming that takes place on the Pacific islands is at a subsistence level, and many people keep pigs and chickens. A few crops are grown for export, especially oil palms, and coconuts, which are dried in the sun to produce copra. Many islanders make their living from the rich fishing grounds of the Pacific. The thick forests of Papua New Guinea are increasingly cut down for timber.

AUSTRALASIA AND OCEANIA

Southwest Pacific

LAND USE

- Fishing
- Bananas
- Cocoa
- Coconuts
- Coffee
- Oil palms
- Rubber
- Timber
- Cropland
- Forest
- Wetland
- Major conurbation

Lae

Port Moresby

Honiara

Port Vila

Suva

Nouméa

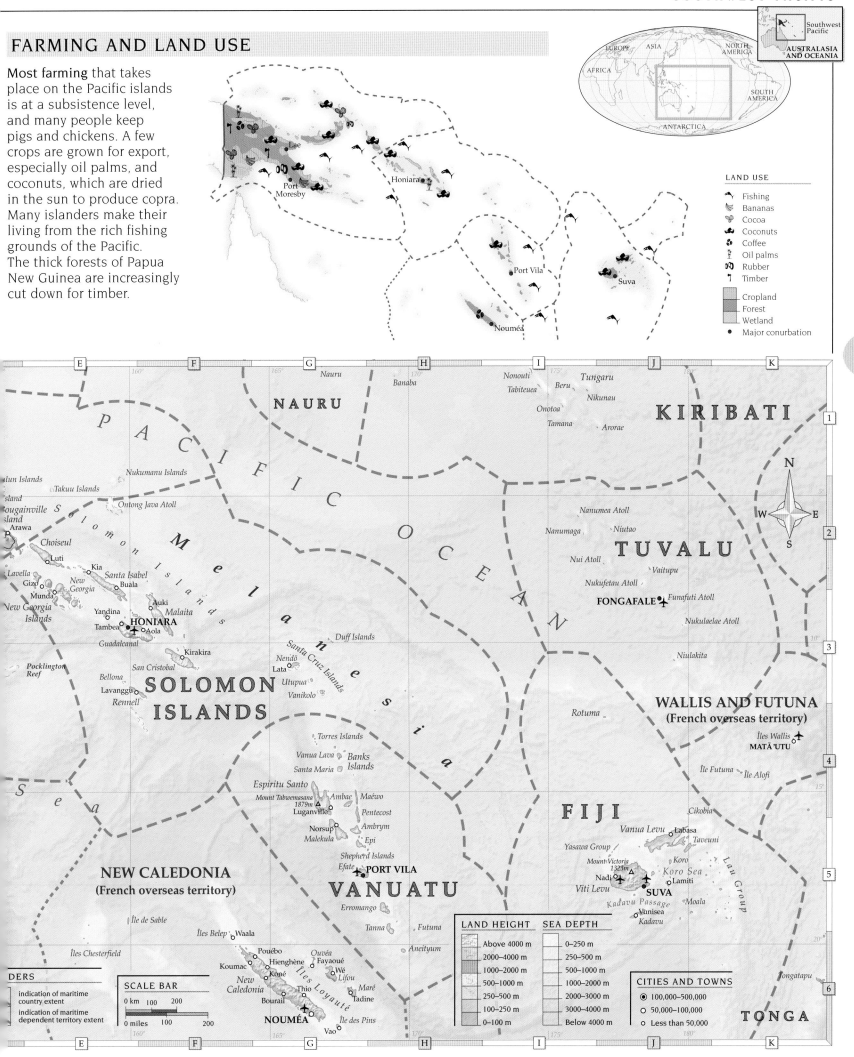

NAURU

Nauru

Banaba

Nonouti
Tabiteuea
Beru
Tungaru
Nikunau

KIRIBATI

Onotoa
Tamana
Arorae

PACIFIC OCEAN

Nukumanu Islands

Takuu Islands

Ontong Java Atoll

Nanumea Atoll

Nanumaga
Niutao

TUVALU

Nui Atoll
Vaitupu

Nukufetau Atoll

FONGAFALE • Funafuti Atoll

Nukulaelae Atoll

...lun Islands
...sland
...ougainville
...sland

Arawa

Choiseul

Luti

Lavella

Gizo
Munda
New Georgia

Kia
Santa Isabel
Buala

Yandina
Malaita
Auki

New Georgia Islands

Tambea
HONIARA
Aola

Guadalcanal

Kirakira

Duff Islands

Niulakita

WALLIS AND FUTUNA
(French overseas territory)

Rotuma

Îles Wallis
MATÂ'UTU

Pocklington Reef

Bellona
Lavanggu
Rennell

San Cristobal

SOLOMON ISLANDS

Nendö
Lata
Santa Cruz Islands
Utupua
Vanikolo

Torres Islands

Île Futuna
Île Alofi

Sea

Vanua Lava
Santa Maria
Banks Islands

Espiritu Santo

Mount Tabwemasana 1879m △
Luganville

Ambae
Maéwo
Pentecost

Norsup
Malekula
Ambrym
Epi

Cikobia

FIJI

Vanua Levu
Labasa
Taveuni

Yasawa Group
Koro

Mount Victoria 1323m △
Nadi
Koro Sea
Lamiti

Viti Levu
SUVA

Moala

NEW CALEDONIA
(French overseas territory)

Shepherd Islands

Efate
PORT VILA

VANUATU

Erromango

Kadavu Passage
Vunisea
Kadavu

Île de Sable

Tanna
Futuna

Îles Belep
Waala

Aneityum

Tongatapu

Îles Chesterfield

Pouébo
Hienghène
Koumac
Koné

Ouvéa
Fayaoué
Wé
Lifou

New Caledonia

Îles Loyauté

Maré
Tadine

Thio
Bourail

TONGA

NOUMÉA

Île des Pins

Vao

LAND HEIGHT

- Above 4000 m
- 2000–4000 m
- 1000–2000 m
- 500–1000 m
- 250–500 m
- 100–250 m
- 0–100 m

SEA DEPTH

- 0–250 m
- 250–500 m
- 500–1000 m
- 1000–2000 m
- 2000–3000 m
- 3000–4000 m
- Below 4000 m

CITIES AND TOWNS

- ⊙ 100,000–500,000
- ○ 50,000–100,000
- ○ Less than 50,000

...DERS

indication of maritime country extent

indication of maritime dependent territory extent

SCALE BAR

0 km   100   200

0 miles   100   200

ANTARCTICA

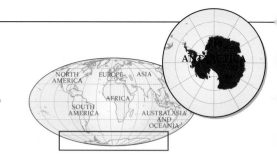

The continent of Antarctica has no permanent human population and very few animals can survive on the frozen land, although the surrounding seas teem with fish and mammals. Even in the summer the temperature is rarely above freezing and the sea-ice only partly melts; in winter, temperatures plummet to –80°C. The only people who live in Antarctica are teams of scientists who study the wildlife and monitor the ice for changes in the Earth's atmosphere.

THE LANDSCAPE

Antarctica is the world's most southerly continent. It is also the world's coldest continent and its highest, mainly due to the great ice sheet – up to 2 km thick in parts – which lies over the mountains of the Antarctic Peninsula and the plateau of East Antarctica.

Frozen seas
During the cold winter months, the seas surrounding Antarctica freeze, almost doubling the size of the continent.

Transantarctic Mountains (C 5)
The Transantarctic Mountains run across the continent, splitting it into East and West Antarctica.

Lambert Glacier (E 4)
The Lambert Glacier is the world's largest series of glaciers. It is 80 km wide at the coast and reaches more than 300 km inland.

Ice sheet
A massive sheet of ice, about 4,800 m thick at its deepest point, covers almost the entire area of Antarctica. It contains most of the fresh water on Earth. The weight of the ice pushes the land down below sea level.

The Ross Ice Shelf (C 5)
The Ross Sea is part of the Southern Ocean. This deep bay is covered by a thick sheet of ice which floats on the ocean.

RESOURCES

The mountains of Antarctica have rich mineral reserves. Gold, iron and coal are found, and there is natural gas in the surrounding seas. The unique and abundant marine wildlife is Antarctica's greatest resource. Colonies of penguins breed on the ice sheet, and whales, seals and many bird and fish species thrive in the icy waters.

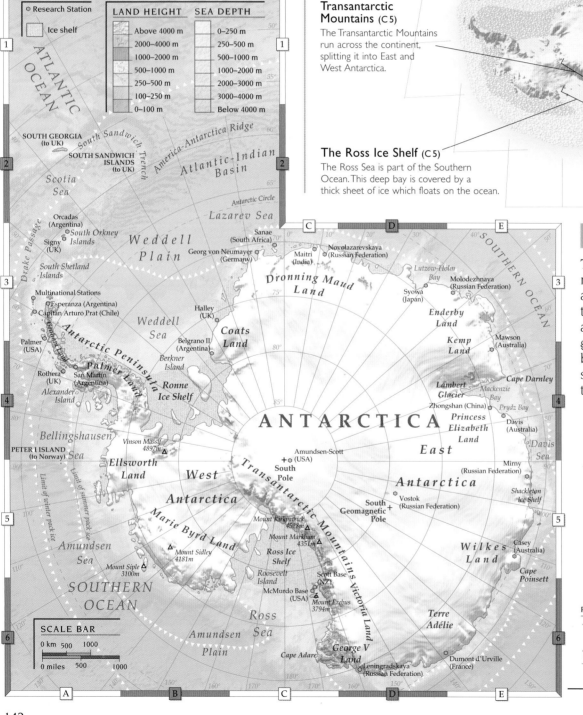

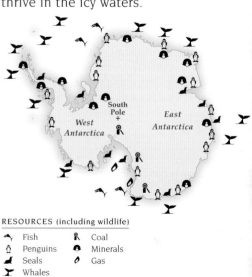

RESOURCES (including wildlife)

Fish	Coal
Penguins	Minerals
Seals	Gas
Whales	

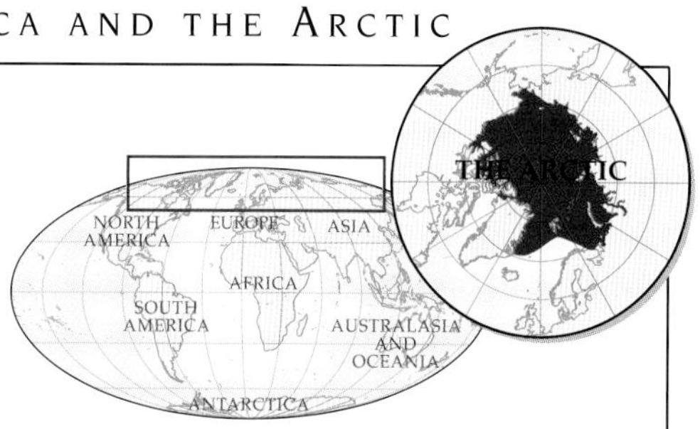

THE ARCTIC

The ice-covered **Arctic Ocean** is encircled by the most northerly parts of Europe, North America and Asia. Very few people live in the often freezing conditions. Those who do, including the Sami of northern Scandinavia, the Siberian Yugyt and Nenet people and the Canadian Inuit, were nomads who lived by hunting and herding. Some live like this today, but many have now settled in small towns.

THE LANDSCAPE

The Arctic Ocean is the smallest ocean in the world, covering a total area of 15,100,000 sq km. The ocean is divided into two large basins, divided by three great underwater mountain ranges including the Lomonosov Ridge which is more than 3,000 m high on average.

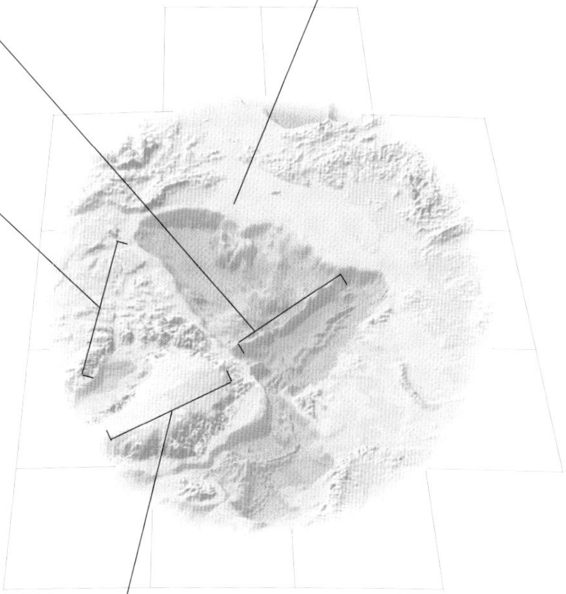

Lomonosov Ridge (C 4)

Arctic islands (A 4)
In the far north of Canada, there are many thousands of islands including Baffin Island and Victoria Island. Many of them are almost entirely surrounded by pack-ice.

Pack-ice
Much of the Arctic Ocean is permanently covered by pack-ice. When the ice breaks up, it forms enormous floating ice-masses called icebergs.

Greenland (A 3)
Greenland is the world's largest island. It is covered by a huge ice sheet, more than 1,683,400 sq km across. The weight of the ice has pushed most of the land below sea level.

Sastrugi
Snow, blown by strong winds can scratch deep patterns in the snow. These patterns are known as sastrugi and line up with the direction of the wind.

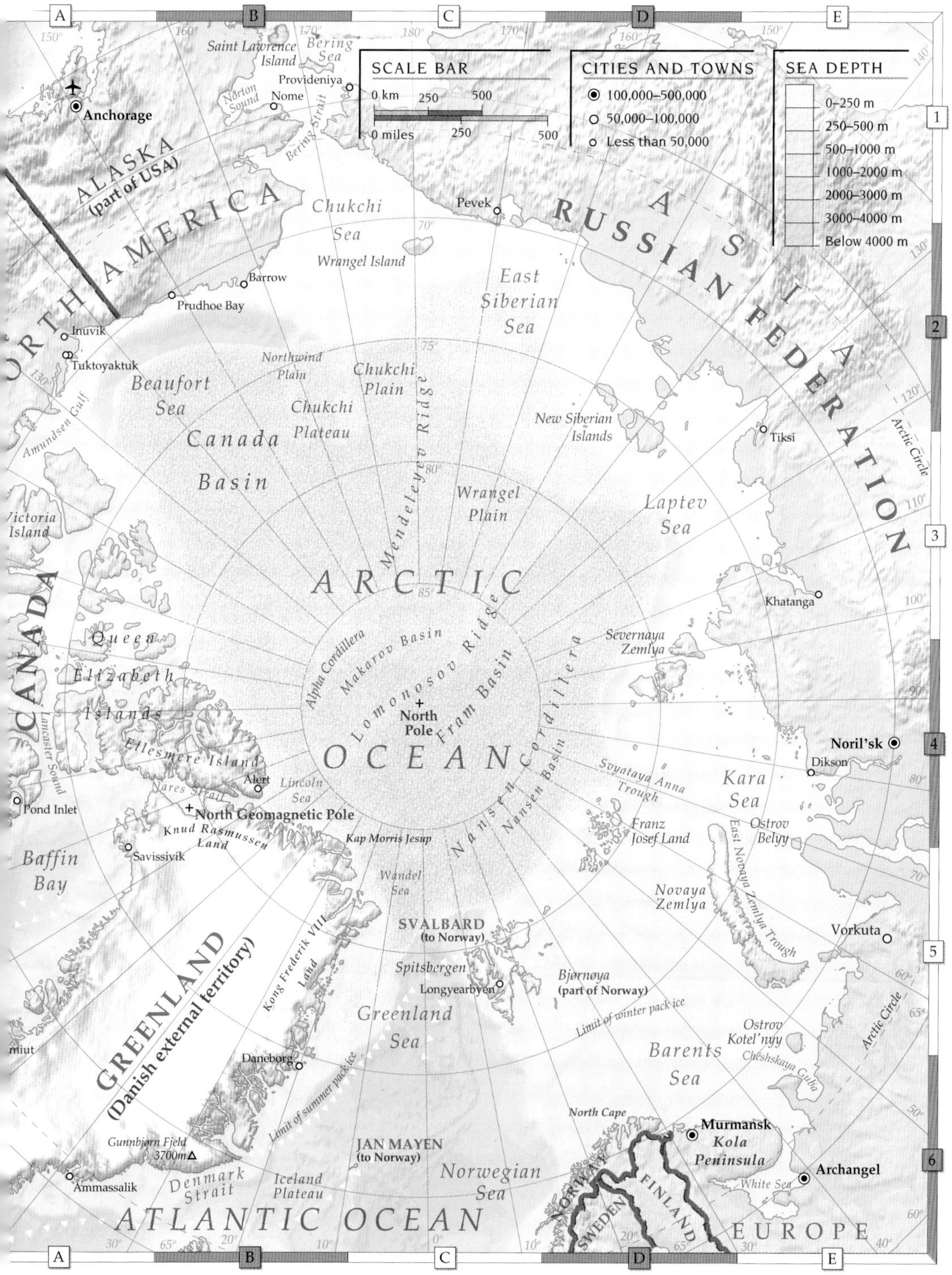

RESOURCES

Coal, oil and gas are found beneath the Arctic Ocean and in Canada, Alaska and Russia. Fears about damage to the environment and the cost of extracting these resources have restricted the quantities removed. Overfishing has reduced fish stocks to very low levels. Quotas have been put in place to allow them to revive.

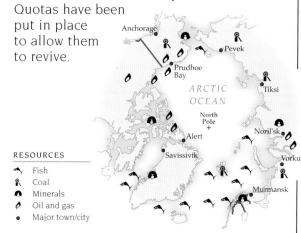

RESOURCES
- ⌐ Fish
- 🏋 Coal
- 🏋 Minerals
- ◊ Oil and gas
- ● Major town/city

(Map of The Arctic region with the following labelled features:)

SCALE BAR 0 km 250 500 / 0 miles 250 500

CITIES AND TOWNS
- ◉ 100,000–500,000
- ○ 50,000–100,000
- ○ Less than 50,000

SEA DEPTH
- 0–250 m
- 250–500 m
- 500–1000 m
- 1000–2000 m
- 2000–3000 m
- 3000–4000 m
- Below 4000 m

THE ARCTIC

NORTH AMERICA EUROPE ASIA
SOUTH AMERICA AFRICA AUSTRALASIA AND OCEANIA
ANTARCTICA

Saint Lawrence Island
Bering Sea
Provid;niya
Nome
Norton Sound
Anchorage
ALASKA (part of USA)
Chukchi Sea
Pevek
Wrangel Island
Barrow
Prudhoe Bay
Inuvik
Tuktoyaktuk
Beaufort Sea
Northwind Plain
Chukchi Plateau
Chukchi Plain
East Siberian Sea
New Siberian Islands
Tiksi
NORTH AMERICA
Canada Basin
Wrangel Plain
Mendeleyev Ridge
Laptev Sea
RUSSIAN FEDERATION
ASIA
Arctic Circle
Victoria Island
CANADA
Queen Elizabeth Islands
Alpha Cordillera
Makarov Basin
ARCTIC OCEAN
North Pole
Lomonosov Ridge
Fram Basin
Nansen Cordillera
Khatanga
Severnaya Zemlya
Lancaster Sound
Ellesmere Island
Pond Inlet
Alert
Lincoln Sea
Nares Strait
North Geomagnetic Pole
Nansen Basin
Nansen Basin
Svyataya Anna Trough
Kara Sea
Noril'sk
Dikson
Baffin Bay
Knud Rasmussen Land
Kap Morris Jesup
Franz Josef Land
Ostrov Belyy
East Novaya Zemlya Trough
Savissivik
Wandel Sea
Novaya Zemlya
Vorkuta
GREENLAND (Danish external territory)
Kong Frederik VIII Land
SVALBARD (to Norway)
Spitsbergen
Longyearbyen
Bjørnøya (part of Norway)
Limit of winter pack-ice
Ostrov Kotel'nyy
Cheshskaya Guba
miut
Greenland Sea
Limit of summer pack-ice
Barents Sea
Arctic Circle
Gunnbjørn Field 3700m△
Daneborg
JAN MAYEN (to Norway)
North Cape
Murmansk
Kola Peninsula
Archangel
White Sea
Ammassalik
Denmark Strait
Iceland Plateau
Norwegian Sea
NORWAY
SWEDEN
FINLAND
EUROPE
ATLANTIC OCEAN

(Resources map labels:)
Anchorage
Pevek
Prudhoe Bay
Tiksi
ARCTIC OCEAN
North Pole
Alert
Noril'sk
Savissivik
Vorkuta
Murmansk

STANDARD TIME ZONES

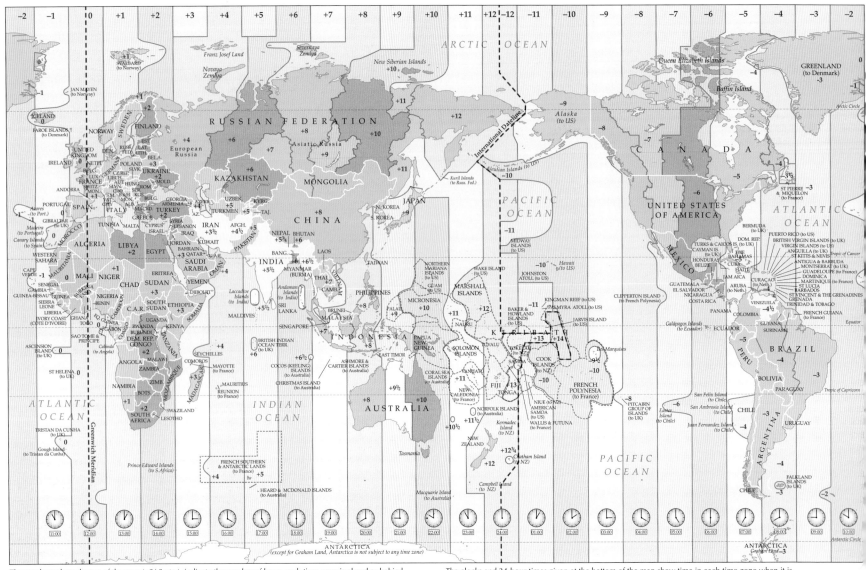

The numbers along the top of the map (+2/-2 etc.), indicate the number of hours each time zone is ahead or behind UTC (Coordinated Universal Time)

The clocks and 24-hour times given at the bottom of the map show time in each time zone when it is 12.00 hours noon UTC

Time Zones

The Earth is a rotating sphere, and because of this the Sun only shines on half of its surface at any one time. This means that it is morning, evening and night time in different parts of the world (*see diagram below*). Because of these differences, each country or part of a country uses a local time. A region of Earth's surface which uses a single local time is called a time zone. There are 24 one-hour time zones around the world, arranged roughly in vertical longitudinal bands.

Day and night around the world

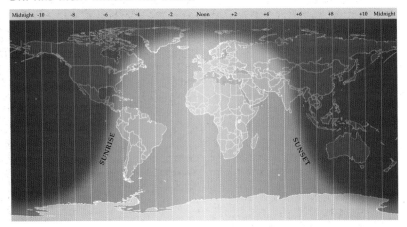

Standard Time

Standard time is the official local time in a particular country or part of a country. Although time zones are arranged roughly in longitudinal bands, in many places the borders of a zone do not fall exactly along a line of longitude, as can be seen on the map, but are determined by geographical factors or by borders between countries.

Most countries have just one time zone, but some large countries (such as the USA, Canada and Russia) are split between several time zones, so standard time varies across those countries. For example, mainland USA crosses four time zones and so has four standard times, called the Eastern, Central, Mountain and Pacific standard times. China is unusual in that just one standard time is used for the whole country, even though it extends across 60° of longitude from west to east.

Coordinated Universal Time (UTC)

Coordinated Universal Time (UTC) is an international reference used to set the local time in each time zone. For example, Australian Western Standard Time (the local time in Western Australia) is set 8 hours ahead of UTC (it is UTC+8), so if it were 12.00 noon UTC in London, UK, it would be 8.00pm in Perth, Western Australia. UTC has replaced Greenwich Mean Time (GMT) because UTC is based on an atomic clock, which is more accurate and convenient than GMT. Greenwich Mean Time was determined by the Sun's position in the sky relative to the 0° line of longitude, also known as the Greenwich Meridian, which runs through Greenwich, UK.

The International Dateline

The International Dateline is an imaginary line from pole to pole that roughly corresponds to the 180° line of longitude. It is an arbitrary marker between calendar days. The dateline is needed because of the use of local times around the world rather than a single universal time. When moving from west to east across the dateline, travellers have to set their watches back one day. Those travelling in the opposite direction, from east to west, must add a day.

Daylight saving time

Daylight saving is a summertime adjustment to the local time in a country or region, designed to increase the hours of daylight that occur during people's normal waking hours. To follow the system, clocks are advanced by an hour on a pre-decided date in spring and reverted back in autumn. About half of the world's nations use daylight saving.

LARGEST COUNTRIES

Russian Federation	17,075,200 sq km (6,592,735 sq miles)
Canada	9,984,670 sq km (3,885,171 sq miles)
USA	9,826,675 sq km (3,794,100 sq miles)
China	9,596,960 sq km (3,705,386 sq miles)
Brazil	8,511,965 sq km (3,286,470 sq miles)
Australia	7,686,850 sq km (2,967,893 sq miles)
India	3,287,590 sq km (1,269,339 sq miles)
Argentina	2,766,890 sq km (1,068,296 sq miles)
Kazakhstan	2,717,300 sq km (1,049,150 sq miles)
Algeria	2,381,740 sq km (919,590 sq miles)

SMALLEST COUNTRIES

Vatican City	0.44 sq km (0.17 sq miles)
Monaco	1.95 sq km (0.75 sq miles)
Nauru	21 sq km (8.1 sq miles)
Tuvalu	26 sq km (10 sq miles)
San Marino	61 sq km (24 sq miles)
Liechtenstein	160 sq km (62 sq miles)
Marshall Islands	181 sq km (70 sq miles)
St. Kitts & Nevis	261 sq km (101 sq miles)
Maldives	300 sq km (116 sq miles)
Malta	316 sq km (122 sq miles)

MOST POPULOUS COUNTRIES

China	1,393,800,000
India	1,267,400,000
USA	322,600,000
Indonesia	252,800,000
Brazil	202,120,000
Pakistan	185,100,000
Nigeria	178,500,000
Bangladesh	155,500,000
Russian Federation	142,500,000
Japan	127,000,000

LEAST POPULOUS COUNTRIES

Vatican City	800
Nauru	9500
Tuvalu	10,800
Palau	21,200
San Marino	32,700
Monaco	37,000
Liechtenstein	37,300
St. Kitts & Nevis	51,500
Marshall Islands	71,000
Dominica	73,400

MOST DENSELY POPULATED COUNTRIES

Monaco	18,949 per sq km (49,078 people per sq mile)
Singapore	9016 per sq km (23,351 people per sq mile)
Vatican City	1914 per sq km (4957 people per sq mile)
Bahrain	1841 per sq km (4768 people per sq mile)
Maldives	1333 per sq km (3452 people per sq mile)
Malta	1250 per sq km (3237 people per sq mile)
Bangladesh	1184 per sq km (3066 people per sq mile)
Taiwan	725 per sq km (1877 people per sq mile)
Barbados	698 per sq km (1808 people per sq mile)
Mauritius	645 per sq km (1670 people per sq mile)

MOST SPARSELY POPULATED COUNTRIES

Mongolia	2 per sq km (4 people per sq mile)
Namibia	3 per sq km (7 people per sq mile)
Australia	3 per sq km (7 people per sq mile)
Suriname	3 per sq km (8 people per sq mile)
Iceland	3 per sq km (8 people per sq mile)
Botswana	4 per sq km (9 people per sq mile)
Mauritania	4 per sq km (9 people per sq mile)
Canada	4 per sq km (9 people per sq mile)
Libya	4 per sq km (9 people per sq mile)
Guyana	4 per sq km (10 people per sq mile)

RICHEST COUNTRIES (GNI PER CAPITA, IN US$)

Monaco	186,950
Liechtenstein	136,770
Norway	102,610
Switzerland	90,760
Qatar	86,790
Luxembourg	69,900
Australia	65,390
Sweden	61,760
Denmark	61,680
Singapore	54,040

POOREST COUNTRIES (GNI PER CAPITA, IN US$)

Burundi	260
Malawi	270
Somalia	288
Central African Republic	320
Niger	400
Liberia	410
Congo, Democratic Republic of	430
Madagascar	440
Guinea	460
Ethiopia	470

MOST WIDELY SPOKEN LANGUAGES

1. Chinese (Mandarin)
2. English
3. Hindi, Hindustani, Urdu
4. Spanish
5. Russian
6. Arabic
7. Bengali
8. Portuguese
9. Malay-Indonesian
10. French

LARGEST DESERTS

Sahara	9,065,000 sq km (3,450,000 sq miles)
Gobi	1,295,000 sq km (500,000 sq miles)
Empty Quarter (Ar Rub al Khali)	750,000 sq km (289,600 sq miles)
Great Victorian	647,000 sq km (249,800 sq miles)
Sonoran	311,000 sq km (120,000 sq miles)
Kalahari	310,800 sq km (120,000 sq miles)
Garagum	300,000 sq km (115,800 sq miles)
Takla Makan	260,000 sq km (100,400 sq miles)
Namib	135,000 sq km (52,100 sq miles)
Thar	130,000 sq km (33,670 sq miles)

NB – Most of Antarctica is a polar desert, with only 50 mm (2 inches) of precipitation annually

LARGEST ISLANDS

Greenland	2,200,000 sq km (849,400 sq miles)
New Guinea	808,000 sq km (312,000 sq miles)
Borneo	757,050 sq km (292,222 sq miles)
Madagascar	594,000 sq km (229,300 sq miles)
Sumatra	524,000 sq km (202,300 sq miles)
Baffin Island	476,000 sq km (183,800 sq miles)
Honshu	230,000 sq km (88,800 sq miles)
Britain	229,800 sq km (88,700 sq miles)
Victoria Island	212,000 sq km (81,900 sq miles)
Ellesmere Island	196,000 sq km (75,700 sq miles)

HIGHEST MOUNTAINS (HEIGHT ABOVE SEA LEVEL)

Everest	8848 m (29,029 ft)
K2	8611 m (28,253 ft)
Kanchenjunga I	8598 m (28,210 ft)
Makalu I	8463 m (27,767 ft)
Cho Oyu	8201 m (26,907 ft)
Dhaulagiri I	8167 m (26,796 ft)
Manaslu I	8163 m (26,783 ft)
Nanga Parbat I	8126 m (26,661 ft)
Annapurna I	8091 m (26,547 ft)
Gasherbrum I	8068 m (26,471 ft)

DEEPEST OCEAN FEATURES

Challenger Deep, Mariana Trench (Pacific)	10,920 m (35,826 ft)
Vityaz III Depth, Tonga Trench (Pacific)	10,882 m (35,704 ft)
Vityaz Depth, Kurile-Kamchatka Trench (Pacific)	10,542 m (34,588 ft)
Cape Johnson Deep, Philippine Trench (Pacific)	10,497 m (34,441 ft)
Kermadec Trench (Pacific)	10,047 m (32,964 ft)
Ramapo Deep, Japan Trench (Pacific)	9984 m (32,758 ft)
Milwaukee Deep, Puerto Rico Trench (Atlantic)	9200 m (30,185 ft)
Argo Deep, Torres Trench (Pacific)	9165 m (30,070 ft)
Meteor Depth, South Sandwich Trench (Atlantic)	9144 m (30,000 ft)
Planet Deep, New Britain Trench (Pacific)	9140 m (29,988 ft)

LARGEST BODIES OF INLAND WATER (AREA & DEPTH)

Caspian Sea	371,000 sq km (143,243 sq miles) 980 m (3215 ft)
Lake Superior	83,270 sq km (32,151 sq miles) 393 m (1289 ft)
Lake Victoria	68,880 sq km (26,560 sq miles) 100 m (328 ft)
Lake Huron	60,700 sq km (23,436 sq miles) 229 m (751 ft)
Lake Michigan	58,020 sq km (22,402 sq miles) 281 m (922 ft)
Lake Tanganyika	32,900 sq km (12,703 sq miles) 1435 m (4700 ft)
Great Bear Lake	31,790 sq km (12,274 sq miles) 319 m (1047 ft)
Lake Baikal	30,500 sq km (11,776 sq miles) 1741 m (5712 ft)
Great Slave Lake	28,440 sq km (10,981 sq miles) 140 m (459 ft)
Lake Erie	25,680 sq km (9915 sq miles) 60 m (197 ft)

LONGEST RIVERS

Nile (NE Africa)	6695 km (4160 miles)
Amazon (South America)	6516 km (4049 miles)
Yangtze (China)	6299 km (3915 miles)
Mississippi/Missouri (US)	5969 km (3710 miles)
Ob'-Irtysh (Russ. Fed.)	5570 km (3461 miles)
Yellow River (China)	5464 km (3395 miles)
Congo (Central Africa)	4667 km (2900 miles)
Mekong (Southeast Asia)	4425 km (2749 miles)
Lena (Russian Federation)	4400 km (2734 miles)
Mackenzie (Canada)	4250 km (2640 miles)
Yenisey (Russian Federation)	4090 km (2541 miles)

GREATEST WATERFALLS (MEAN FLOW OF WATER)

Boyoma (Congo)	17,000 cu.m/sec (600,400 cu. ft/sec)
Khône (Laos/Cambodia)	11,600 cu.m/sec (410,000 cu. ft/sec)
Niagara (USA/Canada)	5500 cu.m/sec (195,000 cu. ft/sec)
Grande (Uruguay)	4500 cu.m/sec (160,000 cu. ft/sec)
Paulo Afonso (Brazil)	2800 cu.m/sec (100,000 cu. ft/sec)
Urubupunga (Brazil)	2750 cu.m/sec (97,000 cu. ft/sec)
Iguaçu (Argentina/Brazil)	1700 cu.m/sec (62,000 cu. ft/sec)
Maribondo (Brazil)	1500 cu.m/sec (53,000 cu. ft/sec)
Victoria (Zimbabwe)	1100 cu.m/sec (39,000 cu. ft/sec)
Kabalega (Uganda)	1200 cu.m/sec (42,000 cu. ft/sec)
Churchill (Canada)	1000 cu.m/sec (35,000 cu. ft/sec)
Cauvery (India)	900 cu.m/sec (33,000 cu. ft/sec)

HIGHEST WATERFALLS

Angel (Venezuela)	979 m (3212 ft)
Tugela (South Africa)	948 m (3110 ft)
Utigard (Norway)	800 m (2625 ft)
Mongefossen (Norway)	774 m (2539 ft)
Mtarazi (Zimbabwe)	762 m (2500 ft)
Yosemite (USA)	739 m (2425 ft)
Ostre Mardola Foss (Norway)	657 m (2156 ft)
Tyssestrengane (Norway)	646 m (2119 ft)
*Cuquenan (Venezuela)	610 m (2001 ft)
Sutherland (New Zealand)	580 m (1903 ft)
*Kjellfossen (Norway)	561 m (1841 ft)

* indicates that the total height is a single leap

	GENERAL FACTS				
Country	**Capital city**	**Land area (sq km)**	**Main languages spoken**	**Unit of currency**	**Population (2014)**
NORTH AMERICA					
Antigua & Barbuda	St John's	442	English, English patois	East Caribbean dollar	91 3
Bahamas, The	Nassau	13 940	English, English Creole, French Creole	Bahamian dollar	400 0
Barbados	Bridgetown	430	Bajan (Barbadian English), English	Barbados dollar	300 0
Belize	Belmopan	22 966	English Creole, Spanish, English, Mayan, Garifuna (Carib)	Belizean dollar	300 0
Canada	Ottawa	9 984 670	English, French, Chinese, Italian, German, Ukrainian, Portuguese, Inuktitut, Cree	Canadian dollar	35 500 0
Costa Rica	San José	51 100	Spanish, English Creole, Bribri, Cabecar	Costa Rican colón	4 900 0
Cuba	Havana	110 860	Spanish	Cuban peso	11 300 0
Dominica	Roseau	754	French Creole, English	East Caribbean dollar	73 4
Dominican Republic	Santo Domingo	48 380	Spanish, French Creole	Dominican Republic peso	10 500 0
El Salvador	San Salvador	21 040	Spanish	Salvadorean colón, US $	6 400 0
Grenada	St George's	340	English, English Creole	East Caribbean dollar	110 0
Guatemala	Guatemala City	108 890	Quiché, Mam, Cakchiquel, Kekchí, Spanish	Quetzal	15 900 0
Haiti	Port-au-Prince	27 750	French Creole, French	Gourde	10 500 0
Honduras	Tegucigalpa	112 090	Spanish, Garífuna (Carib), English Creole	Lempira	8 300 0
Jamaica	Kingston	10 990	English Creole, English	Jamaican dollar	2 800 0
Mexico	Mexico City	1 972 550	Spanish, Nahuatl, Mayan, Zapotec, Mixtec, Otomi, Totonac, Tzotzil, Tzeltal	Mexican peso	123 800 0
Nicaragua	Managua	129 494	Spanish, English Creole, Miskito	Córdoba oro	6 200 0
Panama	Panama City	78 200	English Creole, Spanish, Amerindian languages, Chibchan languages	Balboa, US dollar	3 900 0
St Kitts & Nevis	Basseterre	261	English, English Creole	East Caribbean dollar	51 5
St Lucia	Castries	620	English, French Creole	East Caribbean dollar	200 0
St Vincent & the Grenadines	Kingstown	389	English, English Creole	East Caribbean dollar	103 0
Trinidad & Tobago	Port-of-Spain	5 128	English Creole, English, Hindi, French, Spanish	Trinidad and Tobago dollar	1 300 0
United States	Washington D.C.	9 826 675	English, Spanish, Chinese, French, German, Tagalog, Vietnamese, Italian, Korean, Russian, Polish	US dollar	322 600 0
SOUTH AMERICA					
Argentina	Buenos Aires	2 766 890	Spanish, Italian, Amerindian languages	Argentine peso	41 800 0
Bolivia	La Paz/Sucre	1 098 580	Aymara, Quechua, Spanish	Boliviano	10 800 0
Brazil	Brasília	8 511 965	Portuguese, German, Italian, Spanish, Polish, Japanese, Amerindian languages	Real	202 000 0
Chile	Santiago	756 950	Spanish, Amerindian languages	Chilean peso	17 800 0
Colombia	Bogotá	1 138 910	Spanish, Wayuu, Páez, other Amerindian languages	Colombian peso	48 900 0
Ecuador	Quito	283 560	Spanish, Quechua, other Amerindian languages	US dollar	16 000 0
Guyana	Georgetown	214 970	English Creole, Hindi, Tamil, Amerindian languages, English	Guyanese dollar	800 0
Paraguay	Asunción	406 750	Guaraní, Spanish, German	Guaraní	6 900 0
Peru	Lima	1 285 200	Spanish, Quechua, Aymara	New sol	30 800 0
Suriname	Paramaribo	163 270	Sranan (creole), Dutch, Javanese, Sarnami Hindi, Saramaccan, Chinese, Carib	Surinamese dollar	500 0
Uruguay	Montevideo	176 220	Spanish	Uruguayan peso	3 400 0
Venezuela	Caracas	912 050	Spanish, Amerindian languages	Bolívar fuerte	30 900 0
AFRICA					
Algeria	Algiers	2 381 740	Arabic, Tamazight (Kabyle, Shawia, Tamashek), French	Algerian dinar	39 900 0
Angola	Luanda	1 246 700	Portuguese, Umbundu, Kimbundu, Kikongo	Readjusted kwanza	22 100 0
Benin	Porto-Novo	112 620	Fon, Bariba, Yoruba, Adja, Houeda, Somba, French	CFA franc	10 600 0
Botswana	Gaborone	600 370	Setswana, English, Shona, San, Khoikhoi, isiNdebele	Pula	2 000 0
Burkina Faso	Ouagadougou	274 200	Mossi, Fulani, French, Tuareg, Dyula, Songhai	CFA franc	17 400 0
Burundi	Bujumbura	27 830	Kirundi, French, Kiswahili	Burundian franc	10 500 0
Cameroon	Yaoundé	475 400	Bamileke, Fang, Fulani, French, English	CFA franc	22 800 0
Cape Verde	Praia	4 033	Portuguese Creole, Portuguese	Escudo	500 0
Central African Republic	Bangui	622 984	Sango, Banda, Gbaya, French	CFA franc	4 700 0
Chad	N'Djamena	1 284 000	French, Sara, Arabic, Maba	CFA franc	13 200 0
Comoros	Moroni	2 170	Arabic, Comoran, French	Comoros franc	800 0
Congo, Democratic Republic	Kinshasa	2 345 410	Kiswahili, Tshiluba, Kikongo, Lingala, French	Congolese franc	69 400 0

POPULATION					HEALTH AND EDUCATION					ECONOMIC DEVELOPMENT			TECHNOLOGICAL DEVELOPMENT		
Population density per sq km (2014)	Birth rate per 1 000 population (2012)	Death rate per 1 000 population (2012)	Life expectancy at birth (years; 2013–2014)		Medical doctors per 10 000 people (2004–2013)	Infant mortality (deaths per 1 000 live births; 2013)	Adult literacy rate (percentage of adults over 15; 2015)		Average calorie intake per person (2011)	GNI per person (US$; 2013)	Annual electricity consumption per person (kWh; 2012)	Annual military expenditure as percentage of GDP (2009–2014)	Mobile telephones per 1 000 population (2013)	Internet users per 1 000 population (2013)	ICT Dev. Index (IDI), compiled by the ITU (2013)
			Male	Female			Male	Female							
207	17	7	74	78	1.7	8	98.4	99.0	2 396	13 050	3 291	0.7	1 271	634	57
40	15	6	72	78	28.2	10	95.0	96.7	2 575	21 570	4 290	0.7	761	720	-
698	13	7	73	78	18.1	13	99.0	99.0	3 047	15 080	3 127	0.7	1 081	750	35
13	24	4	71	77	8.3	14	76.7	77.1	2 757	4 510	2 017	1.0	526	317	-
4	11	7	79	84	20.7	5	99.0	99.0	3 419	52 200	15 125	1.0	806	858	23
96	15	4	78	82	11.1	8	97.7	97.8	2 898	9 550	1 872	0.7	1 460	460	55
102	10	8	77	81	67.2	5	99.0	99.0	3 277	5 890	1 290	3.3	177	257	125
98	16	7	74	80	15.9	10	94.0	94.0	3 047	6 930	1 227	0.0	1 300	590	83
217	21	5	70	77	14.9	24	91.2	92.3	2 597	5 770	1 167	0.6	884	459	102
309	20	7	68	77	16.0	14	90.4	86.0	2 513	3 720	899	1.1	1 362	231	110
324	19	7	70	75	6.6	11	96.0	96.0	2 453	7 490	1 633	-	1 256	350	76
147	31	6	69	76	9.3	26	87.4	76.3	2 502	3 340	541	0.5	1 404	197	118
381	26	9	61	65	2.5	55	64.3	57.3	2 105	810	44	0.2	694	106	-
74	26	5	72	76	3.7	19	88.4	88.6	2 651	2 180	637	1.2	959	178	119
259	18	7	71	76	4.1	14	84.0	93.1	2 789	5 220	1 074	0.8	1 022	378	97
65	19	5	75	80	21.0	12	96.2	94.2	3 024	9 940	2 015	0.6	858	435	95
52	23	5	72	78	3.7	20	82.4	83.2	2 564	1 790	593	0.8	1 120	155	120
51	20	5	75	81	15.5	15	95.7	94.1	2 644	10 700	1 984	1.1	1 630	429	82
143	14	9	73	78	11.7	8	-	-	2 507	13 890	2 567	-	1 421	800	54
328	16	7	72	78	4.7	13	89.5	90.6	2 629	7 060	2 074	0.0	1 163	352	79
303	17	6	70	75	5.3	17	96.0	96.0	2 960	6 460	1 231	0.0	1 146	520	72
253	15	9	66	74	11.8	19	99.0	99.0	2 889	15 760	5 975	0.8	1 449	638	67
35	13	8	77	81	24.5	6	99.0	99.0	3 639	53 470	12 140	3.8	955	842	14
15	17	8	73	80	32.1	12	98.0	98.1	3 155	6 290	2 849	0.7	1 625	599	59
10	26	7	65	70	4.7	31	97.8	93.6	2 254	2 550	633	1.5	977	395	107
24	15	7	70	78	18.9	12	92.2	92.9	3 287	11 690	2 437	1.4	1 353	516	65
24	14	5	77	83	10.3	7	97.6	97.4	2 989	15 230	3 643	2.0	1 343	665	56
47	19	4	70	78	14.7	14	94.6	94.8	2 593	7 590	1 037	3.4	1 041	517	77
58	21	5	74	79	16.9	19	95.4	93.5	2 477	5 760	1 277	3.0	1 115	404	88
4	21	8	64	69	2.1	30	87.2	89.8	2 648	3 750	698	1.1	694	330	111
17	24	5	70	75	11.1	19	96.1	95.0	2 698	4 010	1 213	1.6	1 037	369	109
24	20	4	72	78	11.3	13	97.3	91.7	2 624	6 270	1 202	1.4	981	392	105
3	18	4	68	74	9.1	20	96.1	95.0	2 727	9 370	3 144	1.1	1 611	374	98
19	15	9	74	81	37.4	10	98.2	99.0	2 939	15 180	2 811	1.9	1 546	581	48
35	20	5	72	78	19.4	13	96.4	96.2	2 880	12 550	3 267	1.2	1 016	549	80
17	25	6	69	73	12.1	22	87.2	73.1	3 220	5 330	1 174	5.0	1 008	165	114
18	45	14	50	53	1.7	102	82.0	60.7	2 400	5 170	240	4.9	619	191	139
96	37	10	58	61	0.6	56	49.9	27.3	2 594	790	97	1.0	933	49	149
4	24	8	62	67	3.4	36	88.0	88.9	2 285	7 770	1 530	2.0	1 606	150	104
64	41	10	56	57	0.5	64	43.0	29.3	2 655	670	56	1.4	664	44	156
409	45	12	52	56	0.3	55	88.2	83.1	1 604	260	33	2.2	250	13	-
49	38	11	54	56	0.8	61	81.2	68.9	2 586	1 290	270	1.3	704	64	140
124	20	5	71	79	3.0	22	92.1	83.1	2 716	3 620	571	0.5	1 001	375	93
8	35	14	48	52	0.5	96	50.7	24.4	2 154	320	37	2.6	295	35	166
10	46	14	50	52	0.4	88	48.5	31.9	2 061	1 030	16	2.0	356	23	164
359	36	8	60	62	1.5	58	81.8	73.7	2 139	840	50	2.8	473	65	-
31	43	14	48	52	1.1	86	78.1	50.0	1 585	430	105	1.3	418	22	157

			GENERAL FACTS		
Country	**Capital city**	**Land area (sq km)**	**Main languages spoken**	**Unit of currency**	**Population (2014)**
Congo	Brazzaville	342 000	Kongo, Teke, Lingala, French	CFA franc	4 600 000
Djibouti	Djibouti	22 000	Somali, Afar, French, Arabic	Djibouti franc	900 000
Egypt	Cairo	1 001 450	Arabic, French, English, Berber	Egyptian pound	83 400 000
Equatorial Guinea	Malabo	28 051	Spanish, Fang, Bubi, French	CFA franc	800 000
Eritrea	Asmara	121 320	Tigrinya, English, Tigre, Afar, Arabic, Saho, Bilen, Kunama, Nara, Hadareb	Nakfa	6 500 000
Ethiopia	Addis Ababa	1 127 127	Amharic, Tigrinya, Galla, Sidamo, Somali, English, Arabic	Birr	96 500 000
Gabon	Libreville	267 667	Fang, French, Punu, Sira, Nzebi, Mpongwe	CFA franc	1 700 000
Gambia	Banjul	11 300	Mandinka, Fulani, Wolof, Jola, Soninke, English	Dalasi	1 900 000
Ghana	Accra	238 540	Twi, Fanti, Ewe, Ga, Adangbe, Gurma, Dagomba (Dagbani), English	Cedi	26 400 000
Guinea	Conakry	245 857	Pulaar, Malinké, Soussou, French	Guinea franc	12 000 000
Guinea-Bissau	Bissau	36 120	Portuguese Creole, Balante, Fulani, Malinké, Portuguese	CFA franc	1 700 000
Ivory Coast (Côte d'Ivoire)	Yamoussoukro	322 460	Akan, French, Krou, Voltaïque	CFA franc	20 800 000
Kenya	Nairobi	582 650	Kiswahili, English, Kikuyu, Luo, Kalenjin, Kamba	Kenya shilling	45 500 000
Lesotho	Maseru	30 355	English, Sesotho, isiZulu	Loti, S African rand	2 100 000
Liberia	Monrovia	111 370	Kpelle, Vai, Bassa, Kru, Grebo, Kissi, Gola, Loma, English	Liberian dollar	4 400 000
Libya	Tripoli	1 759 540	Arabic, Tuareg	Libyan dinar	6 300 000
Madagascar	Antananarivo	587 040	Malagasy, French, English	Ariary	23 600 000
Malawi	Lilongwe	118 480	Chewa, Lomwe, Yao, Ngoni, English	Malawi kwacha	16 800 000
Mali	Bamako	1 240 000	Bambara, Fulani, Senufo, Soninke, French	CFA franc	15 800 000
Mauritania	Nouakchott	1 030 700	Arabic, Hassaniyah Arabic, Wolof, French	Ouguiya	4 000 000
Mauritius	Port Louis	1 860	French Creole, Hindi, Urdu, Tamil, Chinese, English, French	Mauritian rupee	1 200 000
Morocco	Rabat	446 300	Arabic, Tamazight (Berber), French, Spanish	Moroccan dirham	33 500 000
Mozambique	Maputo	801 590	Makua, Xitsonga, Sena, Lomwe, Portuguese	New metical	26 500 000
Namibia	Windhoek	825 418	Ovambo, Kavango, English, Bergdama, German, Afrikaans	Namibian $, S African rand	2 300 000
Niger	Niamey	1 267 000	Hausa, Djerma, Fulani, Tuareg, Teda, French	CFA franc	18 500 000
Nigeria	Abuja	923 768	Hausa, English, Yoruba, Ibo	Naira	178 500 000
Rwanda	Kigali	26 338	Kinyarwanda, French, Kiswahili, English	Rwanda franc	12 100 000
São Tomé & Príncipe	São Tomé	1 001	Portuguese Creole, Portuguese	Dobra	200 000
Senegal	Dakar	196 190	Wolof, Pulaar, Serer, Diola, Mandinka, Malinké, Soninké, French	CFA franc	14 500 000
Seychelles	Victoria	455	French Creole, English, French	Seychelles rupee	91 700
Sierra Leone	Freetown	71 740	Mende, Temne, Krio, English	Leone	6 200 000
Somalia	Mogadishu	637 657	Somali, Arabic, English, Italian	Somali shilin	10 800 000
South Africa	Pretoria/Cape Town/Bloemfontein	1 219 912	English, isiZulu, isiXhosa, Afrikaans, Sepedi, Setswana, 5 other official languages	Rand	53 100 000
South Sudan	Juba	644 329	Arabic, Dinka, Nuer, Zande, Bari, Shilluk, Lotuko, English	South Sudan pound	11 700 000
Sudan	Khartoum	1 861 481	Arabic, Nubian, Beja, Fur	New Sudanese pound	38 800 000
Swaziland	Mbabane	17 363	English, siSwati, isiZulu, Xitsonga	Lilangeni	1 300 000
Tanzania	Dodoma	945 087	Kiswahili, Sukuma, Chagga, Nyamwezi, Hehe, Makonde, Yao, Sandawe, English	Tanzanian shilling	50 800 000
Togo	Lomé	56 785	Ewe, Kabye, Gurma, French	CFA franc	7 000 000
Tunisia	Tunis	163 610	Arabic, French	Tunisian dinar	11 100 000
Uganda	Kampala	236 040	Luganda, Nkole, Chiga, Lango, Acholi, Teso, Lugbara, English	Uganda shilling	38 800 000
Western Sahara (occupied by Morocco)	Laâyoune	266 000	Arabic, Hassaniyah Arabic, Tamazight (Berber), Spanish	Moroccan dirham	555 000
Zambia	Lusaka	752 614	Bemba, Tonga, Nyanja, Lozi, Lala-Bisa, Nsenga, English	New Zambian kwacha	15 000 000
Zimbabwe	Harare	390 580	Shona, isiNdebele, English	US dollar, S African rand*	14 600 000
EUROPE					
Albania	Tirana	28 748	Albanian, Greek	Lek	3 200 000
Andorra	Andorra la Vella	468	Spanish, Catalan, French, Portuguese	Euro	85 500
Austria	Vienna	83 858	German, Croatian, Slovenian, Hungarian (Magyar)	Euro	8 500 000
Belarus	Minsk	207 600	Belarussian, Russian	Belarussian rouble	9 300 000
Belgium	Brussels	30 510	Dutch, French, German	Euro	11 100 000
Bosnia & Herzegovina	Sarajevo	51 129	Bosnian, Serbian, Croatian	Marka	3 800 000
Bulgaria	Sofia	110 910	Bulgarian, Turkish, Romani	Lev	7 200 000
Croatia	Zagreb	56 542	Croatian	Kuna	4 300 000

* Zimbabwe dollar suspended in 2009; US dollar, South African rand, euro, UK pound, Botswanan pula, Australian dollar, Chinese yuan, Indian rupee, and Japanese yen are legal tend

POPULATION					HEALTH AND EDUCATION					ECONOMIC DEVELOPMENT			TECHNOLOGICAL DEVELOPMENT		
Population density per sq km (2014)	Birth rate per 1 000 population (2012)	Death rate per 1 000 population (2012)	Life expectancy at birth (years; 2013–2014)		Medical doctors per 10 000 people (2004–2013)	Infant mortality (deaths per 1 000 live births; 2013)	Adult literacy rate (percentage of adults over 15; 2015)		Average calorie intake per person (2011)	GNI per person (US$; 2013)	Annual electricity consumption per person (kWh; 2012)	Annual military expenditure as percentage of GDP (2009–2014)	Mobile telephones per 1 000 population (2013)	Internet users per 1 000 population (2013)	ICT Dev. Index (IDI), compiled by the ITU (2013)
			Male	Female			Male	Female							
13	38	10	57	60	1.0	36	86.4	72.9	2 195	2 590	176	5.6	1 048	66	137
39	28	9	60	63	2.3	57	79.9	61.4	2 526	1 030	346	3.5	280	95	141
84	24	6	69	74	28.3	19	82.2	65.4	3 557	3 140	1 614	1.7	1 215	496	89
29	36	12	52	55	3.0	69	97.4	93.0	-	14 320	133	1.0	675	164	-
55	37	7	61	65	0.5	36	82.4	65.5	1 640	490	51	4.2	56	9	163
87	34	8	62	65	0.2	44	57.2	41.1	2 105	470	60	0.8	273	19	162
7	32	9	62	65	2.9	39	85.3	81.0	2 781	10 650	1 050	1.3	2 148	92	126
190	43	8	58	60	0.4	49	63.9	47.6	2 849	500	121	1.6	1 000	140	135
115	31	8	60	62	1.0	52	82.0	71.4	3 003	1 770	334	0.5	1 082	123	113
49	37	10	55	57	1.0	65	38.1	22.8	2 553	460	86	3.8	633	16	161
60	38	12	53	56	0.5	78	71.8	48.3	2 304	590	29	1.7	741	31	154
65	37	13	50	52	1.4	71	53.1	32.5	2 781	1 450	230	1.5	954	26	151
80	36	9	60	64	1.8	48	81.1	74.9	2 189	1 160	155	1.6	718	390	124
69	28	14	49	50	0.5	73	70.1	88.3	2 595	1 500	321	2.1	863	50	132
46	36	8	60	62	0.1	54	62.4	32.8	2 251	410	66	0.7	594	46	153
4	21	4	74	77	19.0	12	96.7	85.6	3 211	12 930	4 236	6.2	1 650	165	-
41	35	7	63	66	1.6	40	66.7	62.6	2 092	440	86	0.5	369	22	160
179	40	10	55	55	0.2	44	73.0	58.6	2 334	270	128	1.4	323	54	158
13	47	12	55	55	0.8	78	48.2	29.2	2 833	670	54	1.4	1 291	23	143
4	35	8	60	63	1.3	67	62.6	41.6	2 791	1 060	267	3.6	1 025	62	147
645	12	7	70	77	10.6	12	92.9	88.5	3 055	9 290	1 902	0.2	1 232	390	70
75	23	6	69	73	6.2	26	78.6	58.8	3 334	3 020	819	3.9	1 285	560	96
34	39	12	49	51	0.4	62	73.3	45.4	2 267	610	461	1.0	480	54	159
3	26	6	62	67	3.7	35	79.2	84.5	2 086	5 870	1 582	3.0	1 184	139	117
15	50	10	58	59	0.2	60	27.3	11.0	2 546	400	56	1.1	393	17	165
196	42	12	52	53	4.0	74	69.2	49.7	2 724	2 710	149	0.5	733	380	133
485	36	7	62	66	0.6	37	73.2	68.0	2 148	630	32	1.1	568	87	148
208	35	7	64	68	4.9	37	81.8	68.4	2 676	1 470	302	0.5	649	230	-
75	38	7	62	65	0.6	44	69.7	46.6	2 426	1 050	197	0.01	929	209	130
339	17	7	69	78	15.1	12	91.4	92.3	2 426	13 210	3 264	0.9	1 473	504	75
87	37	17	45	46	0.2	107	58.7	37.7	2 333	660	22	0.01	657	17	-
17	44	14	53	57	0.4	90	49.7	25.8	1 696	288	30	0.9	494	15	-
43	21	12	55	59	7.8	33	95.5	93.1	3 007	7 190	4 173	1.2	1 456	489	90
18	37	12	54	56	-	64	40.0	16.0	-	950	173	9.3	253	-	-
21	34	8	60	64	2.8	51	83.3	68.6	2 346	1 550	173	1.3	729	227	122
76	30	12	50	48	1.7	56	87.4	87.5	2 275	2 990	1 079	3.0	715	247	128
57	40	8	60	63	0.1	36	75.9	65.4	2 167	630	95	1.1	557	44	152
129	37	10	56	57	0.5	56	78.3	55.3	2 366	530	155	1.6	625	45	-
71	17	6	74	78	12.2	13	89.6	74.2	3 362	4 200	1 244	2.0	1 156	438	99
194	44	10	58	60	1.2	44	85.3	71.5	2 279	550	79	2.2	441	162	146
2	31	8	60	65	4.4	56	-	-	-	2 500	151	-	-	-	-
20	43	10	56	60	0.7	56	70.9	56.0	1 937	1 810	599	1.4	715	154	144
38	32	10	59	61	0.6	55	88.5	84.6	2 210	860	525	2.6	963	185	121
117	13	9	75	81	11.5	13	98.4	96.9	3 023	4 710	1 268	1.3	1 162	601	84
184	9	8	79	86	39.1	2	99.0	99.0	-	43 110	-	0.0	807	940	20
103	10	9	79	84	48.3	3	99.0	99.0	3 784	50 430	7 620	0.8	1 562	806	24
45	11	13	64	76	37.6	4	99.0	99.0	3 253	6 730	3 503	1.3	1 188	542	38
338	12	10	78	83	29.0	4	99.0	99.0	3 793	46 290	7 583	1.0	1 109	822	25
74	9	9	74	79	16.9	6	99.0	97.5	3 130	4 780	3 218	1.1	911	679	69
65	10	15	70	77	38.1	10	99.0	98.1	2 877	7 360	4 216	1.5	1 452	531	49
76	10	12	74	80	30.0	4	99.0	99.0	3 052	13 430	4 461	1.7	1 145	667	37

	GENERAL FACTS				
Country	Capital city	Land area (sq km)	Main languages spoken	Unit of currency	Population (2014)
Cyprus	Nicosia	9 250	Greek, Turkish	Euro; Turkish lira in TRNC	1 200 000
Czech Republic	Prague	78 866	Czech, Slovak, Hungarian (Magyar)	Czech koruna	10 700 000
Denmark	Copenhagen	43 094	Danish	Danish krone	5 600 000
Estonia	Tallinn	45 226	Estonian, Russian	Euro	1 300 000
Finland	Helsinki	337 030	Finnish, Swedish, Sámi	Euro	5 400 000
France	Paris	547 030	French, Provençal, German, Breton, Catalan, Basque	Euro	64 600 000
Germany	Berlin	357 021	German, Turkish	Euro	82 700 000
Greece	Athens	131 940	Greek, Turkish, Macedonian, Albanian	Euro	11 100 000
Hungary	Budapest	93 030	Hungarian (Magyar)	Forint	9 900 000
Iceland	Reykjavík	103 000	Icelandic	Icelandic króna	300 000
Ireland	Dublin	70 280	English, Irish	Euro	4 700 000
Italy	Rome	301 230	Italian, German, French, Rhaeto-Romanic, Sardinian	Euro	61 100 000
Kosovo (disputed)	Pristina	10 908	Albanian, Serbian, Bosniak, Gorani, Roma, Turkish	Euro	1 900 000
Latvia	Riga	64 589	Latvian, Russian	Euro	2 000 000
Liechtenstein	Vaduz	160	German, Alemannish dialect, Italian	Swiss franc	37 300
Lithuania	Vilnius	65 200	Lithuanian, Russian	Euro	3 000 000
Luxembourg	Luxembourg-Ville	2 586	Luxembourgish, German, French	Euro	500 000
Macedonia	Skopje	25 333	Macedonian, Albanian, Turkish, Romani, Serbian	Macedonian denar	2 100 000
Malta	Valletta	316	Maltese, English	Euro	400 000
Moldova	Chisinau	33 843	Moldovan, Ukrainian, Russian	Moldovan leu	3 500 000
Monaco	Monaco-Ville	2	French, Italian, Monégasque, English	Euro	37 000
Montenegro	Podgorica	13 812	Montenegrin, Serbian, Albanian, Bosniak, Croatian	Euro	600 000
Netherlands	Amsterdam/The Hague	41 526	Dutch, Frisian	Euro	16 800 000
Norway	Oslo	324 220	Norwegian (*Bokmål* "book language" and *Nynorsk* "new Norsk"), Sámi	Norwegian krone	5 100 000
Poland	Warsaw	312 685	Polish	Zloty	38 200 000
Portugal	Lisbon	92 391	Portuguese	Euro	10 600 000
Romania	Bucharest	237 500	Romanian, Hungarian (Magyar), Romani, German	New Romanian leu	21 600 000
Russian Federation	Moscow	17 075 200	Russian, Tatar, Ukrainian, Chavash, various other national languages	Russian rouble	142 500 000
San Marino	San Marino	61	Italian	Euro	32 700
Serbia	Belgrade	77 453	Serbian, Hungarian (Magyar)	Serbian dinar	9 500 000
Slovakia	Bratislava	48 845	Slovak, Hungarian (Magyar), Czech	Euro	5 500 000
Slovenia	Ljubljana	20 253	Slovenian	Euro	2 100 000
Spain	Madrid	504 782	Spanish, Catalan, Galician, Basque	Euro	47 100 000
Sweden	Stockholm	449 964	Swedish, Finnish, Sámi	Swedish krona	9 600 000
Switzerland	Bern	41 290	German, Swiss-German, French, Italian, Romansch	Swiss franc	8 200 000
Ukraine	Kiev	603 700	Ukrainian, Russian, Tatar	Hryvna	44 900 000
United Kingdom	London	244 820	English, Welsh, Scottish Gaelic, Irish	Pound sterling	63 500 000
Vatican City	Vatican City	0.4	Italian, Latin	Euro	800
ASIA					
Afghanistan	Kabul	647 500	Pashtu, Tajik, Dari, Farsi, Uzbek, Turkmen	Afghani	31 300 000
Armenia	Yerevan	29 800	Armenian, Azeri, Russian	Dram	3 000 000
Azerbaijan	Baku	86 600	Azeri, Russian	New manat	9 500 000
Bahrain	Manama	620	Arabic	Bahraini dinar	1 300 000
Bangladesh	Dhaka	144 000	Bengali, Urdu, Chakma, Marma (Magh), Garo, Khasi, Santhali, Tripuri, Mro	Taka	158 500 000
Bhutan	Thimphu	47 000	Dzongkha, Nepali, Assamese	Ngultrum	800 000
Brunei	Bandar Seri Begawan	5 770	Malay, English, Chinese	Brunei dollar	400 000
Cambodia	Phnom Penh	181 040	Khmer, French, Chinese, Vietnamese, Cham	Riel	15 400 000
China	Beijing	9 596 960	Mandarin, Wu, Cantonese, Hsiang, Min, Hakka, Kan	Renminbi (known as yuan)	1 393 800 000
East Timor	Dili	14 874	Tetum (Portuguese/Austronesian), Bahasa Indonesia, Portuguese	US dollar	1 200 000
Georgia	Tbilisi	69 700	Georgian, Russian, Azeri, Armenian, Mingrelian, Ossetian, Abkhazian	Lari	4 300 000
India	New Delhi	3 287 590	Hindi, English, Urdu, Bengali, Marathi, Telugu, Tamil, Bihari, Gujarati, Kanarese	Indian rupee	1 267 400 000

POPULATION					HEALTH AND EDUCATION					ECONOMIC DEVELOPMENT			TECHNOLOGICAL DEVELOPMENT		
Population density per sq km (2014)	Birth rate per 1 000 population (2012)	Death rate per 1 000 population (2012)	Life expectancy at birth (years; 2013–2014)		Medical doctors per 10 000 people (2004–2013)	Infant mortality (deaths per 1 000 live births; 2013)	Adult literacy rate (percentage of adults over 15; 2015)		Average calorie intake per person (2011)	GNI per person (US$; 2013)	Annual electricity consumption per person (kWh; 2012)	Annual military expenditure as percentage of GDP (2009–2014)	Mobile telephones per 1 000 population (2013)	Internet users per 1 000 population (2013)	ICT Dev. Index (IDI), compiled by the ITU (2013)
			Male	Female			Male	Female							
130	12	6	78	82	22.9	3	99.0	99.0	2 661	25 210	3 905	2.1	964	654	51
136	11	10	75	81	36.2	3	99.0	99.0	3 292	18 950	5 712	1.0	1 277	741	41
132	11	10	77	82	34.2	3	99.0	99.0	3 363	61 680	5 708	1.4	1 271	946	1
29	11	12	69	80	32.6	3	99.0	99.0	3 214	17 690	6 323	1.9	1 597	800	21
18	11	9	77	84	29.1	2	99.0	99.0	3 285	48 820	15 192	1.2	1 716	915	8
117	12	9	78	85	31.8	4	99.0	99.0	3 524	43 460	7 104	2.2	985	819	18
237	8	11	78	83	38.1	3	99.0	99.0	3 539	47 270	6 587	1.3	1 209	840	17
85	10	10	78	83	61.7	4	99.0	96.9	3 433	22 690	5 064	2.5	1 168	599	39
107	10	13	71	79	29.6	5	99.0	99.0	2 968	13 260	3 713	0.9	1 164	726	46
3	15	6	80	84	34.8	2	99.0	99.0	3 339	46 400	56 467	0.1	1 081	966	4
68	16	6	79	83	27.2	3	99.0	99.0	3 591	43 110	5 270	0.5	1 028	782	26
208	9	9	80	85	40.9	3	99.0	99.0	3 539	35 860	4 969	1.5	1 588	585	36
174	18	7	68	72	10.8	11	95.3	90.1	-	3 940	2 676	-	845	766	-
31	11	14	67	78	28.8	7	99.0	99.0	3 293	15 280	3 246	1.0	2 284	752	33
233	10	12	80	84	13.1	8	99.0	99.0	-	136 770	-	0.0	1 041	938	-
46	11	12	66	78	41.2	4	99.0	99.0	3 463	14 900	2 928	0.8	1 513	684	40
193	12	7	78	83	28.2	2	99.0	99.0	3 568	69 900	12 216	0.5	1 486	938	10
82	11	9	73	78	26.3	6	99.0	96.8	2 923	4 870	3 516	1.2	1 062	612	60
1 250	9	7	78	82	35.0	5	93.1	95.8	3 389	20 980	4 630	0.6	1 298	689	30
104	12	12	65	73	28.6	13	99.0	99.0	2 837	2 470	1 445	0.3	1 060	488	61
18 949	7	9	86	94	71.7	3	99.0	99.0	-	186 950	-	0.0	937	907	15
43	12	9	73	77	19.8	5	99.0	98.0	3 568	7 250	5 440	1.6	1 599	568	63
495	11	8	79	83	28.6	3	99.0	99.0	3 147	51 060	6 436	1.2	1 137	940	7
17	13	8	79	84	37.4	2	99.0	99.0	3 484	102 610	23 101	1.4	1 163	950	6
125	11	10	72	81	22.0	4	99.0	99.0	3 485	13 240	3 629	1.8	1 491	628	44
115	9	9	77	83	38.7	3	97.1	94.4	3 456	21 260	4 355	2.1	1 130	621	43
94	10	12	70	78	23.9	10	99.0	99.0	3 363	9 060	2 157	1.3	1 056	498	58
8	12	15	62	74	43.1	9	99.0	99.0	3 358	13 850	6 232	4.2	1 528	614	42
537	9	10	81	86	51.3	3	99.0	99.0	-	51 470	-	-	1 170	508	-
123	10	12	71	77	21.1	6	99.0	97.2	2 724	6 050	2 709	2.0	1 194	515	50
112	11	9	72	79	30.0	6	99.0	99.0	2 902	17 810	4 683	1.0	1 139	779	45
104	10	9	76	83	25.2	2	99.0	99.0	3 173	23 210	6 512	1.1	1 102	727	31
94	11	9	79	85	37.0	4	99.0	97.5	3 183	29 920	5 195	0.9	1 069	716	28
23	12	10	80	84	37.7	2	99.0	99.0	3 160	61 760	13 738	1.1	1 244	948	3
206	10	8	80	85	39.4	4	99.0	99.0	3 487	90 760	7 534	0.7	1 368	867	13
74	11	15	63	74	35.3	9	99.0	99.0	3 142	3 960	3 559	2.9	1 381	418	73
263	12	9	79	83	27.9	4	99.0	99.0	3 414	41 680	5 082	2.2	1 246	898	5
1 914	-	-	80	85	-	-	99.0	99.0	-	-	-	0.0	-	570	-
48	35	8	60	62	2.3	70	52.0	24.2	2 107	690	117	6.4	707	59	155
101	14	12	71	78	26.9	14	99.0	99.0	2 809	3 800	1 627	4.1	1 124	463	74
110	18	6	68	74	34.3	30	99.0	99.0	2 952	7 350	1 893	4.7	1 076	587	64
1 841	16	2	76	78	9.1	5	96.9	93.5	-	19 700	8 349	3.8	1 659	900	27
1 184	20	6	70	72	3.6	33	64.6	58.5	2 430	1 010	272	1.2	744	65	145
17	20	7	68	69	2.6	30	73.1	55.0	-	2 330	2 052	1.0	722	299	123
76	16	4	77	81	15.0	8	97.5	94.5	2 949	31 590	8 628	2.6	1 122	645	66
87	26	6	69	75	2.2	32	84.5	70.5	2 411	950	207	1.6	1 339	60	127
149	13	7	74	77	19.4	11	98.2	94.5	3 074	6 560	3 300	2.1	887	458	86
82	36	6	66	69	0.7	46	71.5	63.4	2 083	3 580	-	2.3	574	11	-
62	14	13	71	78	42.4	12	99.0	99.0	2 731	3 570	1 969	2.7	1 150	431	78
426	21	8	65	68	7.0	41	81.3	60.6	2 459	1 570	687	2.4	708	151	129

Country	Capital city	Land area (sq km)	Main languages spoken	Unit of currency	Population (2014)
			GENERAL FACTS		
Indonesia	Jakarta	1 919 440	Javanese, Sundanese, Madurese, Bahasa Indonesia, Dutch	Rupiah	252 800 0
Iran	Tehran	1 648 000	Farsi, Azeri, Luri, Gilaki, Mazanderani, Kurdish, Turkmen, Arabic, Baluchi	Iranian rial	78 500 0
Iraq	Baghdad	437 072	Arabic, Kurdish, Turkic languages, Armenian, Assyrian	New Iraqi dinar	34 800 0
Israel	Jerusalem (disputed)	20 770	Hebrew, Arabic, Yiddish, German, Russian, Polish, Romanian, Persian	Shekel	7 800 0
Japan	Tokyo	377 835	Japanese, Korean, Chinese	Yen	127 000 0
Jordan	Amman	92 300	Arabic	Jordanian dinar	7 500 0
Kazakhstan	Astana	2 717 300	Kazakh, Russian, Ukrainian, German, Uzbek, Tatar, Uighur	Tenge	16 600 0
Kuwait	Kuwait City	17 820	Arabic, English	Kuwaiti dinar	3 500 0
Kyrgyzstan	Bishkek	198 500	Kyrgyz, Russian, Uzbek, Tatar, Ukrainian	Som	5 600 0
Laos	Vientiane	236 800	Lao, Mon-Khmer, Yao, Vietnamese, Chinese, French	Kip	6 900 0
Lebanon	Beirut	10 400	Arabic, French, Armenian, Assyrian	Lebanese pound	5 000 0
Malaysia	Kuala Lumpur/Putrajaya	329 750	Bahasa Malaysia, Malay, Chinese, Tamil, English	Ringgit	30 200 0
Maldives	Male'	300	Dhivehi (Maldivian), Sinhala, Tamil, Arabic	Rufiyaa	400 0
Mongolia	Ulan Bator	1 565 000	Khalkha Mongolian, Kazakh, Chinese, Russian	Tugrik (tögrög)	2 900 0
Myanmar (Burma)	Nay Pyi Taw	678 500	Burmese (Myanmar), Shan, Karen, Rakhine, Chin, Yangbye, Kachin, Mon	Kyat	53 700 0
Nepal	Kathmandu	140 800	Nepali, Maithili, Bhojpuri	Nepalese rupee	28 100 0
North Korea	Pyongyang	120 540	Korean	North Korean won	25 000 0
Oman	Muscat	212 460	Arabic, Baluchi, Farsi, Hindi, Punjabi	Omani rial	3 900 0
Pakistan	Islamabad	803 940	Punjabi, Sindhi, Pashtu, Urdu, Baluchi, Brahui	Pakistani rupee	185 100 0
Philippines	Manila	300 000	Filipino, English, Tagalog, Cebuano, Ilocano, Hiligaynon, many other local languages	Philippine peso	100 100 0
Qatar	Doha	11 437	Arabic	Qatar riyal	2 300 0
Saudi Arabia	Riyadh	1 960 582	Arabic	Saudi riyal	29 400 0
Singapore	Singapore	648	Mandarin, Malay, Tamil, English	Singapore dollar	5 500 0
South Korea	Seoul/Sejong City	98 480	Korean	South Korean won	49 500 0
Sri Lanka	Colombo/Sri Jayewardenepura Kotte	65 610	Sinhala, Tamil, Sinhala-Tamil, English	Sri Lanka rupee	21 400 0
Syria	Damascus	184 180	Arabic, French, Kurdish, Armenian, Circassian, Turkic languages, Assyrian, Aramaic	Syrian pound	22 000 0
Taiwan	Taipei	35 980	Amoy Chinese, Mandarin Chinese, Hakka Chinese	Taiwan dollar	23 400 0
Tajikistan	Dushanbe	143 100	Tajik, Uzbek, Russian	Somoni	8 400 0
Thailand	Bangkok	514 000	Thai, Chinese, Malay, Khmer, Mon, Karen, Miao	Baht	67 200 0
Turkey	Ankara	780 580	Turkish, Kurdish, Arabic, Circassian, Armenian, Greek, Georgian, Ladino	Turkish lira	75 800 0
Turkmenistan	Ashgabat	488 100	Turkmen, Uzbek, Russian, Kazakh, Tatar	New manat	5 300 0
United Arab Emirates	Abu Dhabi	82 880	Arabic, Farsi, Indian and Pakistani languages, English	UAE dirham	9 400 0
Uzbekistan	Tashkent	447 400	Uzbek, Russian, Tajik, Kazakh	Som	29 300 0
Vietnam	Hanoi	329 560	Vietnamese, Chinese, Thai, Khmer, Muong, Nung, Miao, Yao, Jarai	Dông	92 500 0
Yemen	Sana	527 970	Arabic	Yemeni rial	25 000 0
AUSTRALASIA & OCEANIA					
Australia	Canberra	7 686 850	English, Italian, Cantonese, Greek, Arabic, Vietnamese, Aboriginal languages	Australian dollar	23 600 0
Fiji	Suva	18 270	Fijian, English, Hindi, Urdu, Tamil, Telugu	Fiji dollar	900 0
Kiribati	Bairiki (Tarawa Atoll)	717	English, Kiribati	Australian dollar	104 0
Marshall Islands	Majuro	181	Marshallese, English, Japanese, German	US dollar	71 0
Micronesia	Palikir (Pohnpei Island)	702	Trukese, Pohnpeian, Kosraean, Yapese, English	US dollar	106 0
Nauru	None	21	Nauruan, Kiribati, Chinese, Tuvaluan, English	Australian dollar	9 5
New Zealand	Wellington	268 680	English, Maori	New Zealand dollar	4 600 0
Palau	Ngerulmud	458	Palauan, English, Japanese, Angaur, Tobi, Sonsorolese	US dollar	21 2
Papua New Guinea	Port Moresby	462 840	Pidgin English, Papuan, English, Motu, around 800 native languages	Kina	7 500 0
Samoa	Apia	2 860	Samoan, English	Tala	200 0
Solomon Islands	Honiara	28 450	English, Pidgin English, Melanesian Pidgin, around 120 native languages	Solomon Islands dollar	600 0
Tonga	Nuku'alofa	748	English, Tongan	Pa'anga (Tongan dollar)	106 0
Tuvalu	Fongafale (Funafuti Atoll)	26	Tuvaluan, Kiribati, English	Australian $, Tuvaluan $	10 8
Vanuatu	Port Vila	12 200	Bislama (Melanesian pidgin), English, French, other indigenous languages	Vatu	300 0

POPULATION					HEALTH AND EDUCATION					ECONOMIC DEVELOPMENT			TECHNOLOGICAL DEVELOPMENT		
Population density per sq km (2014)	Birth rate per 1 000 population (2012)	Death rate per 1 000 population (2012)	Life expectancy at birth (years; 2013–2014)		Medical doctors per 10 000 people (2004–2013)	Infant mortality (deaths per 1 000 live births; 2013)	Adult literacy rate (percentage of adults over 15; 2015)		Average calorie intake per person (2011)	GNI per person (US$; 2013)	Annual electricity consumption per person (kWh; 2012)	Annual military expenditure as percentage of GDP (2009–2014)	Mobile telephones per 1 000 population (2013)	Internet users per 1 000 population (2013)	ICT Dev. Index (IDI), compiled by the ITU (2013)
			Male	Female			Male	Female							
141	19	6	69	73	2.0	24	96.3	91.5	2 713	3 580	684	0.9	1 254	158	106
48	19	5	72	76	8.9	14	91.2	82.5	3 058	5 780	2 584	2.1	842	314	94
80	32	5	66	73	6.1	28	85.7	73.7	2 489	6 720	1 332	3.4	961	92	-
384	21	5	80	84	33.5	3	99.0	99.0	3 619	33 930	6 893	5.6	1 228	708	29
337	8	9	80	87	23.0	2	99.0	99.0	2 719	46 330	7 287	1.0	1 176	863	11
84	28	4	72	76	25.6	16	97.7	92.9	3 149	4 950	2 138	3.6	1 418	442	87
6	21	10	61	72	35.8	15	99.0	99.0	3 107	11 550	4 896	1.2	1 847	540	53
196	21	2	74	76	17.9	8	96.5	95.8	3 471	45 130	17 242	3.3	1 903	755	-
28	27	7	63	72	19.6	22	99.0	99.0	2 828	1 210	1 841	3.2	1 214	234	108
30	27	7	67	70	1.8	54	87.1	72.8	2 356	1 450	449	0.2	681	125	134
489	13	5	78	82	32.0	8	96.0	91.8	3 181	9 870	3 009	4.4	806	705	62
92	18	5	73	77	12.0	7	96.2	93.2	2 855	10 430	4 046	1.5	1 447	670	71
1 333	22	4	77	79	14.2	8	99.0	99.0	2 722	5 600	890	4.0	1 812	441	85
2	23	7	64	72	27.6	26	98.2	99.0	2 463	3 770	1 502	1.1	1 242	177	92
82	17	8	63	67	6.1	40	95.2	91.2	2 528	578	159	4.3	128	12	150
205	22	7	67	70	2.1	32	76.4	53.1	2 580	730	104	1.4	768	133	131
208	14	9	66	73	32.9	22	99.0	99.0	2 103	555	639	22.3	97	-	-
18	21	3	75	79	22.2	10	93.6	85.6	-	25 150	7 020	11.6	1 546	664	52
240	26	7	66	68	8.3	69	69.5	45.8	2 428	1 360	427	3.5	701	109	142
336	25	6	65	72	11.5	24	95.8	96.8	2 608	3 270	635	1.3	1 045	370	103
209	11	1	78	80	77.4	7	97.4	96.8	-	86 790	16 069	1.5	1 526	853	34
14	20	3	74	78	9.4	13	97.0	91.1	3 122	26 260	8 070	9.0	1 842	605	47
9 016	10	4	80	85	19.2	2	99.0	95.0	-	54 040	8 303	3.3	1 559	730	16
501	10	5	78	85	21.4	3	99.0	99.0	3 329	25 920	9 926	2.6	1 110	848	2
331	18	7	71	77	6.8	8	93.6	91.7	2 488	3 170	480	2.7	955	219	116
120	24	6	72	78	15.0	12	91.7	81.0	3 106	1 850	1 218	4.2	561	262	112
725	9	7	77	83	19.0	4	99.0	97.0	2 959	20 690	9 628	2.0	1 275	800	-
59	33	6	64	71	19.0	41	99.0	99.0	2 101	990	2 031	1.1	918	160	-
132	11	8	71	78	3.9	11	96.6	96.7	2 757	5 340	2 230	1.5	1 401	289	81
98	17	6	72	79	17.1	16	98.4	91.8	3 680	10 970	2 645	2.3	930	463	68
11	22	9	61	70	23.9	47	99.0	99.0	2 883	6 880	2 259	1.6	1 169	96	-
112	15	1	76	78	19.3	7	93.1	95.8	3 215	38 360	11 517	5.0	1 719	880	32
65	22	6	65	72	23.8	37	99.0	99.0	2 675	1 880	1 609	3.5	743	382	115
284	16	6	71	81	11.6	19	96.3	92.8	2 703	1 740	1 207	2.2	1 309	439	101
44	32	7	62	65	2.0	40	85.1	55.0	2 185	1 330	150	3.9	690	200	138
3	13	6	80	85	32.7	3	99.0	99.0	3 265	65 390	9 721	1.6	1 068	830	12
49	21	7	67	73	4.3	20	95.9	92.9	2 930	4 370	864	1.4	1 056	371	91
147	23	8	66	72	3.8	45	99.0	99.0	3 022	2 620	237	0.0	166	115	-
392	28	7	70	75	4.4	31	93.6	93.7	-	4 310	-	0.0	70	117	-
151	24	6	68	70	1.8	30	91.0	88.0	-	3 280	-	0.0	303	278	-
452	27	4	62	70	7.1	30	-	-	-	3 433	2 479	0.0	678	540	-
17	14	6	79	83	27.4	5	99.0	99.0	3 170	35 550	8 956	1.0	1 058	828	19
42	11	6	69	76	13.8	15	99.0	99.0	-	10 970	-	0.0	858	310	-
17	29	8	60	65	0.5	47	65.6	62.8	2 193	2 010	433	0.6	410	65	-
71	27	5	70	77	4.8	16	99.0	99.0	2 872	3 970	452	0.0	914	153	-
21	32	5	66	69	2.2	25	83.7	69.0	2 473	1 600	132	0.0	576	80	136
148	26	7	70	76	5.6	10	99.0	99.0	-	4 490	421	0.9	546	350	-
415	23	9	64	68	10.9	24	-	-	-	5 840	-	0.0	344	370	-
25	27	5	70	74	1.2	15	86.6	83.8	2 820	3 130	164	0.0	503	113	-

GLOSSARY

This glossary defines certain geographical and technical terms used in this Atlas.

Acid rain Rain, sleet, snow or mist that has absorbed waste gases from fossil-fuelled power stations and vehicle exhausts, becoming acidic and poisonous.

Alluvium Material deposited by a river, such as silt, sand and mud.

Archipelago A group, or chain, of islands.

Atoll A circular or horseshoe-shaped coral reef enclosing a shallow area of water (lagoon).

Aquifer A body of rock that can absorb water. It may be a source of water for wells or springs.

Bar, coastal An offshore strip of sand or shingle, either above or below the water.

Biodiversity The quantity of different animal or plant species in a given area.

Birth rate The number of live births per 1000 individuals annually within a population.

Cash crop Agricultural produce grown for sale, often for foreign export, rather than to be consumed within the country or area in which it was grown.

Climate The long-term trends in weather conditions for an area.

Coniferous forest A type of forest containing trees or shrubs, like pines and firs, which have needles instead of leaves. They are found in temperate zones.

Continental plates The huge interlocking plates which make up the Earth's surface. A plate boundary is an area where two plates meet, and is the point at which earthquakes occur most frequently.

Conurbation A large urban area created by the merging of several towns.

Coral reef An underwater barrier created by colonies of coral polyps. The polyps secrete a protective skeleton of calcium carbonate, and reefs develop as live polyps build on the skeletons of dead generations.

Core The layers of liquid rock and solid iron at the centre of the Earth.

Crust The hard, thin outer shell of the Earth. The crust floats on the mantle, which is softer, but more dense.

Deciduous forest A type of broadleaf forest found in temperate regions.

Deforestation Cutting down trees or forest for timber or farmland. It can lead to soil erosion, flooding and landslides.

Delta A low-lying, fan-shaped area at a river mouth, formed by the deposition of successive layers of sediment. Slowing as it enters the sea, a river deposits sediment and may, as a result, split into many smaller channels called distributaries.

Deposition The laying down of material broken down by erosion or weathering and transported by the wind, water or gravity.

Desertification The spread of desert conditions into a region which was not previously a desert.

Drainage basin The land drained by a river and its tributaries.

Drought A long period of continuously low rainfall.

Earthquake A trembling or shaking of the ground caused by the sudden movement of rocks in the Earth's crust – and sometimes deeper than the crust. Earthquakes occur most frequently along continental plate boundaries.

Economy The organization of a country's finances, exports, imports, industry, agriculture and services.

Ecosytem A community of species dependent on each other and on the habitat in which they live.

Equator The 0° line of latitude. Equatorial climates are hot and there is plenty of rain.

Erosion The wearing down of the land surface by running water, waves, moving ice, wind and weather.

Estuary The mouth of a river, where the salt water from the sea meets the fresh water of the river.

Fault A crack or fracture in the Earth along which there has been movement of the rock masses relative to one another.

Fjord A coastal valley that has been was sculpted by glacial action.

Flood plain The broad, flat part of a river valley, next to the river itself, formed by sediment deposited during flooding.

Geyser A fountain of hot water or steam that erupts periodically as a result of underground streams coming into contact with hot rocks.

GDP Gross Domestic Product. The total value of goods and services produced by a country, excluding income from foreign countries.

GIS Geographical Information System. A computerized system for the collection, storage and retrieval of geographical data.

Glacier A huge mass of ice made up of compacted and frozen snow which moves slowly, eroding and depositing rock.

Glaciation The moulding of the land by a glacier or ice sheet.

GNI Gross National Income. The total value of goods and services produced by a country.

Groundwater Water that has seeped into the pores, cavities and cracks of rocks or into soil and water held in an aquifer or permeable rock.

Gully A deep, narrow chasm eroded in the landscape by a fast-flowing stream.

Heavy industry Industry that uses large amounts of energy and raw materials to produce heavy goods, such as machinery, ships or locomotives.

Humidity The moisture content of the air.

Hurricane A Violent tropical storm, also known as a cyclone in the Indian Ocean and a typhoon in the Pacific Ocean.

Hydro-electric power Energy produced by harnessing the rapid movement of water down steep mountain slopes to drive turbines to generate electricity.

Ice Age Periods of time in the past when much of the Earth's surface was covered by massive ice sheets. The most recent Ice Age began two million years ago and ended 10,000 years ago.

Iceberg A floating mass of ice that has broken off from a glacier or ice sheet.

Ice sheet A massive area of ice, thousands of metres thick.

Irrigation The artificial supply of water to dry areas – mainly for agricultural use. Water is carried or pumped to the area through pipes or ditches.

Lagoon A shallow stretch of coastal salt water behind a partial barrier such as a sandbank or coral reef.

Latitude The distance north or south of the Equator, measured in degrees, and shown on a globe as imaginary circles running around the Earth parallel to the Equator.

Lava The molten rock, magma, which erupts onto the Earth's surface through a volcano or through a fault or crack in the Earth's crust. Lava refers to the rock both in its liquid and its later, solidified form.

Load The material that is carried by a river or stream.

Longitude The distance, measured in degrees, east or west of the Prime Meridian.

Limestone A type of rock, formed by sediment, through which water can pass.

Magma Underground, molten rock, which is very hot and highly charged with gas. It originates in the Earth's lower crust or mantle.

Mantle The layer of the Earth's interior between the crust and the core. It is about 2,900 km thick.

Map projection A mathematical formula that is used to show the curved surface of the Earth on a flat map.

Market gardening The intensive growing of fruit and vegetables close to large local markets.

Meander A loop-like bend in a river. As a river nears the sea, it tends to wind more and more. The bigger the river and the shallower its slope, the more likely it is that meanders will form.

Mediterranean climate A temperate climate of hot, dry summers and warm, damp winters.

Meltwater Water which has melted from glaciers or ice sheets.

Mestizo A person of mixed native American and European origin.

Mineral A chemical compound that occurs naturally in the Earth.

Monsoon Winds that change direction according to the seasons. They are most common in South and East Asia, where they blow from the southwest in summer, bringing heavy rainfall, and the northeast in winter.

Moraine Sand and gravel that have been deposited by a glacier or ice sheet.

Nomads (nomadic) Wandering communities who move around in search of suitable pasture for their herds of animals.

Oasis A fertile area in a desert, usually watered by an underground aquifer.

Pack ice Ice masses more than three metres thick which form on the sea surface and are not attached to a landmass.

Pacific Rim The name given to the economically dynamic countries bordering the Pacific Ocean.

Peat Decomposed vegetation found in bogs. It can be dried and used as fuel.

Per capita A latin term meaning 'for each person'.

Plantation A large farm on which only one crop is usually grown, e.g. bananas or coffee.

Plain A flat, level region of land, often relatively low-lying.

Plateau A large area of high, flat land. When surrounded by steep slopes it is called a tableland.

Peninsula A thin strip of land surrounded on three of its sides by water. Large examples include Italy, Florida and Korea.

Permafrost Permanently frozen ground, in which temperatures have remained below 0°C for more than two years.

Precipitation The fall of moisture from the atmosphere onto the surface of the Earth, as dew, hail, rain, sleet or snow.

Prairie A Spanish-American term for grassy plains, with few or no trees.

Prime Meridian 0° longitude. Also known as the Greenwich Meridian because it runs through Greenwich in England.

Rainforest Dense forests in tropical zones with high rainfall, temperature and humidity.

Rainshadow An area downwind from high terrain which has little or no rainfall because it has fallen upon the high relief.

Remote-sensing A way of obtaining information about the environment by using unmanned equipment, such as a satellite, which relays the information to a point where it is collected.

Ria A flooded V-shaped river valley or estuary flooded by a rise in sea level or sinking land.

Rift valley A long, narrow depression in the Earth's crust, formed by the sinking of rocks between two faults.

Savannah Open grassland, where an annual dry season prevents the growth of most trees. They lie between the tropical rainforest and hot desert regions.

Scale The relationship between distance on a map and on the Earth's surface.

Sediment Grains of rock transported and deposited by rivers, sea, ice or wind.

Semi-arid Areas between deserts and better-watered areas, where there is sufficient moisture to support a little more vegetation than in a true desert.

Service industry An industry that supplies services, such as banking, rather than producing manufactured goods.

Shanty town An area in or around a city where people live in temporary shacks, usually without basic facilities such as running water.

Silt Small particles, finer than sand, often carried by water and deposited on river banks, at river mouths and harbours.

Soil A thin layer of rock particles mixed with the remains of dead plants and animals. Soil occurs naturally on the surface of the Earth and provides a medium for plants to grow.

Soil erosion The wearing away of soil more quickly than it is replaced by natural processes. Over-grazing and the clearing of land for farming speeds up the process.

Sorghum A type of grass found in South America, similar to sugar cane.

Spit A narrow bank of shingle or sand extending out from the sea shore. Spits are made out of material transported along the coast by currents, wind and waves.

Staple crop The main food crop grown in a region, for example rice in Southeast Asia.

Steppe Large areas of dry grassland in the northern hemisphere – particularly found in southeast Europe and central Asia.

Subsistence farming A method of farming where enough food is produced to feed farmers and their families but not providing any extra to generate an income.

Taiga A Russian name given to the belt of coniferous forest found in Russia, which borders tundra in the north and mixed forests and grasslands in the south.

Temperate The mild, variable climate found in areas between the tropics and cold polar regions.

Terrace Steps cut into steep slopes to create flat surfaces for cultivating crops.

Tropics An area between the Equator and the Tropic of Cancer and Tropic of Capricorn that has heavy rainfall and high temperatures, and lacks any clear seasonal variation.

Tundra The land area lying in the very cold northern regions of Europe, Asia and Canada, where winters are long and cold and the ground beneath the surface is permanently frozen.

U-shaped valley A river valley that has been deepened and widened by a glacier. They are flat-bottomed and steep-sided, and usually much deeper than river valleys.

V-shaped valley A typical valley eroded by a river in its upper course.

Volcano An opening or vent in the Earth's crust where magma erupts. Volcanos are caused by the movement of the Earth's plates. When the plates collide or spread apart, magma is forced to the surface, at or near the place where the plates meet.

Watershed The dividing line between one drainage basin and another.

INDEX

◆ Administrative region   ◆ Country   ● Country capital   ◇ Dependent territory   ◇ Dependent territory capital   ▲ Mountain range   ▲ Mountain   ◊ Volcano   ≈ River   ◎ Lake   ◙ Reservoir

155

B

BROOKS RANGE

Beaverton *49 B3* Oregon, NW USA
Beawar *127 D3* N India
Beccles *95 H2* E England, United Kingdom
Béchar *70 D2* W Algeria
Beckley *39 G2* West Virginia, NE USA
Bedford *95 F2* E England, United Kingdom
Bedford *40 D7* Indiana, N USA
Bedford Level *95 F2 physical region* E England, United Kingdom
Bedum *84 F2* NE Netherlands
Bedworth *93 D6* C England, United Kingdom
Be'er Menuha *123 H7* S Israel
Beernem *84 B6* NW Belgium
Be'er Sheva *123 G6* S Israel
Beesel *84 E6* SE Netherlands
Beeston *93 E5* C England, United Kingdom
Beeville *44 G5* Texas, SW USA
Bega *137 G6* New South Wales, SE Australia
Beihai *129 F6* S China
Beijing *129 F3* ● E China
Beilen *84 E3* NE Netherlands
Beinn Dearg *91 D3* ▲ N Scotland, United Kingdom
Beira *76 E5* C Mozambique
Beirut *123 A2* ● W Lebanon
Beja *99 B5* SE Portugal
Béjar *99 C3* N Spain
Békéscsaba *105 F8* SE Hungary
Bekobod *125 F3* E Uzbekistan
Belarus *109 C2* ◆ *republic* E Europe
Bełchatów *105 E4* C Poland
Belcher Islands *35 C2 island group* Nunavut, SE Canada
Beledweyne *75 F4* C Somalia
Belém *63 G3* N Brazil
Belén *55 D5* SW Nicaragua
Belen *44 D2* New Mexico, SW USA
Belep, Îles *141 F6 island group* W New Caledonia
Belfast *89 F2 National region capital*, E Northern Ireland, United Kingdom
Belfield *43 A2* North Dakota, N USA
Belfort *97 F3* E France
Belgaum *127 D6* W India
Belgium *84 B7* ◆ *monarchy* NW Europe
Belgorod *111 A6* W Russian Federation
Belgrade *107 D2* ● N Serbia
Belgrano II *142 B4 Argentinian research station* Antarctica
Belitung, Pulau *131 C7 island* W Indonesia
Belize *55 B2* ◆ *commonwealth republic* Central America
Belize *55 B1* ~ Belize/Guatemala
Belize City *55 C1* NE Belize
Belkofski *50 C3* Alaska, USA
Bellananagh *89 D3* N Ireland
Bellavary *89 B3* NW Ireland
Belle Île *97 A3 island* NW France
Belle Isle, Strait of *35 G3 strait* Newfoundland and Labrador, E Canada
Belleville *40 B7* Illinois, N USA
Bellevue *43 D5* Nebraska, C USA
Bellevue *49 B2* Washington, NW USA
Bellingham *49 B1* Washington, NW USA
Bellingshausen Sea *142 A4 sea* Antarctica
Bellinzona *101 B8* S Switzerland
Bello *63 B2* W Colombia
Bellona *141 E3 island* S Solomon Islands
Bellville *76 C7* SW South Africa
Belmopan *55 B2* ● C Belize
Belmullet *89 B3* W Ireland
Belo Horizonte *63 G7* SE Brazil
Belomorsk *111 B3* NW Russian Federation
Beloretsk *111 D6* W Russian Federation
Belorussia *see* Belarus
Belozersk *111 B4* NW Russian Federation
Belper *93 D5* C England, United Kingdom
Belton *44 H4* Texas, SW USA
Belturbet *89 D3* N Ireland
Belukha, Gora *118 D5* ▲ Kazakhstan/Russian Federation
Belyy, Ostrov *118 D2 island* N Russian Federation
Bemaraha *76 G5* ▲▲ W Madagascar
Bemidji *43 E2* Minnesota, N USA
Bemmel *84 E4* SE Netherlands
Benavente *99 C2* N Spain
Benbecula *91 A3 island* NW Scotland, United Kingdom
Bend *49 B4* Oregon, NW USA
Bendery *see* Tighina
Bendigo *137 F6* Victoria, SE Australia
Benešov *105 B5* W Czech Republic
Benevento *103 D6* S Italy
Bengbu *129 G4* E China
Benghazi *70 G2* NE Libya
Bengkulu *131 B7* Sumatra, W Indonesia
Benguela *76 B4* W Angola
Ben Hope *91 D2* ▲ N Scotland, United Kingdom
Beni *76 D1* NE Dem. Rep. Congo
Benidorm *99 F4* SE Spain
Beni-Mellal *70 C2* C Morocco
Benin *72 D4* ◆ *republic* W Africa
Benin, Bight of *72 E5 gulf* W Africa
Benin City *72 E5* SW Nigeria
Beni, Río *65 A2* ~ N Bolivia
Ben Klibreck *91 C2* ▲ N Scotland, United Kingdom
Ben Lawers *91 D5* ▲ C Scotland, United Kingdom
Ben Lui *91 C5* ▲ C Scotland, United Kingdom
Ben Macdui *91 E4* ▲ C Scotland, United Kingdom
Ben More *91 B5* ▲ W Scotland, United Kingdom
Ben More *91 D5* ▲ C Scotland, United Kingdom
Ben More Assynt *91 D2* ▲ N Scotland, United Kingdom
Ben Nevis *91 C4* ▲ N Scotland, United Kingdom
Benson *44 C3* Arizona, SW USA
Benton *39 B4* Arkansas, C USA
Benton Harbor *40 D5* Michigan, N USA
Benue *72 F5* ~ Cameroon/Nigeria
Beograd *see* Belgrade
Berat *107 D4* C Albania
Berau, Teluk *131 H7 bay* Papua, E Indonesia
Berbera *75 F3* NW Somalia
Berbérati *72 G5* SW Central African Republic
Berck-Plage *97 D1* N France
Berdyans'k *109 G6* SE Ukraine
Bereket *125 C3* W Turkmenistan
Berettyó *105 F8* ~ Hungary/Romania
Berettyóújfalu *105 F7* E Hungary
Berezniki *111 D5* NW Russian Federation
Berga *99 G2* NE Spain
Bergamo *103 B2* N Italy
Bergen *101 D2* NE Germany
Bergen *84 C3* NW Netherlands
Bergen *83 A5* S Norway
Bergerac *97 C5* SW France
Bergeyk *84 D6* S Netherlands
Bergse Maas *84 D5* ~ S Netherlands
Beringen *84 D6* NE Belgium
Bering Sea *50 B1 sea* N Pacific Ocean
Bering Strait *50 D1 strait* Bering Sea/Chukchi Sea
Berja *99 E6* S Spain
Berkeley *49 B7* California, W USA
Berkhamsted *95 F3* SE England, United Kingdom
Berkner Island *142 B4 island* Antarctica
Berlin *101 D3* ● NE Germany
Berlin *37 F3* New Hampshire, NE USA
Bermejo, Río *65 B3* ~ N Argentina
Bermeo *99 E1* N Spain
Bermuda *26 UK* ◇ NW Atlantic Ocean
Bern *101 A8* ● W Switzerland
Bernau *101 D3* NE Germany
Bernburg *101 D4* C Germany
Berner Alpen *101 A8* ▲▲ SW Switzerland
Berneray *91 A4 island* NW Scotland, United Kingdom
Bernier Island *137 A4 island* Western Australia
Berry *97 D3 cultural region* C France
Berry Islands *57 C1 island group* N Bahamas
Bertoua *72 G5* E Cameroon
Berwick-upon-Tweed *93 D1* N England, United Kingdom
Besançon *97 E4* E France
Bessbrook *89 E3* S Northern Ireland, United Kingdom
Betafo *76 G5* C Madagascar
Betanzos *99 B1* NW Spain
Bethlehem *76 D6* C South Africa
Bethlehem *37 D5* Pennsylvania, NE USA
Bethlehem *123 H6* C West Bank
Béticos, Sistemas *99 D5* ▲▲ S Spain
Bétou *76 C1* N Congo
Bette, Picco *70 G4* ▲ S Libya
Betws-y-Coed *93 B5* N Wales, United Kingdom
Beulah *40 D3* Michigan, N USA
Beveren *84 C6* N Belgium
Beverley *93 F4* E England, United Kingdom
Bexhill *95 G4* SE England, United Kingdom
Beyla *72 C4* SE Guinea
Beyrouth *see* Beirut
Beyşehir Gölü *120 B4* ◎ C Turkey
Béziers *97 D6* S France
Bhadravati *127 D6* SW India
Bhagalpur *127 F3* NE India
Bhaktapur *127 F3* C Nepal
Bharuch *127 C4* W India
Bhavnagar *127 C4* W India
Bhopal *127 D4* C India
Bhubaneshwar *127 F4* E India
Bhusawal *127 D4* C India
Bhutan *127 G3* ◆ *monarchy* S Asia
Biak, Pulau *131 H6 island* E Indonesia
Biała Podlaska *105 G3* E Poland
Białogard *105 C2* NW Poland
Białystok *105 G2* NE Poland
Biarritz *97 B6* SW France
Bicester *95 E3* C England, United Kingdom
Biddeford *37 F3* Maine, NE USA
Bideford *95 B4* SW England, United Kingdom
Biel *101 A8* W Switzerland
Bielefeld *101 B4* NW Germany
Bielsko-Biała *105 E5* S Poland
Bielsk Podlaski *105 G3* E Poland
Biên Hoa *131 C4* S Vietnam
Bienville, Lac *35 D3* ◎ Québec, C Canada
Bié Plateau *76 C4 plateau* C Angola
Big Bend National Park *44 E5 national park* Texas, S USA
Bigbury Bay *95 B6 bay* SW England, United Kingdom
Big Cypress Swamp *39 G8 wetland* Florida, SE USA
Biggleswade *95 F2* C England, United Kingdom
Bighorn Mountains *47 E3* ▲▲ Wyoming, C USA
Bighorn River *47 E3* ~ Montana/Wyoming, NW USA
Big Sioux River *43 D4* ~ Iowa/South Dakota, N USA
Big Smoky Valley *47 B6 valley* Nevada, W USA
Big Spring *44 F3* Texas, SW USA
Bihać *107 B2* NW Bosnia and Herz.
Bihar *127 F3 cultural region* N India Asia
Biharamulo *75 C6* NW Tanzania
Bihar Sharif *127 F3* NE India
Bihosava *109 C1* NW Belarus
Bijelo Polje *107 D3* E Montenegro
Bikaner *127 D3* NW India
Bikin *118 H5* SE Russian Federation
Bilaspur *127 E4* C India
Biläsuvar *121 I3* SE Azerbaijan
Bila Tserkva *109 D4* N Ukraine
Bilauktaung Range *131 B4* ▲▲ Myanmar (Burma)/Thailand
Bilbao *99 E1* N Spain
Bilecik *120 B3* NW Turkey
Billingham *93 E2* N England, United Kingdom
Billings *47 E2* Montana, NW USA
Bilma, Grand Erg de *72 G2 desert* NE Niger
Biloela *137 H4* Queensland, E Australia
Biloxi *39 C6* Mississippi, S USA
Biltine *72 H3* E Chad
Bilzen *84 D6* NE Belgium
Bimini Islands *57 C1 island group* W Bahamas
Binche *84 C7* S Belgium
Binghamton *37 D4* New York, NE USA
Bingöl *121 F3* E Turkey
Bintulu *131 D6* C Malaysia
Binzhou *129 G3* E China
Bío Bío, Río *65 A6* ~ C Chile
Bioco, Isla de *72 F6 island* NW Equatorial Guinea
Birak *70 F3* C Libya
Birao *72 I4* NE Central African Republic
Biratnagar *127 F3* SE Nepal
Birdhill *89 D5* S Ireland
Birhar Sharif *127 F3* N India
Birjand *123 F2* E Iran
Birkenfeld *101 A6* SW Germany
Birkenhead *93 C4* NW England, United Kingdom
Birmingham *93 D6* C England, United Kingdom
Birmingham *39 D4* Alabama, S USA
Bir Mogreïn *72 B1* N Mauritania
Birnin Kebbi *72 E4* NW Nigeria
Birnin Konni *72 E3* SW Niger
Birobidzhan *118 H5* SE Russian Federation
Birr *89 D4* C Ireland
Birsk *111 D6* W Russian Federation
Birżebbuġa *112 B6* SE Malta
Bisbee *44 C4* Arizona, SW USA
Biscay, Bay of *97 B4 bay* France/Spain
Bishah, Wadi *123 B5 dry watercourse* C Saudi Arabia
Bishkek *125 H2* ● N Kyrgyzstan
Bishop *49 C7* California, W USA
Bishop Auckland *93 D2* N England, United Kingdom
Biskra *70 E1* NE Algeria
Biskupiec *105 F2* NE Poland
Bislig *131 G5* S Philippines
Bismarck *43 B2 state capital* North Dakota, N USA
Bismarck Archipelago *141 B1 island group* NE Papua New Guinea
Bismarck Sea *141 B1 sea* W Pacific Ocean
Bissau *72 A4* ● W Guinea-Bissau
Bistriţa *109 B6* N Romania
Bitam *76 A1* N Gabon
Bitburg *101 A5* SW Germany
Bitlis *121 G4* SE Turkey
Bitola *107 D4* S Macedonia
Bitonto *103 E6* SE Italy
Bitterfeld *101 D4* E Germany
Bitterroot Range *47 C2* ▲▲ Idaho/Montana, NW USA
Biu *72 G4* E Nigeria
Biwa-ko *133 E6* ◎ Honshu, SW Japan
Bizerte *70 F1* N Tunisia
Bjørnøya *143 D5 island* N Norway
Blackall *137 G4* Queensland, E Australia
Blackburn *93 C4* NW England, United Kingdom
Black Drin *107 D3* ~ Albania/Macedonia
Blackfoot *47 D4* Idaho, NW USA
Black Forest *101 B7* ▲▲ SW Germany
Black Hills *43 A4* ▲▲ South Dakota/Wyoming, N USA
Black Mountain *47 D5* ▲ Colorado, C USA
Black Mountains *93 C6* ▲▲ SE Wales, United Kingdom
Blackpool *93 C4* NW England, United Kingdom
Black Range *44 D3* ▲▲ New Mexico, SW USA
Black River *131 B2* ~ China/Vietnam
Black Rock Desert *47 A4 desert* Nevada, W USA
Black Sea *78 sea* Asia/Europe
Black Sea Lowland *109 E6 depression* SE Europe
Blacksod Bay *89 A3 inlet* W Ireland
Black Volta *72 D4* ~ W Africa
Blackwater *89 E6* SE Ireland
Blackwater *89 D6* ~ S Ireland
Blackwater *89 E2* ~ Ireland/Northern Ireland, United Kingdom
Blaenavon *93 C7* SE Wales, United Kingdom
Blagoevgrad *107 E3* W Bulgaria
Blagoveshchensk *118 H5* SE Russian Federation
Blairgowrie *91 E5* C Scotland, United Kingdom
Blakeney Point *95 G1 headland* E England, United Kingdom
Blanca, Bahía *65 B6 bay* E Argentina
Blanca, Costa *99 F5 physical region* SE Spain
Blanche, Lake *137 F4* ◎ South Australia
Blanc, Mont *97 F5* ▲ France/Italy
Blanco, Cape *49 A4 headland* Oregon, NW USA
Blandford Forum *95 D5* S England, United Kingdom
Blanes *99 H2* NE Spain
Blankenberge *84 B5* NW Belgium
Blankenheim *101 A5* W Germany
Blanquilla, Isla *57 I7 island* N Venezuela
Blantyre *76 E4* S Malawi
Blaricum *84 D4* C Netherlands
Blenheim *139 C5* South Island, New Zealand
Blida *70 D1* N Algeria
Bloemfontein *76 D6* ● C South Africa
Blois *97 C3* C France
Bloody Foreland *89 C1 headland* NW Ireland
Bloomfield *44 C1* New Mexico, SW USA
Bloomington *40 B6* Illinois, N USA
Bloomington *40 D7* Indiana, N USA
Bloomington *43 E3* Minnesota, N USA
Bloomsburg *37 D5* Pennsylvania, NE USA
Bloomsbury *137 G3* Queensland, NE Australia
Bluefield *39 G2* West Virginia, NE USA
Bluefields *55 E4* SE Nicaragua
Blue Mountains *137 G6* ▲▲ New South Wales, SE Australia
Blue Mountains *49 C3* ▲▲ Oregon/Washington, NW USA
Blue Nile *75 C3* ~ Ethiopia/Sudan
Bluff *47 D6* Utah, W USA
Blumenau *63 F8* S Brazil
Blyth *93 D2* N England, United Kingdom
Blythe *49 E9* California, W USA
Blytheville *39 C3* Arkansas, C USA
Bo *72 B5* S Sierra Leone
Boaco *55 D4* S Nicaragua
Boa Vista *63 E3* NW Brazil
Bobaomby, Tanjona *76 G4 headland* N Madagascar
Bobo-Dioulasso *72 C4* SW Burkina Faso
Bobruysk *see* Babruysk
Boca Raton *39 G8* Florida, SE USA
Bocay *55 D3* N Nicaragua
Bocholt *101 A4* W Germany
Bochum *101 A4* W Germany
Bodaybo *118 F4* E Russian Federation
Boden *83 D3* N Sweden
Bodmin *95 B5* SW England, United Kingdom
Bodmin Moor *95 B5 moorland* SW England, United Kingdom
Bodø *83 C2* C Norway
Bodrum *120 A4* SW Turkey
Boende *76 C2* C Dem. Rep. Congo
Bofin, Lough *89 D3* ◎ N Ireland
Bogalusa *39 C6* Louisiana, S USA
Bogatynia *105 B4* SW Poland
Boğazlıyan *121 D3* C Turkey
Boggeragh Mountains *89 C6* ▲▲ S Ireland
Bogia *141 B1* N Papua New Guinea
Bognor Regis *95 F5* SE England, United Kingdom
Bogor *131 C8* Java, C Indonesia
Bogotá *63 B2* ● C Colombia
Bo Hai *129 G3 gulf* NE China
Bohemia *105 B6 cultural region* W Czech Republic
Bohemian Forest *101 D6* ▲▲ C Europe
Bohol Sea *131 F5 sea* S Philippines
Bohoro Shan *129 B2* ▲▲ NW China
Boise *47 B3 state capital* Idaho, NW USA
Boise City *43 A7* Oklahoma, C USA
Boizenburg *101 C3* N Germany
Bojnūrd *123 E1* N Iran
Boké *72 A4* W Guinea
Bol *72 G3* W Chad
Bolesławiec *105 C4* SW Poland
Bolgatanga *72 D4* N Ghana
Bolivia *65 A2* ◆ *republic* W South America
Bollene *97 E6* SE France
Bollnäs *83 C5* C Sweden
Bollon *137 G4* Queensland, C Australia
Bologna *103 C3* N Italy
Bol'shevik, Ostrov *118 F2 island* Severnaya Zemlya, N Russian Federation
Bol'shezemel'skaya Tundra *111 E3 physical region* NW Russian Federation
Bol'shoy Lyakhovskiy, Ostrov *118 G2 island* NE Russian Federation
Bolton *93 C4* NW England, United Kingdom
Bolu *121 C2* NW Turkey
Bolungarvík *83 A1* NW Iceland
Bolus Head *89 A6 headland* SW Ireland
Bolzano *103 C1* N Italy
Boma *76 B3* W Dem. Rep. Congo
Bombay *see* Mumbai
Bomu *76 C1* ~ Central African Republic/Dem. Rep. Congo
Bonaire *57 H7 Dutch* ◇ S Caribbean Sea
Bonanza *55 E3* NE Nicaragua
Bonaparte Archipelago *137 B2 island group* Western Australia
Bon, Cap *112 E4 headland* N Tunisia
Bondo *76 C1* N Dem. Rep. Congo
Bondoukou *72 D5* E Ivory Coast
Bone, Teluk *131 F7 bay* Celebes, C Indonesia
Bongaigaon *127 G3* NE India
Bongo, Massif des *72 H4* ▲▲ NE Central African Republic
Bongor *72 G4* SW Chad
Bonifacio *97 G6* Corsica, France
Bonifacio, Strait of *103 A5 strait* C Mediterranean Sea
Bonin Trench *15 undersea feature* NW Pacific Ocean
Bonn *101 A5* W Germany
Boonville *37 D3* New York, NE USA
Boosaaso *75 F3* N Somalia
Boothia, Gulf of *33 H3 gulf* Nunavut, NE Canada
Boothia Peninsula *33 H3 peninsula* Nunavut, NE Canada
Boppard *101 B5* W Germany
Boquete *55 F6* W Panama
Boquillas *53 D2* NE Mexico
Bor *107 D2* E Serbia
Bor *75 C4* C South Sudan
Borah Peak *47 B3* ▲ Idaho, NW USA
Borås *83 C6* S Sweden
Bordeaux *97 B5* SW France
Bordj Omar Driss *70 E3* E Algeria
Bordon *95 F4* S England, United Kingdom
Børgefjelt *83 C3* ▲▲ C Norway
Borger *84 F2* NE Netherlands
Borger *44 F2* Texas, SW USA
Borgholm *83 C6* S Sweden
Borisoglebsk *111 B6* W Russian Federation
Borisov *see* Barysaw
Borlänge *83 C5* C Sweden
Borne *84 F4* E Netherlands
Borneo *131 D7 island* Brunei/Indonesia/Malaysia
Bornholm *83 C7 island* E Denmark
Borovichi *111 A4* W Russian Federation
Borriana *99 F3* E Spain
Borrisokane *89 C5* S Ireland
Bosanski Novi *107 B1* Republika Srpska, NW Bosnia and Herzegovina
Boskovice *105 C6* SE Czech Republic
Bosna *107 C2* ~ N Bosnia and Herzegovina
Bosna I Hercegovina, Federacija *107 C2 republic* Bosnia and Herzegovina
Bosnia and Herzegovina *107 C2* ◆ *republic* SE Europe
Boso-hanto *133 G6 peninsula* S Japan
Bosporus *120 B2 strait* NW Turkey
Bossangoa *72 H5* C Central African Republic
Bossembélé *72 H5* C Central African Republic
Bossier City *39 B5* Louisiana, S USA
Bosten Hu *129 C3* ◎ NW China
Boston *93 F5* E England, United Kingdom
Boston *37 F4 state capital* Massachusetts, NE USA
Boston Mountains *39 B3* ▲▲ Arkansas, C USA
Botany Bay *137 H6 inlet* New South Wales, SE Australia
Boteti *76 C5* ~ N Botswana
Bothnia, Gulf of *83 D4 gulf* N Baltic Sea
Botoșani *109 C5* NE Romania
Botrange *84 E7* ▲ E Belgium
Botswana *76 C5* ◆ *republic* S Africa
Bouar *72 G5* W Central African Republic
Bou Craa *70 B3* NW Western Sahara
Bougainville Island *141 D2 island* NE Papua New Guinea
Bougaroun, Cap *112 D4 headland* NE Algeria
Bougouni *72 C4* SW Mali
Boujdour *70 A3* W Western Sahara
Boulder *47 F5* Colorado, C USA
Boulder *47 D2* Montana, NW USA
Boulogne-sur-Mer *97 D1* N France
Boûmdeïd *72 B3* S Mauritania
Boundiali *72 C4* N Ivory Coast
Bountiful *47 D5* Utah, W USA
Bourail *141 G6* C New Caledonia
Bourbonnais *97 D4 cultural region* C France
Bourg-en-Bresse *97 E4* E France
Bourges *97 D4* C France
Bourgogne *see* Burgundy
Bourke *137 G5* New South Wales, SE Australia
Bournemouth *95 E5* S England, United Kingdom
Boutilimit *72 A3* SW Mauritania
Bowen *137 G3* Queensland, NE Australia
Bowland, Forest of *93 C3 forest* N England, United Kingdom
Bowling Green *39 E3* Kentucky, S USA
Bowling Green *40 E5* Ohio, N USA
Bowman *43 A2* North Dakota, N USA
Boxmeer *84 E5* SE Netherlands
Boyle *89 C3* C Ireland
Boyne *89 E4* ~ E Ireland
Boysun *125 F3* S Uzbekistan
Bozeman *47 D3* Montana, NW USA
Bozüyük *120 B3* NW Turkey
Brač *107 B3 island* S Croatia
Brades *57 J5* ○ Montserrat
Bradford *93 D4* N England, United Kingdom
Bradford *37 B4* Pennsylvania, NE USA
Brady *44 G4* Texas, SW USA
Brae *91 A6* NE Scotland, United Kingdom
Braemar *91 E4* NE Scotland, United Kingdom
Braga *99 B2* NW Portugal
Bragança *99 C2* NE Portugal
Brahmanbaria *127 G3* E Bangladesh
Brahmapur *127 F5* E India
Brahmaputra *127 H3* ~ S Asia
Brăila *109 D7* E Romania
Braine-le-Comte *84 C7* SW Belgium
Brainerd *43 E2* Minnesota, N USA
Braintree *95 G3* SE England, United Kingdom
Brampton *35 D6* Ontario, S Canada
Brampton *93 C2* NW England, United Kingdom
Brandberg *76 B5* ▲ NW Namibia
Brandenburg *101 D3* NE Germany
Brandon *33 H7* Manitoba, S Canada
Brandon *89 A6* SW Ireland
Brandon Bay *89 A6 bay* SW Ireland
Brandon Mountain *89 A6* ▲ SW Ireland
Braniewo *105 E2* NE Poland
Brasília *63 G6* ● C Brazil
Brașov *109 C6* C Romania
Bratislava *105 D7* ● W Slovakia
Bratsk *118 F5* C Russian Federation
Braunschweig *101 C4* N Germany
Brava, Costa *99 H2 coastal region* NE Spain
Bravo, Río *53 D2* ~ Mexico/USA North America
Brawley *49 D9* California, W USA
Bray *89 E4* E Ireland
Brazil *63 C4* ◆ *federal republic* South America
Brazil Basin *14 undersea feature* W Atlantic Ocean
Brazilian Highlands *63 G6* ▲▲ E Brazil
Brazos River *44 H4* ~ Texas, SW USA
Brazzaville *76 B2* ● S Congo
Brechin *91 E4* E Scotland, United Kingdom
Brecht *84 C5* N Belgium
Brecon *93 C6* E Wales, United Kingdom
Brecon Beacons *93 B7* ▲▲ S Wales, United Kingdom
Breda *84 D5* S Netherlands
Bree *84 D6* NE Belgium
Bregalnica *107 E3* ~ E Macedonia
Bremen *101 B3* NW Germany
Bremerhaven *101 B3* NW Germany
Bremerton *49 B2* Washington, NW USA
Brenham *44 H4* Texas, SW USA
Brenner Pass *101 C8 pass* Austria/Italy
Brentwood *95 G3* E England, United Kingdom
Brescia *103 C2* N Italy
Bressanone *103 C1* N Italy
Bressay *91 B6 island* NE Scotland, United Kingdom
Brest *109 B3* SW Belarus
Brest *97 A2* NW France
Bretagne *see* Brittany
Brewton *39 D6* Alabama, S USA
Bria *72 H5* C Central African Republic
Briançon *97 F5* SE France
Bride *93 B3* N Isle of Man
Bridgend *93 B7* S Wales, United Kingdom
Bridgeport *49 C6* California, W USA
Bridgeport *37 E5* Connecticut, NE USA
Bridgetown *57 K6* ● SW Barbados
Bridgetown *89 E6* SE Ireland
Bridgwater *95 D4* SW England, United Kingdom
Bridgwater Bay *95 C4 bay* SW England, United Kingdom
Bridlington *93 F3* E England, United Kingdom
Bridlington Bay *93 F3 bay* E England, United Kingdom
Bridport *95 D5* S England, United Kingdom
Brig *101 B8* SW Switzerland
Brigg *93 E4* N England, United Kingdom
Brigham City *47 D4* Utah, W USA
Brighton *95 F5* SE England, United Kingdom
Brighton *47 F5* Colorado, C USA
Brindisi *103 F6* SE Italy
Brisbane *137 H4 state capital* Queensland, E Australia
Bristol *95 D4* SW England, United Kingdom
Bristol *37 E4* Connecticut, NE USA
Bristol *39 F3* Virginia, NE USA North America
Bristol Bay *50 C2 bay* Alaska, USA
Bristol Channel *95 C4 inlet* England/Wales, United Kingdom
British Columbia *33 E5* ⬖ *province* SW Canada
British Indian Ocean Territory *27 UK* ◇ C Indian Ocean
British Isles *78 island group* NW Europe
British Virgin Islands *57 I4 UK* ◇ E West Indies
Brittany *97 B2 cultural region* NW France Europe
Brive-la-Gaillarde *97 C5* C France
Brixham *95 C5* SW England, United Kingdom
Brno *105 C6* SE Czech Republic
Broad Bay *91 C2 bay* NW Scotland, United Kingdom
Broadford *91 C4* N Scotland, United Kingdom
Broad Haven *89 B2 inlet* NW Ireland
Broad Law *91 E6* ▲ S Scotland, United Kingdom
Broadstairs *95 H4* SE England, United Kingdom
Broads, The *95 H2 wetland* E England, United Kingdom
Brockton *37 F4* Massachusetts, NE USA
Brodeur Peninsula *33 H3 peninsula* Baffin Island, Nunavut, NE Canada
Brodick *91 C6* W Scotland, United Kingdom
Brodnica *105 E2* C Poland
Broek-in-Waterland *84 D3* C Netherlands
Broken Hill *137 F5* New South Wales, SE Australia
Bromley *95 F4* SE England, United Kingdom
Bromsgrove *93 D6* W England, United Kingdom
Brookhaven *39 C5* Mississippi, S USA
Brookings *43 D3* South Dakota, N USA
Brooks Range *50 E2* ▲▲ Alaska, USA

⬖ Administrative region ◆ Country ● Country capital ◇ Dependent territory ○ Dependent territory capital ▲▲ Mountain range ▲ Mountain ϟ Volcano ~ River ◎ Lake ⊠ Reservoir

C

❖ Administrative region   ◆ Country   ● Country capital   ◇ Dependent territory   ○ Dependent territory capital   ▲▲ Mountain range   ▲ Mountain   ☇ Volcano   ☇ River   ○ Lake   ▢ Reservoir

159

◆ Administrative region　◆ Country　● Country capital　◇ Dependent territory　○ Dependent territory capital　▲ Mountain range　▲ Mountain　℞ Volcano　∻ River　☉ Lake　☒ Reservoir

161

H

◆ Administrative region   ◆ Country   ● Country capital   ◇ Dependent territory   ○ Dependent territory capital   ▲ Mountain range   ▲ Mountain   ☒ Volcano   ☇ River   ○ Lake   ☒ Reservoir

JAMAICA CHANNEL

Hastings 139 E4 North Island, New Zealand
Hastings 95 G4 SE England, United Kingdom
Hastings 43 C5 Nebraska, C USA
Hatch 44 D3 New Mexico, SW USA
Hatfield 95 F3 E England, United Kingdom
Hattem 84 E3 E Netherlands
Hatteras, Cape 39 I3 headland North Carolina, SE USA
Hattiesburg 39 C6 Mississippi, S USA
Hat Yai 131 B5 SW Thailand
Haugesund 83 A5 S Norway
Haukeligrend 83 B5 S Norway
Haukivesi 83 F4 ◎ SE Finland
Hauraki Gulf 139 D2 gulf North Island, N New Zealand
Hauroko, Lake 139 A8 ◎ SW New Zealand
Hautes Fagnes 84 E7 ⛰ E Belgium
Hauts Plateaux 70 D2 plateau Algeria/Morocco
Hauzenberg 101 E6 SE Germany
Havana 57 B2 ● W Cuba
Havant 95 F5 S England, United Kingdom
Havelock 39 H4 North Carolina, SE USA
Havelock North 139 E4 North Island, New Zealand
Haverfordwest 93 A7 SW Wales, United Kingdom
Haverhill 95 G2 E England, United Kingdom
Havířov 105 D5 E Czech Republic
Havre 47 D1 Montana, NW USA
Havre-St-Pierre 35 F4 Québec, E Canada
Hawi 51 D2 Hawaii, USA
Hawaii 51 C1 ◐ state USA, C Pacific Ocean
Hawaiʻi 51 D3 island USA, C Pacific Ocean
Hawea, Lake 139 B7 ◎ South Island, New Zealand
Hawera 139 D4 North Island, New Zealand
Hawes 93 D3 N England, United Kingdom
Hawick 91 E6 SE Scotland, United Kingdom
Hawke Bay 139 E4 bay North Island, New Zealand
Hawthorne 47 A6 Nevada, W USA
Hay 137 F6 New South Wales, SE Australia
Hayden 44 B3 Arizona, SW USA
Hayes 35 A2 ~ Manitoba, C Canada
Hay-on-Wye 93 C6 E Wales, United Kingdom
Hay River 33 G5 Northwest Territories, W Canada
Hays 43 C6 Kansas, C USA
Haysyn 109 D5 C Ukraine
Haywards Heath 95 G4 SE England, United Kingdom
Hazar 125 B3 W Turkmenistan
Hearne 44 H4 Texas, SW USA
Hearst 35 C4 Ontario, S Canada
Hebbronville 44 G6 Texas, SW USA
Hebrides, Sea of the 91 B4 sea NW Scotland, United Kingdom
Hebron 123 H6 S West Bank
Heemskerk 84 C3 W Netherlands
Heerde 84 E3 E Netherlands
Heerenveen 84 E2 N Netherlands
Heerhugowaard 84 D3 NW Netherlands
Heerlen 84 E6 SE Netherlands
Hefa see Haifa
Hefei 129 G4 E China
Hegang 129 H1 NE China
Heide 101 B2 N Germany
Heidelberg 101 B6 SW Germany
Heidenheim an der Brenz 101 C6 S Germany
Heilbronn 101 B6 SW Germany
Heilong Jiang see Amur
Heiloo 84 C3 NW Netherlands
Heimdal 83 B4 S Norway
Hekimhan 121 E3 C Turkey
Helena 47 D2 state capital Montana, NW USA
Helensburgh 91 D5 W Scotland, United Kingdom
Helensville 139 D2 North Island, New Zealand
Helgoländer Bucht 101 B2 bay NW Germany
Hellevoetsluis 84 C5 SW Netherlands
Hellín 99 E4 C Spain
Hells Canyon 49 D3 valley Idaho/Oregon, NW USA
Helmand, Darya-ye 125 D6 ~ Afghanistan/Iran
Helmond 84 E5 S Netherlands
Helmsdale 91 E2 N Scotland, United Kingdom
Helmsley 93 E3 N England, United Kingdom
Helsingborg 83 C7 S Sweden
Helsinki 83 E5 ● S Finland
Helston 95 A6 SW England, United Kingdom
Helvellyn 93 C3 ▲ NW England, United Kingdom
Henderson 47 C7 Nevada, W USA
Henderson 44 H3 Texas, SW USA
Hengduan Shan 129 D5 ⛰ SW China
Hengelo 84 F4 E Netherlands
Hengyang 129 F5 S China
Heniches'k 109 F6 S Ukraine
Henley-on-Thames 95 F3 C England, United Kingdom
Hennebont 97 B3 NW France
Herat 125 D5 W Afghanistan
Heredia 55 E6 C Costa Rica
Hereford 93 C6 W England, United Kingdom
Hereford 44 F2 Texas, SW USA
Herford 101 B4 NW Germany
Herk-de-Stad 84 D6 NE Belgium
Herm 95 G6 island Channel Islands
Herma Ness 91 B5 headland NE Scotland, United Kingdom
Hermansverk 83 B5 S Norway
Hermiston 49 C3 Oregon, NW USA
Hermit Islands 141 B1 island group N Papua New Guinea
Hermon, Mount 123 H5 ▲ S Syria
Hermosillo 53 B2 NW Mexico
Herrera del Duque 99 C4 W Spain
Herselt 84 D6 C Belgium
Herstal 84 E7 E Belgium
Hessen 101 C5 state C Germany
Hessle 93 F4 N England, United Kingdom
Hettinger 43 B3 North Dakota, N USA
Hexham 93 D2 N England, United Kingdom
Hidalgo del Parral 53 D3 N Mexico
Hida-sanmyaku 133 E5 ⛰ Honshū, S Japan
Hienghène 141 G6 C New Caledonia
High Atlas 70 C2 ⛰ C Morocco
High Point 39 G3 North Carolina, SE USA
High Willhays 95 C5 ▲ SW England, United Kingdom
High Wycombe 95 F3 SE England, United Kingdom
Higüero, Punta 51 headland W Puerto Rico
Hiiumaa 83 D6 island W Estonia
Hikurangi 139 D2 North Island, New Zealand
Hildesheim 101 C4 N Germany
Hill Bank 55 B1 N Belize
Hillegom 84 C4 W Netherlands
Hillsborough 89 E2 E Northern Ireland, United Kingdom
Hilo 51 D3 Hawaii, USA, C Pacific Ocean
Hilversum 84 D4 C Netherlands
Himalayas 127 E2 ⛰ S Asia
Himeji 133 E6 SW Japan
Hims 123 B2 C Syria
Hinchinbrook Island 137 G2 island Queensland, NE Australia
Hinds 139 C6 SW New Zealand
Hindu Kush 125 F4 ⛰ Afghanistan/Pakistan
Hinesville 39 G5 Georgia, SE USA
Hinnøya 83 C2 island C Norway
Hinthada 131 A3 SW Burma (Myanmar)
Hirfanlı Barajı 121 C3 ⊠ C Turkey
Hirosaki 133 F3 C Japan
Hiroshima 133 D7 SW Japan
Hirson 97 E2 N France
Hisiu 141 B3 SW Papua New Guinea
Hispaniola 57 F4 island Dominion Republic/Haiti
Hitachi 133 G5 S Japan
Hitra 83 B4 island S Norway
Hjälmaren 83 C6 ◎ C Sweden
Hjørring 83 B6 N Denmark
Hkakabo Razi 131 A1 ▲ Burma (Myanmar)/China
Hlukhiv 109 E3 NE Ukraine
Hlybokaye 109 C2 N Belarus
Hoang Lien Son 131 C2 ⛰ N Vietnam
Hobart 137 G7 state capital Tasmania, SE Australia
Hobbs 44 E3 New Mexico, SW USA
Hobro 83 B6 N Denmark
Ho Chi Minh 131 C4 S Vietnam
Hocking River 40 F7 ~ Ohio, N USA
Hodeida 123 B6 W Yemen
Hódmezővásárhely 105 E8 SE Hungary
Hodna, Chott El 112 D4 salt lake N Algeria
Hodonín 105 D6 SE Czech Republic
Hoeryong 133 C3 NE North Korea
Hof 101 D5 SE Germany
Hofu 133 D7 SW Japan
Hohenems 101 C7 W Austria
Hohe Tauern 101 D8 ⛰ W Austria
Hohhot 129 F3 N China
Hokianga Harbour 139 C2 inlet SE Tasman Sea
Hokitika 139 B6 South Island, New Zealand
Hokkaido 133 F1 island NE Japan
Holbrook 44 C2 Arizona, SW USA
Holden 47 D5 Utah, W USA
Holguín 57 D3 SE Cuba
Holin Gol 129 G2 N China
Hollabrunn 101 F6 NE Austria
Holland see Netherlands
Holly Springs 39 C4 Mississippi, S USA
Hollywood 39 G8 Florida, SE USA
Holman 33 G3 Victoria Island, Northwest Territories, N Canada
Holmsund 83 D4 N Sweden
Holon 123 G6 C Israel
Holstebro 83 B6 W Denmark
Holt 95 H1 E England, United Kingdom
Holycross 89 D5 S Ireland
Holyhead 93 A4 NW Wales, United Kingdom
Holy Island 93 D1 island NE England, United Kingdom
Holyoke 37 E4 Massachusetts, NE USA
Hombori 72 D3 S Mali
Homyel' 109 D3 SE Belarus
Hondo 44 G5 Texas, SW USA
Hondo 55 B1 ~ Central America
Honduras 55 C3 ◆ republic Central America
Honduras, Gulf of 55 C2 gulf W Caribbean Sea
Hønefoss 83 B5 S Norway
Honey Lake 49 B6 ◎ California, W USA
Hong Kong 129 H6 S China
Honiara 141 E3 ● C Solomon Islands
Honiton 95 C5 SW England, United Kingdom
Honjo 133 F4 C Japan
Honolulu 51 B1 state capital Oʻahu, Hawaii, USA
Honshu 133 G5 island SW Japan
Hoogeveen 84 E3 NE Netherlands
Hoogezand-Sappemeer 84 F2 NE Netherlands
Hoorn 84 D3 NW Netherlands
Hoover Dam 47 C7 dam Arizona/Nevada, W USA
Hopa 121 G2 NE Turkey
Hope 33 D4 British Columbia, SW Canada
Hope 50 E3 Alaska, USA
Hopedale 35 F2 Newfoundland and Labrador, NE Canada
Hopkinsville 39 D3 Kentucky, S USA
Horasan 121 G3 NE Turkey
Horki 109 D2 E Belarus
Horley 95 F4 SE England, United Kingdom
Horlivka 109 G5 E Ukraine
Hormuz, Strait of 123 E4 strait Iran/Oman
Horn, Cape 65 B9 cape S Chile
Horncastle 93 F5 E England, United Kingdom
Hornsea 93 F4 E England, United Kingdom
Horoshiri-dake 133 G2 ▲ Hokkaidō, N Japan
Horseleap 89 D4 C Ireland
Horsham 137 F6 Victoria, SE Australia
Horsham 95 F4 SE England, United Kingdom
Horst 84 E5 SE Netherlands
Horten 83 B5 S Norway
Horyn' 109 C4 ~ NW Ukraine
Hosingen 84 F8 NE Luxembourg
Hotan 129 B3 NW China
Hotazel 76 C6 N South Africa
Hoting 83 C4 C Sweden
Hot Springs 39 B4 Arkansas, C USA
Houayxay 131 B2 N Laos
Houghton 40 C2 Michigan, N USA
Houghton Lake 40 D4 Michigan, N USA
Houilles 97 C6 N France
Houlton 37 G1 Maine, NE USA
Houma 39 C6 Louisiana, S USA
Houston 44 H4 Texas, SW USA
Hovd 129 C2 W Mongolia
Hove 95 F5 SE England, United Kingdom
Hoverla, Hora 109 B5 ▲ W Ukraine
Hövsgöl Nuur 129 D1 ◎ N Mongolia
Howar, Wadi 75 B2 ~ Chad/Sudan
Howth 89 E4 E Ireland
Hoy 91 E1 island N Scotland, United Kingdom
Hoyerswerda 101 E4 E Germany
Hradec Králové 105 C5 N Czech Republic
Hranice 105 D6 E Czech Republic
Hrodna 109 B2 W Belarus
Huaihua 129 F5 S China
Huajuapan 53 F5 SE Mexico
Hualapai Peak 44 A2 ▲ Arizona, SW USA
Huambo 76 B4 C Angola
Huancayo 63 B5 C Peru
Huangshi 129 G4 C China
Huánuco 63 B5 C Peru
Huanuni 65 A2 W Bolivia
Huaraz 63 B5 W Peru
Huatabampo 53 C3 NW Mexico
Hubli 127 D6 SW India
Huch'ang 133 B4 N North Korea
Hucknall 93 D5 C England, United Kingdom
Huddersfield 93 D4 N England, United Kingdom
Hudiksvall 83 D4 C Sweden
Hudson Bay 35 B2 bay NE Canada
Hudson River 37 E4 ~ New Jersey/New York, NE USA
Hudson Strait 33 J4 strait Northwest Territories/Québec, NE Canada
Hue 131 C3 C Vietnam
Huehuetenango 55 A3 W Guatemala
Huelva 99 B5 SW Spain
Huesca 99 F2 NE Spain
Huéscar 99 E5 S Spain
Hughenden 137 G3 Queensland, NE Australia
Hugo 43 D9 Oklahoma, C USA
Huich'on 133 B4 C North Korea
Huíla Plateau 76 B4 plateau S Angola
Huixtla 53 H6 SE Mexico
Hull 35 D5 Québec, SE Canada
Hull 93 E4 ~ N England, United Kingdom
Hulst 84 C6 SW Netherlands
Hulun Buir 129 G1 NE China
Hulun Nur 129 F2 ◎ NE China
Humacao 51 E Puerto Rico
Humaitá 63 D4 N Brazil
Humber 93 F4 estuary E England, United Kingdom
Humboldt River 47 B5 ~ Nevada, W USA
Humphreys Peak 44 A2 ▲ Arizona, SW USA
Humpolec 105 C6 C Czech Republic
Hunedoara 109 B6 SW Romania
Hünfeld 101 C5 C Germany
Hungary 105 D8 ◆ republic C Europe
Hunstanton 95 G1 E England, United Kingdom
Hunter Island 137 F7 island Tasmania, SE Australia
Huntingdon 95 F2 E England, United Kingdom
Huntington 39 F2 West Virginia, NE USA
Huntington Beach 49 C9 California, W USA
Huntly 139 D3 North Island, New Zealand
Huntly 91 E3 NE Scotland, United Kingdom
Huntsville 39 E4 Alabama, S USA
Huntsville 44 H4 Texas, SW USA
Huon Gulf 141 B2 gulf E Papua New Guinea
Hurghada see Al Ghurdaqah
Huron 43 C3 South Dakota, N USA
Huron, Lake 40 E3 ◎ Canada/USA
Hurunui 139 C6 ~ South Island, New Zealand
Húsavík 83 A1 NE Iceland
Husum 101 B2 N Germany
Hutchinson 43 C6 Kansas, C USA
Huy 84 D7 E Belgium
Hvannadalshnúkur 83 B1 ※ S Iceland
Hvar 107 B3 island S Croatia
Hwange 76 D5 W Zimbabwe
Hyargas Nuur 129 D2 ◎ NW Mongolia
Hyderabad 127 E5 C India
Hyderabad 127 B3 SE Pakistan
Hyères 97 E7 SE France
Hyères, Îles d' 97 E7 island group S France
Hyesan 133 B4 NE North Korea
Hythe 95 H4 SE England, United Kingdom
Hyvinkää 83 E5 S Finland

I

Ialomiţa 109 C7 ~ SE Romania
Iaşi 109 C6 NE Romania
Ibadan 72 E5 SW Nigeria
Ibar 107 D2 ~ C Serbia
Ibarra 63 B3 N Ecuador
Iberian Peninsula 78 physical region Portugal/Spain
Ibérico, Sistema 99 E2 ⛰ NE Spain
Ibiza 99 G4 island Balearic Islands, Spain
Ica 63 B6 SW Peru
İçel see Mersin
Iceland 83 A1 ◆ republic N Atlantic Ocean
Iceland Plateau 143 B6 undersea feature S Greenland Sea
Idabel 43 E9 Oklahoma, C USA
Idaho 49 D3 ◐ state NW USA
Idaho Falls 47 D3 Idaho, NW USA
Idfu 70 J3 SE Egypt
Idini 72 A2 W Mauritania
Idlib 123 B2 NW Syria
Idre 83 C4 C Sweden
Ieper 84 A6 W Belgium
Iferouâne 72 F2 N Niger
Ifôghas, Adrar des 72 E2 ⛰ NE Mali
Igarka 118 E3 N Russian Federation
Iglesias 103 A6 Sardinia, Italy
Igloolik 33 I3 Nunavut, N Canada
Igoumenitsa 107 D5 W Greece
Iguaçu, Rio 63 F8 ~ Argentina/Brazil
Iguala 53 F5 S Mexico
Iguazu Falls 65 D4 waterfall Brazil/Argentina
Iguidi, 'Erg 70 C3 desert Algeria/Mauritania
Ihosy 76 G5 S Madagascar
Iisalmi 83 E4 C Finland
IJssel 84 E4 ~ Netherlands
IJsselmeer 84 D3 ◎ N Netherlands
IJsselmuiden 84 E3 E Netherlands
Ijzer 84 A6 ~ W Belgium
Ikaahuk see Sachs Harbour
Ikaluktutiak see Cambridge Bay
Ikaría 107 F6 island Dodecanese, Greece
Ikela 76 C2 C Dem. Rep. Congo
Iki 133 C7 island SW Japan
Ilagan 131 F3 Luzon, N Philippines
Iława 105 E2 NE Poland
Ilebo 76 C2 W Dem. Rep. Congo
Île-de-France 97 D3 region N France
Ilford 95 G3 SE England, United Kingdom
Ilfracombe 95 B4 SW England, United Kingdom
Ílhavo 99 B3 N Portugal
Iliamna Lake 50 D2 ◎ Alaska, USA
Iligan 131 F5 S Philippines
Ilkeston 93 E5 C England, United Kingdom
Ilkley 93 D4 N England, United Kingdom
Illapel 65 A5 C Chile
Illichivs'k 109 E6 SW Ukraine
Illinois 40 B7 ◐ state C USA
Illinois River 40 B6 ~ Illinois, N USA
Iloilo 131 F4 Panay Island, C Philippines
Ilorin 72 E4 W Nigeria
Ilovlya 111 B7 SW Russian Federation
Imatra 83 F4 SE Finland
Imisli 121 I2 C Azerbaijan
Imola 103 C3 N Italy
Imperatriz 63 G4 NE Brazil
Imperia 103 A3 NW Italy
Imphal 127 H3 NE India
Inagh 89 B5 W Ireland
Inarajan 51 SE Guam
Inarijärvi 83 E1 ◎ N Finland
Inawashiro-ko 133 F5 ◎ Honshu, C Japan
İncesu 121 D4 Turkey
Incheon 133 B5 NW South Korea
Independence 43 E6 Missouri, C USA
Independence Mountains 47 B4 ⛰ Nevada, W USA
India 127 D4 ◆ republic S Asia
Indiana 37 B5 Pennsylvania, NE USA
Indiana 40 C6 ◐ state N USA
Indianapolis 40 D7 state capital Indiana, N USA
Indian Church 55 B1 N Belize
Indian Ocean 15 ocean
Indianola 43 E5 Iowa, C USA
Indigirka 118 G2 ~ NE Russian Federation
Indonesia 131 C7 ◆ republic SE Asia
Indore 127 D4 C India
Indus 127 B3 ~ S Asia
Indus, Mouths of the 127 B3 delta S Pakistan
İnebolu 121 D2 N Turkey
Infiernillo, Presa del 53 E5 ⊠ S Mexico
Ingleborough 93 C4 ▲ N England, United Kingdom
Ingolstadt 101 C6 S Germany
Inhambane 76 E6 SE Mozambique
Inishannon 89 C7 S Ireland
Inishbofin 89 A4 island W Ireland
Inishcrone 89 C3 N Ireland
Inishkea North 89 A3 island NW Ireland
Inishkea South 89 A3 island NW Ireland
Inishmore 89 B4 island W Ireland
Inishshark 89 A4 island W Ireland
Inishtrahull 89 D1 island NW Ireland
Inishturk 89 A3 island W Ireland
Inn 101 D7 ~ C Europe
Inner Hebrides 91 B5 island group W Scotland, United Kingdom
Inner Sound 91 C3 strait NW Scotland, United Kingdom
Innisfail 137 G2 Queensland, NE Australia
Innsbruck 101 C7 W Austria
Inowrocław 105 D3 C Poland
I-n-Sakane, 'Erg 72 D2 desert N Mali
I-n-Salah 70 D3 C Algeria
Inta 111 E3 NW Russian Federation
Interlaken 101 B8 SW Switzerland
International Falls 43 E1 Minnesota, N USA
Inukjuak 35 D2 Québec, NE Canada
Inuvik 33 F4 Northwest Territories, NW Canada
Inver 89 C2 N Ireland
Inveraray 91 C5 W Scotland, United Kingdom
Inverbervie 91 F4 NE Scotland, United Kingdom
Invercargill 139 B8 Sw New Zealand
Invergordon 91 D3 N Scotland, United Kingdom
Inverness 91 D3 N Scotland, United Kingdom
Inverurie 91 F3 NE Scotland, United Kingdom
Investigator Strait 137 E6 strait South Australia
Inyangani 76 E5 ▲ NE Zimbabwe
Ioánnina 107 D5 W Greece
Iola 43 E7 Kansas, C USA
Iona 91 B5 island W Scotland, United Kingdom
Iónia Nisiá see Ionian Islands
Ionian Islands 107 D5 island group W Greece
Ionian Sea 112 G3 sea C Mediterranean Sea
Íos 107 F6 island Cyclades, Greece
Iowa 43 E5 ◐ state C USA
Iowa City 43 F5 Iowa, C USA
Iowa Falls 43 E4 Iowa, C USA
Iowa River 40 A5 ~ Iowa, C USA
Ipel' 105 E7 ~ Hungary/Slovakia
Ipoh 131 B5 W Malaysia
Ippy 72 H5 C Central African Republic
Ipswich 137 H5 Queensland, E Australia
Ipswich 95 H2 E England, United Kingdom
Iqaluit 33 J3 province capital Baffin Island, Nunavut, NE Canada
Iquique 65 A3 N Chile
Iquitos 63 C4 N Peru
Irákleio 107 F7 Crete, Greece
Iran 123 E2 ◆ republic SW Asia
Iranian Plateau 123 E3 plateau N Iran
Irapuato 53 E4 C Mexico
Iraq 123 B2 ◆ republic SW Asia
Irbid 123 A2 N Jordan
Ireland 89 C4 ◆ republic NW Europe
Irian Jaya see Papua
Iringa 75 D7 C Tanzania
Iriomote-jima 133 A8 island Sakishima-shoto, SW Japan
Iriona 55 D2 NE Honduras
Irish Sea 87 C6 sea C British Isles
Irkutsk 118 F5 S Russian Federation
Iroise 97 A2 sea NW France
Iron Mountain 40 C3 Michigan, N USA
Ironwood 40 B2 Michigan, N USA
Irrawaddy 131 A2 ~ W Burma (Myanmar)
Irrawaddy, Mouths of the 131 A3 delta SW Burma (Myanmar)
Irtysh 118 D4 ~ C Asia
Irún 99 E1 N Spain
Iruña see Pamplona
Irvine 91 D6 W Scotland, United Kingdom
Irvinestown 89 D2 W Northern Ireland, United Kingdom
Isabela, Isla 63 A7 island Galapagos Islands, Ecuador
Isabella, Cordillera 55 D4 ⛰ NW Nicaragua
Isachsen 33 G2 Ellef Ringnes Island, Nunavut, N Canada
Ísafjörður 83 A1 NW Iceland
Isbister 91 A6 NE Scotland, United Kingdom
Ise 133 F6 SW Japan
Isère 97 E5 ~ E France
Isernia 103 D5 C Italy
Ise-wan 133 F6 bay S Japan
Isfahan 123 D2 C Iran
Ishigaki-jima 133 A8 island Sakishima-shoto, SW Japan
Ishikari-wan 133 F2 bay Hokkaidō, NE Japan
Ishim 118 C4 C Russian Federation
Ishim 118 D4 ~ Kazakhstan/Russian Federation
Ishinomaki 133 G4 C Japan
Ishkoshim 125 G4 S Tajikistan
Isiro 76 D1 NE Dem. Rep. Congo
İskenderun 121 E5 S Turkey
Iskur 107 E3 ~ NW Bulgaria
Iskur, Yazovir 107 E3 ⊠ W Bulgaria
Isla Cristina 99 B5 SW Spain
Islamabad 127 D1 ● NE Pakistan
Islay 91 B6 island SW Scotland, United Kingdom
Isle 97 C5 ~ W France
Isle of Man 93 B3 UK ◇ NW Europe
Isle of Wight 95 E5 island , United Kingdom
Isles of Scilly 95 A3 island group SW England, United Kingdom
Ismoili Somoní, Qullai 125 G3 ▲ NE Tajikistan
Isna 70 J3 SE Egypt
Isoka 76 E3 NE Zambia
Isparta 120 B4 SW Turkey
İspir 121 F2 NE Turkey
Israel 123 G6 ◆ republic SW Asia
Issoire 97 D5 C France
Issyk-Kul', Ozero 125 H2 ◎ E Kyrgyzstan
Istanbul 120 B2 NW Turkey
Istra 107 A1 cultural region NW Croatia
Itabuna 63 H6 E Brazil
Itagüí 63 B2 W Colombia
Itaipú Dam 65 C4 dam Brazil/Paraguay
Itaipú, Represa de 63 F7 ⊠ Brazil/Paraguay
Itaituba 63 F4 NE Brazil
Italy 103 C4 ◆ republic S Europe
Ithaca 37 D4 New York, NE USA
Itoigawa 133 F5 C Japan
Iturup, Ostrov 118 I5 island Kurile Islands, SE Russian Federation
Itzehoe 101 C2 N Germany
Ivalo 83 E2 N Finland
Ivanhoe 137 F5 New South Wales, SE Australia
Ivano-Frankivs'k 109 B5 W Ukraine
Ivanovo 111 B5 W Russian Federation
Ivoire, Côte d' see Ivory Coast
Ivory Coast 72 C5 ◆ republic W Africa
Ivujivik 35 D1 Québec, NE Canada
Iwaki 133 G5 N Japan
Iwakuni 133 D7 SW Japan
Iwanai 133 F2 NE Japan
Iwate 133 G3 N Japan
Ixtapa 53 E5 S Mexico
Ixtepec 53 G5 SE Mexico
Iyo-nada 133 D7 sea S Japan
Izabal, Lago de 55 B3 ◎ E Guatemala
Izad Khvast 123 D3 C Iran
Izegem 84 B6 W Belgium
Izhevsk 111 D6 NW Russian Federation
Izmayil 109 D7 SW Ukraine
İzmir 120 A4 W Turkey
İzmit 120 B2 NW Turkey
İznik Gölü 120 B2 ◎ NW Turkey
Izu-hanto 133 G6 peninsula Honshu, S Japan
Izu-shoto 133 G6 island group S Japan

J

Jabal ash Shifa 123 A3 desert NW Saudi Arabia
Jabalpur 127 E4 C India
Jaca 99 F2 NE Spain
Jacaltenango 55 A3 W Guatemala
Jackman 37 F2 Maine, NE USA
Jackpot 47 C4 Nevada, W USA
Jackson 43 G7 Missouri, C USA
Jackson 39 D3 Tennessee, S USA
Jackson 39 C5 state capital Mississippi, S USA
Jacksonville 39 G6 Florida, SE USA
Jacksonville 40 B6 Illinois, N USA
Jacksonville 39 H4 North Carolina, SE USA
Jacksonville 44 H3 Texas, SW USA
Jacmel 57 F4 S Haiti
Jacobabad 127 C3 SE Pakistan
Jaén 99 D5 S Spain
Jaffna 127 E7 N Sri Lanka
Jagdalpur 127 E5 C India
Jagdaqi 129 G1 N China
Jaipur 127 D3 N India
Jaisalmer 127 C3 NW India
Jakarta 131 C7 ● Java, C Indonesia
Jakobstad 83 E4 W Finland
Jalalabad 125 G5 E Afghanistan
Jalandhar 127 D2 N India
Jalapa 55 D3 NW Nicaragua
Jalpa 53 E4 C Mexico
Jalu 70 H3 NE Libya
Jamaame 75 E5 S Somalia
Jamaica 57 C5 ◆ commonwealth republic W West Indies
Jamaica Channel 57 E4 channel Haiti/Jamaica

◐ Administrative region ◆ Country ● Country capital ◇ Dependent territory ○ Dependent territory capital ⛰ Mountain range ▲ Mountain ※ Volcano ~ River ◎ Lake ⊠ Reservoir

K

◆ Administrative region   ◆ Country   ● Country capital   ◇ Dependent territory   ○ Dependent territory capital   🜄 Mountain range   🜄 Mountain   🜄 Volcano   🜄 River   ◎ Lake   ◎ Reservoir

◆ Administrative region   ● Country   ● Country capital   ◇ Dependent territory   ○ Dependent territory capital   ▲ Mountain range   ▲ Mountain   🜂 Volcano   ✍ River   ⊗ Lake   ▨ Reservoir

165

M

◆ Administrative region ◆ Country ● Country capital ◇ Dependent territory ◎ Dependent territory capital ▲ Mountain range ▲ Mountain ⛰ Volcano ↘ River ◎ Lake ⊡ Reservoir

167

◊ Administrative region   ◆ Country   ● Country capital   ◊ Dependent territory   ○ Dependent territory capital   ▲ Mountain range   ▲ Mountain   ℞ Volcano   ↫ River   ⊗ Lake   ▣ Reservoir

PASŁĘK

North Frisian Islands 101 B2 *island group* N Germany
North Geomagnetic Pole 143 A4 *pole* Arctic Ocean
North Island 139 B2 *island* N New Zealand
North Korea 133 C4 ◆ *republic* E Asia
Northland 139 C1 *cultural region* North Island, New Zealand
North Las Vegas 47 B7 Nevada, W USA
North Little Rock 39 C4 Arkansas, C USA
North Platte 43 B5 Nebraska, C USA
North Platte River 43 B5 ~ C USA
North Pole 143 C4 *pole* Arctic Ocean
North Ronaldsay 91 F1 *island* NE Scotland, United Kingdom
North Saskatchewan 33 G6 ~ Alberta/Saskatchewan, S Canada
North Sea 78 *sea* NW Europe
North Siberian Lowland 118 E3 *lowlands* N Russian Federation
North Sound 89 B4 *sound* W Ireland
North Sound, The 91 E1 *sound* N Scotland, United Kingdom
North Taranaki Bight 139 C3 *gulf* North Island, New Zealand
North Tyne 93 D2 ~ N England, United Kingdom
North Uist 91 A3 *island* NW Scotland, United Kingdom
North West Highlands 91 C3 ⛰ N Scotland, United Kingdom
Northwest Pacific Basin 15 *undersea feature* NW Pacific Ocean
Northwest Territories 33 F4 ◐ *territory* NW Canada
Northwich 93 C5 C England, United Kingdom
Northwind Plain 143 B2 *undersea feature* Arctic Ocean
North York Moors 93 E3 *moorland* N England, United Kingdom
Norton Sound 50 D1 *inlet* Alaska, USA
Norway 83 A4 ◆ *monarchy* N Europe
Norwegian Sea 83 A4 *sea* NE Atlantic Ocean
Norwich 95 H2 E England, United Kingdom
Noshiro 133 F3 C Japan
Nosop 76 C6 ~ E Namibia
Noteć 105 D3 ~ NW Poland
Nottingham 93 E5 C England, United Kingdom
Nouâdhibou 72 A2 W Mauritania
Nouakchott 72 A2 ● SW Mauritania
Nouméa 141 G6 ○ S New Caledonia
Nova Gorica 101 E8 W Slovenia
Nova Iguaçu 63 G7 SE Brazil
Novara 103 B2 NW Italy
Nova Scotia 37 H2 ◐ *province* SE Canada
Novaya Sibir', Ostrov 118 G2 *island* NE Russian Federation
Novaya Zemlya 111 E1 *island group* N Russian Federation
Novi Sad 107 D1 N Serbia
Novoazovs'k 109 G5 E Ukraine
Novocheboksarsk 111 C6 W Russian Federation
Novocherkassk 111 A7 SW Russian Federation
Novodvinsk 111 C3 NW Russian Federation
Novokuznetsk 118 E5 S Russian Federation
Novolazarevskaya 142 C3 *Russian research station* Antarctica
Novo mesto 101 E9 SE Slovenia
Novomoskovsk 111 B6 W Russian Federation
Novomoskovs'k 109 F5 E Ukraine
Novorossiysk 111 A8 SW Russian Federation
Novopolotsk *see* Navapolatsk
Novoshakhtinsk 111 A7 SW Russian Federation
Novosibirsk 118 D5 C Russian Federation
Novotroitsk 111 D7 W Russian Federation
Novyy Buh 109 E5 S Ukraine
Nowogard 105 C2 NW Poland
Nowy Dwór Mazowiecki 105 E3 C Poland
Nowy Sącz 105 F6 S Poland
Nowy Tomyśl 105 C3 C Poland
Noyon 97 D2 N France
Ntomba, Lac 76 B2 ◎ NW Dem. Rep. Congo
Nubian Desert 75 C1 *desert* NE Sudan
Nueces River 44 G5 ~ Texas, SW USA
Nueva Gerona 57 B3 NW Cuba
Nueva Guinea 55 E5 SE Nicaragua
Nueva Ocotepeque 55 B3 W Honduras
Nueva Rosita 53 E2 NE Mexico
Nuevitas 57 D3 E Cuba
Nuevo Casas Grandes 53 C2 N Mexico
Nuevo, Golfo 65 B7 *gulf* S Argentina
Nuevo Laredo 53 E2 NE Mexico
Nui Atoll 141 I2 *atoll* W Tuvalu
Nuku'alofa 135 ● Tongatapu, S Tonga
Nukufetau Atoll 141 I2 *atoll* C Tuvalu
Nukulaelae Atoll 141 J3 *atoll* E Tuvalu
Nukumanu Islands 141 E1 *island group* NE Papua New Guinea
Nukus 125 D2 W Uzbekistan
Nullarbor Plain 137 D5 *plateau* South Australia/Western Australia
Nunavut 33 H4 ◐ *territory* N Canada
Nuneaton 93 D6 C England, United Kingdom
Nunivak Island 50 C2 *island* Alaska, USA
Nunspeet 84 E4 E Netherlands
Nuoro 103 A6 Sardinia, Italy
Nuremberg 101 C6 S Germany
Nurmes 83 F4 E Finland
Nürnberg *see* Nuremberg
Nurota 125 E3 C Uzbekistan
Nusaybin 121 G4 SE Turkey
Nyagan' 118 D3 N Russian Federation
Nyainqentanglha Shan 129 C4 ⛰ W China
Nyala 75 B3 W Sudan
Nyamtumbo 75 D7 S Tanzania
Nyandoma 111 B4 NW Russian Federation
Nyantakara 75 C6 NW Tanzania
Nyasa, Lake 76 E4 ◎ Malawi/Mozambique/Tanzania/Zambia
Nyeri 75 D5 C Kenya
Nyíregyháza 105 F7 NE Hungary
Nykøbing 83 B7 SE Denmark
Nyköping 83 D6 S Sweden
Nylstroom *see* Modimolle
Nyngan 137 G5 New South Wales, SE Australia
Nyurba 118 F4 NE Russian Federation
Nzega 75 C6 C Tanzania
Nzérékoré 72 B5 SE Guinea
N'Zeto 76 B3 NW Angola

O

Oahe, Lake 43 C3 ⊠ North Dakota/South Dakota, N USA
Oa'hu 51 B1 *island* Hawai'ian Islands, Hawaii, USA
Oakham 93 E5 C England, United Kingdom
Oak Harbor 49 B2 Washington, NW USA
Oakland 49 B7 California, W USA
Oakley 43 B6 Kansas, C USA
Oamaru 139 B7 South Island, New Zealand
Oa, Mull of 91 B6 *headland* W Scotland, United Kingdom
Oaxaca 53 F5 SE Mexico
Ob' 118 D3 ~ C Russian Federation
Oban 91 C5 W Scotland, United Kingdom
Ob', Gulf of 118 D3 *gulf* N Russian Federation
Obihiro 133 G2 NE Japan
Obo 72 I5 E Central African Republic
Obock 75 E3 E Djibouti
Oborniki 105 C3 W Poland
Ocala 39 F7 Florida, SE USA
Ocaña 99 D3 C Spain
O Carballiño 99 B2 NW Spain
Occidental, Cordillera 65 A2 ⛰ Bolivia/Chile
Ocean Falls 33 E6 British Columbia, SW Canada
Oceanside 49 D9 California, W USA
Ochamchire 121 G1 W Georgia
Ochil Hills 91 E5 ⛰ C Scotland, United Kingdom
Ocotal 55 D4 NW Nicaragua
Ocozocuautla 53 G5 SE Mexico
October Revolution Island 118 F2 *island* N Russian Federation
Ocú 55 G7 S Panama
Odate 133 G3 C Japan
Ödemiş 120 A4 SW Turkey
Odense 83 B7 C Denmark
Oder 101 E3 ~ C Europe
Oderhaff 105 B2 *bay* Germany/Poland
Odesa 109 E6 SW Ukraine
Odessa 44 F4 Texas, SW USA
Odienné 72 C4 NW Ivory Coast
Odisha 127 F5 *state* NE India
Odoorn 84 F2 NE Netherlands
Odra *see* Oder
Of 121 F2 NE Turkey
Ofanto 103 E6 ~ S Italy
Offenbach 101 B5 W Germany
Offenburg 101 B7 SW Germany
Ofu 51 *island* E American Samoa
Ogaden 75 F4 *plateau* Ethiopia/Somalia
Ogaki 133 F6 SW Japan
Ogallala 43 B5 Nebraska, C USA
Ogbomosho 72 E5 W Nigeria
Ogden 47 D5 Utah, W USA
Ogdensburg 37 D2 New York, NE USA
Ohio 40 E6 ◐ *state* N USA
Ohio River 40 F7 ~ N USA
Ohrid, Lake 107 D4 ◎ Albania/Macedonia
Ohura 139 D3 North Island, New Zealand
Oil City 37 B4 Pennsylvania, NE USA
Oirschot 84 D5 S Netherlands
Oise 97 D2 ~ N France
Oita 133 D7 Kyushu, SW Japan
Ojinaga 53 D2 N Mexico
Ojos del Salado, Cerro 65 A4 ▲ W Argentina
Okaihau 139 C1 North Island, New Zealand
Okanogan River 49 C1 ~ Washington, NW USA
Okara 127 D2 E Pakistan
Okavango 76 C5 ~ S Africa
Okavango Delta 76 C5 *wetland* N Botswana
Okayama 133 E6 SW Japan
Okazaki 133 F6 C Japan
Okeechobee, Lake 39 F8 ◎ Florida, SE USA
Okefenokee Swamp 39 F6 *wetland* Georgia, SE USA
Okehampton 95 C5 SW England, United Kingdom
Okhotsk 118 H3 E Russian Federation
Okhotsk, Sea of 118 H4 *sea* NW Pacific Ocean
Okhtyrka 109 F4 NE Ukraine
Okinawa 133 A8 SW Japan
Okinawa-shoto 133 A8 *island group* SW Japan
Oki-shoto 133 D6 *island group* SW Japan
Oklahoma 43 C8 ◐ *state* C USA
Oklahoma City 43 D8 *state capital* Oklahoma, C USA
Okmulgee 43 D8 Oklahoma, C USA
Oko, Wadi 75 D1 ~ NE Sudan
Oktyabr'skiy 111 D6 SW Russian Federation
Okushiri-to 133 F2 *island* NE Japan
Öland 83 D7 *island* S Sweden
Olavarría 65 C6 E Argentina
Oława 105 D4 SW Poland
Olbia 103 B5 Sardinia, Italy
Oldebroek 84 E3 E Netherlands
Oldenburg 101 B3 NW Germany
Oldenburg 101 C2 N Germany
Oldenzaal 84 F4 E Netherlands
Oldham 93 D4 NW England, United Kingdom
Old Head of Kinsale 89 C7 *headland* SW Ireland
Olëkma 118 G4 ~ C Russian Federation
Olëkminsk 118 G4 NE Russian Federation
Oleksandriya 109 E5 C Ukraine
Olenegorsk 111 B2 NW Russian Federation
Olenek 118 F3 NE Russian Federation
Olenëk 118 F3 ~ NE Russian Federation
Oléron, Île d' 97 B4 *island* W France
Olevs'k 109 C4 N Ukraine
Ölgiy 129 C1 W Mongolia
Olhão 99 B5 S Portugal
Olifa 76 B4 NW Namibia
Oliva 99 F4 E Spain
Olivet 97 D3 C France
Olmaliq 125 F3 E Uzbekistan
Olomouc 105 D6 E Czech Republic
Olonets 111 B4 NW Russian Federation
Olosega 51 *island* E American Samoa
Olovyannaya 118 G5 S Russian Federation
Olpe 101 B5 W Germany
Olsztyn 105 E2 N Poland
Olt 109 B7 ~ S Romania
Olvera 99 C6 SW Spain
Olympia 49 B2 *state capital* Washington, NW USA
Olympic Mountains 49 A2 ⛰ Washington, NW USA
Olympus, Mount 107 D4 ▲ N Greece
Omagh 89 D2 W Northern Ireland, United Kingdom
Omaha 43 D5 Nebraska, C USA
Oman 123 E6 ◆ *monarchy* SW Asia
Oman, Gulf of 123 F4 *gulf* N Arabian Sea
Omboué 76 A2 W Gabon
Omdurman 75 C2 C Sudan
Ometepe, Isla de 55 D5 *island* S Nicaragua
Ommen 84 E3 E Netherlands
Omsk 118 D5 C Russian Federation
Omuta 133 D7 SW Japan
Onda 99 F3 E Spain
Öndörhaan 129 F2 E Mongolia
Onega 111 B3 NW Russian Federation
Onega 111 B4 ~ NW Russian Federation
Onega, Lake 111 B4 ◎ NW Russian Federation
Oneida Lake 37 D3 ◎ New York, NE USA
O'Neill 43 C4 Nebraska, C USA
Oneonta 37 D4 New York, NE USA
Onex 101 A8 SW Switzerland
Ongjin 133 A5 SW North Korea
Ongole 127 E6 E India
Onitsha 72 F5 S Nigeria
Onon Gol 129 F2 ~ N Mongolia
Onslow 137 A3 Western Australia
Onslow Bay 39 H4 *bay* North Carolina, E USA
Ontario 35 B4 ◐ *province* S Canada
Ontario, Lake 37 C3 ◎ Canada/USA
Ontinyent 99 F4 E Spain
Ontong Java Atoll 141 E2 *atoll* N Solomon Islands
Oostakker 84 B6 NW Belgium
Oostburg 84 B5 SW Netherlands
Oostende *see* Ostend
Oosterbeek 84 E4 SE Netherlands
Oosterhout 84 D5 S Netherlands
Opava 105 D5 E Czech Republic
Opelika 39 E5 Alabama, S USA
Opelousas 39 B6 Louisiana, S USA
Opmeer 84 D3 NW Netherlands
Opochka 111 A4 W Russian Federation
Opole 105 D5 S Poland
Oporto 99 B3 NW Portugal
Opotiki 139 E3 North Island, New Zealand
Oqtosh 125 E3 C Uzbekistan
Oradea 109 B6 NW Romania
Oran 70 D1 NW Algeria
Orange 137 G5 New South Wales, SE Australia
Orange 97 E6 SE France
Orangeburg 39 G4 South Carolina, SE USA
Orange River 76 C6 ~ S Africa
Orange Walk 55 C1 N Belize
Oranienburg 101 D3 NE Germany
Oranjemund 76 B6 SW Namibia
Oranjestad 57 G7 ○ W Aruba
Oranmore 89 C4 W Ireland
Orbetello 103 C4 C Italy
Orcadas 142 A2 *Argentinian research station* South Orkney Islands, Antarctica
Orchard Homes 47 C2 Montana, NW USA
Ord River 137 D2 ~ N Australia Oceania
Ordu 121 E2 N Turkey
Örebro 83 C5 C Sweden
Oregon 49 B4 ◐ *state* NW USA
Oregon City 49 B3 Oregon, NW USA
Orël 111 A6 W Russian Federation
Orem 47 D5 Utah, W USA
Ore Mountains 101 D5 ⛰ Czech Republic/Germany
Orenburg 111 D7 W Russian Federation
Orense *see* Ourense
Orford Ness 95 H2 *cape* E England, United Kingdom
Organ Peak 44 D3 ▲ New Mexico, SW USA
Oriental, Cordillera 65 B3 ⛰ Bolivia/Peru
Orihuela 99 F5 E Spain
Orikhiv 109 F5 SE Ukraine
Orin 47 F4 Wyoming, C USA
Orinoco, Río 63 D2 ~ Colombia/Venezuela
Oriomo 141 A3 SW Papua New Guinea
Orissa *see* Odisha
Oristano 103 A6 Sardinia, Italy
Orkney Islands 91 D1 *island group* N Scotland, United Kingdom
Orlando 39 G7 Florida, SE USA
Orléanais 97 D3 *cultural region* C France
Orléans 97 D3 C France
Orleans 37 G4 Massachusetts, NE USA
Ormskirk 93 C4 NW England, United Kingdom
Örnsköldsvik 83 D4 C Sweden
Orohena, Mont 141 B6 ▲ Tahiti, W French Polynesia
Oromocto 35 F5 New Brunswick, SE Canada
Orsha 109 D2 NE Belarus
Orsk 111 D7 W Russian Federation
Orthez 97 B6 SW France
Ortona 103 D5 C Italy
Oruro 65 A2 W Bolivia
Orwell 95 H2 ~ E England, United Kingdom
Osaka 133 E6 SW Japan
Osa, Península de 55 E7 *peninsula* S Costa Rica
Osborne 43 C6 Kansas, C USA
Osh 125 G3 SW Kyrgyzstan
Oshakati 76 B5 N Namibia
Oshawa 35 D6 Ontario, SE Canada
Oshikango 76 B4 N Namibia
O-shima 133 G6 *island* S Japan
Oshkosh 40 C4 Wisconsin, N USA
Osijek 107 C1 E Croatia
Oskaloosa 43 F5 Iowa, C USA
Oskarshamn 83 C6 S Sweden
Oslo 83 B5 ● S Norway
Osmaniye 121 E5 S Turkey
Osnabrück 101 B4 NW Germany
Osorno 65 A7 C Chile
Oss 84 D5 S Netherlands
Ossa, Serra d' 99 B4 ⛰ SE Portugal
Ossora 118 I3 E Russian Federation
Ostend 84 A6 NW Belgium
Östersund 83 C4 C Sweden
Ostfriesische Inseln *see* East Frisian Islands
Ostiglia 103 C2 N Italy
Ostrava 105 D5 E Czech Republic
Ostróda 105 E2 NE Poland
Ostrołęka 105 F3 C Poland
Ostrov 111 A4 W Russian Federation
Ostrowiec Świętokrzyski 105 F4 C Poland
Ostrów Mazowiecka 105 F3 NE Poland
Ostrów Wielkopolski 105 D4 C Poland
Osumi-shoto 133 A7 *island group* SW Japan
Osumit, Lumi i 107 D4 ~ SE Albania
Osuna 99 C5 SW Spain
Oswego 37 D3 New York, NE USA
Oswestry 93 C5 W England, United Kingdom
Otago Peninsula 139 B7 *peninsula* South Island, New Zealand
Otaki 139 D5 North Island, New Zealand
Otaru 133 F2 NE Japan
Otavi 76 B5 N Namibia
Otira 139 C6 South Island, New Zealand
Otjiwarongo 76 B5 N Namibia
Otley 93 D4 N England, United Kingdom
Otorohanga 139 D3 North Island, New Zealand
Otranto 112 G3 SE Italy
Otranto, Strait of 103 F7 *strait* Albania/Italy
Otrokovice 105 D6 E Czech Republic
Ōtsu 133 E6 Honshu, SW Japan
Ottawa 35 D5 ● Ontario, SE Canada
Ottawa 40 B5 Illinois, N USA
Ottawa 43 E6 Kansas, C USA
Ottawa Islands 35 C2 *island group* Nunavut, C Canada
Otterburn 93 D2 N England, United Kingdom
Ottignies 84 C7 C Belgium
Ottumwa 43 F5 Iowa, C USA
Ouachita Mountains 39 A3 ⛰ Arkansas/Oklahoma, C USA
Ouachita River 39 B5 ~ Arkansas/Louisiana, C USA
Ouagadougou 72 D4 ● C Burkina Faso
Ouahigouya 72 D3 NW Burkina Faso
Oualâta 72 C3 SE Mauritania
Ouanda Djallé 72 I4 NE Central African Republic
Ouarâne 72 B2 *desert* C Mauritania
Ouargla 70 E2 NE Algeria
Ouarzazate 70 C2 S Morocco
Oubangui 72 H5 ~ C Africa
Ouessant, Île d' 97 A2 *island* NW France
Ouésso 76 B1 NW Congo
Oughterard 89 B4 W Ireland
Oujda 70 D1 NE Morocco
Oujeft 72 B2 C Mauritania
Oulu 83 E3 C Finland
Oulujärvi 83 E3 ◎ C Finland
Oulujoki 83 E3 ~ C Finland
Ounasjoki 83 E2 ~ N Finland
Ounianga Kébir 72 H2 N Chad
Oupeye 84 D7 E Belgium
Our 84 E8 ~ NW Europe
Ourense 99 B2 NW Spain
Ourique 99 B5 S Portugal
Ourthe 84 E8 ~ E Belgium
Ou-sanmyaku 133 G3 ⛰ Honshū, C Japan
Ouse 93 E4 ~ N England, United Kingdom
Outer Hebrides 91 A3 *island group* NW Scotland, United Kingdom
Outes 99 B1 NW Spain
Out Skerries 91 B6 *island group* NE Scotland, United Kingdom
Ouvéa 141 G6 *island* Îles Loyauté, NE New Caledonia
Ouyen 137 F6 Victoria, SE Australia
Ovalle 65 A5 N Chile
Ovar 99 B3 N Portugal
Overflakkee 84 B5 *island* SW Netherlands
Overijse 84 C7 C Belgium
Oviedo 99 C1 NW Spain
Owando 76 B2 C Congo
Owase 133 F6 SW Japan
Owatonna 43 E4 Minnesota, N USA
Owen, Mount 139 C5 ▲ South Island, New Zealand
Owensboro 39 D2 Kentucky, S USA
Owens Lake 49 D7 *salt flat* California, W USA
Owen Stanley Range 141 B3 ⛰ S Papua New Guinea
Owerri 72 F5 S Nigeria
Owyhee River 49 D4 ~ Idaho/Oregon, NW USA
Oxford 139 C6 South Island, New Zealand
Oxford 95 E3 S England, United Kingdom
Oxford Canal 95 E2 *canal* S England, United Kingdom
Oxkutzcab 53 H4 SE Mexico
Oxnard 49 C8 California, W USA
Oyama 133 G5 Honshu, S Japan
Oyem 76 A1 N Gabon
Oykel 91 D3 ~ N Scotland, United Kingdom
Oyo 76 B2 C Congo
Oyo 72 E5 W Nigeria
Ozark 39 E6 Alabama, S USA
Ozark Plateau 43 E7 *plain* Arkansas/Missouri, C USA
Ozarks, Lake of the 43 F6 ⊠ Missouri, C USA
Ózd 105 E7 NE Hungary
Ozieri 103 A5 Sardinia, Italy

P

Pabbay 91 A3 *island* NW Scotland, United Kingdom
Pabna 127 G3 W Bangladesh
Pachuca 53 F5 C Mexico
Pacific Ocean 14 *ocean*
Padang 131 B6 Sumatra, W Indonesia
Paderborn 101 B4 NW Germany
Padova *see* Padua
Padre Island 44 H6 *island* Texas, SW USA
Padua 103 C2 NE Italy
Paducah 39 D2 Kentucky, S USA
Paektu-san 133 B3 ▲ China/North Korea
Paeroa 139 D3 North Island, New Zealand
Páfos 112 C6 W Cyprus
Pag 107 B2 *island* C Croatia
Page 44 B1 Arizona, SW USA
Pago Pago 135 ○ W American Samoa
Pāhala 51 D3 Hawaii, USA
Pahiatua 139 D4 North Island, New Zealand
Pāhoa 51 D3 Hawaii, USA
Paignton 95 C5 SW England, United Kingdom
Paihia 139 D1 North Island, New Zealand
Päijänne 83 E4 ◎ S Finland
Pailolo Channel 51 C2 *channel* Hawaii, USA
Paine, Cerro 65 A9 ▲ S Chile
Painted Desert 47 D7 *desert* Arizona, SW USA
Paisley 91 D6 W Scotland, United Kingdom
País Valenciano 99 F3 *cultural region* NE Spain
País Vasco *see* Basque Country, The
Pakistan 127 B2 ◆ *republic* S Asia
Pakokku 131 A2 C Myanmar (Burma)
Pakruojis 83 E7 N Lithuania
Paks 105 E8 S Hungary
Pakwach 75 C5 NW Uganda
Pakxe 131 C3 S Laos
Palafrugell 99 H2 NE Spain
Palagruža 107 B3 *island* SW Croatia
Palamós 99 H2 NE Spain
Palanpur 127 C4 W India
Palapye 76 D5 SE Botswana
Palatka 39 G6 Florida, SE USA
Palau 131 H6 ◆ *republic* W Pacific Ocean
Palawan 131 E5 *island* W Philippines
Palawan Passage 131 E4 *passage* W Philippines
Palembang 131 C7 W Indonesia
Palencia 99 D2 NW Spain
Palermo 103 C7 Sicily, Italy
Palestine 44 H3 Texas, SW USA
Pali 127 C3 N India
Palikir 135 ● Pohnpei, E Micronesia
Palk Strait 127 E7 *strait* India/Sri Lanka
Palliser, Cape 139 D5 *headland* North Island, New Zealand
Palma 99 H4 Balearic Islands, E Spain
Palma del Río 99 C5 S Spain
Palmar Sur 55 F6 SE Costa Rica
Palma Soriano 57 E4 E Cuba
Palmer 37 F4 Massachusetts, NE USA
Palmer 142 A4 *US research station* Antarctica
Palmer Land 142 B4 *physical region* Antarctica
Palmerston North 139 D4 North Island, New Zealand
Palmi 103 E8 SW Italy
Palm Springs 49 D9 California, W USA
Palmyra Atoll 135 *US* ◇ C Pacific Ocean
Palo Alto 49 B7 California, W USA
Palu 131 E6 Celebes, C Indonesia
Pamiers 97 C7 S France
Pamir 125 G4 ~ Afghanistan/Tajikistan
Pamirs 125 G4 ⛰ C Asia
Pamlico Sound 39 I3 *sound* North Carolina, SE USA
Pampa 44 F2 Texas, SW USA
Pampas 65 B6 *plain* C Argentina
Pamplona 99 E2 N Spain
Panaji 127 C6 W India
Panama 55 G7 ◆ *republic* Central America
Panama Canal 55 G6 *shipping canal* E Panama
Panama City 55 H6 ● C Panama
Panama City 39 E6 Florida, SE USA
Panama, Gulf of 55 H7 *gulf* S Panama
Panama, Isthmus of 55 H6 *isthmus* E Panama
Panay Island 131 E4 *island* C Philippines
Pančevo 107 D2 N Serbia
Panevėžys 83 E7 C Lithuania
Pangkalpinang 131 C7 W Indonesia
Panguitch 47 C6 Utah, W USA
Pantanal 63 E6 *swamp* SW Brazil
Pantelleria 103 B8 Sicily, Italy
Pantelleria, Isola di 112 F4 *island* SW Italy
Pánuco 53 F4 E Mexico
Paola 112 B6 E Malta
Papagayo, Golfo de 55 D5 *gulf* NW Costa Rica
Papakura 139 D2 North Island, New Zealand
Papantla 53 F4 E Mexico
Papa Stour 91 A6 *island* NE Scotland, United Kingdom
Papa Westray 91 E1 *island* NE Scotland, United Kingdom
Papeete 141 A5 ○ W French Polynesia
Papillion 43 D5 Nebraska, C USA
Papua 131 I7 *province* E Indonesia
Papua, Gulf of 141 B3 *gulf* S Papua New Guinea
Papua New Guinea 141 B2 ◆ *commonwealth republic* NW Melanesia
Papuk 107 C1 ⛰ NE Croatia
Pará 63 F4 *state* NE Brazil
Paracel Islands 131 C3 *Disputed* ◇ SE Asia
Paraguay 65 B3 ◆ *republic* C South America
Paraguay 65 C3 ~ C South America
Paraíba 63 I5 *state* E Brazil
Parakou 72 E4 C Benin
Paramaribo 63 F2 ● N Suriname
Paramushir, Ostrov 118 I4 *island* SE Russian Federation
Paraná 65 C5 E Argentina
Paraná 63 F8 *state* S Brazil
Paraná 65 C5 ~ C South America
Paraparaumu 139 D5 North Island, New Zealand
Parchim 101 C3 N Germany
Parczew 105 G4 E Poland
Pardubice 105 C5 C Czech Republic
Parecis, Chapada dos 65 B1 ⛰ W Brazil
Parepare 131 E7 Celebes, C Indonesia
Paria, Gulf of 57 J7 *gulf* Trinidad and Tobago/Venezuela
Paris 97 D2 ● N France
Paris 44 H2 Texas, SW USA
Parkersburg 39 F1 West Virginia, NE USA
Parkes 137 G5 New South Wales, SE Australia
Parma 103 C3 N Italy
Parnaíba 63 H4 E Brazil
Pärnu 83 E6 SW Estonia
Páros 107 F6 *island* SE Greece
Parral 65 A6 C Chile
Parramatta 137 G6 New South Wales, SE Australia
Parras 53 E3 NE Mexico
Parrett 95 D4 ~ SW England, United Kingdom
Parsons 43 E7 Kansas, C USA
Partney 93 F5 E England, United Kingdom
Partry 89 B3 NW Ireland
Partry Mountains 89 B4 ⛰ W Ireland
Pasadena 49 C8 California, W USA
Pasadena 44 H4 Texas, SW USA
Pasco 49 C3 Washington, NW USA
Pasewalk 101 E3 NE Germany
Pasinler 121 G3 NE Turkey
Pasłęk 105 E2 NE Poland

◐ Administrative region ◆ Country ● Country capital ◇ Dependent territory ○ Dependent territory capital ⛰ Mountain range ▲ Mountain ※ Volcano ~ River ◎ Lake ⊠ Reservoir

◆ Administrative region ◆ Country ● Country capital ◇ Dependent territory ⊘ Dependent territory capital ▲ Mountain range ▲ Mountain ☒ Volcano ≈ River ⊘ Lake ▥ Reservoir

SALISBURY

Quincy *40 A6* Illinois, N USA
Quito *63 B3* ● N Ecuador
Qurghonteppa *125 F4* SW Tajikistan
Quy Nhon *131 D4* C Vietnam

R

Raahe *83 E3* W Finland
Raalte *84 E3* E Netherlands
Raamsdonksveer *84 D5* S Netherlands
Raasay *91 B3 island* NW Scotland, United Kingdom
Rába *105 C8* ≋ Austria/Hungary
Rabat *70 C1* ● NW Morocco
Rabat *112 A5* W Malta
Rabaul *141 D1* E Papua New Guinea
Rabinal *55 B3* C Guatemala
Rabka *105 E6* S Poland
Rabyanah Ramlat *70 G4 desert* SE Libya
Race, Cape *35 H4 cape* Newfoundland, E Canada
Rach Gia *131 C4* S Vietnam
Racine *40 C5* Wisconsin, N USA
Rádeyilikóé *see* Fort Good Hope
Radom *105 F4* C Poland
Radomsko *105 E4* C Poland
Radzyń Podlaski *105 F4* E Poland
Raetihi *139 D4* North Island, New Zealand
Rafaela *65 B5* E Argentina
Raga *75 B4* W South Sudan
Ragged Island Range *57 D3 island group* S Bahamas
Ragusa *103 D8* Sicily, Italy
Rahimyar Khan *127 C3* SE Pakistan
Raichur *127 D5* C India
Rainier, Mount *49 B2* ⩚ Washington, NW USA
Rainy Lake *43 E1* ◎ Canada/USA
Raipur *127 E4* C India
Rajahmundry *127 E5* E India
Rajang, Batang *131 D6* ≋ East Malaysia
Rajapalaiyam *127 D8* SE India
Rajasthan *127 C3 state* NW India
Rajkot *127 C4* W India
Rajshahi *127 G3* W Bangladesh
Rakaia *139 C6* ≋ South Island, New Zealand
Raleigh *39 H3 state capital* North Carolina, SE USA
Râmnicu Vâlcea *109 B7* C Romania
Ramree Island *131 A3 island* W Myanmar (Burma)
Ramsey *93 B3* NE Isle of Man
Ramsgate *95 H4* SE England, United Kingdom
Rancagua *65 A5* C Chile
Ranchi *127 F4* N India
Randers *83 B6* C Denmark
Rangiora *139 C6* South Island, New Zealand
Rangitikei *139 D4* ≋ North Island, New Zealand
Rangoon *see* Yangon
Rangpur *127 G3* N Bangladesh
Rankin Inlet *33 H4* Nunavut, C Canada
Rannoch Moor *91 D4 heathland* C Scotland, United Kingdom
Rapid City *43 A3* South Dakota, N USA
Räpina *83 F6* SE Estonia
Rarotonga *135 island* S Cook Islands
Rasht *123 D1* NW Iran
Ratän *83 C4* C Sweden
Rathfriland *89 E3* SE Northern Ireland, United Kingdom
Rathkeale *89 C5* SW Ireland
Rathlin Island *89 E1 island* N Northern Ireland, United Kingdom
Ráth Luirc *89 C6* S Ireland
Rathmelton *89 D1* N Ireland
Rathmore *89 B6* SW Ireland
Rathmullan *89 D1* N Ireland
Rathnew *89 E5* E Ireland
Rat Islands *50 A1 island group* Aleutian Islands, Alaska, USA
Ratlam *127 D4* C India
Ratnapura *127 E8* S Sri Lanka
Raton *44 E1* New Mexico, SW USA
Rättvik *83 C5* C Sweden
Raufarhöfn *83 B1* NE Iceland
Raukumara Range *139 E3* ⛰ North Island, New Zealand
Raurkela *127 F4* E India
Rauma *83 D5* SW Finland
Ravenglass *93 B3* NW England, United Kingdom
Ravenna *103 C3* N Italy
Ravi *127 C2* ≋ India/Pakistan
Rawalpindi *127 D1* NE Pakistan
Rawa Mazowiecka *105 E4* C Poland
Rawicz *105 C4* C Poland
Rawlinna *137 C5* Western Australia
Rawlins *47 E4* Wyoming, C USA
Rawson *65 B7* SE Argentina
Rayong *131 B4* S Thailand
Razazah, Buhayrat ar *123 B2* ◎ C Iraq
Razgrad *107 F2* N Bulgaria
Razim, Lacul *109 D7 lagoon* NW Black Sea
Reading *95 F4* S England, United Kingdom
Reading *37 D5* Pennsylvania, NE USA
Real, Cordillera *58* ⛰ C Ecuador
Realicó *65 B5* C Argentina
Rebecca, Lake *137 C5* ◎ Western Australia
Rebun-to *133 F1 island* NE Japan
Recife *63 I5* E Brazil
Recklinghausen *101 A4* W Germany
Recogne *84 D8* SE Belgium
Reconquista *65 C4* C Argentina
Red Bluff *49 B5* California, W USA
Redcar *93 E2* N England, United Kingdom
Red Deer *33 G7* Alberta, SW Canada
Redding *49 B5* California, W USA
Redditch *93 D6* W England, United Kingdom
Redhill *95 F4* SE England, United Kingdom
Redon *97 B3* NW France
Red River *43 D1* ≋ Canada/USA
Red River *131 B2* ≋ China/Vietnam
Red River *44 G2* ≋ S USA
Red River *39 B6* ≋ Louisiana, S USA
Redruth *95 A6* SW England, United Kingdom
Red Sea *123 A4 sea* Africa/Asia
Red Wing *43 F3* Minnesota, N USA
Reefton *139 C5* South Island, New Zealand
Ree, Lough *89 D4* ◎ C Ireland
Reese River *47 B5* ≋ Nevada, W USA
Refahiye *121 F3* C Turkey
Regensburg *101 D6* SE Germany
Regenstauf *101 D6* SE Germany
Regestan *125 E6 desert region* S Afghanistan
Reggane *70 D3* C Algeria
Reggio di Calabria *103 E8* SW Italy
Reggio nell'Emilia *103 C3* N Italy
Regina *33 H7 province capital* Saskatchewan, S Canada
Rehoboth *76 B5* C Namibia
Rehovot *123 G6* C Israel
Reid *137 D5* Western Australia
Ré, Île de *97 B4 island* W France
Reims *97 E2* N France
Reindeer Lake *33 H5* ◎ Manitoba/ Saskatchewan, C Canada
Reinga, Cape *139 C1 headland* North Island, New Zealand
Reinosa *99 D1* N Spain
Reliance *33 G5* Northwest Territories, C Canada
Rendsburg *101 C2* N Germany
Rengat *131 B6* Sumatra, W Indonesia
Rennell *141 E3 island* S Solomon Islands
Rennes *97 B3* NW France
Reno *47 A5* Nevada, W USA
Republican River *47 G5* ≋ Kansas/ Nebraska, C USA
Repulse Bay *33 I3* Northwest Territories, N Canada
Resistencia *65 C4* NE Argentina
Reşiţa *109 A7* W Romania
Resolute *33 H2* Cornwallis Island, Nunavut, N Canada
Resolution Island *35 E1 island* Nunavut, NE Canada
Réthymno *107 F7* SE Greece
Réunion *76 H6 French* ◇ W Indian Ocean
Reus *99 G3* E Spain
Reutlingen *101 B7* S Germany
Reuver *84 E6* SE Netherlands
Revillagigedo, Islas *53 B5 island group* W Mexico
Rexburg *47 D3* Idaho, NW USA
Reyes *65 A2* NW Bolivia
Rey, Isla del *55 H6 island* Archipiélago de las Perlas, SE Panama
Reykjavík *83 A1* ● W Iceland
Reynosa *53 F3* C Mexico
Rezé *97 B3* NW France
Rhein *see* Rhine
Rheine *101 B4* NW Germany
Rheinisches Schiefergebirge *101 A5* ⛰ W Germany
Rhine *84 E4* ≋ W Europe
Rhinelander *40 B3* Wisconsin, N USA
Rho *103 B2* N Italy
Rhode Island *37 F5* ◐ *state* NE USA
Rhodes *107 G6 island* Dodecanese, Greece
Rhodope Mountains *107 E3* ⛰ Bulgaria/Greece
Rhône *97 E6* ≋ France/Switzerland
Rhossili *93 B7* S Wales, United Kingdom
Rhum *91 B4 island* W Scotland, United Kingdom
Ribble *93 C4* ≋ NW England, United Kingdom
Ribeira *99 A2* NW Spain
Ribeirão Preto *63 G7* S Brazil
Riberalta *65 B1* N Bolivia
Rice Lake *40 A3* Wisconsin, N USA
Richard Toll *72 A3* N Senegal
Richfield *47 D6* Utah, W USA
Richland *49 C3* Washington, NW USA
Richmond *139 C5* South Island, New Zealand
Richmond *93 D3* N England, United Kingdom
Richmond *39 E2* Kentucky, S USA
Richmond *39 H2 state capital* Virginia, NE USA
Richmond Range *139 C5* ⛰ South Island, New Zealand
Ricobayo, Embalse de *99 B2* ⊠ NW Spain
Ridder *118 D5* E Kazakhstan
Ridgecrest *49 D8* California, W USA
Ridsdale *93 D2* N England, United Kingdom
Ried im Innkreis *101 D7* NW Austria
Riemst *84 D7* NE Belgium
Riesa *101 D4* E Germany
Riga *83 E6* ● C Latvia
Riga, Gulf of *83 E6 gulf* Estonia/Latvia
Riggins *47 B3* Idaho, NW USA
Riihimäki *83 E5* S Finland
Rijeka *107 B1* NW Croatia
Rijn *see* Rhine
Rijssen *84 E4* E Netherlands
Rimah, Wadi ar *123 C4 dry watercourse* C Saudi Arabia
Rimini *103 D3* N Italy
Rimouski *35 E4* Québec, SE Canada
Ringebu *83 B4* S Norway
Ringkøbing Fjord *83 A7 fjord* W Denmark
Ringvassøya *83 C1 island* N Norway
Ringwood *95 E5* S England, United Kingdom
Rio Branco *63 D5* W Brazil
Río Bravo *53 F3* C Mexico
Río Cuarto *65 B5* C Argentina
Rio de Janeiro *63 H7* SE Brazil
Río Gallegos *65 B9* S Argentina
Río Grande *65 B9* S Argentina
Rio Grande *63 F9* S Brazil
Río Grande *53 D4* C Mexico
Rio Grande *47 F7* ≋ Texas, SW USA
Rio Grande do Norte *63 I4 state* E Brazil
Rio Grande do Sul *63 F8 state* S Brazil
Ríohacha *63 C1* N Colombia
Río Lagartos *53 I4* SE Mexico
Riom *97 D5* C France
Río Verde *53 E4* C Mexico
Ripoll *99 G2* NE Spain
Ripon *93 D3* N England, United Kingdom
Rishiri-to *133 F1 island* NE Japan
Ritidian Point *51 headland* N Guam
Rivas *55 D5* SW Nicaragua
Rivera *65 C5* NE Uruguay
River Falls *40 A3* Wisconsin, N USA
Riverside *49 D9* California, W USA
Riverstown *89 C6* S Ireland
Riverton *139 A8* South Island, New Zealand
Riverton *47 E4* Wyoming, C USA
Riviera *44 G6* Texas, SW USA
Rivière-du-Loup *35 E5* Québec, SE Canada
Rivne *109 C4* NW Ukraine
Rivoli *103 A2* NW Italy
Riyadh *123 C4* ● C Saudi Arabia
Rize *121 F2* NE Turkey
Rkîz *72 A3* W Mauritania
Road Town *57 I4* ○ C British Virgin Islands
Roag, Loch *91 A2 inlet* NW Scotland, United Kingdom
Roanne *97 E4* E France
Roanoke *39 G2* Virginia, NE USA
Roanoke River *39 H3* ≋ North Carolina/Virginia, SE USA
Roatán *55 D2* N Honduras
Robin Hood's Bay *93 E3* N England, United Kingdom
Robson, Mount *33 F6* ▲ British Columbia, SW Canada
Robstown *44 H5* Texas, SW USA
Roca Partida, Isla *53 B5 island* W Mexico
Rocas, Atol das *63 I4 island* E Brazil
Rochdale *93 D4* NW England, United Kingdom
Rochefort *84 D8* SE Belgium
Rochefort *97 B4* W France
Rochester *43 F4* Minnesota, N USA
Rochester *37 F3* New Hampshire, NE USA
Rochester *37 C3* New York, NE USA
Rockford *40 B5* Illinois, N USA
Rockhampton *137 H4* Queensland, E Australia
Rock Hill *39 G4* South Carolina, SE USA
Rock Island *40 B5* Illinois, N USA
Rock Sound *57 E2* Eleuthera Island, C Bahamas
Rock Springs *47 E4* Wyoming, C USA
Rocky Mount *39 H3* North Carolina, SE USA
Rocky Mountains *28* ⛰ Canada/USA
Roden *84 E2* NE Netherlands
Rodez *97 D6* S France
Rodos *see* Rhodes
Roermond *84 E6* SE Netherlands
Roeselare *84 B6* W Belgium
Rogers *39 B3* Arkansas, C USA
Roi Et *131 C3* E Thailand
Rokiškis *83 F7* NE Lithuania
Rokycany *105 B5* W Czech Republic
Rolla *43 F6* Missouri, C USA
Roma *137 G4* Queensland, E Australia
Roma *see* Rome
Roman *109 C6* NE Romania
Romania *109 B6* ◆ *republic* SE Europe
Rome *103 C5* ● C Italy
Rome *39 E4* Georgia, SE USA
Romford *95 G3* SE England, United Kingdom
Romney Marsh *95 G4 physical region* SE England, United Kingdom
Romny *109 E4* NE Ukraine
Rømø *83 A7 island* SW Denmark
Romsey *95 E4* S England, United Kingdom
Ronda *99 C6* S Spain
Rondônia *63 D5 state* W Brazil
Rondonópolis *63 F6* W Brazil
Rønne *83 C7* E Denmark
Ronne Ice Shelf *142 B4 ice shelf* Antarctica
Roosendaal *84 C5* S Netherlands
Roosevelt Island *142 C6 island* Antarctica
Roraima *63 D3 state* N Brazil
Roraima, Mount *63 D2* ▲ N South America
Røros *83 B4* S Norway
Rosa, Lake *57 E3* ◎ S Bahamas
Rosalia, Punta *141 C5 headland* Easter Island, Chile
Rosario *65 C5* C Argentina
Rosario *65 C3* C Paraguay
Rosarito *53 A1* NW Mexico
Roscommon *89 C4* C Ireland
Roscommon *40 D4* Michigan, N USA
Roscrea *89 D5* C Ireland
Roseau *57 K5* ● SW Dominica
Roseburg *49 B4* Oregon, NW USA
Rosenberg *44 H4* Texas, SW USA
Rosengarten *101 C3* N Germany
Rosenheim *101 D7* S Germany
Roslavl' *111 A5* W Russian Federation
Rosmalen *84 D5* S Netherlands
Ross *139 B6* SW New Zealand
Rossano *103 E7* SW Italy
Ross Carbery *89 B7* S Ireland
Ross Ice Shelf *142 C5 ice shelf* Antarctica
Rosslare *89 E6* SE Ireland
Rosslare Harbour *89 E6* SE Ireland
Rosso *72 A3* SW Mauritania
Ross-on-Wye *93 C6* W England, United Kingdom
Rossosh' *111 A7* W Russian Federation
Ross Sea *142 C6 sea* Antarctica
Rostock *101 D2* NE Germany
Rostov-na-Donu *111 A7* SW Russian Federation
Roswell *44 E3* New Mexico, SW USA
Rother *95 F4* ≋ S England, United Kingdom
Rothera *142 A4 UK research station* Antarctica
Rotherham *93 E4* N England, United Kingdom
Rothesay *91 C6* W Scotland, United Kingdom
Rotorua *139 D3* North Island, New Zealand
Rotorua, Lake *139 D3* ◎ NE New Zealand
Rotterdam *84 C4* SW Netherlands
Rottweil *101 B7* S Germany
Rotuma *141 I4 island* NW Fiji
Roubaix *97 D1* N France
Rouen *97 D2* N France
Round Rock *44 G4* Texas, SW USA
Roundstone *89 B4* W Ireland
Roundwood *89 E5* E Ireland
Rousay *91 E1 island* N Scotland, United Kingdom
Roussillon *97 D7 cultural region* S France
Rouyn-Noranda *35 D5* Québec, SE Canada
Rovaniemi *83 E3* N Finland
Rovigo *103 C3* NE Italy
Rovuma, Rio *76 F4* ≋ Mozambique/ Tanzania
Roxas City *131 F4* C Philippines
Royale, Isle *40 C1 island* Michigan, N USA
Royal Leamington Spa *93 D6* C England, United Kingdom
Royal Tunbridge Wells *95 G4* SE England, United Kingdom
Royan *97 B4* W France
Royston *95 G3* E England, United Kingdom
Rožňava *105 E6* E Slovakia
Ruapehu, Mount *139 D4* ⩚ North Island, New Zealand
Ruapuke Island *139 B8 island* SW New Zealand
Ruatoria *139 E3* North Island, New Zealand
Ruawai *139 D2* North Island, New Zealand
Rubizhne *109 G4* E Ukraine
Ruby Mountains *47 B5* ⛰ Nevada, W USA
Rudnyy *118 C4* N Kazakhstan
Rufiji *75 D7* ≋ E Tanzania
Rufino *65 B5* C Argentina
Rugby *93 E6* C England, United Kingdom
Rugeley *93 D5* C England, United Kingdom
Rügen *101 D2 cape* NE Germany
Ruhr Valley *101 A4 industrial region* W Germany
Rukwa, Lake *75 C7* ◎ SE Tanzania
Rumbek *75 B4* C South Sudan
Rum Cay *57 E2 island* C Bahamas
Rumia *105 D1* N Poland
Runanga *139 C5* South Island, New Zealand
Runcorn *93 C4* C England, United Kingdom
Rundu *76 C5* NE Namibia
Ruoqiang *129 C3* NW China
Rupel *84 C6* ≋ N Belgium
Rupert, Rivière de *35 D4* ≋ Québec, C Canada
Ruse *107 F2* N Bulgaria
Rushden *95 F2* C England, United Kingdom
Rushmore, Mount *43 A4* ▲ South Dakota, N USA
Russellville *39 B3* Arkansas, C USA
Russian Federation *118 D4* ◆ *republic* Asia/Europe
Rustavi *121 H2* SE Georgia
Ruston *39 B5* Louisiana, S USA
Rutland *37 E3* Vermont, NE USA
Rutland Water *93 E5* ◎ C England, United Kingdom
Rutog *129 A4* W China
Ruvuma *75 D7* ≋ Mozambique/ Tanzania
Ruwenzori *75 B5* ⛰ Dem. Rep. Congo/ Uganda
Ružomberok *105 E6* N Slovakia
Rwanda *75 B6* ◆ *republic* C Africa
Ryazan' *111 B6* W Russian Federation
Rybinsk *111 B5* W Russian Federation
Rybnik *105 D5* S Poland
Rye *95 G4* SE England, United Kingdom
Rye *93 E3* ≋ N England, United Kingdom
Ryki *105 F4* E Poland
Rypin *105 E3* C Poland
Rysy *105 E6* ▲ S Poland
Ryukyu Islands *133 A7 island group* SW Japan
Rzeszów *105 F5* SE Poland
Rzhev *111 A5* W Russian Federation

S

Saale *101 D4* ≋ C Germany
Saalfeld *101 C5* C Germany
Saarbrücken *101 A6* SW Germany
Saaremaa *83 D6 island* W Estonia
Saariselkä *83 E2* N Finland
Šabac *107 D2* W Serbia
Sabadell *99 G2* E Spain
Sabah *131 E5 cultural region* Borneo, E Malaysia Asia
Sab'atayn, Ramlat as *123 C7 desert* C Yemen
Sabaya *65 A3* S Bolivia
Saberi, Hamun-e *123 F3* ◎ Afghanistan/ Iran
Sabha *70 F3* C Libya
Sabinas *53 E2* NE Mexico
Sabinas Hidalgo *53 E3* NE Mexico
Sabine Lake *39 A6* ◎ Louisiana/ Texas, S USA
Sabine River *44 I4* ≋ Louisiana/ Texas, SW USA
Sable, Cape *39 G9 headland* Florida, SE USA
Sable, Île de *141 E5 island* NW New Caledonia
Sable Island *35 G5 island* Nova Scotia, SE Canada
Sabzevar *123 E1* NE Iran
Sachsen *see* Saxony
Sachs Harbour *33 F3* Banks Island, Northwest Territories, N Canada
Sacramento *49 B6 state capital* California, W USA
Sacramento Mountains *44 D3* ⛰ New Mexico, SW USA
Sacramento River *49 B6* ≋ California, W USA
Sacramento Valley *49 B6 valley* California, W USA
Sa'dah *123 C6* NW Yemen
Sado *133 F4 island* C Japan
Säffle *83 C5* C Sweden
Safford *44 C3* Arizona, SW USA
Saffron Walden *95 G3* SE England, United Kingdom
Safi *70 B2* W Morocco
Safīd Kuh, Selseleh-ye *125 D5* ⛰ W Afghanistan
Saga *133 D7* Kyūshū, SW Japan
Sagaing *131 A2* C Myanmar (Burma)
Sagami-nada *133 G6 inlet* SW Japan
Saganaga Lake *43 F1* ◎ Minnesota, N USA
Sagar *127 E4* C India
Saginaw *40 E4* Michigan, N USA
Saginaw Bay *40 E4 lake bay* Michigan, N USA
Sagua la Grande *57 C2* C Cuba
Sagunt *see* Sagunto
Sagunto *99 F4* E Spain
Sahara *72 D2 desert* Libya/Algeria
Saharan Atlas *70 D2* ⛰ Algeria/Morocco
Sahel *72 E3 physical region* C Africa
Sahiwal *127 D2* E Pakistan
Saidpur *127 F3* NW Bangladesh
Saimaa *83 F4* ◎ SE Finland
St Albans *95 F3* E England, United Kingdom
Saint Albans *39 F2* West Virginia, NE USA
St Aldhelm's Head *95 E5 headland* S England, United Kingdom
St Andrews *91 E5* E Scotland, United Kingdom
St Anne *95 H5* Alderney, Channel Islands
St. Anthony *35 G3* Newfoundland, SE Canada
Saint Augustine *39 G6* Florida, SE USA
St Austell *95 B5* SW England, United Kingdom
St Austell Bay *95 B6 bay* SW England, United Kingdom
St-Barthélemy *57 J4 island* N Guadeloupe
St Bees Head *93 B3 headland* NW England, United Kingdom
St-Brieuc *97 B2* NW France
St. Catharines *35 D6* Ontario, S Canada
St Catherine's Point *95 E5 headland* S England, United Kingdom
St-Chamond *97 E5* E France
Saint Clair, Lake *37 A4* ◎ Canada/USA
St-Claude *97 E4* E France
Saint Cloud *43 E3* Minnesota, N USA
St. Croix *51 island* S Virgin Islands (USA)
Saint Croix River *40 A3* ≋ Minnesota/ Wisconsin, N USA
St David's *93 A7* SW Wales, United Kingdom
St-Dié *97 F3* NE France
St-Egrève *97 E5* E France
Saintes *97 B4* W France
St-Étienne *97 E5* E France
St-Flour *97 D5* C France
St-Gaudens *97 C6* S France
Saint George *137 G4* Queensland, E Australia
Saint George *47 C6* Utah, W USA
St. George's *57 K7* ● SW Grenada
St-Georges *35 E5* Québec, SE Canada
St George's Channel *89 F6 channel* Ireland/Wales, United Kingdom
Saint Helena *26 UK* ◇ C Atlantic Ocean
St. Helena Bay *76 B7 bay* SW South Africa
St Helens *93 C4* NW England, United Kingdom
Saint Helens, Mount *49 B2* ⩚ Washington, NW USA
St Helier *95 H6* ○ S Jersey, Channel Islands
Saint Ignace *40 D3* Michigan, N USA
St Ives *95 A6* E England, United Kingdom
St Ives *95 B3* SW England, United Kingdom
St-Jean, Lac *35 E4* ◎ Québec, SE Canada
St. John *35 F5* New Brunswick, SE Canada
St John *95 H6* N Jersey
St. John *51 island* Virgin Islands (USA)
Saint John River *37 G1* ≋ Canada/USA
St John's *57 J4* ● Antigua, Antigua and Barbuda
St. John's *35 H4* Newfoundland, E Canada
Saint Johns *44 C2* Arizona, SW USA
St John's Point *89 F2 headland* N Ireland
Saint Joseph *43 E6* Missouri, C USA
Saint Kitts and Nevis *57 I5* ◆ *commonwealth republic* E West Indies
St. Lawrence, Gulf of *35 F4 gulf* NW Atlantic Ocean
Saint Lawrence Island *50 C1 island* Alaska, USA
Saint Lawrence River *37 D2* ≋ Canada/ USA
St. Lawrence Seaway *35 F4 seaway* Canada/USA North America Gulf of St.Lawrence N Atlantic Ocean
St-Lô *97 C2* N France
St-Louis *97 F3* NE France
Saint Louis *72 A3* NW Senegal
Saint Louis *43 G6* Missouri, C USA
St Lucia *57 J6* ◆ *commonwealth republic* SE West Indies
St. Lucia Channel *57 K6 channel* Martinique/Saint Lucia North America Atlantic Ocean
St Magnus Bay *91 A6 bay* N Scotland, United Kingdom
St-Malo *97 B2* NW France
St-Malo, Golfe de *97 B2 gulf* NW France
St Margaret's Hope *91 E1* NE Scotland, United Kingdom
St-Martin *57 J4 island* N Guadeloupe
St Mary *95 H6* Jersey, Channel Islands
St. Matthias Group *141 C1 island group* NE Papua New Guinea
St. Moritz *101 C8* SE Switzerland
St-Nazaire *97 B3* NW France
St Neots *95 F2* E England, United Kingdom
St-Omer *97 D1* N France
Saint Paul *43 E3 state capital* Minnesota, N USA
St Peter Port *95 G6* ○ C Guernsey, Channel Islands
Saint Petersburg *111 A4* NW Russian Federation
Saint Petersburg *39 F7* Florida, SE USA
St-Pierre and Miquelon *35 G4 French* ◇ NE North America
St-Quentin *97 D2* N France
St. Thomas *51 island* Virgin Islands (USA)
Saint Vincent *57 J6 island* N Saint Vincent and the Grenadines
Saint Vincent and the Grenadines *57 I6* ◆ *commonwealth republic* SE West Indies
Saint Vincent Passage *57 K6 passage* Saint Lucia/Saint Vincent and the Grenadines
Sajama, Nevado *65 A2* ▲ W Bolivia
Sajószentpéter *105 F7* NE Hungary
Sakakawea, Lake *43 B2* ⊠ North Dakota, N USA
Sakata *133 F4* C Japan
Sakhalin *118 I4 island* SE Russian Federation
Saki *121 I2* NW Azerbaijan
Sakishima-shoto *133 A8 island group* SW Japan
Sala *83 C5* C Sweden
Sala Consilina *103 E6* S Italy
Salado, Río *65 B4* ≋ E Argentina
Salado, Río *65 B5* ≋ C Argentina
Salalah *123 E6* SW Oman
Salamá *55 B3* C Guatemala
Salamanca *65 A5* C Chile
Salamanca *99 C3* NW Spain
Salang Tunnel *125 F4 tunnel* C Afghanistan Asia
Salantai *83 E7* NW Lithuania
Salavat *111 D6* W Russian Federation
Šalčininkai *83 F7* SE Lithuania
Salcombe *95 C6* SW England, United Kingdom
Sale *137 G6* Victoria, SE Australia
Salé *70 C1* NW Morocco
Salekhard *118 D3* N Russian Federation
Salelologa *141 A5* C Samoa
Salem *127 D7* SE India
Salem *49 B3 state capital* Oregon, NW USA
Salerno *103 D6* S Italy
Salerno, Gulf of *103 D6 gulf* S Italy
Salford *93 D4* NW England, United Kingdom
Salihorsk *109 C3* S Belarus
Salina *43 D6* Kansas, C USA
Salina *47 D6* Utah, W USA
Salina Cruz *53 G6* SE Mexico
Salinas *49 B7* California, W USA
Salisbury *95 E4* S England, United Kingdom

◐ Administrative region ◆ Country ● Country capital ◇ Dependent territory ○ Dependent territory capital ⛰ Mountain range ▲ Mountain ⩚ Volcano ≋ River ◎ Lake ⊠ Reservoir

171

◆ Administrative region   ◆ Country   ● Country capital   ◇ Dependent territory   ○ Dependent territory capital   ▲ Mountain range   ▲ Mountain   ☼ Volcano   ☒ River   ☒ Lake   ☒ Reservoir

◆ Administrative region ◆ Country ● Country capital ◇ Dependent territory ○ Dependent territory capital ▲▲ Mountain range ▲ Mountain ☒ Volcano ↶ River ◎ Lake ⊡ Reservoir

◈ Administrative region   ◆ Country   ● Country capital   ◇ Dependent territory   ○ Dependent territory capital   ▲ Mountain range   ▲ Mountain   ☈ Volcano   ◈ River   ◎ Lake   □ Reservoir

175

◈ Administrative region   ◆ Country   ● Country capital   ◇ Dependent territory   ○ Dependent territory capital   ▲ Mountain range   ▲ Mountain   ☒ Volcano   ≈ River   ● Lake   ☒ Reservoir

NORTH AMERICA

 CANADA

 UNITED STATES OF AMERICA

 MEXICO

 BELIZE

 COSTA RICA

 EL SALVADOR

 GUATEMALA

 HONDURAS

SOUTH AMERICA

 GRENADA

 HAITI

 JAMAICA

 ST KITTS & NEVIS

 ST LUCIA

 ST VINCENT & THE GRENADINES

 TRINIDAD & TOBAGO

 COLOMBIA

AFRICA

 URUGUAY

 CHILE

 PARAGUAY

 ALGERIA

 EGYPT

 LIBYA

 MOROCCO

 TUNISIA

 LIBERIA

 MALI

 MAURITANIA

 NIGER

 NIGERIA

 SENEGAL

 SIERRA LEONE

 TOGO

 BURUNDI

 DJIBOUTI

 ERITREA

 ETHIOPIA

 KENYA

 RWANDA

 SOUTH SUDAN

 SOMALIA

EUROPE

 SOUTH AFRICA

 SWAZILAND

 ZAMBIA

 ZIMBABWE

 DENMARK

 FINLAND

 ICELAND

NORWAY

 MONACO

 ANDORRA

PORTUGAL

SPAIN

ITALY

SAN MARINO

VATICAN CITY

AUSTRIA

 LIECHTENSTEIN

 CROATIA

 MACEDONIA

 MONTENEGRO

 SERBIA

 KOSOVO (disputed)

 BULGARIA

GREECE

 MOLDOVA

ROMANIA

ASIA

 ARMENIA

 AZERBAIJAN

 GEORGIA

 TURKEY

IRAQ

 ISRAEL

JORDAN

LEBANON

 IRAN

 KAZAKHSTAN

 KYRGYZSTAN

TAJIKISTAN

TURKMENISTAN

UZBEKISTAN

AFGHANISTAN

 PAKISTAN

 TAIWAN

 JAPAN

 BRUNEI

 INDONESIA

 EAST TIMOR

 MALAYSIA

 SINGAPORE

 MYANMAR (BURMA)

AUSTRALASIA & OCEANIA

 MAURITIUS

 SEYCHELLES

AUSTRALIA

NEW ZEALAND

PAPUA NEW GUINEA

SOLOMON ISLANDS

MARSHALL ISLANDS

 MICRONESIA